Markets and Exchanges in Pre-modern and Traditional Societies

Multidisciplinary Approaches to Ancient Societies (MAtAS) – Interpreting Ancient Egypt

Chief Editors
Gianluca Miniaci (University of Pisa)
Juan Carlos Moreno García (CNRS, France)

Volume 1. *Markets and Exchanges in Pre-modern and Traditional Societies* (ed. Juan Carlos Moreno García)
Volume 2. *Breaking Images: Damage and Mutilation of Ancient and Modern Statues and Figurines* (ed. Gianluca Miniaci)
Volume 3. *From House Societies to States: Early political organization, from Antiquity to the Middle Ages* (ed. Juan Carlos Moreno García)

Markets and Exchanges in Pre-modern and Traditional Societies

Edited by

Juan Carlos Moreno García

Multidisciplinary Approaches to Ancient Societies:
Interpreting Ancient Egypt
Volume 1

OXBOW | books
Oxford & Philadelphia

Published in the United Kingdom in 2021 by
OXBOW BOOKS
The Old Music Hall, 106–108 Cowley Road, Oxford OX4 1JE

and in the United States by
OXBOW BOOKS
1950 Lawrence Road, Havertown, PA 19083

Hardback Edition: ISBN 978-1-78925-611-6
Digital Edition: ISBN 978-1-78925-612-3 (ePub)

A CIP record for this book is available from the British Library

Library of Congress Control Number: 2021934388

Printed in the United Kingdom by Short Run Press

Typeset by Versatile PreMedia Service (P) Ltd

For a complete list of Oxbow titles, please contact:

UNITED KINGDOM
Oxbow Books
Telephone (01865) 241249
Email: oxbow@oxbowbooks.com
www.oxbowbooks.com

UNITED STATES OF AMERICA
Oxbow Books
Telephone (610) 853-9131, Fax (610) 853-9146
Email: queries@casemateacademic.com
www.casemateacademic.com/oxbow

Oxbow Books is part of the Casemate Group

Front cover: Nubian tribute in the tomb of Huy https://commons.wikimedia.org/wiki/File:Nubian_Tribute_Presented_to_the_King,_Tomb_of_Huy_MET_DT221112.jpg.
Back cover: Kurchi market https://commons.wikimedia.org/wiki/File:Kurchi_market.jpg.

Contents

Contributors

Gary M. Feinman
Field Museum of National History of Chicago
gfeinman@fieldmuseum.org

Anne Haour
University of East Anglia
a.haour@uea.ac.uk

Bas van Leeuwen
Utrecht University
B.vanLeeuwen@uu.nl

Christopher M. Monroe
Cornell University
cmountfort@gmail.com

Juan Carlos Moreno García
CNRS (Sorbonne University)
jcmorenogarcia@hotmail.com

Linda M. Nicholas
Field Museum of National History of Chicago
lnicholas@fieldmuseum.org

J.B. Owens
Idaho State University
owenjack@isu.edu

Robin C.M. Philips
Utrecht University
robin.philips@iisg.nl

Reinhard Pirngruber
University of Vienna
reinhard.pirngruber@univie.ac.at

Osamu Saito
Hitotsubashi University
O-Saito@ier.hit-u.ac.jp

Bethany J. Walker
University of Bonn
bwalker@uni-bonn.de

Preface

Comparative research represents a flourishing trend in historical studies. Yet its practical implementation in ancient studies still constitutes a major challenge. In general, comparative ancient history usually consists in the juxtaposition of case studies issued from different areas of the world, each one embedded in its disciplinary traditions, practices, and distinctive topics (Egyptology, Assyriology, Classical Studies, Sinology, and so on). This problem is reinforced by the lack of structured common agendas, of shared sets of concepts, which hamper the effective dialogue between different social disciplines. For instance, history, archaeology, economy, sociology, human geography, psychology, cultural studies, or anthropology hardly attempt to engage in really collaborative projects on a particular society, subject, or period of the ancient world. Similar obstacles become too visible between the diverse branches of a single area study. The unfortunate consequence is that ancient history is thus divided into regional and chronological compartments often referred to as 'worlds', such as the Greek, Roman, Egyptian, Mesopotamian, Aegean, Levantine, Mesoamerican, Indian, or Chinese. Such compartmental divisions emphasize borders, differences, and periodization, a sort of retrospective projection into the past of geopolitical divisions and cultural traditions ('Orientalism') that only crystallized in modern times. Inevitably, this approach stresses uniqueness and isolation and favors hyper-specialized research too, thus narrowing the possibility of inter-dialogue with the Other, seen as remote and qualitative different. In the end, it seems as if particular institutions and social features ('market', 'temple', 'rational behavior', 'law') were so idiosyncratic of particular societies, regions, and times that finding any structural commonality proves to be a futile intellectual endeavor.

It is for this reason that the series *Multidisciplinary Approaches to Ancient Societies (MAtAS)* intends to produce a fertile ground on which original, more structured approaches to the comparative study of ancient societies may flourish and favor dialogue. It is essential that the extraordinary wealth of data from ancient societies must be integrated into current general discussions in social sciences. This could not only help renew and enlarge perspectives on sensitive topics, inspire dialogue, and provide a broader pool of human experiences for discussion. It might also make emerge structural features, practices, and social logics common to diverse societies but hidden under cultural and conceptual specificities. Research in social sciences cannot but benefit from such collaboration. Hence, the series aims to promote comparative and transversal research between unusual but carefully chosen case studies, be they geographical, thematic, or conceptual. Finally, the series intends to introduce inspiring theoretical approaches and innovative methods in ancient studies borrowed from other social sciences.

Since ancient Egypt remains marginal in current debates in ancient history and social sciences –notwithstanding its plethora of sources and potentially inspiring case studies – we are convinced that one of the branches of *MAtAS* should target Egyptology: hence the subtitle *Interpreting Ancient Egypt*. The reluctance of mainstream Egyptology to open up to concepts, methods, and debates usual in other disciplines, coupled with its chronic difficulty in generating historical and theoretical models, has resulted in disciplinary isolation and anachronistic views. In return, social sciences hardly benefit at all from the information generated from Ancient Egyptian studies. That is why the series should overcome this lack of dialogue and set the stage to make Ancient Egypt accessible and comprehensible to other disciplines. Only in this way can Ancient Egypt start contributing in a productive way to a better understanding of ancient and modern societies.

Gianluca Miniaci & Juan Carlos Moreno García

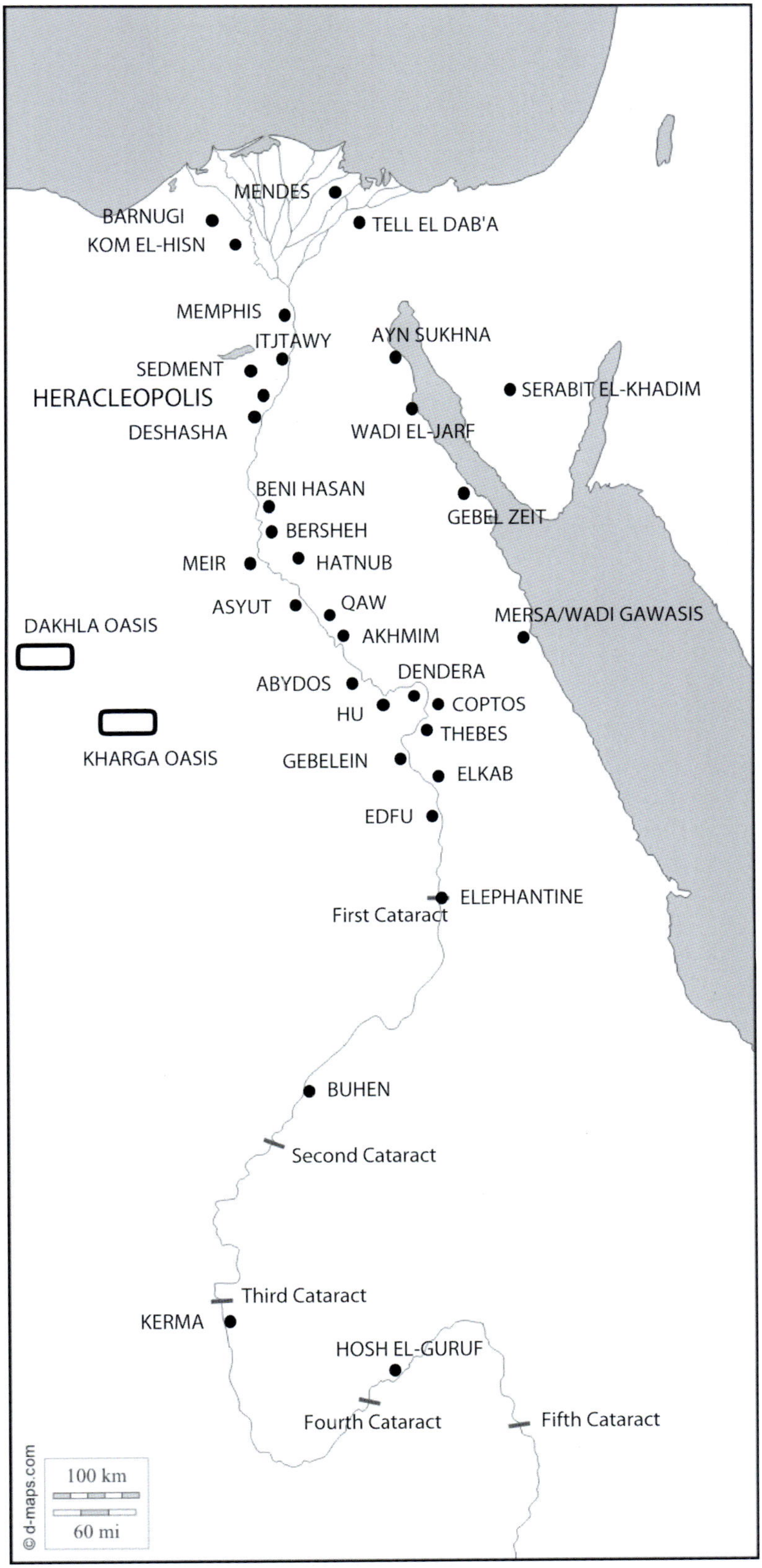

Map of ancient Egypt

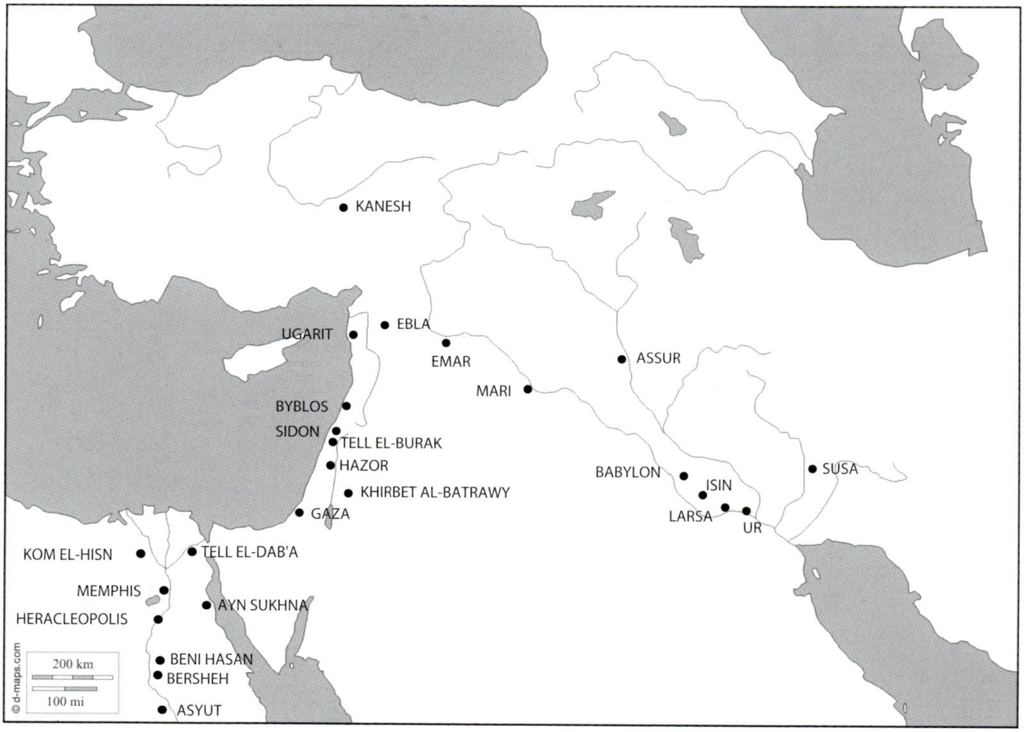

Map of the ancient Near East

Chapter 1

Markets and transactions in pre-modern societies

Juan Carlos Moreno García

In recent years a considerable interest in pre-modern markets and transactions and, more generally, in long-distance exchanges, has increased substantially the empiric evidence available and contributed to renewing historical interpretations. It was common in previous decades that specialists in ancient economies imported models conceived for other periods of history (the Middle Ages, the early modern period) or by anthropologists and that their conclusions hardly reached general debates on economic history. Perhaps the most noticeable exception was Polanyi and the team of collaborators he led. The influential ambitious project they launched aimed to analysing and characterizing other, usually pre-modern, logics of production that escaped to the mere economic utilitarianism and market-oriented goals of industrial societies, considered nevertheless to embody the very essence of rational economic thought and entrepreneurial behaviour (Polanyi *et al.* 1957). Polanyi emphasized instead the importance of social relations and the weight of institutional and social factors that limited, if not utterly prevented, the emergence and generalization of capitalist relations of production in many societies of the world in which markets were common nonetheless. It is not the place here to describe once more the shortages and mistakes that marked his pioneering work. Yet the questions and problems he raised still mark an inescapable intellectual path to get a better comprehension of the economies of the ancient and medieval worlds (Clancier *et al.* 2005). They also suggest an exciting autonomous sphere of historical research in which a careful analysis of pre-modern sources, coupled with the use of archaeology, might help detect other economic logics and, in doing so, to open the scope of what rationality, profit, investment, or enterprise meant in non-Western societies.

From a very different perspective, Max Weber also raised important questions about the organization and limits of pre-modern economies in his inspiring comparative sociology of religion. His classic study on the influence of Protestantism in the development of a modern economic mentality in the West had a reverse: why did other areas of the world, apparently best suited for the emergence of capitalism because of their early extension of trade networks, sophisticated financial tools, and vibrant commercial relations never experience a sustained process of economic growth and capitalist industrial economy? In his opinion, the ethical and religious values promoted by Buddhism, Hinduism, Confucianism, and Islam, among others, limited the mere pursuit of accumulation of wealth, the promotion of sustained investment, and the emergence of individualism as socially prized values. The echoes and influence of the Weberian research program resonated vigorously in the work of influential historians of the ancient economy like Moses Finley and in the debates about primitivism and modernism that characterized the analysis of the Greco-Roman economies in the second half of the 20th century.

In both cases, the impact of the ancient Near East on debates in general economic history or, more specifically, on ancient economies was always quite modest at best. Usually reduced to the specialized competencies of philologists and archaeologists, the economic conclusions obtained by Assyriologists and Egyptologists rarely reached a wider audience and remained confined, on the contrary, to a tiny minority of scholars and rather specialized publications. Little dialogue between 'oriental' disciplines only made things worse. Ignace Gelb, for example, a leading specialist on Mesopotamian economy history, admitted as late as 1980:

> About twenty years ago, while preparing a paper on Social Stratification in the Old Akkadian Period for the Twenty-fifth International Congress of Orientalists in Moscow, I made a discovery which was destined to influence my scholarly orientation in the years to come. Strange as it may seem, I suddenly found that the Old Akkadian texts, which I had been studying for so many years from the point of view of writing, grammar, and lexicon, have not only form, but also content; and that their content is of fundamental importance for the understanding of the social and economic history of ancient Mesopotamia, and with it, of the history of mankind (Gelb 1980: 29).

Things have changed in the last decades, particularly since the late 1990s and the early 2000s. The reasons for this shift are diverse, but the most important seem related to the explosion of archaeological research and the generalization of new techniques (remote sensing, landscape archaeology, zooarchaeology, and paleobotany) and approaches that are more sophisticated. Hence, integrative multidisciplinary projects focused on particular sites, regions, or materials have contributed to renewing discussions and perspectives of research that were still rooted, in many cases, on topics current in the 1950s (birth of urbanism and agriculture, nature of states and chiefdoms, economic and bureaucratic centralization, etc.). In turn, this has stimulated comparative analyses of economic features present in diverse regions of the world to characterize their commonalities and their idiosyncrasies too (Andreau *et al.* 1997; Hudson and Levine 1999; Hudson and van de Mieroop 2002; Hudson and Wunsch 2004; Steinkeller and Hudson 2015; Hudson 2018). The study of pre-industrial markets has not escaped from this move as well (Roman and Dalaison 2008; Feinman and Garraty 2010; Garraty and Stark 2010; Hahn and Schmitz 2018).

Another reason is the gradual self-awareness of the decline of the West in a world of accelerated geopolitical and economic changes. New actors risen to a central economic and geopolitical position (China, India, East Asia), capable of challenging the predominance of the West in the last three centuries, reject that the historical path followed by the West represents the ultimate model to imitate in order to reach modernity, economic prosperity, and political maturity. In doing so, these actors criticize the dominant Eurocentric historical narrative. On the contrary, they advocate for their own distinctive trajectories, based on their own cultural values and socio-political traditions, as alternatives that, in the end, have proven to be successful in promoting economic growth, prosperity, and modernity too. The 'Great Divergence' debate is perhaps the most influential example of this change of perception. A consequence is that the historical analysis of markets, trade, finance, investment, and enterprise no longer follows exclusively their conceptualization by generations of Western scholars and reveals itself more open to other historical and regional experiences instead.

A third cause is the very idea of globalization. Since the seminal studies by Braudel, Wallerstein, and others, it was assumed that the European discovery of America and the penetration of Western traders in the Indian Ocean in modern times launched a period of global economic integration and consolidation of capitalist economic relations on a worldwide scale. Regional specialization and division of labor, coupled with the emergence of sophisticate financial tools and commercial organization (joint-stock companies, stock exchange, etc.) and the expansion of trade, inaugurated a period of accumulation centred in Europe and the first economic globalization. Yet such view has been contested in recent times, as economic and archaeological research reveals early forms of globalization, certainly limited and relatively short-lived that connected, nevertheless, vast areas of Eurasia and Africa, from the Bronze Age to the Greco-Roman period and the Middle Ages (Hodos 2017). It was in these periods that commercial networks crossed these regions and trading activities expanded, not necessarily on the initiative of states and powerful institutions (temples, nobility, etc.). At their core, powerful merchants and trade diaspores organized caravans, fleets of ships, credit, joint ventures, etc., and made it possible the circulation of particularly coveted items, usually textiles, metals, and luxury products (cosmetics, wine, high-quality pottery, ornaments, etc.). Strategic crossroads situated at the borders of competing political powers and spheres of influence proved ideal to the emergence of specialized trading communities, like Ugarit, Phoenicia, Palmyra, and many others.

The identification of these early globalizations opens many questions about the real impact of trade in ancient societies. Usually regarded as fundamentally agrarian, the synchrony of major periods of political centralization and collapse across vast areas of the ancient world suggests some sort of economic integration, no matter how modest or limited it was. In other words, trade may prove less marginal and less centred on central powers than it was assumed by previous generations of scholars, as herders, sailors, maritime communities, mobile populations, etc., promoted and boosted circuits of exchanges and technical innovations subsequently captured by states. In other cases, some seasonal activities practised by peasants, like mining, gathering, etc., also played a crucial role in the provision of highly demanded goods

(Wilkinson *et al.* 2011; Boivin 2018; Kristiansen *et al.* 2018). Finally, archaeology also reveals the extension and intensity of commercial and economic contacts from the analysis of prices or the use of weight measures. Warburton observes for instance that silver unified the values of all the articles traded on the markets of the ancient Near East (Warburton 2013). As for weights and measures, the introduction and exploitation of balances, weights, and systems of measurements by traders and the major states of the ancient Near East facilitated the creation of equivalences which offered the basis for prices and market activities over vast geographical areas (Rahmstorf 2012; Warburton 2013; 2018; Wilkinson 2014; Rahmstorf and Stratford 2019; *cf.* however Ialongo *et al.* 2018). In all, these developments promoted the expansion of international commerce and the circulation of certain goods over vast distances in some of the earliest 'globalizations', more particularly around 2000 BC and in the Late Bronze Age (Sherratt 2003; Warburton 2007; 2011).

In the end, the outcome of all these changes of perspective is what can be defined as a more uninhibited approach to markets, trade, and ancient economies, one emancipated from older dichotomies like the modernism/primitivism debate. One that does not hesitate to detect the early traces of 'commercial capitalism', 'market performance', and 'market economies' in antiquity and to use modern concepts such as 'privatization' (Hudson and Levine 1996), 'enterprise' (Landes *et al.* 2010) long before their emergence in Europe in the late Middle Ages. Thus, in his broad-scoping study of 'commercial capitalism' in world history, Jairus Banaji, for instance, discusses a rich body of evidence from pre-modern India, the Muslim world, and China that reveals the extent, complexity, and economic integration achieved through trade and markets located far from Europe (Banaji 2020). 'Industrial' crops employed in the textile industry, the cultivation of tea, coffee, etc., connected the cities and their rural hinterland and integrated peasants in market production through a diversity of commercial agents. The networks controlled by the latter penetrated deeply into the peasant sphere and oriented its production toward commercial crops and craft activities that complemented or utterly replaced subsistence agriculture. Capitals circulated, guilds of traders financed maritime trade as well as caravan routes and peasant production, whereas credit permeated the entire economy and led to the accumulation of wealth re-invested in the economic circuits they controlled. So, putting-out systems were operative in many parts of the world, when traders provided tools and capital to peasant families who produced textile fibres, commercial crops, or particular items (nails, etc.) for traders. Far from 'primitivist' views about ancient peasant economies, as well as about over-simplistic 'modernist' interpretations, his conclusions may be linked to the work of specialists of pre-modern economies like Huang. He realized that, in some cases and under specific circumstances, peasant families produced for markets, yet the considerable extent of commercial production thus obtained prevented, nevertheless, the expansion of cities and factories. It also avoided the implosion of domestic peasant units of production thanks to an intensive use of their workforce mostly oriented toward market production, a process that hampered the disintegration of families, the migration of their members to cities and the loss of their land. In this way, the interplay of markets, cities, commercialization of crops, and an intensive use of labor did not necessarily result in the emergence of capitalist relations of production, as it happened in Europe in the Modern Period (Huang 1990).

In other cases, institutional storage and state redistribution of cereals were not only not incompatible with market transactions but rather complemented and promoted market economy. An example can be found in some East Asian dynastic states, most notably Ming/Ching China and Choseon Korea, which dealt with popular welfare through both a state redistribution system and conventional practices of mutual aid and reciprocity prevalent in rural communities. In the case of Choseon Korea, the redistribution system was built upon a network of state granaries that extracted resources (grain and other goods) from the peasant population and that functioned as the focal point of the circulation of principal goods, particularly for rice. The royal house and central administrative agencies drew upon those granaries to provide themselves with necessary supplies, yet the grain also helped prevent disasters, such as drought, famine, and foreign invasions. However, this system proved inefficient because the collection of tribute taxes involved heavy transaction costs, such as the transport of goods. Therefore, since the early 17th century the government relied upon the market to be supplied with necessary goods, instead of upon the previous tribute tax. To this effect, it employed purchasing agents, or government-licensed merchants who supplied government offices with goods purchased on the market. With the new taxation system, peasants were able to pay the tribute tax in rice or hemp, and the government purchased necessary goods on the market and promoted market development. At the same time, the state allowed local granaries to meet people's needs by exchanging reserves for other goods not produced locally. The resulting growth of market economy made the Choseon monarchy increase the number of state granaries, further reinforcing the state system of grain storage, instead of promoting civilian and private initiatives to address subsistence problems, as it happened in China. In the end, Choseon market growth was in no way opposed to the redistributive economy promoted by the state but it served to supplement the latter (Kang and Choi 2016; 2017; from a broader geographical perspective, *cf.* Will and Wong 1991).

The renewed view about markets in pre-modern times emphasizes that markets for labor, land, and capital played important roles in the long-term evolution of economies and encouraged that prices were mainly determined by supply and demand. These exchanges increasingly replaced other systems of exchange and allocation, such as those by way of tribute, voluntary redistribution, or systems applying some type of coercion, as in the manorial system (van Bavel *et al.* 2009b: 9). The result is sustained attention to the role played by markets in a comparative perspective that encompasses either a global view (an example: van Bavel *et al.* 2009a), a particular region of the world, such as the Middle East (van Bavel 2014) or the particular contribution of some agricultural or technological device, such as mills (an example: van Bavel *et al.* 2018). This helps reintroduce 'great narratives' and great historical frescoes about the structural features that promoted, prevented, or precipitated the demise of societies in which markets played a crucial economic role. Just to take two recent examples. The book by Anievas and Nişancıoğlu (2015) builds on the debate about the transition to capitalism, its first steps in diverse European territories, the reasons that led to the 'great divergence' between, principally, Britain and East Asia, and the structural characteristics of tributary states in Asia that blocked the predominance of capitalist relations of production. In the case of van Bavel (2016), he emphasizes that factor markets were not a modern development born in Europe but dominated in some economies and societies in a more ancient past, such as Iraq in the early Islamic period, the Italian cities in the Middle Ages, and the Low Countries in the late Middle Ages and the early modern period. These societies were institutionally quite different, but their market economies initiated a process of accumulative economic growth. However, the social and political polarization it generated, together with wealth inequality, ended in institutional sclerosis while markets stagnated and declined.

Which are the potential contributions that ancient Near Eastern economies, including pharaonic Egypt, may produce to enrich these discussions? Several approaches appeared in recent decades prove particularly fertile.

A good starting point is the research project initiated by Assyriologist Govert van Driel in the late 1990s. His seminal article in the collective volume *Landless and Hungry* as well as subsequent publications explored the organization of institutional agriculture in Mesopotamia as well as the limitations of the sources derived from temples, great domains and the crown. Other actors were present there too, most noticeably private economy and private actors with their own interests. This situation opened spheres of complementarity and collaboration between the 'great institutions' and a myriad of individuals, from agricultural 'entrepreneurs' to merchants, from landless peasants to priests owners of land tenures, etc. He also analysed the impact of silver and the potential commercialization of crops in the agricultural economy as well as the paths taken by investment and capital formation in the rural world (van Driel 1997; 1999a; 1999b; 1999–2000; 2000). As for the series of seminars on comparative research (MOS Studies) that he devoted to the role of money and finances, to the place of entrepreneurial initiatives in the management of land, or the regional characteristics of agriculture and crop production in Mesopotamia, they opened new perspectives about the importance of non-institutional economy. Finally, he also showed that the circulation of precious metals and the traces of pre-monetary uses of silver, trade, and investment in ancient Mesopotamia were more relevant than previously thought, especially in remote periods of history still characterized as heavily dependent on the impact and demand of the Near Eastern monarchies (van Driel 2002).

A second point derives from the publication and analysis of archives that reveal in detail the activities of traders, the extent of their networks, and their economic strategies. From the study of the archives of several Mesopotamian traders from the late 3rd millennium BC, Garfinkle showed that they were far from being mere agents of the crown, a sort of specialized civil servants who simply executed the commercial missions that the kings trusted to them. Quite the contrary, they acted on their own initiative, so their experience, contacts, and capacity to commercialize crops and transform them into 'cash' (silver) made them indispensable for institutions in their quest for the goods and commodities they needed. At the same time, these traders carried on their own business. Their 'commercial firms' were usually small and took the form of family affairs (Garfinkle 2012; 2020). Another excellent archive comes from Kültepe (ancient Kanesh), the commercial colony of the Assyrian merchants in Anatolia during the early 2nd millennium BC. The abundance and quality of the texts provide a unique glimpse into the complex trading networks that covered part of Anatolia, the organization and financing of caravans, the commodities exchanged, the profit obtained, and the institutional setting at the capital city of Assur itself that promoted the interests of the traders (Larsen 2015). The archaeological record also reveals that Syrian (Ebla) and Mesopotamian (Assur, Sippar) traders divided Anatolia into three spheres of influence, respectively, which were forbidden to the competition by commercial treaties (Barjamovic 2019). Finally, archaeological and textual evidence from the Levantine harbor city of Ugarit, dating from the Late Bronze Age, helps complete this picture from a Late Bronze Age perspective (Monroe 2009; 2015). As for the re-investment of the wealth thus accumulated, Mesopotamian evidence from different periods shows the preference of traders for real estate, orchards, slaves, money lending, leases, and temple prebends.

Only in later times do massive textual sources make it possible to quantify data and to address crucial questions about the modalities of management, returns, monetization, crop commercialization, etc., in exceptionally well-documented regions, such as Babylonia. Perhaps the best example is the ground-breaking monograph written by Michael Jursa and his collaborators in 2010 (Jursa 2010). Their conclusions, summarized in many other publications too, have since then been well integrated in collective works on general economic history (for example, Jursa 2014a; 2014b; or his contributions in Baker and Jursa 2014; van der Spek *et al.* 2015; van der Spek and van Leeuwen 2018) and have revealed their potential in renewing the interpretation of the ancient Mesopotamian economy (Kozuh 2015; Pirngruber 2017; 2018). What is more, they provide a broader and deeper perspective about the role played by markets since antiquity. What emerges from this impressive study is the diversity of economic strategies and investment patterns discernible from the Neo-Babylonian documentation recovered in temples, from private investments in date plantations and houses to the accumulation of prebends and money lending. It is possible too to discern patterns of increasing monetization of transactions and use of silver as well as general trends in the evolution of prices during the so-called 'long 6th century' BC. Contrary to previous assumptions about the non-institutional (or 'private') sector of the economy, seen as characterized by the predominance of subsistence farming and a mentality typical of 'traditional peasant societies', the Neo-Babylonian (626–539 BC) documentation reveals instead that silver was currently used, it was weighed, and much attention was given to its physical characteristics and its fineness. As for the institutional household economy, money-based exchange was an indispensable part of it in the 6th century and silver was the near-exclusive means of payment for all transactions reaching beyond the confines of the temple households. In terms of numbers of transactions, external exchange accounts for 30–50% of the total of economic activities conducted by the temples as documented by the samples. Owing primarily to the importance of cash-crop agriculture (the principal source of the temple's money income) and of hired labor which was paid for in silver, the temples could not have functioned without monetized exchange with the outside economy. So the temples engaged in a commercial exchange with other institutions but also with wholesale traders and, in the case of small-scale transactions, with 'private' individuals, many of whom bought basic staples from the temples or sold some of their own surplus (staples, animals, etc.) to them: the temple archives, therefore, shed light also on the non-institutional economy, and the means of payment current in this sector. The importance of silver-based transactions for the non-institutional sector of the economy emerges also from the private archives of city dwellers. Silver money was used for hiring labor (both free and slave), to the point that hired mass labor, rather than compelled work, was the backbone of the labor force temples provided for the ambitious building projects to which they were required by the crown to contribute. These undertakings must have brought large amounts of money into circulation among the less affluent strata of the free population, both urban and rural. In the realm of taxation and payments for substitute labor service, silver money predominated.

The archives also cast some light on the activities of particular 'firms' that operated partially at the service of institutions (van Driel 1999a or b; Bongenaar 2000; Jursa 2010; Wunsch 2010), like the Egibis (Abraham 2004; Wunsch 2007) and the Murashu (Stolper 1985; 2005) and their diversified portfolio. Institutions (temples, the crown) employed rent farmers to cultivate their extensive domains (grain fields or date orchards), in exchange for a fixed delivery quota of commodities and cash. This opened many opportunities for 'entrepreneurs' like the Egibis, capable to turn commodities into money by creating a marketing plan that integrated agricultural production, tax payments, and the shipment of crops to the cities along Babylon's canal system. The Egibi family typically conducted its business in partnership arrangements with others, usually on-the-spot entrepreneurs whom they found and backed. These partnerships involved a specific activity, such as brewing date-beer or buying local crops and selling them in Babylon. The Egibi prepared regular accounts for these ventures to calculate the surplus. These businesses usually maintained their working capital at a steady level, distributing profits to the individual partners to do with as they chose. Rather than using them to expand the joint venture, partners typically took their profits out of the business to invest in their own, for instance, to buy land, houses, slaves, and luxury goods whenever opportunities were available. They also lent money, participated in real estate transactions, etc. The wealth they amassed was such that when the Egibi inheritance was divided among the fourth-generation sons in 508 BC, the family owned 16 houses in Babylon and Borsippa and more than 100 slaves, not to mention agricultural land. However, two major obstacles menaced these 'firms'. On the one hand, political lobbying because businessmen engaged in rent or tax farming depended upon certain political institutions and officials to develop their commercial operations. Such undertakings demand care of political relationships, so rent or tax farmers may have had to spend a great deal of time establishing and maintaining such contacts and expended resources on prestige goods given as presents, incentives, or bribes. On the other hand are inheritance divisions, which put at risk the assets accumulated by a family. However, there existed the institution of 'undivided brothers', allowing the business to be kept running as a single entity for a considerable period of time after the father's death. Without any need for legal formalities, the eldest son succeeded to his father's business and represented the heirs collectively.

Many more examples could be mentioned, particularly from Babylonia in the Hellenistic period. In all, the combined analyses of all this material have modified our understanding of the ancient Near Eastern economies and provided substantial comparative evidence currently discussed in general studies on ancient markets and trade. Some examples are the books recently edited by Robartus van der Spek (van der Spek *et al.* 2015; van der Spek and van Leeuwen 2018) as well as others that integrate Near Eastern data in ancient economic history works (de Callataÿ 2014; Kleber and Pirngruber 2016) and use models that have become popular in ancient economies, such as neo-institutional economics (Jursa 2010; 2014a; 2014b; Droß-Krüpe *et al.* 2016). In other cases, wide-ranging comparative studies based on a combination of archaeological and textual data, from antiquity to medieval times, prove more and more attentive to the use of ancient near eastern evidence (Kristiansen *et al.* 2018; Rahmstorf and Stratford 2019). Finally, the study of the characteristics of a specific feature in two or more very different societies, distant both geographically and chronologically, helps understand their distinctive responses as well as the socioeconomic and political basis that produced such differences. An example is the comparative analysis of medieval England and Hellenistic Babylonia led by van Leeuwen, Földvári and Pirngruber (2011). It reveals a low level of inter-annual storage in both economies and thus helps us compare the costs and benefits in each society, costs being largely equated with interest rates and benefits with seasonal price changes. Unlike in England, Babylonia's dual crop structure (barley and dates) reduced seasonality and thus the potential benefits of storage. There is no evidence, however, that storage costs – that is, interest rates – were likewise lower. This suggests that interest rates were primarily determined in the urban and commercial sectors, not the agricultural one. Consequently, the authors conclude that measures of seasonal price changes in pre-modern economies may tell us relatively little about interest rates. Similar examples could be cited too (Scheidel 2010; Földvári and van Leeuwen 2012; Baker and Jursa 2014; de Callataÿ 2014; Kehoe *et al.* 2017; Ponchia 2018).

The degree of 'monetization' of the Near Eastern economies and, more particularly, the use of silver in economic transactions, in taxes, etc., represents a major theme of research and has inspired comparative studies about the early use of silver in other parts of the world, like Scandinavia in the Viking period (Kleber and Pirngruber 2016; Brandherm *et al.* 2018; Heymans and Termeer 2020). The Late Bronze Age was a period in which archaeological and textual evidence refers to the increasing circulation of precious metals in everyday operations, including discs, rings, wires, pieces of metal, etc., that were stocked, cut, exchanged, and held in houses. The discovery at the Ramesside garrison city of Beith Shean, in Israel, of three small silver hoards found in the 20th dynasty levels (11th–12th centuries BC) is of particular interest, since they contained 'chocolate bar' silver ingots and used silver objects that had a monetary function, and could have been used to pay the wages of Egyptian officials or mercenaries. The silver found there came from southeast Turkey and Greece. The discovery of many other small hoards from Late Bronze and Early Iron Age contexts in the Levant proves the extent of the use of precious metals in everyday economic operations. Yet the precedents of these practices can be traced back even earlier, to the late 3rd and early 2nd millennium, as revealed by about a dozen hoards of silver from beneath the floors of private houses in several Mesopotamian cities as well as from the Assyrian colony at Kanesh/Kültepe, in Anatolia, and from Mesopotamia and Syria. Also since the middle of the 2nd millennium, but especially from the 1st millennium BC onwards, silver and precious metals also circulated in the form of sealed bags of a given weight, both in Egypt and the Near East. In the case of ancient Mesopotamia, silver replaced copper as a weight currency from the late Early Dynastic III. Yet the tendency to establish value rates on silver became further fixed and standardized when administrative unification and standardization accompanied the rise of the Akkadian empire. In fact, the use of silver, the commercialization of agricultural produce through markets and the crucial mediating role played by merchants between institutions and producers are well attested from the 3rd millennium. The sophistication of the commercial operations and the uses of silver involved in them is apparent in the extraordinary archive of the Old Assyrian merchants at Kanesh/Kültepe, in Anatolia, who transported textiles and tin to Anatolia in exchange for silver and gold carried back to their homeland (with profits of 100% on tin and 200% on textiles). Silver unambiguously functioned as money and not only as a standard of value and means of payment, but also as an indirect means of exchange, while markets, fluctuating prices, creditors and credits, assurances, long-term trade ventures, etc., are also well documented in the texts from Kanesh. The importance of silver in private and institutional economic operations continued during the 2nd millennium and expanded in the 1st millennium, during the Neo-Babylonian period (Moreno García 2016: 18–22, with bibliography). In fact, the transition between the Late Bronze and Early Iron Age in the Levant not only did not suffer from a reduction of hoards but they actually increased, thus revealing that trade routes, demand, and silver did not collapse with the end of some of the dominant political powers in this region (Jurman 2015; Sherratt 2016; 2019; Pappa 2017; Wood *et al.* 2019; 2020).

A final point concerns the impact of trade and exchanges on the political organization and the settlement structure of ancient regions and states. In the case of ancient Egypt, for instance, the historical episodes of unification and division of the monarchy into several regional polities follow very closely periods in which international commerce increased. Quite paradoxically, it was when the pharaonic central power collapsed that trade flourished and some regions in the Nile Valley thrived. Then, some of these regions tried to capture the flows of wealth that crossed the Valley and the neighbouring areas (Western and Eastern Desert, Nubia, the Red Sea, the Southern Levant) and to eliminate rivals. Political re-unification ensued, yet regional actors remained powerful enough in the restored monarchy so as to preserve their own political and commercial agendas, thus limiting the formal 'absolutist' claims of the new pharaohs (Moreno García 2018; 2019). Another consequence is that the main actors involved in these networks of exchange developed strategies seeking to avoid the privileged or monopolistic positions enjoyed by others. One of them consisted of bypassing routes controlled by a particular power by developing alternative circuits and a direct access to the source of coveted goods (a desert route instead of a maritime one and vice-versa). Pharaohs themselves did not hesitate to promote initiatives of this kind. For example, when they launched maritime expeditions to the land of Punt (southern Red Sea) in their quest of incense and other aromatic plants, or when they organized complex desert logistics to favour land routes instead of the Nile, thus avoiding a myriad of mediators that increased the final price. From another point of view, the expansion of towns at the turn of the 3rd millennium BC was concomitant with the use of a term, *demi* ('harbor area of a town'), which became the synonym of town/city. The sources of this period show that fluvial trade increased in this period indeed and that this process left its mark in the settlement organization of Egypt (Moreno García 2018; 2019; in press).

In the case of other cases from the ancient Near East, Barjamovic has observed that a recurring feature in the sociopolitical organization of those polities that were specialized in long-distance trade is the dominance of parliamentary institutions controlling political and executive power (Barjamovic 2018: 128–129). In the case of Assur, the oligarchic nature of its political organization has long been linked to the city's commercial specialization in the Middle Bronze Age, particularly visible in the extensive network of trading colonies documented in Anatolia and, quite probably, in the Levant too (Collon 2008), but similar institutional frameworks occurred in many other places. Thus, other cities that specialized in overland trade had 'republican constitutions', like Emar and Tuttul in Syria and Sippar in Babylonia, where various forms of collective governance were in place. So, Barjamovic concludes that the apparent connection between political configuration and trade specialization suggests that state support and regulation was vital for the success of the system.

Commerce was stimulated by abolishing taxation on the import of trade goods, negotiations with foreign powers and partners, and the operation of a reliable legal system. At the same time, the governing institutions (whose members, it should be emphasized, were for the most part themselves involved in the trade) left the actual running of the business to private enterprise (Barjamovic 2018: 129; cf. also Barjamovic and Yoffee 2020). Finally, his analysis of the archives of the Assyrian traders found at Kültepe/Kanesh through a structural gravity model to locate lost ancient cities suggests notable parallels with Egypt. On the one hand, it shows that the relative sizes of ancient cities are explained by their position in the network of natural trade routes. It also reveals that the key to the hierarchy of the urban system in Anatolia is the ability of cities to access natural routes, and integrate into the broader trading network (Barjamovic *et al.* 2019).

Many more aspects relating to markets and exchanges could be evoked like, for instance, the much-debated theme of economic growth in ancient societies and the structural features that blocked the emergence of fully capitalist conditions in areas of the world where markets, regional economic specialization, the use of 'money', and extensive commercial networks were operative in pre-industrial times (Erdkamp 2015; 2016; Ogilvie and Carus 2014; Warburton 2014; in press). Contributions from anthropology and ethnology remain crucial too in order to assess the complex web of moral values, identities, and social practices and networks that surround apparently modest transactions between individuals, from barter to loans and debts, not to speak of the introduction of money in traditional societies (some examples in Izquierdo Martín 2002; Sánchez León and Izquierdo Martín 2002; Ferraro 2004; 2011; Zhang 2017). These contributions reveal too that documents that might be easily interpreted as mere land sales or grants do not record definitive and undisputed economic operations. In fact, the additional information provided by oral informants refers to key features of the land in question never mentioned in the texts, such as lineage connections, marriage alliances, or how a particular piece of land fits into the strategies of those acquiring and granting land, from kings to individuals and kin groups. They also give vital information about the location, size and yields of the fields involved in the dealings as well as about their place and function in the local social hierarchy (an example in La Rue 2016).

What is missing from this general overview is any significant contribution from Egyptology. It is not the place here to discuss why economic history has played and still plays a marginal role in the study of pre-Hellenistic Egypt, and why so few Egyptologists devote some attention to the analysis of markets, transactions and non-institutional trade (a summary in Moreno García 2014 and van Rinsveld 2014; cf. however the monumental study of Warburton 2016). This book aims to cast some light on these topics by suggesting a comparative perspective of research in which Egyptology could not but benefit from innovative perspectives from other disciplines. This is the case of the chapters in this volume devoted to grain markets (van Leeuwen and Philips), to peasant production and cash crops (Saito, Walker), to the organization of markets and seasonal meeting points in Africa (Haour), and America (Feinman and Nicholas), to trade diaspores (Owens) and, from a specifically ancient Near Eastern perspective, to the importance and role of markets in the Middle and Late Bronze Ages (Monroe), as well as in the Iron Age (Pirngruber). In the final chapter of this book, I will propose some venues of research in which pharaonic sources, both textual and archaeological may, in turn, prove useful for historians and archaeologists working on these same themes.

Bibliography

Abraham, K. (2004). *Business and Politics under the Persian Empire. The Financial Dealings of Marduk-nāṣir-apli of the House of Egibi*. Bethesda MD: CDL Press.

Andreau, J., Briant, P. and Descat, R. (eds) (1997). *Economie antique. Prix et formation des prix dans les économies antiques*. Saint-Bertrand-de-Comminges: Musée archéologique départamental.

Anievas, A. and Nişancıoğlu, K. (2015). *How the West Came to Rule. The Geopolitical Origins of Capitalism*. London: Pluto Press.

Baker, H. and Jursa, M. (eds) (2014). *Documentary Sources in Ancient Near Eastern and Greco-Roman Economic History: Methodology and Practice*. Oxford: Oxbow Books.

Banaji, J. (2020). *A Brief History of Commercial Capitalism*. Chicago IL: Haymarket Books.

Barjamovic, G. (2018). Interlocking commercial networks and the infrastructure of trade in Western Asia during the Bronze Age. In: Kristiansen *et al.* (eds) 2018, 113–142.

Barjamovic, G. (2019). Silver, markets and long-distance Trade in the Konya Region, 2400–1700 BCE. In: Maner, C. (ed.) *Crossroads. Konya Plain from Prehistory to the Byzantine Period*. Istanbul: Ege Yayınları, 71–81.

Barjamovic, G. and Yoffee, N. (2020). Working at home, traveling abroad: Old Assyrian trade and archaeological theory. In: Mas, J. and Notizia, P. (eds) *Working at Home in the Ancient Near East*. Oxford: Archaeopress, 107–116.

Barjamovic, G., Chaney, T., Coşar, K. and Hortaçsu, A. (2019). Trade, merchants, and the lost cities of the Bronze Age. *Quarterly Journal of Economics* 134, 1455–1503.

Boivin, N. (ed.) (2018). *Globalization in Prehistory. Contact, Exchange, and the 'People without History'*. Cambridge: Cambridge University Press.

Bongenaar, A.C.V.M. (ed.) (2000). *Interdependency of Institutions and Private Entrepreneurs: Proceedings of the Second MOS Symposium (Leiden 1998)*. Istanbul: Nederlands Historisch-Archaeologisch Instituut te Istanbul/Leiden: Nederlands Instituut voor het Nabije Oosten.

Brandherm, D., Heymans, E. and Hofmann, D. (eds) (2018). *Gifts, Goods and Money. Comparing Currency and Circulation Systems in Past Societies*. Oxford: Archaeopress.

Clancier, P., Joannès, F., Rouillard, P. and Tenu, A. (eds) (2005). *Autour de Polanyi. Vocabulaire, théories et modalités des échanges*. Paris: De Boccard.

Collon, D. (2008). Cappadocia and the Eastern Mediterranean. In: Michel, C. (ed.) *Old Assyrian Studies in Memory of Paul Garelli*. Leiden: Nederlands Instituut voor het Nabije Oosten, 91–100.

de Callataÿ, F. (ed.) (2014). *Quantifying the Greco-Roman Economy and Beyond*. Bari: Edipuglia.

Droβ-Krüpe, K., Föllinger, S. and Ruffing, K. (eds) (2016). *Antike Wirtschaft und ihre kulturelle Pragung - The Cultural Shaping of the Ancient Economy*. Wiesbaden: Otto Harrassowitz.

Erdkamp, P. (2015). Agriculture, division of labor, and the paths to economic growth. In: Erdkamp, P., Verboven, K. and Zuiderhoek, A. (eds) *Ownership and Exploitation of Land and Natural Resources in the Roman world*. Oxford: Oxford University Press, 18–39.

Erdkamp. P. (2016). Economic growth in the Roman Mediterranean world: An early good-bye to Malthus? *Explorations in Economic History* 60, 1–20.

Feinman, G. and Garraty, C.P. (2010). Preindustrial markets and marketing: Archaeological perspectives. *Annual Review of Anthropology* 39, 167–191.
Ferraro, E. (2004). Owing and being in debt. A contribution from the northern Andes of Ecuador. *Social Anthropology* 12, 77–94.
Ferraro, E. (2011). *Trueque*: An ethnographic account of barter, trade and money in Andean Ecuador. *Journal of Latin American and Caribbean Anthropology* 16, 168–184.
Földvári, P and van Leeuwen, B. (2012). Comparing per capita income in the Hellenistic world: The case of Mesopotamia. *Review of Income and Wealth* 58(3), 550–568.
Garfinkle, S.J. (2012). *Entrepreneurs and Enterprise in Early Mesopotamia. A Study of Three Archives from the Third Dynasty of Ur*. Bethesda MD: CDL Press.
Garfinkle, S.J. (2020). The house of Ur-saga: Ur III merchants in their non-institutional context. In Mas, J. and Notizia, P. (eds) *Working at Home in the Ancient Near East*. Oxford: Archaeopress, 71–82.
Garraty, C.P. and Stark, B.L. (eds) (2010). *Archaeological Approaches to Market Exchange in Ancient Societies*. Boulder CO: University Press of Colorado.
Gelb, I.J. (1980). Comparative method in the study of the society and economy of the ancient Near East. *Rocznik Orientalistyczny* 41(2), 29–36.
Hahn, H.P. and Schmitz, G. (eds) (2018). *Market as Place and Space of Economic Exchange: Perspectives from Archaeology and Anthropology*. Oxford: Oxbow Books.
Heymans, E.D. and Termeer, M.K. eds 2020. *Politics of Value: New Approaches to Early Money and the State*. Heidelberg: Propylaeum.
Hodos, T. (ed.) (2017). *The Routledge Handbook of Archaeology and Globalization*. London-New York: Routledge.
Huang, P.C. (1990). *The Peasant Family and Rural Development in the Yangzi Delta, 1350–1988*. Stanford CA: Stanford University Press.
Hudson, M. (2018). *... And Forgive Them Their Debts. Lending, Foreclosure and Redemption from Bronze Age Finance to the Jubilee Year*. Dresden: ISLET.
Hudson, M. and Levine, B. (eds) (1996). *Privatization in the Ancient Near East and Classical Antiquity*. Cambridge MA: Peabody Museum.
Hudson, M. and Levine, B. (eds) (1999). *Urbanization and Land Ownership in the Ancient Near East*. Cambridge MA: Peabody Museum.
Hudson, M. and van de Mieroop, M. (eds) (2002). *Debt and Economic Renewal in the Ancient Near East*. Baltimore MD: CDL Press.
Hudson, M. and Wunsch, C. (eds) (2004). *Creating Economic Order. Record-Keeping, Standardization, and the Development of Accounting in the Ancient Near East*. Baltimore MD: CDL Press.
Ialongo, N., Vacca, A. and Peyronel, L. (2018). Breaking down the bullion. The compliance of bullion-currencies with official weight-systems in a case-study from the ancient Near East. *Journal of Archaeological Science* 91, 20–32.
Izquierdo Martín, J. (2002). *El rostro de la comunidad. La identidad del campesino en la Castilla del Antiguo Régimen*. Madrid: Consejo Económico y Social de Madrid.
Jurman, C. (2015). Silver of the treasury of Herishef. Considering the origin and economic significance of silver in Egypt during the Third Intermediate Period. In: Babbi, A,, Bubenheimer-Erhart, F., Marin-Aguilera, B. and Muhl, S. (eds) *The Mediterranean Mirror. Cultural Contacts in the Mediterranean Sea between 1200 and 750 BC*. Mainz: Verlag der Römisch-Germanisen Zentralmuseums, 51–68.
Jursa, M. (2010). *Aspects of the Economic History of Babylonia in the First Millennium BC: Economic Geography, Economic Mentalities, Agriculture, the Use of Money and the Problem of Economic Growth*. Münster: Ugarit.
Jursa, M. (2014a). Factor markets in Babylonia from the late 7th to the 3rd century BC. *Journal of the Economic and Social History of the Orient* 57, 173–202.

Jursa, M. (2014b). Babylonia in the first millennium BCE – economic growth in times of empire. In: Neal, L. and Williamson, J.G. (eds) *The Cambridge History of Capitalism. Vol. I: The Rise of Capitalism, from Ancient Origins to 1848*. Cambridge: Cambridge University Press, 24–42.

Kang, S. and Choi, J. (2016). Confucian business ethics in Korea: pre-modern welfare state. *Asia Pacific Business Review* 22(3), 422–438.

Kang, S. and Choi, J. (2017). Business ethics and government intervention in the market in *Joseon*. In: Oh, I. and Park, G.-S. (eds) *The Political Economy of Business Ethics in East Asia: A Historical and Comparative Perspective*. Cambridge MA/Witney: Chandos Publishing, 112–130.

Kehoe, D.P., Ratzan, D.M. and Yiftach, U. (eds) (2017). *Law and Transaction Costs in the Ancient Economy*. Ann Arbor MI: University of Michigan Press.

Kleber, K. and Pirngruber, R. (eds) (2016). *Silver, Money and Credit. A Tribute to Robartus J. van der Spek on the Occasion of his 65th Birthday*. Louvain: Peeters.

Kozuh, M. (2015). A hand anything but hidden: Institutions and markets in first millennium BCE Mesopotamia. In: Howe, T. (ed.) *Traders in the Ancient Mediterranean*. Chicago: Ares, 73–100.

Kristiansen, K., Lindkvist, T. and Myrdal, J. (eds) (2018). *Trade and Civilisation. Economic Networks and Cultural Ties, from Prehistory to the Early Modern Era*. Cambridge: Cambridge University Press.

Landes, D.S., Mokyr, J. and Baumol, W.J. (eds) (2010). *The Invention of Enterprise: Entrepreneurship from Ancient Mesopotamia to Modern Times*. Princeton NJ: Princeton University Press.

Larsen, M.T. (2015). *Ancient Kanesh: A Merchant Colony in Bronze Anatolia*. Cambridge, Cambridge University Press.

La Rue, G.M. (2016). Land documents in Dār Fūr sultanate (Sudan, 1785–1875): Between memory and archives. *Afriques - Débats, méthodes et terrains d'histoire* 7 http://journals.openedition.org/afriques/1896

Monroe, C.M. (2009). *Scales of Fate: Trade, Tradition and Transformation in the Eastern Mediterranean ca. 1350–1175 BCE*. Münster: Ugarit.

Monroe, C.M. (2015). Tangled in blue: Material and other relations of exchange in the Late Bronze Age. In: Howe, T. (ed.) *Traders in the Ancient Mediterranean*. Chicago IL: Ares, 7–46.

Moreno García, J.C. (2014). Penser l'économie pharaonique. *Annales. Histoire, Sciences Sociales* 69(1), 7–38.

Moreno García, J.C. (2016). Economies in transition: trade, 'money', labor and nomads at the turn of the 1st millennium BC. In: Moreno García, J.C. (ed.) *Dynamics of Production in the Ancient Near East, 1300–500 BC*. Oxford: Oxbow Books, 1–39.

Moreno García, J.C. (2018). Divergent trajectories on the Nile: Polities, wealth and power between 4000–1600 BCE. In: Meller, H., Risch, R. and Gronenborn, D. (eds) *Surplus without State - Political Forms in Prehistory*. Halle: Landesmuseum für Vorgeschichte Halle (Saale), 337–372.

Moreno García, J.C. (2019). Marketplaces and hubs of trade in Egypt at the end of the 3rd millennium BC: Heracleopolis Magna in context. In: Rahmstorf and Stratford (eds) 2019, 185–202.

Moreno García, J.C. (in press). Trade, statehood and configurations of power in ancient Egypt (Early–Middle Bronze Age). In: Cooney, K., Ben-Marzouk, N. and Candelora, D. (eds) *Challenging Assumptions: A Critical Social History of Ancient Egypt*. London: Routledge.

Ogilvie, S. and Carus, A.W. (2014). Institutions and economic growth in historical perspective. In: Aghion, Ph. and Durlauf, S. (eds) *Handbook of Economic Growth*, Vol. 2A. Amsterdam: Elsevier, 403–513.

Pappa, E. (2017). 'You give me letters instead of money?' Commercial transactions in the Near East and the Western Mediterranean ca. 1100–600 BCE: social innovation and institutional inhibition of Phoenician commerce. *Revista do Museu de Arqueologia e Etnologia* 28: 1–30.

Pirngruber, R. (2017). *The Economy of Late Achaemenid and Seleucid Babylonia*. Cambridge: Cambridge University Press.

Pirngruber, R. (2018). Towards a framework for interpreting social and economic change in Babylonia during the long 6th century BCE. In: Waerzeggers, C. and Seire, M. (eds) *Xerxes and Babylonia: The Cuneiform Evidence*. Leuven-Paris-Bristol CT: Peeters, 19–33.
Polanyi, K., Arensberg, C.M. and Pearson, H.W. (eds) (1957). *Trade and Market in the Early Empires*. Glencoe IL: The Free Press & Falcon's Wing Press.
Ponchia, S. (ed.) (2018). Slavery from Babylon to Rome. *Journal of Global Slavery*, 3(1–2). Leiden-Boston MA: Brill.
Rahmstorf, L. (2012). Control mechanisms in Mesopotamia, the Indus Valley, the Aegean and Central Europe, *c.* 2600–200 BC, and the question of social power in early complex societies. In: Kienlin, T.L. and Zimmermann, A. (eds) *Beyond Elites: Alternatives to Hierarchical Systems in Modelling Social Formations*, Vol. II. Bonn: Habelt, 311–326.
Rahmstorf, L. and Stratford, E. (eds) (2019). *Weights and Marketplaces from the Bronze Age to the Early Modern Period*. Kiel-Hamburg: Wachholz Verlag & Murmann Publishers.
Roman, Y. and Dalaison, J. (eds) (2008). *L'économie antique, une économie de marché?* Paris: De Boccard.
Sánchez León, P. and Izquierdo Martín, J. (2002). L'autismo della microeconomia. Per un'interpretazione non utilitarista della storia agraria. *Meridiana* 45, 179–197.
Scheidel, W. (2010). Real wages in early economies: Evidence for living standards from 1800 BCE to 1300 CE. *Journal of the Economic and Social History of the Orient* 53, 425–462.
Sherratt, S. (2003). The Mediterranean economy: 'Globalization' at the end of the second millennium BCE. In: Dever, W.G. and Gitin, S. (eds) *Symbiosis, Symbolism and the Power of the Past. Canaan, Ancient Israel, and Their Neighbors from the Late Bronze Age through Roman Palaestina*. Winona Lake IN: Eisenbrauns, 37–62.
Sherratt, S. (2016). From 'institutional' to 'private': Traders, routes and commerce from the Late Bronze Age to the Iron Age. In: Moreno García, J.C. (ed.) *Dynamics of Production in the Ancient Near East 1300–500 BC*. Oxford: Oxbow Books, 289–301.
Sherratt, S. (2019). Phoenicians in the Aegean and Aegean silver, 11th–9th centuries BC. In: Bonadies, L., Chirpanlieva, I. and Guillon, É. (eds) *Les Phéniciens, les Puniques et les autres: échanges et identités en Méditerranée ancienne*. Paris: De Boccard, 129–158.
Steinkeller, P. and Hudson, M. (eds) (2015). *Labor in the Ancient World*. Dresden: ISLET.
Stolper, M.W. (1985) *Entrepreneurs and Empire: The Murašû Archive, the Murašû Firm, and Persian Rule in Babylonia*. Leiden: Nederlands Instituut voor het Nabije Oosten.
Stolper, M.W. (2005) Farming with the Murašûs and others: costs and returns of cereal agriculture in fifth-century Babylonian texts. In: Baker, H.D. and Jursa, M. (eds) *Approaching the Babylonian Economy: Proceedings of the START Project Symposium Held in Vienna, 1-3 July 2004*. Münster: Ugarit, 323–342.
van Bavel, B. (ed.) (2014). *Emerging and Declining Markets for Land, Labor and Capital: Iraq from* c. *700 BC to* c. *1100 AD*. Journal of the Economic and Social History of the Orient 57(2). Leiden-Boston: Brill.
van Bavel (2016). *The Invisible Hand? How Market Economies Have Emerged and Declined since AD 500*. Oxford: Oxford University Press.
van Bavel, B., Buring, E. and Dijkman, J. (2018). Mills, cranes, and the great divergence: the use of immovable capital goods in western Europe and the Middle East, ninth to sixteenth centuries. *Economic History Review* 71(1), 31–54.
van Bavel, B., de Moor, T. and van Zanden, J.L. (2009a). Special Issue: Factor Markets in Global Economic History. *Continuity and Change* 24(1). Cambridge: Cambridge University Press.
van Bavel, B., de Moor, T. and van Zanden, J.L. (2009b). Introduction: Factor markets in global economic history. In van Bavel *et al.* 2009a, 9–21.
van der Spek, R.J. and van Leeuwen, B. (eds) (2018). *Money, Currency and Crisis. In Search of Trust, 200 BC to AD 2000*. London-New York: Routledge.

van der Spek, R.J., van Leeuwen, B. and van Zanden, J.L. (eds) (2015). *A History of Market Performance. From Ancient Babylonia to the Modern World*. Abingdon-New York: Routledge.

van Driel, G. (1997). Land in ancient Mesopotamia: 'That what remains undocumented does not exist.' In: Haring, B. and de Maaijer, R. (eds) *Landless and Hungry? Access to Land in Ancient and Traditional Societies*. Leiden: Research School CNWS, 19–49.

van Driel, G. (1999a). Capital formation and investment in an institutional context in ancient Mesopotamia. In Dercksen, J.G. (ed.) *Trade and Finance in Ancient Mesopotamia*. Leiden: Nederlands Instituut voor het Nabije Oosten, 25–42.

van Driel, G. (1999b). Agricultural entrepreneurs in Mesopotamia. In: Klengel, H. and Renger, J. (eds) *Landwirtschaft im Alten Orient (CRRAI 41, 1994)*. Berlin: Reimer, 213–223.

van Driel, G. (1999–2000). The size of institutional Umma. *Archiv für Orientforschung* 46–47, 80–91.

van Driel, G. (2000). Institutional and non-institutional economy in ancient Mesopotamia. In: Bongenaar (ed.) 2000, 5–23.

van Driel, G. (2002). *Elusive Silver: In Search of a Role for a Market in an Agrarian Environment. Aspects of Mesopotamia's Society*. Istanbul: Nederlands Instituut voor het Nabije Oosten.

van Leeuwen, B., Földvári, P. and Pirngruber, R. (2011). Markets in pre-industrial societies: storage in Hellenistic Babylonia in the medieval English mirror. *Journal of Global History* 6(2), 169–193.

van Rinsveld, B. (2014). Le marché local au carrefour de l'égyptologie, de l'économie et de l'histoire. À propos d'un livre récent. *Bibliotheca Orientalis* 71, 5–29.

Warburton, D. (2007). What happened in the Near East ca. 2000 BC? In: Seland, E.H. (ed.) *The Indian Ocean in the Ancient Period: Definite Places, Translocal Exchange*. Oxford: British Archaeological Report S1593, 9–22.

Warburton, D. (2011). What might *the* Bronze Age world system look like? In: Wilkinson *et al.* (eds) 2011, 120–134.

Warburton, D. (2013). Integration by price in the Bronze Age. In: Frenez, D. and Tosi, M. (eds) *South Asian Archaeology 2007. Volume I: Prehistoric Periods*. Oxford: British Archaeological Report S2454, 287–296.

Warburton, D. (2014). Understanding economic growth: The importance of money in economic history and theory. In: Csabai, Z. (ed.) *Studies in Economic and Social History of the Ancient Near East in Memory of Péter Vargyas*. Budapest: University of Pécs & L'Harmattan, 423–481.

Warburton, D. (2016). *The Fundamentals of Economics. Lessons from the Bronze Age Near East*. Grand-Saconnex: Recherches et Publications.

Warburton, D. (2018). Prices and values: Origins and early history in the Near East. In: Kristiansen *et al.* (eds) 2018, 56–86.

Warburton, D. (ed.) (in press). *Economic Growth in Antiquity*. Louvain: Peeters.

Wilkinson, T.C. (2014). *Tying the Threads of Eurasia. Trans-Regional Routes and Material Flows in Transcaucasia, Eastern Anatolia and Western Central Asia, c. 3000–1500 BC*. Leiden: Sidestone Press.

Wilkinson, T.C., Sherratt, S. and Bennet, J. (eds) (2011). *Interweaving Worlds: Systemic Interactions in Eurasia, 7th to 1st Millennia BC*. Oxford: Oxbow Books.

Will, P.-E. and Wong, R.B. (1991). *Nourish the People, the State Civilian Granary System in China, 1650–1850*. Ann Arbor MI: Center for Chinese Studies Publication, University of Michigan.

Wood, J.R., Bell, C. and Montero Ruiz, I. (2020). The origin of Tel Dor hacksilver and the westward expansion of the Phoenicians in the Early Iron Age: The Cypriot connection. *Journal of Eastern Mediterranean Archaeology and Heritage Studies* 8(1), 1–21.

Wood, J.R., Montero Ruiz, I. and Martinón Torres, M. (2019). From Iberia to the Southern Levant: The movement of silver across the Mediterranean in the Early Iron Age. *Journal of World Prehistory* 32, 1–31.

Wunsch, C. (2007). The Egibi Family. In: Leick, G. (ed.) *The Babylonian World*. London: Routledge, 232–243.

Wunsch, C. (2010). Neo-Babylonian entrepreneurs. In: Landes, D.S., Mokyr, J. and Baumol, W.J. (eds) *The Invention of Enterprise: Entrepreneurship from Ancient Mesopotamia to Modern Times*. Princeton NJ: Princeton University Press, 40–61.

Zhang, T. (2017). Moral economies in early modern land markets: history and theory. *Law and Contemporary Problems* 80, 107–133.

Chapter 2

A key commodity: The role of cowries in West Africa

Anne Haour

Introduction

This chapter considers one of the key economic products of the pre-modern world: cowrie shells. Part of the complexity of the story of these shells lies in their global spread and appeal and they took on major importance in several areas of the world, such as West Africa, China, Bengal, and northern Europe. They had economic significance: used as loose currency or strung together to form numerical quantities of value. They also took on a range of other functions, combined with other elements to form charms, added onto textiles and other materials as decorative elements, grouped for use as vehicles of divination, given as votive offerings, or deposited as grave goods. To achieve these uses the shells were adapted through different types of processing and were physically incorporated in a number of ways. Crucially, though, they first had to be sourced and classical economic models have argued that scarcity drives value.

Cowries are a type of marine mollusc and hundreds of species exist but some of the most valued species were *Monetaria moneta* and *M. annulus*, known as the money cowrie and the ring cowrie respectively (Fig. 2.1). Their natural range is the Indo-Pacific, and *moneta* for its part 'covers the greatest area of any cowrie' (Burgess 1970: 344). Thus, though their natural range is huge, these cowries were not native to China, Bengal, northern Europe, or indeed West Africa. In the case of West Africa, the usual model is that they were brought through two main channels: via the Sahara first, then, after the development of Atlantic trade routes, via the coast. In this latter phase, traders carried the shells to West Africa as capital to buy slaves; there, the shells were absorbed into local economies and used for a variety of purposes, including as a medium of exchange for small transactions.

While the lack of local availability may be a prerequisite of a successful currency, *moneta* and *annulus* cowries confound expectations in being deeply rooted culturally in many parts of West Africa. Perhaps even more than gold, cowries have, suggests Félix Iroko (1987: 80–88), been the subject of myths and popular beliefs. This brings in the

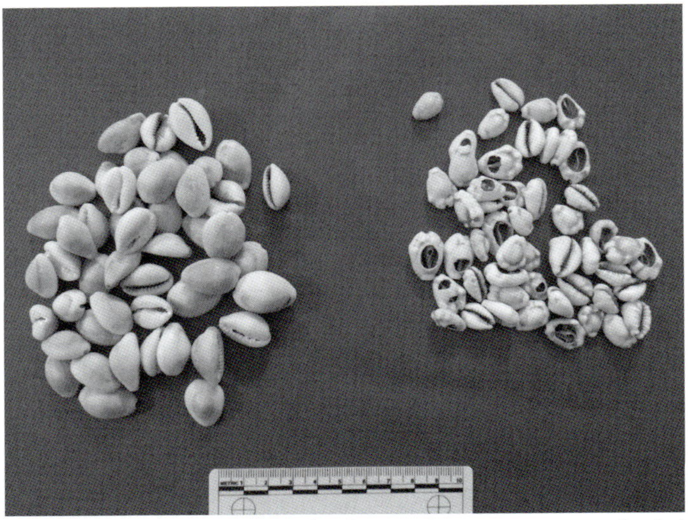

Figure 2.1. The ring cowrie (left) and the money cowrie (right) (courtesy of Malik Saako, image by Anne Haour).

question of the creation of economic and cultural value by communities. The aim of this chapter is therefore not to offer a conclusive summary of the role of cowries in markets – an impossible task given the diversity of uses to which they were put – but, rather, to give a sense of the myriad and regionally-specific ways in which economic and cultural spheres interrelated – and indeed, the difficulties in defining these as separate in the first place. The question of the motivation of past traders, and of the mechanisms behind their activities, has been the subject of some debate: capitalist desire for gain, gift-exchange aiming to foster social ties, a combination of both? It might be useful here to remind ourselves that British anthropologist Alison Hingston Quiggin's much-reprinted book *A Survey of Primitive Money: The beginnings of currency* (1949) tackles this dual role head-on. Her book begins with a chapter on cowries and beads, the 'most universal of all forms of primitive money, [which] have magical as well as monetary value' (Quiggin 1949: 322). This dual role will be a thread running through this chapter.

The cultural uses of cowries have been well discussed, and a substantial debate has developed over their symbolism, pitting 'verticalists' vs. 'horizontalists' in the words of one author (Gregory 1996: 214). In a nutshell, this debate centers on whether the shell resembles an eye, or the female genitals – and from there, what its role may be: protection against the evil eye or prophylactic against infertility.[1] The use of cowries as a means of transmitting messages and for divination has been well covered also, most famously for the Yorùbá world (Bloxam 1887; Iroko 1987; Bascom 1993). The commercial value of the cowrie has equally challenged scholars (Hiskett 1966; Johnson 1970; Hogendorn and Johnson 1986). Spanning the 'mercantile' and the 'ritual' spheres is the important work of Ogundiran (2002) on the Yorùbá world, which examines the manner in which cowries, once they began to arrive in large numbers through the Atlantic trade, could be incorporated into existing ways of relating to objects in West Africa.

Overviews of the spread of cowries into Africa have tended to apply principles of formal economic anthropology, with a rather narrow time depth and little consideration of the social creation of value. The work of Karl Polanyi (1966), who popularized cowries as an 'archaic currency' in pre-colonial Dahomey (17th–19th centuries), involving central issue and regulated importation, is an example of this. Hogendorn and Johnson (1986) too have tended to consider classic topics such as rates of exchange, profit, etc. through their study of historical sources. However, while economic history has often considered the uncertainties in long-distance trade as logistical and symptomatic of pre-modern conditions, recent currents in economic anthropology have pointed out the importance of studying people and their behavior as well as rules of the market (Forrest and Haour 2018). As such, the present chapter attempts to keep uppermost a concern with how past West African communities procured, valued, and modified these shells. To repeat: the cowries most prized, *moneta* and *annulus*, are not native to this coastline. Almost the entirety of the western side of Africa, from Mauretania to South Africa, is dominated by deposits deriving from material eroded from the land – there is often a heavy sediment load – and coral only occurs on three islands in the Gulf of Guinea (Longhurst and Pauly 1987: 9). This is not a conducive environment for *moneta* and *annulus*. Other cowrie species occur along this coastline but, *contra* York (1972: 100), it seems highly unlikely that coastal peoples would have used these locally occurring cowries 'as a free source of income'. None of these native species is at all similar to *moneta* and *annulus*, they would probably not have occurred in the huge amounts required by cowrie traders, and any shell recovered as beach wash would be much less attractive to consumers than specimens collected live (Hogendorn and Johnson 1986; Haour and Christie 2019).

This chapter will briefly outline the distribution of cowries in West Africa over time as seen through archaeological and historical sources, then survey the various mentions made of them by early European sources; this discussion draws on both archaeological and historical data and underscores some of the issues in identifying cowries and their meaning in the past. A relatively recent example, that of the kingdom of Dahomey, offers us an opportunity to examine the issues in more detail. Dahomey (in present-day Republic of Benin) was one of the hegemonic powers, along with Benin and Ọyọ (both in present-day Nigeria), which expanded greatly in the 18th century, a period marked by an increase in the trade of slaves and of cowries.

Cowries in West Africa

The popularity of cowries with West African consumers is well attested in the earliest historical sources describing West Africa, those by Middle Eastern and North African writers, which show that cowries were a key item of trans-Saharan trade. The first mention of their use in sub-Saharan Africa appears to date to the late 10th or early 11th centuries, when the author of the *Akhbār al-zamān*, writing in Egypt, reports that they were used as ornaments in women's hair (Levtzion and Hopkins 2000: 35). In the 11th century al-Bakrī, writing in southern Spain, states that cowries were among the main goods exported to a place in West Africa called Kūgha (Levtzion and Hopkins

2000: 83). His statement seems to imply that, at this period, cowries were not used as currency as the assumption is that he would have said so if this was the case (Hiskett 1966: 345, see also Levtzion and Hopkins, 2000: 83, n. 48). In the 12th century, al-Zuhri mentions that Jewish communities along the Niger River imported cowries among other goods (Levtzion and Hopkins 2000: 99–100).

The first mention of cowries as currency seems to be in the first half of the 14th century, when al-'Umarī described them used as such in two parts of West Africa (Levtzion and Hopkins 2000: 260, 269, 276). But cowries rarely operated as a single currency. In Kanem, al-'Umarī tells us that metal bars and textiles were also used; glass, fragments of copper, and hammered iron are mentioned. Twenty years later, ibn Baṭṭūṭa also mentions cowries as currency, including the comment that they sold at a rate of 1150 to the gold dinar (Levtzion and Hopkins 2000: 281, 300).[2] Alvise Cadamosto, a Venetian slave trader who visited the Senegambian coast in the 1450s on behalf of the Portuguese crown, reported that in the Songhai kingdom 'they use little white shells which are brought to Venice from the Levant, of which they pay certain numbers according to the goodness of what they want to buy' (Jeffreys 1948: 47). Here too, however, he is told that other items – salt, for example – circulated and were highly prized (Iroko 1987: 203).

The above historical data suggest that in some parts of West Africa cowries were valued both as adornment and as currency, in the latter case often parallel with other items. The sources also clearly show that the use of cowries in sub-Saharan Africa was not the result of European influence and of the opening of global maritime routes in the 1400/1500s but occurred earlier.

The fullest data on the distribution of cowries in West Africa come from archaeological results. In this respect, as a classificatory exercise, finds might be allocated to several broad groups. The first is that of funerary contexts. In many such instances, cowries appear highly valued, used quite ostentatiously as items of personal adornment and associated with often exotic grave goods. The second category is that of ritual use, suggested by the intentional deposition of cowries within architectural features or shrines – or of course within graves. Thirdly are the large assemblages of dozens or even hundreds of shells, sometimes recovered as caches, and which point most clearly to economic uses. Needless to say, categories often overlap and some finds do not fit any category. Yet, in general terms cowries force us to think about the challenges and opportunities faced by communities, associated with expanding global connections.

At current state of research, the earliest presently known use of cowries in West Africa is from a funerary context, at Kissi, in northeast Burkina Faso (Magnavita 2015). The site consists of an extensive cluster of settlement areas and several burial grounds. The place was occupied by sedentary millet farmers who kept small livestock; they were pottery and iron producers from the onset of settlement in the first few centuries AD, leading to the build-up of large mounds and the site was abandoned around the 13th century. Although the excavations carried out in the habitation

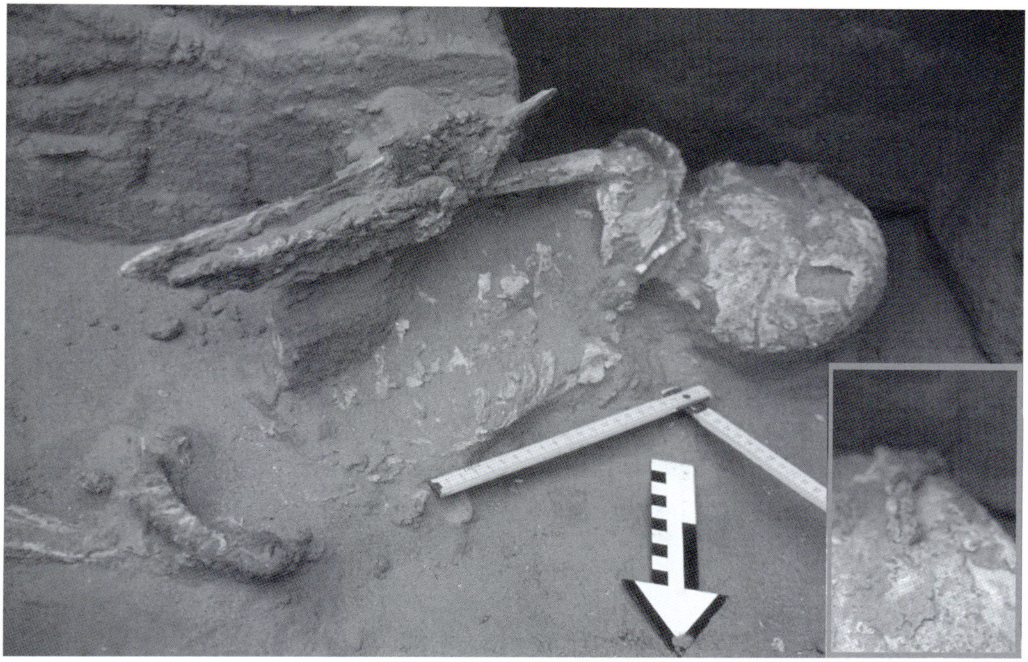

Figure 2.2. Kissi 3, Grave 10 (courtesy of Sonja Magnavita, image edited by Giulia Nazzaro).

area yielded evidence broadly in line with expectations, the funerary data yielded an unexpected picture of a hierarchical society in which trade and trading networks played an important role (Fig. 2.2). The dead were buried with items such as brass jewelry, weapons, glass beads, and a handful of *moneta* cowries, seemingly used as body adornments and dating to between the 5th and 7th centuries AD (Magnavita 2015). The finds from Kissi show that artifacts from far away were finding their way into the West African Sahel much earlier, and on a larger scale, than previously thought. And Kissi was a mere village; that its inhabitants had access to such exotic goods leaves one to wonder what might have been accessible to people living in a major trading settlement.

Cowries have also been reported singly in Saharan graves, such as at Taqallit near Jarma (Libya) (Mattingly *et al.* 2009) and Iwelen in the Aïr massif of Niger (Paris 1990). Both these instances are 2000–2500 years old. The use of cowries as grave goods is documented into the 1st and early 2nd millennia AD, for example at Daima, Nigeria (Connah 1981) or Ain Farah, Sudan (Mohammed 1986). These are just a few examples over a wide region, so it is difficult to extrapolate, but the African archaeological record is notoriously patchy. The fact that cowries occur in much smaller numbers than other goods may indicate scarcity and/or value. For example at Daima, a sub-adult individual was interred with 4163 beads of glass, ostrich eggshell, and stone, and just 18 perforated *moneta,* while one infant burial wore a belt decorated with eight perforated cowries and over 465 ostrich eggshell beads (Connah 1981: 150, 177, 178). At Ain Farah, Sudan, a flexed burial was recovered accompanied by over 200 iron beads, an ostrich eggshell necklace, iron jewelry, and just one perforated cowrie (Mohammed 1986).

The ritual use of cowries is also evidenced archaeologically. A remarkable instance is reported by Eluyemi (1977) at Isoya, near Ife, Nigeria, from excavations at the reported location of a collapsed mud building and in a low midden, contexts thought to date to the late 19th century. Cowries were plentiful, occurring both in deposits and as grave goods: over 2700 were recovered, with *annulus* more common than *moneta.* Several arrangements were reported that are thought to have a ritual function: for example, a concentric arrangement of cowries identified as having supernatural powers to counter evil intentions (Eluyemi 1977: 109). In Ghana, archaeological excavations yielded evidence of the 1826 Battle of Katamansu fought between the Asante and the Ga and their coastal allies, including what appear to be the remains of a shrine, featuring numerous cowrie shells (Apoh and Gavua 2010).

It is difficult to infer meaning from archaeological finds, and it is not easy to point to instances where there is incontrovertible evidence that cowries had a monetary function. The suggestion that large numbers of cowries reflect a commercial function remains just that. However, some very large assemblages, such as the 12,373 cowries, seemingly once contained in a pottery vessel, recovered at a possible miners' camp at Logofiela (Burkina Faso) by a team led by Kiéthéga (1983), must point to a monetary use. So, too, is a 17th century shipwreck off the coast of Elmina (Ghana), which carried items such as European ceramics dating to between the mid-16th and the 19th centuries, and thousands of cowries (Cook 2012; 2014; Pietruszka 2011). The cowries are described as being abundant and apparently uniform and the small representative sample collected suggests a strong predominance of *moneta* shells (Pietruszka 2011: 113).

Through these material remains we obtain an indication of the movement of goods without knowing for sure how they circulated.

The organization of trade

Written sources (which for most of West Africa appear in the 19th century) for some areas speak of common monetary zones, royal mandates, and conquest; a highly centralized and bureaucratic society (see *e.g.* account by Lovejoy 1985). I have elsewhere (*e.g.* Haour 2003; 2007) advanced the idea that there is little evidence for such systems in earlier periods and that rulers probably merely took over and enhanced existing trade networks, alongside a host of other players, for the extraction of tolls and tribute rather than control. Key among these other actors were trade diasporas organized along family, ethnic, or religious lines.[3] Johnson (1976), examining the affairs of trans-Saharan traders in the late 19th century and suggesting that a 'family firm' might out-compete

European traders, pointed out the parallel with the 13th century business of the al-Maqqarī brothers. As described by a slightly later source, this involved five brothers settled at different points along a trans-Saharan route (in Levtzion and Hopkins 2000: 307–308). Another, later, example is that of the family of Abū Bakr al-Siddīq, born about AD 1790 in Timbuktu, whose trader relatives represented family interests throughout an area 'not much smaller than the Iberian peninsula' (Perinbam 1973: 425). In short, I would argue we need to be very cautious in extrapolating back in time models derived from classical economics or from relatively well-described later time periods.

In terms of cowries, the speed at which they were adopted on the West African coast after the arrival of European traders is surprising. The coast was reached in AD 1471–1472 by Portuguese sailors, probably at the same time as they encountered São Tomé, and as early as March 1515 a merchant in the São Tomé trade was given licence to import from India 500 quintals of cowries yearly, coming as ballast without paying duties or freightage (Ryder 1959). It may be, thinks Ryder, that this contract marks the beginning of the seaborne importation of cowries into the coastal areas. Cowries appear gradually in the accounts of the fort at Elmina, now in Ghana. Blake (1942: I, 107) reproduces a March 1510 account that states that in just under 2.5 years the factor of Sao Jorge da Mina took in 1133 shells (against 287, 813 manillas of brass and copper). In June 1519 the Treasurer of the Casa da Mina acknowledged receipt of 27 quintals of cowries for the São Tomé trade; in July 1520, he acknowledged another 20 quintals (Ryder 1959).

Texts relating to this early encounter between Europeans and West Africans are difficult to use. The term 'cowrie' only became established on the Atlantic coast after a certain period, replacing earlier terms. The accountancy book of the *Samta Maria*, a Portuguese ship which sailed from São Tomé to the Niger River Delta in the spring of AD 1522, shows that the ship came equipped with more than 15 quintals of *buzeos da India* or *iguos*, as means of payment for a range of goods but in particular for the slaves needed to work on the plantations of São Tomé (Ryder 1959: 301; Mauny 1967: 518). In Mauny's mind (1967: 522 n. 1), these are *moneta* cowries. In Ryder's (1959: 301, n. 4), these shells came from the Malabar coast. In around 1540, an anonymous Portuguese pilot wrote that the people of São Tomé sold locally-produced sugar to the ships that came yearly against, among other things, 'shells, which in Italia are called *porcellette* [porcelains] – little white ones – which we call *buzios*, and which are used for money in Ethiopia' (Blake 1942: I, 157). The term *boesjes* remained current for at least two centuries. It is used in the mid-17th century by Olfert Dapper in his 'Accurate Descriptions of the African Regions' (Hiskett 1966: 351). Two British traders at Wydah in September 1721 use the terms 'Bouges' and 'boogees' (Hogendorn and Johnson 1986). The French version *bouge* is also well documented: for instance Savary Des Bruslons (1742: 1107), Inspector General of the Manufactures for the King at the Paris Customs, explains as part of a long entry in his compendium of items relating to commerce: 'Les Cauris des Maldives fervent auffi au commerce, que les Européens font fur les Côtes de Guinée, où les Négres qui les eftiment beaucoup les appellent des

Bouges' ('The cowries of the Maldives also serve for the commerce that the Europeans undertake on the Guinea coast, where the Negroes, who estimate them greatly, call them *Bouges*'). He also indicates that as well as currency they serve for adornment.

According to Quiggin (1949: 30), the Portuguese *buzio* or French *bouges* arises from the Divehi (Maldivian) term *boli.* In the Edo polity of Benin (now in Nigeria), she says, the word appeared as *abuy*, and in Dahomey as *akwe*. However, there has in fact been debate over whether terms such as *bozy*, *bochie*, or *boesjes*, were imported words (stemming from the Portuguese *buzio*/French *bouges*) for cowries, or a general trading term of a West African coastal language used to describe any medium of exchange and later specialized to mean cowries (Hiskett 1966). In fact, and speaking generally, Hiskett (1966: 352) commented that 'the cowry words of West Africa are an enigma. We are faced with the fact that an article of such basic market importance, which is obviously exotic, failed to carry with it its own loan-word, but is described by a variety of words most of which appear to be unrelated'. This is surprising[4] and to me argues, again, for a deep embeddedness within West African thought.

The immediate acceptance of cowries suggests that they may have already been in use (Johnson 1970). De Corse (1989) remarks as a general point that the first European traders on the West African coast probably made a conscious effort to offer items for which there was already a demand. Their arrival did not create new trade patterns but utilized and expanded existing networks. The story of the cowrie seems to fit this – the shells were eagerly accepted. One can only assume that the European traders knew that cowries would be welcomed because they had heard this from accounts from trans-Saharan connections. This may also imply that cowries traded through Saharan routes had reached as far as the Atlantic coast. The crew of the *Samta Maria* purchased some cowries on the West African coast, selling some red caps to procure them; possibly, thinks Ryder (1959), because they were short of cowries. This is an unusual feature not seen in later voyages, perhaps indicating that shells were not a completely inconvertible currency at this date, suggest Hogendorn and Johnson (1986: 109). It strengthens the feeling that cowries were already well known there.

The structure and volume of the cowrie trade changed over time but its height was in the period of European mercantile imperialism. The numbers of cowries shipped by Europeans are mind-boggling. By the mid-16th century the Portuguese were transporting in the region of 120 million cowries a year to Africa for sale as money, estimates Alpern (1995: 24). Holland, England, and France would soon get into this lucrative act. The Dutch and English together shipped more than 10,000 million cowries to West Africa from 1700 to 1790; the English alone about 5,500 million from 1800 to 1850. In 1773 a single French slave ship carried 35 million strung cowries to Ouidah. It is recorded that 32,000 pounds (around 14.5 tons) of cowries were imported into Mogador (now Essaouira, Morocco) from Amsterdam in the year 1805 (Hiskett 1966: 343). By the time the cowrie trade ended in the early 20th century, European ships may have disgorged 50,000 million shells on the coastline between Liberia and Nigeria (Alpern 1995: 24).

Hogendorn and Johnson (1986: 88–91) have outlined the European part of the journey. Ships loaded with cowries from the Maldives arrived in Europe, principally to the ports of Amsterdam and London, after Lisbon declined in the 17th century, during the summer months of July and August. At this stage, the shells were cleaned, sorted, and auctioned to West African traders. French buyers frequented the Dutch auctions, and Portugal and Denmark also bought there. The English market saw customers from Portugal, Madeira, Flanders, Denmark, and France while the Dutch and English rather frequently purchased cowries at each other's auctions; there was a 'healthy intra-European traffic' (Hogendorn and Johnson 1986: 91).

Although the low value of cowries made them useful for small purchases, this also entailed two major inconveniences when making larger purchases. The number required were heavy; Monteil (1895: 192) tells us for example that he paid 7000 cowries to cross the Niger on his way to Hausaland in the early 1890s, which would have weighed over 7 kg. Moreover, counting large numbers of cowries was very time-consuming and tedious (Johnson 1970: 41). Heinrich Barth, passing through Tessaoua, Niger, called the counting of shells most tedious: 'in all these inland countries of Central Africa the cowries or kurdi (*Cypraea moneta*) are not, as is customary in some regions near the coast, fastened together in strings of 100 each, but are separate, and must be counted one by one' (cited in Johnson 1970: 41 and Hogendorn and Johnson 1986: 118). Marion Johnson and Jan Hogendorn have suggested that distinct zones existed within West Africa in which cowries were strung, which would make counting easier. The unstrung cowrie shells are known within areas of West Africa that are towards the north and the Sahara such as Bambara to Timbuktu to Hausa land (*i.e.* Borno, Kano), Salaga and Kong, Nupe, and in much of Yorùbá country while the pierced and strung cowrie shells were said to have been used in areas on the Guinea coast, on the lower Niger, in Dahomey, in inland Ewe country, and in Kwahu (Johnson 1970: 37; Hogendorn and Johnson 1986: 119).

The shell money of the slave trade

The import of cowries into West Africa was intimately linked with the slave trade. As Mauny (1967: 512–513) remarks of the *Samta Maria* the quantities of slaves reported dwarf the remaining items: 137 slaves, 19 ivory tusks, 4029 beads, oil, yams, malaguetta, cloth, basketry, and cane were purchased. At a later date, the coast of what is now the modern Republic of Benin became a key player: the port of Ouidah, and the polity of Dahomey which lay inland, are recurring features of historical accounts. In a perhaps over-emphatic way, Polanyi (1966: 18) speaks of the 'shift in the international economy [which] caused a tidal wave to cross the Atlantic and to hurl itself against a twenty-mile stretch of the West African coast [near Ouidah]'. Ouidah was probably the greatest 18th century importer of cowries, suggest Hogendorn and Johnson (1986: 113).

King Guezo of Dahomey (ruled 1818–1858) famously said that he preferred cowries to gold because they could not be counterfeited (Hogendorn and Johnson 1986: 6).

Unlike other currencies, such as metals, cloth, tobacco, or liquor, there was very little leakage into commodity use: cowries only had the very limited value of their lime content (Einzig 1949: 145; Hogendorn and Johnson 1986: 7).

Of course, the whole region was tied into this trade. As Lovejoy (1974) pointed out some decades ago, the flow of cowrie shells provides a useful indicator for long distance commerce between inland areas and those along the Atlantic coast, whose ports became the main source of supply for cowrie imports. Cowries, textiles, and European manufactures were shipped north against slaves, livestock, salt, textiles, and other goods. Here, transport costs have played a central role in models developed by economists. Einzig (1949: 142–143, 413–414) suggests that the value of cowries rose with the distance from the coast, and that for the same reason cowries also tended to be more expensive as one moved east in French colonial territories.

Polanyi (1966) insists that cowries formed an extremely stable currency within Dahomey, at the rate of 32,000 cowries to the ounce gold from the time of Willem Bosman, merchant in the service of the Dutch West India Company in the 1680s, to the French invasion of Dahomey. Cowries 'gained the status of a currency by virtue of state policy, which regulated its use and guarded against its proliferation by preventing shiploads from being freely imported' (Polanyi 1966: 189). This, in his view (1966: 169), 'formed part of the unchanging archaic monetary system of Dahomey'. Polanyi's idea that cowries were centrally issued in pre-colonial Dahomey because the state regulated their importation has since been discarded (Şaul 2004: 73). What is in fact missing from Polanyi's account is the complexity of levels on which cowries functioned. Skertchly's description of his visit to Dahomey (1874) makes clear, though multiple (usually disparaging) allusions to cowries imported by European merchants from Zanzibar, how common they were both as a medium of exchange and as 'charms' or part of 'fetiches'. He remarks that King Gelele's gate in the Banyanemme palace featured rude wooden doors covered with 'fetiche charms – feathers, cowries – thunder-shrub – blood and similar humbug' and that his formal wear involved numerous accoutrements, for example a musket, covered in cowries, 'a *tout ensemble* truly fetiche in its get up' (Skertchley 1874: 138, 218). Part of the king's largesse involved handing out cowries to assembled subjects (Skertchley 1874: 169, 226–228, 274, 298, 366, 374–376). In one instance the cowrie throwing took place over a period of four hours and elsewhere Skertchly comments he was 'getting rather tired of sitting still for hours and seeing a number of half-naked savages scrambling for cowries' (1874: 228, 376).

As mentioned above, it appears that cowries were strung in Dahomey, which required local industry to pierce the shells. Skertchly (1874: 28), again, observed that cowries were strung on twisted grass stems, 50 strings making a 'head'. Fifty cowries made up a string in Ouidah, but only 46 in Abomey and 'the cowries given by the king, which are strung by the Amazons, average only about forty to a string'. An earlier, 18th century, source reports that strung cowries were one short of the nominal 40, the reward to the stringer for the work of piercing and stringing, while cowries strung at the king's palace by the women there lacked up to six cowries per string (Johnson 1970: 45; Hogendorn and Johnson 1986: 122). Unfortunately, these accounts do not provide much insight into the production process, including information about the equipment used for drilling and other related activities or materials used, but colleagues and I have seen for ourselves archaeological evidence of cowrie working areas in the present-day royal palace of Abomey (Fig. 2.3).

Both economists by training, Jan Hogendorn and Marion Johnson (1986) include much quantitative data and apply the quantity theory of money (which holds that the general price level of goods and services is directly proportional to the amount of money in circulation) and Gresham's Law (which suggests that currency that has a commodity value lower than its nominal value will drive out the more valuable currency) to the cowrie trade. Their approach has been criticized or supplemented by more recent articles by Gregory (1996) and Ogundiran (2002), who consider how the cowrie was incorporated into local systems of value and meaning, exploring the shell's links with wealth and prosperity, on the one hand, but exploitation and inequality on the other. They expose the historical tensions between elite and popular discourses on the origin and meaning of cowries, especially in the Yorùbá area

Figure 2.3. A cowrie-processing area within the UNESCO listed Palace of Abomey, Benin (image by Anne Haour, May 2019).

(Ogundiran 2002) and in Dahomey (Gregory 1996). As part of this work, both Gregory (1996: 195) and Ogundiran (2002: 443–444) reproduce the same story of origin for cowrie money, recorded in 1979 from an Ayizo informant of the Allada region, one of the traditional vassals of Dahomey.

> In the beginning of the world we had the forge and we forged things, we had weaving-looms and we wove our clothes, we had oracle huts where we consulted the oracle, and we had boats from which we caught fish. We had no guns. We had no cowrie-money (*akwá*). If you went to the market you took beans in order to exchange them for sweet potatoes. You exchanged something specific for something else. Then the king brought the cowrie-money. What did the king do in order to bring the cowrie-money? He caught people and broke their legs and their arms. Then he built a hut in a banana plantation, put the people in it, and fed them bananas until they became big and fat. The king killed the people and he gave orders to his servants to attach strings to their bodies and to throw them into the sea where the cowrie-shells (*akwá*) lived. When the cowrie-shells started to eat the corpses they pulled them in, collected the shells, and put the live cowries in hot water to kill them. That is how cowrie-money came to exist.

Cece describes the direct sacrifice of people for cowrie money. The cowrie is something new, something external, and people ('we') have died for it for the benefit of powerful people ('the king'). An opposition is set up between artifacts relating to the production of food and useful items (the forge, weaving-looms, fishing boats) and the duo of cowrie money and guns. Gregory (1996: 197) sees in this mythic narrative 'the elements of a general criticism of the quantity theory of money'. For Cece and others who think like him, money is an instrument of the power of a king over his subjects, and the cowrie money is 'caught' by the king through their sacrifice. For an ordinary person, 'the things produced and exchanged by the labour of farmers and artisans is [*sic*] valued more highly than the inhuman mercantile dealings of a brutal king and his trading partners from over the seas' (Gregory 1996: 197).

In Yorùbá areas farther east vultures, symbolizing greedy and ruthless people, herald the introduction of cowries (Ogundiran 2002: 444–445). This tradition may allude to any of the set of actors: the European slavers who brought cowries to the Bight in large amounts, the local slave raiders and traders whose activities ensured the continuous flow of cowries into the hinterland, or the political elite who legitimized the use of cowries as currency and controlled the trade to the coast. These are part of a group of stories relating to the slave trade in the Gulf of Benin that evoke cowrie fishing at sea or in a large pond, using the body or body parts of a slave. A noteworthy fact is that such traditions also occur inland, but only very rarely – to the extent that they may then be interpreted as an introduction by slave traders (Gosselain and Haour 2018).

The work of Ogundiran (2002) on the Yorùbá world was alluded to above. I would like to mention it briefly here to illustrate that the rather malleable meaning of cowries is a recurring feature. Cowries were 'an important essence of self-realization' within the Bight of Benin generally (Ogundiran 2002: 445). For a start there are the traditions of architectural extravagances. Eighteenth century king of Benin Oba Eresoyen is remembered in oral traditions of the kingdom as having 'built a house of money' because he decorated the walls of his palace with cowries (Ben-Amos 1999: 104) while the house of a slightly later high dignitary was 'elegantly incrusted with small Indian shells, called cauris' (Landolphe 1823, cited in Ogundiran 2002: 446). Ogundiran (2002) suggests that when the Atlantic trade brought new quantities of cowries into the Yorùbá world, a cultural and political economic re-interpretation of an earlier idea of beads as political objects and as objects of social distinction took place. The glass beads used by the Ọyọ polity, and by the Edo Benin polity to the east, derived prestige from their 'long-distance source, rarity, and the control of the local supply by the political elite' (Ogundiran 2002: 435). The post-15th century social valuations of cowries developed from a prior institutionalization of beads as objects of political capital (2002: 429). The acquisition of cowries was not subjected to sumptuary laws such as those which created obstacles for the accumulation of dichroic glass beads, chalcedony, jasper and carnelian, and coral beads, and at the low end of the income distribution were people who never owned another [Atlantic] import but who would frequently have used cowries (Ogundiran 2002).

Such traditions are valuable as they offer alternative views to the use of cowrie currencies in some of the best studied regions of West Africa.

Concluding thoughts

The question of the process whereby money acquires value is a complex one. The example of Dahomey illustrates the myriad uses to which cowries, an alien object, were put in pre-colonial West Africa. Examples could be multiplied. In fact, recent oral tradition interviews seeking to illustrate the integration of cowries into ways of thinking indicated that, even when they have a primarily monetary function, cowries remained surrounded by a range of customary and ritual prohibitions (Iroko 1987: 205–206). Cowries served both as currency and as ritually powerful objects and this example confirms the impression given by archaeological data that it is difficult to separate domains of use for cowries. Value, and the distinction between currency and valuable, are blurry notions. The West African data provide an important illustration of these issues, which are common to the study of other times and peoples.

Notes

1. See a range of anecdotal references in issues of *MAN* 1939–1943.
2. There is considerable cross-over between these two authors, so that their similar accounts cannot be taken as corroborating each other. Al-'Umarī had completed his work at least seven years before ibn Juzayy edited ibn Battuta's account, and it is possible that ibn Juzayy referred to al-'Umarī's work in order to correct names and terms and to add detail to some descriptions (Levtzion and Hopkins 2000, 280).
3. We should note here that it has long been assumed that Islam provides a network to believers, facilitating trade between people even though they may not be personally acquainted, but

archaeological work continues to push back the date of contacts across the Sahara, potentially to a time before the development of the Muslim faith.

4. It is in stark contrast with the situation with terms relating to gold along the eastern arc of the Niger River, for example; as argued by Kuba (2009) variations of the same word *wura*, used in languages from very different phylae and families, between the Tamasheq-speaking area to the north and the Yorùbá-speaking region to the south, suggest it is a loanword and is indicative of a trade connection in the 15th century or before.

Bibliography

Alpern, S. (1995). What Africans got for their slaves: A master list of European trade goods. *History in Africa* 22, 5–43.

Apoh, W. and Gavua, K. (2010). Material Culture and Indigenous Spiritism: the Katamansu Archaeological "Otutu" (Shrine). *African Archaeological Review* 27, 211–235.

Bascom, W. (1993) [1980]. *Sixteen Cowries: Yoruba divination from Africa to the New World*. Bloomington IN: Indiana University Press.

Ben-Amos, P. (1999). *Art, Innovation, and Politics in Eighteenth-Century Benin*. Bloomington IN: Indiana University Press.

Blake, J.W. (ed.) (1942). *Europeans in West Africa, 1450-1560. Documents to Illustrate the Nature and Scope of Portuguese Enterprise in West Africa, the Abortive Attempt of Castilians to Create an Empire There, and the Early English Voyages to Barbary and Guinea*. London: Hakluyt.

Bloxam, G.W. (1887). Exhibition of West African symbolic messages. *Journal of the Anthropological Institute of Great Britain and Ireland* 16, 295–299.

Burgess, C.M. (1970). *The Living Cowries*. London: AS Barnes and Co.

Connah, G. (1981). *Three Thousand Years in Africa. Man and his Environment in the Lake Chad Region of Nigeria*. Cambridge: Cambridge University Press.

Cook, G.D. (2012). The Maritime Archaeology of West Africa in the Atlantic World: Investigations at Elmina. Ghana. Unpublished Ph.D dissertation, Syracuse University. https://surface.syr.edu/ant_etd/99/

Cook, G.D. (2014). Maritime archaeology in Ghana. In: Anquandah, J., Kankpeyeng, B. and Apoh, W. (eds) *Current Perspectives in the Archaeology of Ghana*. Legon: Sub-Saharan Publishers, 89–108.

De Corse, C. (1989). Beads as chronological indicators in West African Archaeology: A reexamination. *BEADS: Journal of the Society of Bead Researchers* 1, 41–53.

Einzig, P. (1949). *Primitive Money in its Ethnological, Historical and Economic Aspects*. London: Eyre & Spottiswoode.

Eluyemi, O. (1977). Excavations at Isoya near Ile-Ife (Nigeria), in 1972. *West African Journal of Archaeology* 7, 97–115.

Forrest, I. and Haour, A. (2018). Trust in long-distance relationships, 1000–1600 CE. *Past and Present* 38(13), 190–213.

Gosselain, O. and Haour, A. (2018). The site within West African political and craft history. In: Haour, A. (ed.) *Two Thousand Years in Dendi, Northern Benin: Archaeology, history and memory*. Leiden: Brill/JAAMS, 294–304.

Gregory, C. (1996). Cowries and conquest: Towards a subalternate Quality Theory of Money. *Comparative Studies in Society and History* 38(2), 195–217.

Haour, A. (2003). *Ethnoarchaeology in the Zinder Region, Republic of Niger: The site of Kufan Kanawa*. Oxford: British Archaeological Report S1133.

Haour, A. (2007). *Rulers, Warriors, Traders and Clerics: The Central Sahel and the North Sea, AD 800-1500*. Oxford: Oxford University Press.

Haour, A. and Christie, A. (2019). Cowries in the archaeology of West Africa: the present picture. *Azania: Archaeological Research in Africa* 54(3), 287–321.

Hiskett, M. (1966). Materials relating to the cowry currency of the Western Sudan–II: Reflections on the provenance and diffusion of the cowry in the Sahara and the Sudan. *Bulletin of the School of Oriental and African Studies* 29(2), 339–366.

Hogendorn, J. and Johnson, M. (1986). *The Shell Money of the Slave Trade*. Cambridge: Cambridge University Press.

Iroko, F. (1987). Les cauris en Afrique occidentale du Xe au XXe siècle. Unpublished Ph,D thesis, Sorbonne, Paris.

Jeffreys, M.D. (1948). The diffusion of cowries and Egyptian culture in Africa. *American Anthropologist* 50(1) Pt 1, 45–53.

Johnson, M. (1970). The cowrie currencies of West Africa Part I. *Journal of African History* 11(1), 17–49.

Johnson, M. (1976). Calico caravans: The Tripoli-Kano trade after 1880. *Journal of African History* 17(1), 95–117.

Kiéthéga, J.-B. (1983). *L'or de la Volta Noire*. Paris: Karthala.

Kuba, R. (2009). Cultural contacts between the savannah and the forest: Trade along the Eastern Niger. In: Magnavita, S., Koté, L., Breunig, P. and Idé, O.A. (eds) *Crossroads/Carrefour Sahel: Cultural and technological developments in first millennium BC/AD West Africa*. Frankfurt: Journal of African Archaeology Monograph Series 2, 147–156.

Levtzion, N. and Hopkins, J.F.P. (2000). *Corpus of Early Arabic Sources for West African history*. Princeton NJ: Markus Wiener.

Longhurst, A.R. and Pauly, D. (eds) (1987). *Ecology of Tropical Islands*. San Diego CA: Academic Press.

Lovejoy, P. (1974). Interregional monetary flows in the precolonial trade of Nigeria. *Journal of African History* 15, 563–585.

Lovejoy, P. (1985). The internal trade of West Africa before 1800. In: Ajayi, J. and Crowder, M. (eds) *History of West Africa: Volume One* (3rd edition). Harlow: Longman, 648–690.

Magnavita, S. (2015). *1500 Jahre am Mare de Kissi: eine Fallstudie zur Besiedlungsgeschichte des Sahel von Burkina Faso*. Frankfurt: Africa Magna.

Mattingly, D., Lahr, M. and Wilson, A. (2009). DMP V: Investigations in 2009 of cemeteries and related sites on the west side of the Taqallit Promontory. *Libyan Studies* 40, 95–131.

Mauny, R. (1967). Le navire de bord du navire Samta Maria da Comçeiça (1522). *Bulletin de l'IFAN, série B* 29, 512–535.

Mohammed, I.M. (1986). *The Archaeology of Central Darfur (Sudan) in the 1st millennium AD*. Oxford: British Archaeological Report S285.

Monteil, P. (1895). *De Saint-Louis à Tripoli par le lac Tchad: voyage au travers du Soudan et du Sahara accompli pendant les années 1890, 1891 et 1892*. Paris: Félix Alcan.

Ogundiran, A. (2002). Of small things remembered: beads, cowries, and cultural translations of the Atlantic experience in Yorubaland. *International Journal of African Historical Studies* 35(2–3), 427–457.

Paris, F. (1990). Les sépultures monumentales d'Iwelen. *Journal des africanistes* 60(1), 47–74.

Perinbam, B.M. (1973). Social relations in the Trans-Saharan and Western Sudanese trade: Aan overview. *Comparative Studies in Society and History* 15(4), 416–436.

Pietruszka, A.T. (2011). Artifacts of Exchange: A multiscalar approach to maritime archaeology at Elmina, Ghana. Unpublished Ph.D dissertation, Syracuse University. https://surface.syr.edu/ant_etd/87/

Polanyi, K. (1966). *Dahomey and the Slave Trade: An analysis of an archaic economy*. Seattle WA and London: University of Washington Press.

Quiggin, A.H. (1949). *A Survey of Primitive Money: The beginnings of currency*. London: Routledge.

Ryder, A.F.C. (1959). An early Portuguese trading voyage to the Forcados River. *Journal of the Historical Society of Nigeria* 1(4), 294–321.

Şaul, M. (2004). Money in colonial transition: cowries and francs in West Africa. *American Anthropologist* 106, 71–84.

Savary Des Bruslons, J. (1742). *Dictionnaire universel de commerce, contenant tout ce qui concerne le commerce qui se fait dans les quatre parties du monde. Tome Premier: A-C.* Geneva: Cramer & Philibert. https://gallica.bnf.fr/ark:/12148/bpt6k55968180

Skertchly, J.A. (1874). *Dahomey as it is; Being a narrative of eight months' residence in that country, with a full account of the notorious annual customs, and the social and religious institutions of the Ffons; also an appendix on Ashantee, and a glossary of Dahoman words and titles.* London: Chapman & Hall.

York, R.N. (1972). Cowries as type-fossils in Ghanaian archaeology. *West African Journal of Archaeology* 2, 93–101.

Chapter 3

Marketplaces and market exchanges in the pre-colonial Americas

Gary M. Feinman and Linda M. Nicholas

From their arrival on the shores of Mesoamerica in AD 1519, few indigenous institutions or practices spurred the admiration of the Spanish invaders more than did the markets of the Aztec (*e.g.*, Díaz del Castillo 1956: 218–219; Cortés 1962: 87–89; López de Gómara 1966: 160). And yet, until recently, only a handful of scholars (*e.g.*, Berdan 1975; 1977; 1980; Smith 1979; 1980; Blanton 1996) envisioned marketplace exchange as a central element of the Aztec economy, with most investigators emphasizing redistribution as the principal mode of this economic system (*e.g.*, Kurtz 1974; Carrasco 1978: 23; 2001: 363; Sanders *et al.* 1979; Evans 1980: 867). Despite the massive size of Aztec-era marketplaces and the broad spatial scope of this macro-regional market system (Blanton 1996; Hirth 2016; 2019), even fewer researchers (*e.g.*, Feinman *et al.* 1984; Winter 1984) recognized that the late pre-colonial Aztec market system must have had historical antecedents in Mesoamerica (Fig. 3.1) or that marketplace exchange likely extended beyond central Mexico, the Aztec heartland. Outside of Mesoamerica, across the pre-colonial Americas, the role and nature of marketplace exchange has remained barely considered.

Until recently, the almost complete dismissal of the core role that markets had in pre-Columbian economies stemmed largely from the paradigmatic frame that dominated the study of pre-industrial economies (Polanyi 1944; 1947; 1957; Polanyi *et al.* 1957), not just in the Americas but globally (Finley 1999). Throughout the social and historical sciences, marketplace exchange and market economies were thought basically to be an exclusively recent phenomenon associated with the rise of Western capitalist economies over the last several centuries. This framing presumption was bolstered in archaeological analyses by the clear methodological challenges faced by researchers who endeavored to document marketplaces or market exchange systems empirically (Towell and Atollini Lecón 2009; Feinman and Garraty 2010; Garraty 2010; Stark and Garraty 2010).

In this essay, we synthesize the rapidly changing perspectives on the importance and workings of marketplace exchange in the pre-colonial Americas. We begin

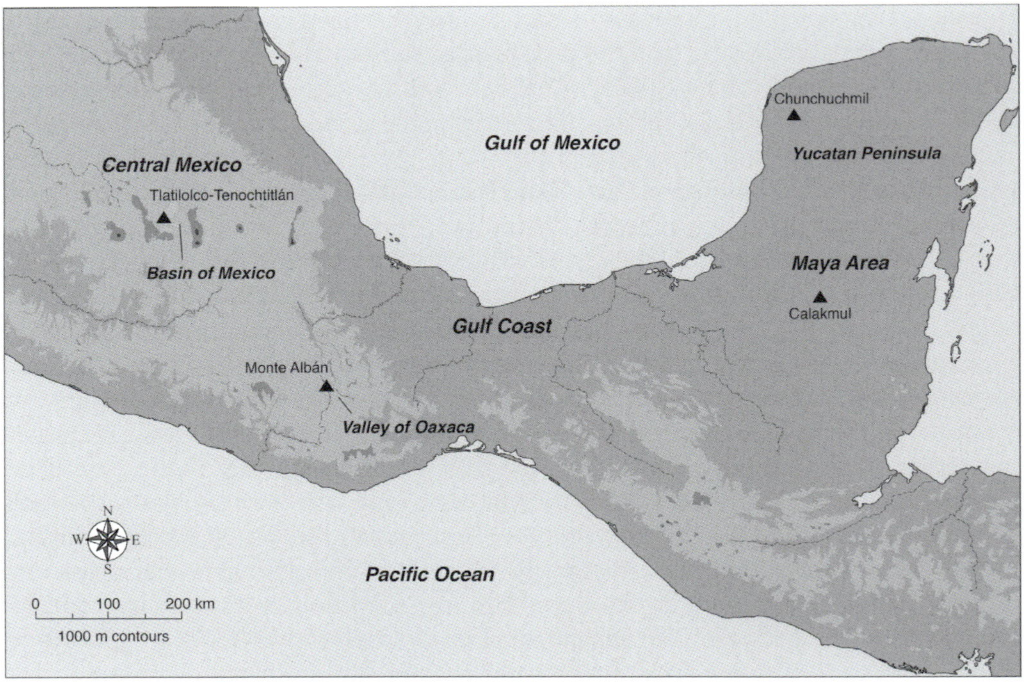

Figure 3.1 Map of Mesoamerica with sites mentioned in text.

coverage, and place our main focus here, on Mesoamerica, both because of the importance of markets as an institution in that macro-region (*e.g.*, Kowalewski 2019) but also because the conceptual consideration of this topic has been explored with greater depth there than elsewhere. Subsequently, we broaden the lens and briefly review the status of scholarly discussions concerning marketplaces and market exchange in Andean South America and select regions north of Mexico. The significant theoretical implications of these changing views on our understanding of pre-industrial economies, pre-modern states, and the interplay between the two is then considered in concluding this work.

Marketplace exchange in the Aztec World

Over the past several decades, scholarly understandings of marketplace and market exchanges in Mesoamerica have been markedly revised in conjunction with a significant uptick in discussions regarding pre-industrial markets more generally (*e.g.*, Feinman and Garraty 2010; Garraty and Stark 2010; Hirth and Pillsbury 2013a; Rahmsdorf and Stratford 2019). This reconceptualization owes much to new empirical findings and re-evaluations of old suites of evidence but it is unquestionably underpinned by major theoretical reconsiderations that followed the diminution of the long and overly polarized formalist-substantivist debate (Halperin 1984; Isaac 1993) and the conceptual advances that followed (*e.g.*, Smith 2004; Blanton and Fargher 2008; 2010; Feinman and Garraty 2010; Garraty and Stark 2010). Our prime focus here is on the current empirical understandings that now situate markets as one of pre-Hispanic Mesoamerica's most important institutions (Feinman and Nicholas 2012; Kowalewski 2012; 2019). For Mesoamerica, we first explore the Aztec, for whom we can draw on both documentary and archaeological sources that allow us to present a fuller picture, then move to other highland contexts before discussing a suite of recent research in lowland regions with a focus on the Maya.

Sixteenth century Spanish sources, which detail the broad spatial scale of the Aztec market system, the enormity of the main market at Tlatilolco-Tenochtitlán, the diversity of goods available, the existence of currencies (Millon 1955), and even an account of the process of haggling between sellers/buyers over transactions (de Torquemada 1943: 580), have long been known to scholars. Cortés (1962: 89) remarked that 'there is nothing to be found in all the land, which is not sold in these markets'. Bernal Díaz del Castillo noted that the market space was so large that more than two days would be necessary for a visitor to see everything (Léon-Portilla 1962: 25). Nevertheless, the role of markets for the Aztec economy was downplayed for decades by a generation of researchers who, constrained by top-down theoretical biases regarding non-Western, pre-industrial polities (Polanyi *et al.* 1957; Wittfogel 1957; Marx 1971; *cf.* Offner 1981; Feinman 2017), instead stressed other aspects of the complex, macro-scale Aztec economy, including tribute and the role of officials in adjudicating market transactions and maintaining law and order in these settings (*e.g.*, Kurtz 1974; Evans 1980; Carrasco 2001).

Although no one contests these political-economic linkages, including that the taxing of market attendance was a revenue source for the Aztec treasury (Smith 2015), it is no longer tenable to use these connections as a basis to argue that the Aztec market system was politically controlled or a variant of a top-down control or redistributive economy. These now-dated arguments reflect previously held false metrics too often applied to the deep (pre-industrial) economic past. After all, all known market systems, past and present, operate in contexts with differing degrees of social embeddedness and governmental oversight (Granovetter 1985; Lie 1991; 1997; Swedberg 1994; 2005; McCloskey 1997; Feinman and Garraty 2010; Blanton 2013). The point is that interrelations between sociopolitical action and market behaviors should not be viewed as necessary signs of market or commercial weakness (Blanton 2013); they may actually be crucial to how most markets were instituted and functioned. For the rulers of the late pre-Hispanic Aztec polity, the implementation of tributary demands and other political/military initiatives helped provoke the flow of market goods and elevate market system participation (Gutiérrez 2013). The rulers of Aztec times did not directly monitor production or control marketplace exchanges but military conquest and subsequent pacification along with certain tributary policies had a role in promoting market vitality and the expansion of the economic network (Blanton and Fargher 2012: 15).

The hierarchical marketplace system of the Aztec extended across the Basin of Mexico and was linked to other regional marketplaces situated throughout the empire and beyond (Blanton 1996; Smith 2012; Hirth 2016; 2019). Aztec marketplaces were centers for a vibrant commercial economy, despite a transport system in which most goods were moved on the backs of porters. Water transport was employed along Mesoamerica's coasts and in the Basin of Mexico's lake system, but the micro-region has few navigable rivers. Yet in scale and diversity of goods, Mesoamerica's markets, in particular the Tlatelolco-Tenochtitán central marketplace with its more than 60,000 buyers and sellers daily, some coming from considerable distances, greatly impressed the Spanish, who gave witness that even in the commercial hub of the Mediterranean there was nothing comparable (Díaz de Castillo 1956: 215; Cortés 1962: 87; López de Gómara 1966: 160).

The Tlatelolco-Tenochtitlán market was crowded and had a diverse array of goods (mundane, rare, local, exotic) crafted or grown by tens of thousands of farmers and artisans. Most participants in the Aztec market were small-scale producers, sellers, and consumers (Hirth 2016: 102–150). A key point is that domestic production was a cornerstone of the Aztec market system. Now, decades of archaeological research illustrate what we knew for the Aztec from historical records and archaeological sources (*e.g.*, Nichols 2013) also applies to the deeper past in this pre-Hispanic world. Most craft production for exchange in ancient Mesoamerica was carried out in domestic contexts (Feinman 1999; 2006; Hirth 2009a; Feinman and Nicholas 2010) rather than non-domestic workshops. These productive activities were largely enacted on a part-time basis (Feinman 1999; Hirth 2009a). Households were not self-sufficient, rather they were interdependent and consumed a broad range of goods that they did not produce themselves, largely through market exchange (Feinman 2006; Hirth 2009b; Feinman and Nicholas 2010; 2012).

Tlatelolco-Tenochtitlán stood at the apex of a hierarchical system of marketplaces in the Basin of Mexico, integrated through a periodic cycle that was expressly tied to the ritual calendar (Smith 1979: 112; Hassig 1982). Larger markets met daily but other smaller venues convened only every five days. According to historical documents, '[t]he marketplace was the center of economic life ... [i]t was a creative, enabling force that ... shaped the structure and organization of prehispanic society' (Hirth 2016: 59). It was a formal institution, with different areas devoted to specific classes of goods (Feldman 1978) and market judges to resolve conflicts. Taxes also were levied on all venders entering the market (Smith 2015; Hirth 2016: 75–79). Economic transactions took place between thousands of merchants and consumers who were not socially related, using an array of currencies (goods with regularized values) in these transactions, including cacao beans and woven textiles. The marketing network was intertwined with other modes of exchange, such as tribute, itinerant peddlers, and the treks of long-distance traders (*e.g.*, Berdan 1977; Gutiérrez 2013; Isaac 2013; Hirth 2016).

Although the Aztec market system lacked printed money and coinage, certain items, such as cacao seeds, quills full of gold dust, and sheets of woven cloth, had standardized values that facilitated marketplace exchanges (Berdan 1982: 43–44). Through barter and haggling specific transactions were consummated, while costs and prices varied with demand for at least some goods, like staple foods (Sahagún 1950–1982: v. 2: 98; Isaac 2013: 438). Aztec tribute demands and equivalencies established over time concerning these exactions appear to have helped set, modify, and expand the spatial range of these values outside the heart of the empire and the core of its market system (Gutiérrez 2013: 158–165). As in many other historical regions (Weatherford 1997: 1–27), the Aztec market system flourished without standardized paper money or coin. Of course, the complex embedded meanings and roles of currencies and money across time (Hudson 2004; Maurer 2006) are illustrative of the weaknesses that fundamentally characterize the categorical, dichotomous frames too-long applied to the study of pre-industrial economies (Polanyi 1957: 264–266; Dalton 1961). The counterfeiting of cacao pods even hints at a motive for profit as does Friar Sahagún's (1950–1982: v. 10: 43, 65, 67, 74) lengthy descriptions of 'bad merchants' as 'stingy, avaricious, greedy, thrifty', and more. One of the first friars (Molina 1972 [translated by Dibble 1988: 71, 73]) to reach central Mexico recounted the following for small traders: 'And when you bought good capes, perhaps you inserted them among the poor ones? And when you filled in the holes of the holey capes, perhaps you did not show your customer that the capes were holey, damaged, whereby you made sport of him?'

An in-depth study of Aztec imperialism (Berdan *et al.* 1996) has documented that, while imperial conquests may have given the Aztec market system a boost, the expansion of the market system preceded the empire's growth. As noted by geographers (Berndt and Boeckler 2009: 536), 'markets do not simply fall out of thin air but are continually produced and constructed socially with the help of actors who are interlinked in dense and extensive webs of social relations'. In fact, they require norms and conventions of cooperation (Blanton 2013). Certainly, this applies to a market system as large as that of the Aztec. In the sections to follow, we broaden the vantage beyond the Aztec, define key terms, and then discuss marketplace exchange in other Mesoamerican regions as well as macro-regional predecessors to the marketplaces of the Aztec.

Definitional perspectives on marketplace exchange

Many economic transfers within the commercialized Aztec exchange system fit comfortably in a more general definition of market exchange as economic transactions where the forces of supply and demand are visible and where prices or exchange equivalences exist (Feinman and Garraty 2010: 169). Likewise, Aztec marketplaces, open plazas with few associated monumental structures, proximity to accessways, and where buyers and sellers congregated, conform to a general classification of marketplaces as physical places in which people congregate and market exchanges are customarily conducted (Feinman and Garraty 2010: 170). Almost every Aztec urban center (Blanton 1996; Smith 2008) had a central marketplace, and both archaeological and ethnohistoric information attest to the flows of goods and people between these centers (Blanton 1996; Hirth *et al.* 2017). Consequently, this network clearly fits the definition of a regional market system, an economically linked network of marketplaces across a regional landscape (Feinman and Garraty 2010: 175).

The detailed accounts of Aztec markets from documentary sources, supplemented by object-based archaeological findings, provide a suite of evidential indicators that can be employed as test implications for marketplaces and market exchange in contexts where textual records are scarce or absent (Feinman and Garraty 2010; Garraty 2010; Kowalewski 2019: 334). Because of the difficulties of the task, convincing assignments likely will require several indicators at multiple analytical scales (Feinman and Nicholas 2010). Large, flat open spaces or plazas that are associated with accessways but not enclosed by an array of monumental buildings serve as a starting point (Feinman and Nicholas 2010; Kowalewski 2019). Within regions, these spaces should correspond roughly to the size of settlements with these features. Mesoamerican markets were goods markets; many of the items consumed were organic, including agricultural produce, food, fiber, and animal products. Micro-remains and sediment residues should reflect these concentrations (Dahlin *et al.* 2007; Hutson *et al.* 2010; Hutson 2017). At the same time, artifactual distributions should reflect the movement of goods beyond local communities and patterns of dispersal in which settlements in regions and households in communities have access to different suites of goods (Hirth 1998). That is, the distributional patterns should not correspond with centralized redistribution or pooling (Feinman and Nicholas 2010; Garraty 2010).

Mesoamerican marketplace exchange

Beyond the Basin of Mexico, brief descriptions of late pre-Hispanic markets exist for other regions, including the highlands and valleys of Oaxaca (Spores 1965; Pohl *et al.* 1997) and the Maya region (Dahlin *et al.* 2010; Tokovinine and Beliaev 2013; Kepecs 2015; King 2015). In Yucatec Mayan, the word for 'market' also means 'plaza' and 'where one buys or sells' (Dahlin *et al.* 2010: 195); there is no distinct/separate word for 'market' or 'plaza' (Shaw 2012; King 2015: 35), which is interpreted to indicate the functional overlap and deep-seated cognitive correspondence between the two (Speal 2014; King 2015: 35). Although the Spanish descriptions of Maya markets are less elaborated than those for the Aztec, they generally describe large plazas where various goods were sold (King 2015: 34–35). In the Mixtec language of highland Oaxaca, the word for 'marketplace' also refers to cost/price (Terraciano 2001; Kowalewski 2019: 325). In contrast to the Aztec, late pre-Hispanic Mixtec market spaces were situated in open areas at the edges of (or even outside) communities (Pohl *et al.* 1997).

Given the ubiquity of marketplaces across late pre-Hispanic Mesoamerica, a key question becomes the time depth of marketplace exchange across the macro-region. Flows of goods and networks of connectivity may reflect that marketplace exchanges were more highly commercialized during the last pre-Hispanic centuries as compared to earlier (Berdan 2003; Berdan *et al.* 2003; Blanton and Fargher 2012). Broad-scale analyses of obsidian transfers across the Mesoamerican world point to a fundamental shift (intensification) in patterns of interaction after AD 900–1200 (Golitko and Feinman 2015: 232–233; Feinman *et al.* 2019: 21). Nevertheless, there is a growing consensus that marketplace exchange was fundamental to Mesoamerican economies by the outset (*c.* AD 200–300) of the Classic period (Kowalewski 2019) if not considerably earlier.

For example, historical linguistic analyses (Tokovinine and Beliaev 2013; Speal 2014) indicate that key Mayan words associated with exchange, like 'sell', have a long history, perhaps extending back to around 1000 BC. Given the deep historical correspondence in meaning between 'marketplace' and 'plaza', it is curious that some of the earliest public spaces at lowland sites of this time (and centuries earlier) were artificially leveled, low, open spaces or plazas (Lesure 1997) as well as long, low platforms (Inomata *et al.* 2019) where gatherings and exchange, of both information and goods, could have taken place. These early open spaces were amplified and shifted in use over time, but they attracted a still-mobile population to these emergent centers.

In the highland Valley of Oaxaca, we (Feinman *et al.* 1984; Blanton *et al.* 1993; 1999) have proposed that markets emerged around 500 BC, as an important mechanism for the provisioning the early hilltop city of Monte Albán. The city population grew rapidly and was situated in a sector of the valley that was not especially productive or risk-free for agriculture. And yet, there is no evidence for centralized granaries or large-scale food storage of the kind that might be expected with centralized redistribution. Domestic artisanry for exchange and householder production for (and participation in) exchange networks, both local and long-distance, were key elements of the economy of the region from this period through the contemporary era (Feinman *et al.* 1984; Feinman and Nicholas 2010; 2012).

The case for marketplace exchange in a suite of Mesoamerican regions during the Classic period (*c.* AD 200–900), including the Maya area (Carrasco Vargas *et al.* 2009; Braswell 2010; Dahlin *et al.* 2010; Masson and Freidel 2012; 2013; Shaw 2012; Tokovinine and Beliaev 2013; Chase and Chase 2014; Chase *et al.* 2015; Eppich and Freidel 2015; Jones 2015; King 2015; Shaw and King 2015; Cap 2019), the Valley of Oaxaca (Feinman and Nicholas 2010; 2012), central Mexico (Sullivan 2007; Carballo 2013), and the Gulf Coast (Stark and Ossa 2010), is now far more empirically robust, grounded in a diversity of evidential sources, as compared to a decade or two ago. Furthermore, we recently have made the argument that the broad adoption of calendrical mechanisms that allowed for the tracking of annual cycles early in (or just prior to) the advent of the Classic period allowed for higher degrees of market-system interconnectivity across Mesoamerica (Feinman and Nicholas 2020). Earlier regional market networks likely became more interconnected with greater volumes of long-distance exchange, illustrated through wider distributions and higher volumes of movement for cacao, cloth, obsidian, feathers, shell, and other items of value (Blanton *et al.* 2005). Without a synchronized means of measuring time that crossed polity/regional boundaries, how would long-distance merchants and traders know when to show up at markets, likely periodically held, outside their local regions?

At the Classic Maya site of Calakmul, a mural, associated with an early building stage of a temple that is adjacent to sizable open spaces, depicts people of all ranks engaged in eating and drinking (Carrasco Vargas *et al.* 2009). Some of the figures in the murals are glyphically identified by monikers that, when translated, identify them as 'salt person' or 'atole [corn gruel] person' (Martin 2012). The positioning of the mural to face outward toward the rest of the site appears to mark this space as being for public food transfer, procurement, and consumption. Although market activities at Calakmul cannot be confirmed at this point, that interpretation seems most salient given the information available.

Beyond the Calakmul mural and the soil chemical analyses implemented in plazas at a set of Classic Maya sites, most notably Chunchucmil (*e.g.*, Dahlin *et al.* 2007; 2010; Terry *et al.* 2015), the lion's share of the evidence for Classic Maya marketplace exchange is derived from the identification of open plaza spaces at large settlements and artifactual distributions that would be hard to explain through any other economic modes of transfer (Masson and Freidel 2012; 2013: 210–212; Shaw 2012). These latter two classes of evidence also provide the strongest indicators for Classic-period marketplace exchange in other regions of Mesoamerica. Because no one criterion is unequivocal, for the Valley of Oaxaca, we outlined an explicitly multi-scalar suite of hypotheses that drew on findings from household artifact distributions and site- and regional-scale settlement patterns to macro-regional patterns of exchange to make a case for a market-based system of exchange (Feinman and Nicholas 2010). For pre-Hispanic Mesoamerica, with debate over the importance of marketplace exchange largely settled, research focus now turns to a new suite of questions that revolve around the causes and consequences of the spatial and temporal differences in these market networks, how these systems emerged, shifts in cross-regional connectivities across time, and the interplays between markets and both other means of economic transfer and the sociopolitical institutions in which these exchange spheres were embedded.

Looking south and north beyond Mesoamerica

As outlined earlier, when they entered the Aztec heartland in the Basin of Mexico, the Spanish invaders were amazed by the scale and diversity of goods in Aztec marketplaces. In marked contrast, the accounts that followed foreign incursions into the Andean core of the Inka domain yielded comparatively few descriptions of markets, but the European intruders did take note of and exploit the storehouses of food that the Inka situated along transport corridors. The differences between these eyewitness texts are meaningful and reflect important distinctions in the economic systems of these late pre-Hispanic empires and the worlds from which they emerged. Clearly, in general, the public sector was more central to the Inka economy than for the Aztec, as the former's government implemented certain allocational functions that were left mostly to markets in the Aztec world (Stanish 2010; Isaac 2013).

It is worth briefly contemplating the history of economic ideas advanced for these late pre-Hispanic empires at a time when top-down substantivist notions regarding pre-industrial states and their economies dominated (Polanyi 1944; 1947; 1957; Polanyi *et al.* 1957). For the Aztec, the vivid descriptions of markets created a degree of empirical dissonance for the redistributive models and command economy biases and generalizations that were in vogue (*e.g.*, Kurtz 1974; Carrasco 1978: 23; 2001: 363; Sanders *et al.* 1979; Evans 1980: 867). Innovative, empirically focused works (*e.g.*, Berdan 1975; Blanton 1985; Smith 1980) ultimately crippled these categorical top-down, managerial perspectives, thereby opening intellectual space for fruitful dialogues regarding the variation in pre-Hispanic markets and economies (and their relations to political institutions) in Mesoamerica that have blossomed subsequently (Blanton and Fargher 2010; Feinman and Garraty 2010).

By comparison, for most of the second half of the 20th century, pre-Hispanic economies in the Andean world (*e.g.*, Murra 1962; Schaedel 1978) were shoe-horned to fit more general expectations of centralized planned economies (Dalton 1975: 92–95; *cf.* Stark and Garraty 2010; Feinman 2013; Hirth and Pillsbury 2013b; Mayer 2013), despite intermittent reference to Spanish accounts that marketplace exchange (Murra 1956; Earle 1985; Mayer 2002) and periodic market fairs (Stanish and Coben 2013) were present both in the Inka heartland as well as more distant reaches of the late pre-Hispanic Andean realm (Salomon 1986). In reality the key issue is not whether these markets were periodic, enacted transactions via barter, dovetailed with ritual cycles, or whether they were intertwined with other modes of transfer, such as reciprocity and redistribution/tribute. In point of fact, globally pre-industrial markets are characterized by these features albeit to different degrees (Feinman and Garraty 2010; Blanton 2013). With the recognition that marketplace exchanges were integral, though perhaps less commercialized and central, to the late pre-Hispanic Andean economy as compared to Mesoamerica, a new research agenda emerged concerning their time depth, articulations with the political realm, variation over space and time, and interrelations with other modes of transfer (*e.g.*, Burger 2013; Nielsen 2013; Stanish and Coben 2013). The cross-cultural theoretical ramifications are significant as well and may, in part, account for the generally smaller city sizes in the Andean world in relation to Mesoamerica, despite the presence of animal transport (camelids) in the former. Sustainable urban provisioning may have posed a greater challenge in the Andes with less commercialized market networks (Stanish 2010; Isaac 2013), thereby contributing to the generally smaller sizes of pre-Hispanic Andean central places as compared to pre-colonial Mesoamerica.

Prior to European incursions, settlement sizes were generally smaller and social formations were less hierarchically complex north of Mesoamerica. Questions regarding the presence of indigenous market exchange only rarely have been considered seriously. The most in-depth arguments for marketplace networks north of Mexico have been centered on the Hohokam of south and central Arizona (Abbott 2010), where a network of more than 230 ballcourts dispersed across almost 200 communities served as loci for ritual ballgames (*c.* AD 1000–1070). People travelled to these events as participants and spectators, leaving open the likelihood that barter and exchanges between strangers took place. Specialized ceramic production for exchange, with specific ceramic forms distributed from select locations to large swaths of the Phoenix Basin is evidenced even prior to the construction of the ballcourts and long-distance exchange goods, including marine shell from California, were acquired by Hohokam householders (Abbott *et al.* 2007; Abbott 2010; Watts and Ossa 2016).

Although no currencies have been proposed for the pre-contact Hohokam exchange network, marine shell beads have been recognized broadly to be a currency in indigenous California based on compilations of both ethnographic (Chagnon 1970) and archaeological evidence (Gamble and King 2011; Burns 2019). Transfers of these beads extended during indigenous times to the greater Southwest. Although the presence of a currency does not uniformly coincide with transfers through marketplace exchanges, it has been documented that networks for the conveyance of goods extended well beyond cultural boundaries, likely among individuals who were not deeply familiar or acquainted with each other. For native California, the explication for shell currency generally is envisioned as a means of forestalling extensive debts. Differential needs could foment imbalances that potentially could rupture incentives for exchange. Currencies help reconcile imbalances, minimize transactions costs, and keep transfers on track (Burns 2019). Nevertheless, this account leaves unsettled key questions including where and how often did these interregional exchange events occur, what was the participatory scale of these episodes of conveyance, and how (through what socioeconomic mechanisms) were cross-regional conventions regarding recognized shell currencies established (*e.g.*, Hudson 2004)?

Conceptual and synthetic implications

In regard to the pre-colonial Americas, the expanded consensus that now recognizes the importance of marketplace exchange, currencies, and other means of interpersonal economic transfers across regions (between both elite and subalterns) forces a re-evaluation of how we conceptualize pre-modern polities and pre-industrial economies both in the Western Hemisphere and globally. For too long studies of pre-modern worlds have adopted an anti-market perspective (Cook 1968; Attwood 1997; Blanton and Fargher 2010; Feinman and Garraty 2010; Feinman 2017) that juxtaposes people in the past from current Westerners, with the latter envisioned as individualized, utility maximizers (*e.g.*, Friedman 1982). Yet, recent events and a growing body of social science research across disciplines has led scholars to question whether terms like 'free market', 'completely disembedded economies', or 'transactional self-regulation' are applicable to any actual behavioral context, even the contemporary (Granovetter 1985;

1992; Lie 1997; Swedberg 2005; Blanton and Fargher 2010). In other words, economies, across time and space, even modern ones, are always embedded in their broader societal contexts, albeit in different ways and to varying degrees (Barber 1995; Krippner 2001; Krugman 2009).

The long-standing social science vision of modern Western economies is relevant to our focus here. For too long supposed 'free market economies' of the modern West were used as a false metric to argue that whatever markets were reported outside the West or in pre-modern times did not operate as 'true' markets because they were intertwined with political institutions or other modes of economic transfer. As McCloskey (1997) put it, Polanyi (1944) was largely right (that economies are embedded), but also wrong (in his blind spot regarding modern Western economies, which do not actually have 'free' markets). Pre-modern markets were an important economic institution historically, including in many areas both in and beyond Europe (Blanton and Fargher 2010; Feinman and Garraty 2010), with pre-colonial Mesoamerica a prime exemplar.

The intellectual stakes of these realizations are broader than may be immediately apparent. For more than a century, a canonical – but from our perspective mistaken – claim of Western social science has advocated two historical pathways. One (Occidental) undergirds the modern world, based on reason, rationality, agency, markets, and elements of democracy. The other (Asiatic) was seen as despotic and/or manipulated through false consciousness, managed from the top down, so that agency was not afforded subalterns (Marx 1971).

When archaeologists and ethnohistorians began to investigate indigenous American economies during the middle of the last century (Feinman and Nicholas 2012), they reflexively elected to draw their framing concepts and tenets from the Asiatic mode. Yet, subsequently, this top-down vision of political economies, controlled by despotic rulers, characterized by redistribution and centralized storage has garnered only the sparest empirical support across the indigenous Americas as the record on production, distribution, and consumption was built through dirt-derived archaeological studies. The actual evidence for large-scale, centralized redistribution has been scanty for decades (*e.g.*, Earle 1977; Feinman and Neitzel 1984), especially beyond the Andes. Findings from household archaeology situate most production for exchange in residential contexts (*e.g.*, Feinman 1999; Hirth 2009a). With this emerging picture, the importance of marketplace exchange should not be a surprise, while knee-jerk presumptions of pre-industrial command economies must be called into question. In fact, beyond the Americas, we suggest that the false barriers between the study of past and present economies need to be broached, if merely to better understand if and how they fundamentally differ (*e.g.*, Smith 2004; Blanton and Fargher 2008; 2010; 2016; Feinman and Garraty 2010).

Minimally, in terms of global histories, it is now evident that pre-industrial economies were more variable than long-presumed and often were not managed from the top down (Feinman 2017). Whether in contexts with or without urban centers, fundamental economic linkages were not strictly local (*e.g.*, Blanton and Feinman

1984; Smith and Berdan 2003; Blanton *et al.* 2005; Nielsen 2013; Golitko and Feinman 2015; Feinman 2019). Furthermore, a revised perspective on pre-modern economies also forces reflection on pre-industrial states. If economies were not administered by managerial or despotic elites, then polities in the past could not have secured the resources necessary to fund the operations of governance simply by controlling production and/or distribution as long thought. Rather, it now appears that the fiscal financing of governance was highly diversified in time, space, and historical context (Monson and Scheidel 2015) and that how government was economically underpinned is, in fact, a key variable that helps account for diversity in the nature of leadership and governance (Blanton and Fargher 2008; 2016). In short, we now have entered a new analytical era for the study of the pre-modern Americas; not only was the nature of governance and political practices more variable than once thought (*e.g.*, Feinman 2018; Carballo and Feinman 2019) but so were the economies that underpinned these indigenous polities. We now know that markets and currencies were a key part of this historical story, but there is still much to be discovered.

Bibliography

Abbott, D.R. (2010). The rise and demise of marketplace exchange among the prehistoric Hohokam of Arizona. In: Garraty, C.P. and Stark, B.L. (eds) *Archaeological Approaches to Market Exchange in Ancient Societies.* Boulder CO: University Press of Colorado, 61–83.

Abbott, D.R., Smith, A.M. and Gallega, E. (2007). Ballcourts and ceramics: The case for Hohokam marketplaces in the Arizona desert. *American Antiquity* 72, 461–484.

Attwood, D.W. (1997). The invisible peasant. In: Blanton, R.E., Peregrine, P.N., Winslow, D. and Hall, T.D. (eds) *Economic Analysis beyond the Local System.* Lanham MD: University Press of America, 147–169.

Barber, B. (1995). All economies are embedded: The career of a concept and beyond. *Social Research* 62, 387–413.

Berdan, F.F. (1975). Trade, Tribute, and Market in the Aztec Empire. Unpublished Ph.D. dissertation, University of Texas.

Berdan, F.F. (1977). Distributive mechanisms in the Aztec economy. In: Halperin, R. and Dow, K. (eds) *Peasant Livelihood: Studies in Economic Anthropology and Cultural Ecology.* New York: St Martins, 91–101.

Berdan, F.F. (1980). Aztec merchants and markets: Local-level economic activity in a non-industrial empire. *Mexicon* 2(3) 37–41.

Berdan, F.F. (1982). *The Aztecs of Central Mexico: An Imperial Society*, New York: Holt, Rinehart and Winston.

Berdan, F.F. (2003). The economy of Postclassic Mesoamerica. In: Smith and Berdan (eds) 2003, 93–95.

Berdan, F.F., Masson, M.A., Gasco, J. and Smith, M.E. (2003). An international economy. In: Smith and Berdan (eds), 2003, 96–108.

Berdan, F.F., Blanton, R.E., Boone, E.H., Hodge, M.G., Smith, M.E and Umberger, E. (1996) *Aztec Imperial Strategies.* Washington DC: Dumbarton Oaks Pre-Columbian Symposia and Colloquia.

Berndt, C. and Boeckler, M. (2009). Geographies of circulation and exchange: Constructions of markets. *Progress in Human Geography* 33, 535–551.

Blanton, R.E. (1985). A comparison of early market systems. In: Plattner, S. (ed.) *Markets and Marketing.* Lanham MD: University Press of America, 399–416.

Blanton, R.E. (1996). The Basin of Mexico market system and the growth of empire. In: Berdan *et al.* 1996, 47–84.

Blanton, R.E. (2013). Cooperation and the moral economy of the marketplace. In: Hirth and Pillsbury (eds) 2006a, 23–49.

Blanton, R. and Fargher, L. (2008). *Collective Action in the Formation of Pre-Modern States*. New York: Springer.

Blanton, R.E. and Fargher, L.F. (2010). Evaluating causal factors in market development in premodern states: A comparative study, with critical comments on the history of ideas about markets. In: Garraty and Stark (eds) 2010, 207–226.

Blanton, R.E. and Fargher, L.F. (2012). Market cooperation and the evolution of the pre-Hispanic Mesoamerican world-system. In: Babones, S.J. and Chase-Dunn, C.K. (eds) *Routledge Handbook of World-Systems Theory and Research*. London: Routledge, 11–20.

Blanton, R.E. and Fargher, L.F. (2016). *How Humans Cooperate: Confronting the Challenges of Collective Action*. Boulder CO: University Press of Colorado.

Blanton, R.E. and Feinman, G.M. (1984). The Mesoamerican world system. *American Anthropologist* 86, 673–682.

Blanton, R.E., Fargher, L.F. and Heredia-Espinoza, V.Y. (2005). The Mesoamerican world of goods and its transformation. In: Blanton, R.E. (ed.) *Settlement, Subsistence, and Social Complexity: Essays Honoring the Legacy of Jeffrey R. Parsons*. Los Angeles CA: Cotsen Institute, 260–294.

Blanton, R.E., Feinman, G.M., Kowalewski, S.A. and Nicholas, L.M. (1999). *Ancient Oaxaca*. Cambridge: Cambridge University Press.

Blanton, R.E., Kowalewski, S.A., Feinman, G.M. and Finsten, L.M. (1993). *Ancient Mesoamerica: A Comparison of Change in Three Regions* (2nd edition). Cambridge: Cambridge University Press.

Braswell, G.E. (2010). The rise and fall of market exchange: A dynamic approach to ancient Maya economy. In: Garraty and Stark (eds) 2010, 127–140.

Burger, R.L. (2013). In the realm of the Incas: An archaeological reconsideration of household exchange, long-distance exchange, and marketplaces in the pre-Hispanic central Andes. In: Hirth and Pillsbury (eds) 2013a, 319–334.

Burns, G.R. (2019). Evolution of Shell Bead Money in Central California: An Isotopic Approach. Unpublished Ph.D dissertation, University of California.

Cap, B. (2019). A Classic Maya marketplace at Xunantunich, Belize. *Research Reports in Belizean Archaeology* 16, 111–122.

Carballo, D.M. (2013). The social organization of craft production and interregional exchange at Teotihuacan. In: Hirth and Pillsbury (eds) 2013a, 113–140.

Carballo, D.M. and Feinman, G.M. (2019). The scale, governance, and sustainability of central places in pre-Hispanic Mesoamerica. In: Lozny, L.R. and McGovern, T.H. (eds) *Global Perspectives on Long Term Community Resource Management*. Cham: Springer, 235–253.

Carrasco, P. (1978). La economía del México prehispánico. In: Carrasco, P. and Broda, J. (eds) *Economía Política e Ideología en el México*. Mexico City: CIS-INAH, Editorial Nueva Imagen, 15–74.

Carrasco, P. (2001). Economic organization and development. In: Carrasco, P. (ed.) *The Oxford Encyclopedia of Mesoamerican Cultures: The Civilizations of Mexico and Central America*. Oxford: Oxford University Press, 363–366.

Carrasco Vargas, R., Vásquez López, V.A. and Martin, S. (2009). Daily life of the ancient Maya recorded on murals at Calakmul, Mexico. *Proceedings of the National Academy of Sciences* 106, 19245–19249.

Chagnon, N.A. (1970). Ecological and adaptive aspects of California shell money. *Annual Reports of the University of California Archaeological Survey* 12: 5–25.

Chase, A.F., Chase, D.Z., Terry, R.E., Horlacher, J.M. and Chase, A.S.Z. (2015). Markets among the ancient Maya: The case of Caracol, Belize. In: King, E.M. (ed.) *The Ancient Maya Marketplace: The Archaeology of Transient Space*. Tucson AZ: University of Arizona Press, 226–250.

Chase, D.Z. and Chase, A.F. (2014). Ancient Maya markets and the economic integration of Caracol, Belize. *Ancient Mesoamerica* 25, 239–250.

Cook, S. (1968). The obsolete 'anti-market' mentality: A critique of the substantivist approach to economic anthropology. In: LeClair, E.E. and Schneider, H.K. (eds) *Economic Anthropology: Readings in Theory and Analysis.* New York: Holt, Rinehart & Winston, 208–228.

Cortés, H. (1962). *Five Letters of Cortés to the Emperor* (ed. and trans. J.B. Morris). New York: Norton.

Dahlin, B.H., Bair, D., Beach, T., Moriarty, M. and Terry, R. (2010). The dirt on food: Ancient feasts and markets among the lowland Maya. In: Staller, J.E. and Carrasco, M.D. (eds) *Pre-Columbian Foodways: Interdisciplinary Approaches to Food, Culture, and Markets in Ancient Mesoamerica.* New York: Springer, 191–232.

Dahlin, B.H., Jensen, C.T., Terry, R.E., Wright, D.R. and Beach, T. (2007). In search of an ancient Maya market. *Latin American Antiquity* 18, 363–384.

Dalton, G. (1961). Economic theory and primitive society. *American Anthropologist* 63, 1–25.

Dalton, G. (1975). Karl Polanyi's analysis of long-distance trade and his wider paradigm. In: Sabloff, J.A. and Lamberg-Karlovsky, C.C. (eds) *Ancient Civilization and Trade.* Albuquerque NM: University of New Mexico Press, 63–132.

Díaz del Castillo, B. (1956). *The Discovery and Conquest of Mexico, 1517-1521.* New York: Farrar, Strauss and Cudahy.

Dibble, C.E. (1988). Molina and Sahagún. In: Josserand, J.K. and Dakin, K. (eds) *Smoke and Mist: Mesoamerican Studies in Memory of Thelma D. Sullivan.* Oxford: British Archaeological Reports S40, 69–76.

Earle, T.K. (1977). A reappraisal of redistribution: Complex Hawaiian chiefdoms. In: Earle, T.K. and Ericson, J.E. (eds) *Exchange Systems in Prehistory.* New York: Academic Press, 213–229.

Earle, T.K. (1985). Commodity exchange and markets in the Inca state: Recent archaeological evidence. In: Plattner, S. (ed.) *Markets and Marketing.* Lanham MD: Monographs in Economic Anthropology 4, 369–397.

Eppich, K. and Freidel, D. (2015). Markets and marketing in the Classic Maya lowlands: A case study from El Perú-Waka'. In: King, E.M. (ed.) *The Ancient Maya Marketplace: The Archaeology of Transient Space.* Tucson AZ: University of Arizona Press, 195–225.

Evans, S. (1980). Spatial analysis of the Basin of Mexico settlement: Problems with the use of the central place model. *American Antiquity* 45, 866–875.

Feinman, G.M. (1999). Rethinking our assumptions: Economic specialization at the household scale in ancient Ejutla, Oaxaca, Mexico. In: Skibo, J.M. and Feinman, G.M. (eds) *Pottery and People: A Dynamic Interaction.* Salt Lake City UT: University of Utah Press, 53–62,

Feinman, G.M. (2006). The economic underpinnings of prehispanic Zapotec civilization: Small-scale production, economic interdependence, and market exchange. In: Marcus, J. and Stanish, C. (eds) *Agricultural Strategies.* Los Angeles: Cotsen Advanced Seminar Series Book 2, 255–280.

Feinman, G.M. (2013). Book review essay: Markets and exchange in the pre-Columbian world. *Latin American Antiquity* 25, 234–236.

Feinman, G.M. (2017). Reframing ancient economies: New models, new questions. In: Fernández-Götz, M. and Krausse, D. (eds) *Eurasia at the Dawn of History.* London and New York: Cambridge Univiersity Press, 139–149.

Feinman, G.M. (2018). The governance and leadership of prehispanic Mesoamerican polities: New perspectives and comparative implications. *Cliodynamics* 9(2) https://escholarship.org/uc/item/29w8q73h.

Feinman, G.M. (2019). The prehispanic Mesoamerican world: Framing interaction. In: Englehardt, J.D. and Carrasco, M.D. (eds) *Interregional Interaction in Ancient Mesoamerica.* Louisville CO: University of Colorado Press, 34–50.

Feinman, G.M. and Garraty, C.P. (2010). Preindustrial markets and marketing: Archaeological perspectives. *Annual Review of Anthropology* 39, 167–191.

Feinman, G.M. and Neitzel, J. (1984). Too many types: An overview of sedentary prestate societies in the Americas. In: Schiffer, M. (ed.) *Advances in Archaeological Method and Theory*. New York: Academic Press, 39–102.

Feinman, G.M. and Nicholas, L.M. (2010). A multiscalar perspective on market exchange in the Classic-period Valley of Oaxaca. In: Garraty and Stark (eds) 2010, 5–98.

Feinman, G.M. and Nicholas, L.M. (2012). The late prehispanic economy of the Valley of Oaxaca, Mexico: Weaving threads from data, theory, and subsequent history. *Research in Economic Anthropology* 32, 225–258.

Feinman, G.M. and Nicholas, L.M. (2020). Teotihuacan and Oaxaca: Assessing prehispanic relations. In: Hirth, K.G., Carballo, D.M. and Arroyo, B. (eds) *Teotihuacan: The World beyond the City*. Washington DC: Dumbarton Oaks Pre-Columbian Symposia and Colloquia, 331–36.

Feinman, G.M., Blanton, R. and Kowalewski, S. (1984). Market system development in the prehispanic Valley of Oaxaca, Mexico. In: Hirth, K.G. (ed.) *Trade and Exchange in Early Mesoamerica*. Albuquerque NM: University of New Mexico Press, 157–178.

Feinman, G.M., Golitko, M. and Nicholas, L.M. (2019). A network analysis of prehispanic obsidian exchange: Implications for macroregional dynamics and ancient economies. In: Kerig, T., Mader, C., Ragkou, K., Reinfeld, M. and Zachar, T. (eds) *Social Network Analysis in Economic Archaeology – Perspectives from the New World*. Bonn: Verlag Dr. Rudolf Habelt GmbH, 13–36.

Feldman, L. (1978). Inside a Mexican market. In: Lee, T. and Navarette, C. (eds) *Mesoamerican Communication Routes and Cultural Contacts*. Provo UT: New World Archaeological Foundation, 219–222.

Finley, M.I. (1999). *The Ancient Economy*. Berkeley CA: University of California Press.

Friedman, M. (1982). *Capitalism and Freedom*. Chicago IL: University of Chicago Press.

Gamble, L.H. and King, C.H. (2011). Beads and ornaments from San Diego: Evidence for exchange networks in southern California and the American Southwest. *Journal of California and Great Basin Anthropology* 31, 155–178.

Garraty, C.P. (2010). Investigating market exchange in ancient societies: A theoretical review. In: Garraty and Stark (eds) 2010, 3–32.

Garraty, C.P. and Stark, B.L. (eds) (2010). *Archaeological Approaches to Market Exchange in Ancient Societies*. Boulder CO: University of Colorado Press.

Golitko, M. and Feinman, G.M. (2015). Procurement and distribution of pre-Hispanic Mesoamerican obsidian 900 BC–AD 1520: A social network analysis. *Journal of Archaeological Method and Theory* 22, 206–247.

Granovetter, M. (1985). Economic action and social structure: The problem of embeddedness. *American Journal of Sociology* 91, 481–510.

Granovetter, M. (1992). The nature of economic relations. In: Ortiz, S. and Lees, S. (eds) *Understanding Economic Process*. Lanham MD: University Press of America, 21–40.

Gutiérrez, G. (2013). Negotiating Aztec tributary demands in the tribute record of *Tlapa*. In: Hirth and Pillsbury (eds) 2013a, 141–167.

Halperin, R.H. (1984). Polanyi, Marx, and the institutional paradigm in economic anthropology. *Research in Economic Anthropology* 6, 245–272.

Hassig, R. (1982). Periodic markets in Precolumbian Mexico. *American Antiquity* 47, 346–355.

Hirth, K.G. (1998). The distributional approach: A new way to identify marketplace exchange in the archaeological record. *Current Anthropology* 39, 451–476.

Hirth, K.G. (ed.) (2009a) *Housework: Craft Production and Domestic Economy in Ancient Mesoamerica*. Washington DC: Archeological Publications of the American Anthropological Society 19.

Hirth, K.G. (2009b). Craft production in a central Mexican marketplace. *Ancient Mesoamerica* 20, 89–102.

Hirth, K.G. (2016). *The Aztec Economic World: Merchants and Markets in Ancient Mesoamerica*. Cambridge: Cambridge University Press.

Hirth, K.G. (2019). Aztec markets and their archaeological signatures. In: Rahmsdorf and Stratford (eds) 2019, 339–354.
Hirth, K.G. and Pillsbury, J. (eds) (2013a). *Merchants, Markets, and Exchange in the Pre-Columbian World.* Washington DC: Dumbarton Oaks Pre-Columbian Symposia and Colloquia.
Hirth, K.G. and Pillsbury, J. (2013b). Redistribution and markets in Andean South America. *Current Anthropology* 54, 642–647.
Hirth, K.G., Smith, M.E., Berdan, F.F. and Nichols, D.L. (2017). Wrapping up objects, economy, and empire: Scale, integration, and change. In: Nichols, D.L., Berdan, F.F. and Smith, M.E. (eds) *Rethinking the Aztec Economy*. Tuscon AZ, University of Arizona Press, 278–291.
Hudson, M. (2004). The archaeology of money: Debt versus barter theories of money's origins. In: Wray, L.R. (ed.) *Credit and State Theories of Money: The Contributions of Mitchell Innes*. Cheltenham: Edward Elgar, 9–127.
Hutson, S.R. (ed.) 2017. *Ancient Maya Commerce: Multidisciplinary Research at Chunchucmil*. Boulder CO: University of Colorado Press.
Hutson, S.R., Dahlin, B.H. and Mazeau, D.E. (2010). Commerce and cooperation among the Classic Maya: The Chunchucmil case. In: Marshall, R.C. (ed.) *Cooperation in Economy and Society.* Lanham MD: Rowman and Littlefield, 81–103.
Inomata, T., Triadan, D., Pinzón, F. and Aoyama, K. (2019). Artificial plateau construction during the Preclassic period at the Maya site of Ceibal, Guatemala. *PloS One* 14(8): e0221943.
Isaac, B.L. (1993). Retrospective on formalist-substantivist debate. *Research in Economic Anthropology* 14, 213–233.
Isaac, B.L. (2013). Discussion. In: Hirth and Pillsbury (eds) 2013a, 435–444.
Jones, C. (2015). The marketplace at Tikal. In: King, E.M. (ed.) *The Ancient Maya Marketplace: The Archaeology of Transient Space.* Tucson AZ: University of Arizona Press, 67–89.
Kepecs, S. (2015). Ek Chuah encounters the Holy Ghost in the colonial labyrinth: Ideology and commerce on both sides of the Spanish invasion. In: Funari, P.P.A. and Senatore, M.X. (eds) *Archaeology of Culture Contact and Colonialism in Spanish and Portuguese America.* Cham: Springer, 103–131.
King, E.M. (2015). The ethnohistoric evidence for Maya markets and its archaeological implications. In: King, E.M. (ed.) *The Ancient Maya Marketplace: The Archaeology of Transient Space.* Tucson AZ: University of Arizona Press, 33–66.
Kowalewski, S.A. (2012). A theory of the Mesoamerican economy. *Research in Economic Anthropology* 32, 187–224.
Kowalewski, S.A. (2019). Finding the marketplaces in prehispanic Mesoamerica: A review. In: Rahmsdorf and Stratford (eds) 2019, 323–338.
Krippner, G.R. (2001). The elusive market: Embeddedness and the paradigm of economic sociology. *Theory and Society* 30, 775–810.
Krugman, P. (2009). How did economists get it so wrong? *New York Times Magazine,* September 6, http://www.nytimes.com/2009/09/06/magazine/06Economic-t.html?
Kurtz, D.V. (1974). Peripheral and transitional markets: The Aztec case. *American Ethnologist* 1, 685–705.
Léon-Portilla, M. (1962). La institución cultural del comercio prehispánico. *Estudios de Cultural Náhuatl* 3, 23–54.
Lesure, R.G. (1997). Early Formative platforms at Paso de la Amada, Chiapas, Mexico. *Latin American Antiquity* 8, 217–235.
Lie, J. (1991). Embedding Polanyi's market society. *Sociological Perspectives* 34, 219–235.
Lie, J. (1997). Sociology of markets. *Annual Review of Sociology* 23, 341–360.
López de Gómara, F. (1966). *The Life of the Conqueror by His Secretary.* Berkeley CA: University of California Press.
Martin, S. (2012). Hieroglyphs from the painted pyramid: The epigraphy of Chiik Nahb Structure Sub 1-4, Calakmul, Mexico. In: Golden, C., Houston, S. and Skidmore, J. (eds) *Maya Archaeology*

2; Featuring the Ancient Maya Murals of Calakmul, Mexico. San Francisco: Precolumbia Mesoweb Press, 60–68.
Marx, K. (1971). *A Contribution to the Critique of Political Economy*. London: Lawrence and Wishart.
Masson, M.A. and Freidel, D.A. (2012). An argument for Classic era Maya market exchange. *Journal of Anthropological Archaeology* 31, 455–484.
Masson, M.A. and Freidel, D.A. (2013). Wide open spaces: A long view of the importance of Maya market exchange. In: Hirth and Pillsbury (eds) 2013a, 201–228.
Maurer, B. (2006). The anthropology of money. *Annual Review of Anthropology* 35, 15–36.
Mayer, E. (2002). *The Articulated Peasant: Household Economies in the Andes.* Boulder CO: University Press of Colorado.
Mayer, E. (2013). In the realm of the Incas. In: Hirth and Pillsbury (eds) 2013a, 309–317.
McCloskey, D.M. (1997). Other things equal: Polanyi was right and wrong. *Eastern Economic Journal* 23, 483–487.
Millon, R.F. (1955). When Money Grew on Trees. A Study of Cacao in Ancient in Ancient Mesoamerica. Unpublished Ph.D dissertation, Columbia University.
Molina, Fray A. de (1972). *Confesionario Mayor en la Lengua Mexicana y Castellana* (ed. R. Moreno). Mexico City: Boletín del Instituto de Investigaciones Bibliográficos 7.
Monson, A. and Scheidel, W. (eds) (2015). *Fiscal Regimes and the Political Economy of Premodern States.* Cambridge: Cambridge University Press.
Murra, J.V. (1956). The Economic Organization of the Inca State. Unpublished Ph.D dissertation, University of Chicago.
Murra, J.V. (1962). Cloth and its function in the Inca state. *American Anthropologist* 64, 710–728.
Nichols, D.L. (2013). Merchants and merchandise: The archaeology of Aztec commerce at Otumba, Mexico. In: Hirth and Pillsbury (eds) 2013a, 49–83.
Nielsen, A.E. (2013). Circulating objects and the constitution of South Andean society (500 BC–AD 1550). In: Hirth and Pillsbury (eds) 2013a, 389–418.
Offner, J. (1981). On the inapplicability of 'oriental despotism' and the 'Asiatic mode of production' to the Aztecs of Texcoco. *American Antiquity* 46, 43–61.
Pohl, J.M.D., Monaghan, J. and Stuiver, L.R. (1997). Religion, economy, and factionalism in Mixtec boundary zones. In: Rueda Smithers, S., Vega Sosa, C. and Martínez Baracs, R. (eds) *Codices y Documentos sobre* México, Segundo *Simposio*, Vol. 1. Mexico City: Instituto Nacional de Antropología e Historia, Direccíon de Estudios Históricos, 205–232.
Polanyi, K. (1944). *The Great Transformation: The Political and Economic Origins of Our Time.* Boston MA: Beacon Press.
Polanyi, K. (1947). Our obsolete market mentality. *Commentary* 3, 109–117.
Polanyi, K. (1957). The economy as instituted process. In: Polanyi *et al.* (eds) 1957, 243–270.
Polanyi, K., Arensberg, C.M. and Pearson, H.W. (eds) (1957). *Trade and Market in the Early Empires.* Chicago IL: Chicago University Press.
Rahmsdorf, L. and Stratford, E. (eds) (2019). *Weights and Marketplaces from the Bronze Age to the Early Modern Period*, Göttingen: Wachhholz.
Sahagún, B. de (1950–1982). *General History of the Things New Spain*. Santa Fe NM: School of American Research.
Salomon, F. (1986). *Native Lords of Quito in the Age of the Incas: The Political Economy of North-Andean Chiefdoms*. Cambridge: Cambridge University Press.
Sanders, W.T., Parsons, J.R. and Santley, R.S. (1979). *The Basin of Mexico: Ecological Processes in the Evolution of a Civilization*. New York: Academic Press.
Schaedel, R.P. (1978). Early state of the Incas. In: Claessen, H.J.M. and Skalník, P. (eds) *The Early State*. The Hague: Mouton, 289–320.
Shaw, L.C. (2012). The elusive Maya marketplace: An archaeological consideration of the evidence. *Journal of Archaeological Research* 20, 117–155.

Shaw, L.C. and King, E.M. (2015). The Maya marketplace at Maax Na, Belize. In: King, E.M. (ed.) *The Ancient Maya Marketplace: The Archaeology of Transient Space.* Tucson AZ: University of Arizona Press, 168–194.

Smith, M.E. (1979). The Aztec marketing system and settlement patterns in the Basin of Mexico: A central place analysis. *American Antiquity* 44, 110–125.

Smith, M.E. (1980). The role of the marketing system in Aztec society and economy: Reply to Evans. *American Antiquity* 45, 876–883.

Smith, M.E. (2004). The archaeology of ancient state economies. *Annual Review of Anthropology* 33, 73–102.

Smith, M.E. (2008). *Aztec City-State Capitals.* Tallahassee FL: University of Florida Press.

Smith, M.E. (2012). *The Aztecs*, Cambridge: Cambridge University Press.

Smith, M.E. (2015). The Aztec empire. In: Monson, A. and Scheidel, W. (eds) *Fiscal Regimes and the Political Economy of Premodern States.* Cambridge: Cambridge University Press, 71–114.

Smith, M.E. and Berdan, F.F. (eds) (2003). *The Postclassic Mesoamerican World.* Salt Lake City UT: University of Utah Press.

Speal, C.S. (2014). The evolution of ancient Maya exchange systems: An epistemological study of economic variability in the Mayan language family. *Ancient Mesoamerica* 25, 69–113.

Spores, R. (1965). The Zapotec and Mixtec at Spanish contact. In: Willey, G.R. (ed.) *The Archaeology of Southern Mesoamerica. Handbook of Middle American Indians* 3, *part* 2. Austin TX: University of Texas Press, 962–987.

Stanish, C. (2010). Labor taxes, market systems, and urbanization in the prehispanic Andes: A comparative perspective. In: Garraty and Stark (eds) 2010, 185–205.

Stanish, C. and Coben, L.S. (2013). Barter markets in the pre-Hispanic Andes. In: Hirth and Pillsbury (eds) 2013a, 419–434.

Stark, B.L. and Garraty, C.P. (2010). Investigating market exchange in archaeology: A methodological review. In: Garraty and Stark (eds) 2010, 33–59.

Stark, B.L. and Ossa, A. (2010). Origins and development of Mesoamerican marketplaces: Evidence from south-central Veracruz, Mexico. In: Garraty and Stark (eds) 2010, 99–126.

Sullivan, K.S. (2007). Commercialization in Early State Economies: Craft Production and Market Exchange in Classic Period Teotihuacan. Unpublished Ph.D dissertation, Arizona State University.

Swedberg, R. (1994). Markets as social structures. In: Smelser, N.J. and Swedberg, R. (eds) *Handbook of Economic Sociology.* Princeton NJ: Princton University Press, 255–282.

Swedberg, R. (2005). Markets in society. In: Smelser, N.J. and Swedberg, R. (eds) *Handbook of Economic Sociology* (2nd edition). Princeton NJ: Princton University Press, 233–253.

Terraciano, K. (2001). *The Mixtecs of Colonial Oaxaca: Nudzahui History, Sixteenth through Eighteenth Centuries.* Stanford CA: Stanford University Press.

Terry, R.E., Bair, D.A. and Coronel, E.G. (2015) Soil chemistry in the search for ancient Maya marketplaces. In: King, E.M. (ed.) *The Ancient Maya Marketplace: The Archaeology of Transient Space.* Tucson AZ: University of Arizona Press, 138–167.

Tokovinine, A. and Beliaev, D. (2013). Traders and travelers in ancient Maya words and images. In: Hirth and Pillsbury (eds) 2013a, 169–200.

Torquemada, J. de (1943). *Monarquia Indiana*, Mexico City: S. Chávez Hayhoe.

Towell, J.L. and Atollini Lecón, A. (eds) (2009). *Caminos y Mercados de México*, Mexico City: Instituto Nacional de Antropología e Historia.

Watts, J. and Ossa, A. (2016). Exchange network topologies and agent-based modeling: Economies of the Sedentary-period Hohokam. *American Antiquity* 81, 623–644.

Weatherford, J. (1997). *The History of Money*. New York: Random House.

Winter, M.C. (1984). Exchange in Formative highland Oaxaca. In: Hirth, K.G. (ed.) *Trade and Exchange in Early Mesoamerica.* Albuquerque NM: University of New Mexico Press, 179–214.

Wittfogel, K. (1957). *Oriental Despotism.* New Haven CT: Yale University Press.

Chapter 4

The enchanting scale: Magic and morality in the Bronze Age economic balance

Chris Monroe

Introduction: in search of balance in economics

I begin from a perspective of equilibrium, an ancient balancing act involving the capitalistic drive in one pan and the social restrictions of profit in the other; this is the perilous and profitable liminal condition in which traders and moneymen practiced in the Bronze Age Eastern Mediterranean and Near Eastern arena. By 2000 BC this area had already been transformed by the widespread emergence of market economies, undermining the state dominance that had characterized prior centuries (Warburton 2016: 388). Two outcomes of the increasingly commercial logics of the 2nd millennium BC concern the balance-pan scale: first, its increasingly ubiquitous presence in everyday life, or at least wherever market economics was practiced; and secondly, the scale becoming a broadly used symbol for social justice. To better understand how this happened, and what it signals about early market-based economic logics, I apply concepts from behavioral neuroeconomics, liminality, materiality or object-agency, and cognitive theories of magic. What this assemblage of perspectives ultimately suggests is that what we have traditionally viewed as a mundane economic tool in fact played an active role in persuading people of moral logics underpinning economic life.

Balance-pans and weights are perhaps the most important type-fossil, or diagnostic artifact type, for identifying market logic in the archaeological record. So it is hardly surprising that scales are common to three of the era's most emblematic witnesses to the lives of Late Bronze Age traders in and around the Eastern Mediterranean from *c.* 1350 to 1175 BCE: Ugarit (Tell Ras Shamra, Syria) has produced the greatest single assemblage of balance-pan weights (over 606 according to Bordreuil 2006); from the Uluburun shipwreck (Turkey) comes the second largest corpus of weights (3–4 sets among 151 overall), plus some pans (Pulak 2000; 2006); and the depiction in Kenamun's tomb shows the use of scales where Syrian ships arrive at a dockside marketplace in 14th century BC Egypt (Fig. 4.1). A number of studies have described the variety of Mediterranean and Near Eastern weighing systems and their physical logics (*e.g.*, Alberti *et al.* 2006; Rahmstorf 2010; Büttner 2017), but here I am exploring the metaphysical implications of the emergence and spread of weighing. One notices that it is the bullion and weight-sets from Uluburun that prevent its strict categorization as a royal shipment, there having always been an allowance for a commercial component to the venture (Pulak 2008: 300). Likewise the copious references to weighing in Bronze Age texts are not merely a mark of equivalencies but of underlying market systems (Warburton 2016, 409).

How did people choose, in a marketplace such as the one shown in Kenamun's tomb? What was the economic logic employed? The paradigm of humans as rational maximizers, a *homo economicus* adapting primarily through self-interest, has already been shattered by game theory: people predictably deny individual self-interest in order to punish wrong-doers, share and cooperate in a variety of experimental games and across cultures (Henrich *et al.* 2001). Building on advances in neural imaging since the 1990s, the nascent field of neuroeconomics also has provided fresh reasons to question choice as a rational, consistent behavior. What we call 'economic logic' has substantial affective components that attempt to factor risk, reward and fairness within uncertain environments that necessarily include the choices and influences of other agents (Reuter and Montag 2016). The ability to monitor cerebral activity while test subjects make economic choices has been used both to confirm classic precepts of 'utility maximization' and to challenge the validity of this rationality axiom that supposedly governs the logic of the theoretical *homo economicus* (Bissonette 2016). And while neuroeconomics may be over-promising on what it can deliver in terms of understanding the physiology of human decision-making (Graziano 2019 discusses some prominent critiques), two questions raised thus far seem particularly germane to the rethinking of ancient economic logics. One concerns how humans adapted (or not) to the relatively sudden appearance of money, a symbolic means of exchange and valuation, after millennia of choosing more tangible, real, and rewarding products of nature – mates, food, shelter, intoxicants, etc. A second stream of neuroeconomics research on ambiguity and risk in information-poor arenas reveals a utility based on past experience and affect that tends to minimize loss rather than maximize gain – even if the result were quantitatively equal, a principle known as 'loss-aversion bias' or 'experienced utility' (Kahneman 1994; Bissonnette 2016: 374–375). Choice appears to involve a neural balancing act pitting observable facts of the moment against learned feelings – satisfaction, dissatisfaction, shame, pleasure. Put another way, if one goes looking for Apollo (an avatar of ancient rationality), the chances are good of encountering Dionysos. It is an old story, certainly, with economic theory slowly catching up to confirm truths both old and new. As one observer remarks on the shifting, blending paradigms in economics:

> the results from studies of social influence and emotion are consistent with Keynes's role of confidence as critical for decision making, and furthermore with his hypothesis that *animal spirits* [my emphasis, for Keynes' term referring to affect] entail variance in choices. (Portelli 2014: 12)

Figure 4.1. Arrival of Syrian ships, weighing, and other dockside activities, Theban Tomb 162 of Kenamun, 14th century BC (Monroe (2009, 212, fig. 6.2), after Davies and Faulkner (1947, pl. 8))

The idea that economic logic is partly moral is not a revelation to all, but game theory and neuroeconomics offer needed corrections to our understanding of decision-making in market and other contexts.

Economic imbalance and awareness in Bronze Age sources

Another implication of Kahneman's 'experienced utility' affects how one may interpret the relationship between palace and trader or between state and market. If decision-makers normatively depart from axioms of rationality and substitute affect for information, then what kind of predictive science (economics, for example) and policy can we assume was practiced by Bronze Age rulers? In texts from Ugarit and Emar, and material from maritime-oriented sites like Uluburun and Ugarit, merchants display considerable agency; as liminal experts who worked in and among the great kingdoms of the time they controlled the wheels of commerce while kings – deftly balancing the sacred ideals of charismatic kingship against the more profane and profitable interests of the mercantile world – went along for the ride (Monroe 2009; 2015; Broodbank 2013: 373–415). And while no one would confuse the Late Bronze Age interregional network with a modern market economy, in a sense the key players pursued their strengths: traders created and extended networks of information concerning commodities; kings conspicuously consumed and dictated legal protections for the traders enriching them. It was the best of times. And then, shockingly, it was not.

As brilliant and familiar as the Late Bronze Age has become – through Mycenaean treasures, the Amarna Letters, Tutankhamun, Uluburun, Rameses II's great endeavours, and Ugarit's textual trove – its collapse has recently become even more heralded, as shown by the success of Eric Cline's *1177: The year civilization collapsed* (2015). Into the familiar weft of Sea Peoples, earthquakes, and broken trade routes Cline weaves climate change into a tale that should chill the bones of contemporary readers. Adding incipient capitalists to Cline's list of corrosive culprits makes it more so. As I argued in *Scales of fate* (Monroe 2009), trade plays both hero and villain in the interconnected Late Bronze scene by creating the economic links of interdependency – if one major partner collapsed, then all might. By commodifying goods, services, and even people, profit-seeking profoundly disturbs the social fabric at every level – individual, household, community, and nation; Schumpeter called this 'the perennial gale of creative destruction' (1994: 82–83). As the post-2008 world is keenly aware, unchecked trade can be as globally consequential as interrupted trade. Trade with China and Russia recently allowed even the historically stagnant North Korean economy to grow at 3.9%, and yet 'the regime does not really want the living standards to rise fast and too much, because that could shake the nation' (Osnos 2017). Indeed, governments somehow balance a love and fear of trade and perhaps it has always been so, especially among those inclined to rule through charismatic appeals. Thus it is fair to ask if any decision-makers could see the end coming *c.* 1177 BC. Were the gods, kings, or anyone else supposedly responsible for economic justice prepared for Schumpeter's 'gale'? What was the thinking, or the logic, if indeed there was any?

Figure 4.2. Top half of the Stele of Hammurabi (https://en.wikipedia.org/wiki/Code_of_Hammurabi#/media/File:P1050763_Louvre_code_Hammurabi_face_rwk.JPG)

Certain sections of Mesopotamian law codes from Ur-Namma's (*c.* 2000 BC) down to Middle Assyrian examples (*c.* 1000 BC) read in part as checks against commercial excess but appear, more generally, to foster the smooth functioning of commerce by protecting property rights and reducing transit costs (Roth 1997). These legal-commercial principles are established by the listing of hypothetical cases – marketplace mishaps often, as many as a hundred in the case of Hammurabi's 18th century BC collection (Fig. 4.2). Despite the sophisticated organization, the laws are myopic as any kind of economic science. They set interest rates, prices on goods and labor, make rules for how one pays off a debt or goes into slavery for insolvency, but there is no analysis regarding whether such practices benefit or harm society, or even just the palace. The best-known exception to this royal myopia is the 17th century BC debt-release or justice (Akkadian *mīšaru*) edict of King Ammisaduqa of Babylon, whose key concern appears to have been checking rampant debt (and implied debt-slavery) suffered by agrarian workers:

> § 4: Whoever has given barley or silver to an Akkadian or an Amorite as an interest bearing loan or as fees, and had a document drawn up – because the king has established justice in the land, his document is voided; he may not collect the barley or silver on the basis of his document. (Van de Mieroop 2007: 94–95)

As Finkelstein (1961: 99–104) made clear, the *mīšaru*-acts referenced by this edict and other Old Babylonian sources made temporary, *ad hoc* corrections (as the term etymologically implies) rather than meaningful or lasting reform. Such measures indicate a system out of control – out of balance – that had reached a critical point at which the king was forced to intervene. As for the 'Akkadian and Amorite' moneylenders, the resulting chaos of such intervention was only compounded by the edict's stipulation that *their* debts would still be due. A Sumerian proverb using folklorish metaphor bears critical insight on the matter: 'A scale set with sinews is a pitfall for the feet. A man should not take a merchant for his friend' (Alster 1997: SP 3.64).

Texts from Ramesside Egypt (*c.* 1300–1100 BC), are even more keenly aware that the socioeconomic times were changing. The *Instructions of Any* for example sets the old familiar tropes of practical advice for bureaucrats alongside emergent cares about personal wealth and its unequal distribution:

> Place wealth where it bears interest (Lichtheim 2006: 138);
> The wise lives off the house of a fool (*ibid.*, 138–139);
> One man is rich, another is poor, but food remains for him who shares it (*ibid.*: 142).

Likewise, the contemporary *Instructions of Amenemope* deals with greed and income inequality throughout its thirty chapters as one might expect for the turbulent times after Ramesses III:

> 6: Better is poverty in the hand of the god, than wealth in the storehouse; better is bread with a happy heart than wealth with vexation
> 7: Do not set your heart on wealth; there is no ignoring Fate and Destiny
> 12: Do not desire a noble's wealth
> 13: Do not cheat a man (through) pen on scroll; the god abhors it; ... If you find a large debt against a poor man, make it into three parts; forgive two, let one stand, ...
> Better is praise with the love of men than wealth in the storehouse
> 16: Do not move the scales nor alter the weights, nor diminish the fractions of the measure; ... Do not covet copper; disdain beautiful linen
> 29: Take the fare from him who's wealthy, and let pass him who is poor (Lichtheim 2006: 146–163).

These concerns, which mostly concern consequences for the individual, echo in Biblical Proverbs and prophecy, especially in the dramatic accusations Isaiah 23 and Ezekiel 27 aimed at Tyre's maritime mercantilism. But even there one finds no awareness that a flood of luxuries might transform the local economy in unpredictable or dangerous ways – no proscription or prescription concerning economic interdependence – other than it somehow resulted in lupine forces descending on the fold.

I have encountered only two Late Bronze Age texts that clearly show royal restriction on foreign commerce. One is the late 13th century BC treaty between Tudḫaliya IV and Šaušgamuwa of Amurru (Beckman 1996: no. 17; Beckman *et al.* 2011: 50–68), which includes the following provision, part of a typical establishment of mutual alliances:

> §13' ... Since the King of Assyria is My Majesty's enemy, he shall be your enemy. Your merchant shall not go to Assyria, and you shall not allow his merchant into your land. He shall not pass through your land. But if he comes into your land, seize him and send him off to My Majesty. §15' [You shall not allow (?) any ship [of] Aḫḫiyawa to go to him (that is, the King of Assyria) ... (Beckman *et al.* 2011: 61–63)

This was not a general restriction of seaborne commerce based on apprehension of a trade imbalance, but a military move against an inland adversary who had the same interests as he in developing commercial ties with Achaean-Mycenaean concerns that had spread from the Aegean to Cyprus. On the other hand an edict of Ḫattušili III clearly recognized the 'burden' the merchants of Ura represented for the king of Ugarit, especially their purchasing of land during the winter:

> His Majesty, Great King, has thus made a regulation concerning the men of Ura in their relations with the men of Ugarit. The men of Ura shall carry on their mercantile activities in the land of Ugarit during the summer, but they will be forced to leave the land of Ugarit for their own land in the winter. The men of Ura shall not live in the land of Ugarit during the winter. They shall not acquire houses or fields (in Ugarit) with their silver. Even if a merchant, a man of Ura, should lose his capital in the land of Ugarit, the king of the land of Ugarit shall not permit him to live in his land. If men of Ugarit owe silver to men of Ura and are not able to pay it off, the king of the land of Ugarit must turn over that man, together with his wife and his sons, to the men of Ura, the merchants. But the men of Ura, the merchants, shall not claim houses or fields of the king of the land of Ugarit. (Beckman 1996: no. 32, 162–163)

The edict, as Ammisaduqa's earlier, notably reveals the threshold at which royals noticed negative effects of foreign trade – when it directly threatened their landholdings. King Niqmepa would allow entire cash-poor families to go into debt-slavery to the Urans, thus profiting the Hittite overlord however indirectly; what he would not tolerate was any loss of domain. Territorial integrity was central to his role as sovereign; and the loss of landholders actually would have allowed Niqmepa opportunities to reward relatives or nobles with estates within the patriarchal land-tenure ideology of the time (Schloen 2001).

Two more examples, from earlier and later in the 2nd millennium BC perhaps illustrate the absence of regulation and the limits of economic analysis vis à vis trade. In terminating his partnership, an Old Assyrian trader named Ennam-Assur justified it thus *c.* 1900 BC:

> In accordance with the policy of the city Assur, any Assyrian will go where it is profitable for him. You went where it was profitable for you and I as well went where it was profitable for me in accordance with the policy of my city. (Larsen 2015: 272, citing text AKT 6b, 493)

It is important to bear in mind, following Larsen (2015: 279), that within this long-distance trade network, arguably the best documented in Antiquity, the royals were deeply involved, not as regulators but *as participants*, playing by the same rules as everyone else. One can only assume Ennam-Assur was quoting city policy accurately, and if so, it appears quite *laissez faire*. Several hundred years later, the king of Ugarit made the following arrangement with a successful maritime merchant that alludes to a similar dynamic:

> From this day forth Ammistamru (II), son of Niqmepa, king of Ugarit, frees from claim Sinaranu, son of Siginu; as Shapshu is clear, so he is clear. His 'grain and beer' and his oil need not enter the palace. His ship is free from claim. If his ship arrives from Kapturi (Crete), he will bring his gift to the king, and the herald will not enter his house... (Monroe 2009: 165–167, translating RS 16.238 + 254/*PRU* 3,107)

The legal exemption granted Sinaranu was clearly an exception to the normal practice of taxing the goods brought in by shippers. It was in the sovereign's economic interest to maximize such trade. The Ugarit documentation differs from the Old Assyrian in that this sort of passive, symbiotic participation through *tamkāru*-merchants is all that is in evidence for the royals.

Thus it has been my working hypothesis that the main political actors of the Bronze Age were largely unaware and unresponsive to local or interregional imbalances and the creeping disruption of capitalist activities (Monroe 2015). It was plausibly unregulated and beyond their control except in such instances that threatened royal holdings directly. This is hardly surprising when one recognizes how much trade was conducted in marginal social and geographic spaces where royal power was already limited. It would also be expected in regimes whose magical thinking rendered them less capable of predicting complex interregional economic outcomes.

The liminal locus of the balancing act

The figure wielding power and authority in the margins was the middleman, the liminal expert, whether he or she was a sailor, merchant, caravaneer, or other professional *passenger* (in the liminal sense). The 'trader's dilemma' studied by economic anthropologists (Evers 1994), and work tying outsiders to the reproduction of political authority (Helms 1988; Kristiansen and Larsson 2005) present the two sides of the liminal coin – the pitfalls and the power of being a expert of the middle, the Other in our midst, both feared and sought after as a source of information, magic, exotica, prestige. Westerdahl (2005) sees the Bronze Age Scandinavian seascape as a contentious margin where rituals helped reduce anxieties inherent to a life divided between land and sea. This sort of ship-to-shore perspective plays a significant role in how Ray (2003) reconstructs Ancient South Asia, as it does also in Malkin's (2011) and Broodbank's (2013) approaches to Mediterranean connectivity. As I have argued elsewhere the Late Bronze Age can be usefully understood in terms of liminality: geographically, as a landscape of shores, islands, and rivers; politically as a blend of middle-grounds and their surrounding terrestrial empires; economically as the field on which the outsider's game of long-distance trade was played; and socially as a condition wherein *communitas* would have replaced more familial and ethnic status distinctions (Monroe 2011).

Aboard ship, in harbors, on the caravan road, or in the merchant quarters, colonies, and marketplaces found where *kārum* occurs in Akkadian texts, liminal experts had the freedom to pursue a mode of accumulation that put them at odds with members of agrarian societies. This social stigma was balanced by considerable power in the ability to state price or equivalence among goods and services – an almost magical sort of transubstantiation of value which could commodify, dis-embed, and threaten local traditions. It was also the power to enslave with debt, to captivate customers with desires for exotica, and to entangle polities into reorganizing their productive capacities for new markets. No wonder that an early 14th century Hittite prince, oppressed by his personal god, prayed to the Sun-god with these words that mark the merchant as either a cheat or false witness:

> My god, you made me, you created me. But now, [wha]t have I, K[antuzili], done to you? The merchant holds the scales towards the Sun-god and falsifies the scales (nevertheless). [But I], what have I done [to] my god? (Schwemer 2015: *CTH* 374, from lines 39'–42')

From considerably later, the Biblical prophet Hosea (12: 8) accusing Ephraim of apostasy, employed a socioeconomic slur not unlike that of the earlier Hittite: 'A trafficker (lit. Canaanite) who has deceitful scales in his hand: he loves to oppress.'

One could say how ironic it is that a poetic device intended to signal exploitation would eventually become a near-universal symbol of justice. And yet status inversions are typical of the liminal state, as understood by Victor Turner (1969; 1974). Sailing merchants such as those lost off Uluburun or Gelidonya were no doubt subject to disapprovals, yet they were also joined in a *communitas* of like-minded outsiders sharing challenges that included the prospect of watery annihilation off foreign shores. A liminal perspective suggests that the external perception of the trader also affords tremendous power in that it helps the subject construct an authority that can convince and coerce (Monroe 2011).

While recognizing the importance of the balance as the chief device wielded by this transformative figure of the merchant, one might mistakenly relegate the object to the class of metaphors, since it vividly captures the merchant's daily 'balancing act' of maintaining social status while transgressing social norms. Westerdahl's (2005) theorizing of the ship itself as a liminal agent is suggestive of yet another process, perhaps less ritual and less human than Turner recognized. And while there's nothing more seductive than a beautiful ship under sail, the ship was not the only form of enchanting technology possessed by the ancient 'trafficker'.

Agency in the balance

The cross-cultural, long-distance trader has obviously played a transformative force in history. It is less obvious that a case be made, following recent anthropological and archaeology trends, for paying some attention to the agency of the trader's equipment itself, *i.e.* the materiality of the balance-pan scale. Archaeologists working in and around the Mediterranean became more interested in materiality around 2010, tapping into the foundational work on object-agency by Latour (1991). Maran and Stockhammer (2012: 2) believe that 'objects have a will of their own' and refer to a 'silent discourse' that constitutes an important aspect of human-object relations. From the same edition, Knapp (2012: 33–34) avows that '[m]ateriality lies at the heart of attempts to engage with objects as an integral dimension of human culture; human behavior cannot be contemplated without taking into account the role of objects, of things in motion'. In response to critiques of over-activating the object, Knapp (2016) has lately preferred the term *affordance* for describing an object's use-potential, as determined primarily by human choice.

Yet an insistence on pure human agency is problematic in some cases where conscious decision-making is not clear. Hodder's engaging book, *Entangled* (2012) wrestles with this question by focusing on webs of dependency, both between humans and things, and between things and things; through *entrapment* material things gain 'potential not just to function, but to take part in social life'. His observations of these relations in the everyday include viewing his sailboat as a network of interdependent systems that happen to include a human pilot. As Westerdahl (2005) he sees boats as having agency. Humans tend to bristle at this idea because if this material dependency (or entrapment) indeed exists, freewill somehow diminishes and the threat of machine overlords somehow becomes (albeit remotely) credible. But to keep things more real than imagined, one may consider the popular biographical vignette concerning the compass given to a young Albert Einstein (Shepler 2020). Without understanding the science, Einstein was fascinated enough to continually question its mechanics and hidden forces until he eventually created a theory of relativity. From there it is a short causal hop to the atomic bomb, Hiroshima, and the threat of global nuclear annihilation looming over generations. Would this condition exist if not for that compass? Did Albert and Compass not have a silent discourse? Did Compass not take part in social life? Exactly how much agency does one grant a machine with a single moving part?

In this context let us return to *c.* 2000 BC and the Sumerian proverb: 'A scale set with sinews is a pitfall for the feet. A man should not take a merchant for his friend' (Alster 1997: SP 3.64). Besides articulating the liminal status which characterizes the merchant's life, the scribe employs a metaphor of entrapment that derives its persuasive logic from a close homology between the straps holding up the pans and other straps that might bind a prisoner. The proverb persuades because the danger of debt-slavery, or economic entrapment, was all too real. But the materialist of our present theoretical era must ask, is the scale just a metaphor for that danger, or was the scale instrumental in, or perceived as instrumental to, the entrapment?

One is forced to repeat the question for the rhetoric employed by the *Eloquent Peasant* from Middle Kingdom Egypt (19th century BC). In his 8th and penultimate petition the lowly Khunanup instructs the high steward Rensi in the philosophy of justice or *ma'at*: 'Can the scales tilt, when theirs are the pans which weigh things' (Parkinson 2012: 286–287, B1 lines 353–355). Early in the 9th petition Khunanup compares his petitions to the essence of justice: 'High steward, my lord! The tongue of men is their balance [*mḫ3t*]; scales [*jwsw*] are what detect deficiency, dealing punishment to the punishable: let the standard be like you!' (*ibid.*: 289–290, B2 lines 92–94). It would be easy to dismiss the agency of the scale represented here as metaphor, since this is an ubiquitous feature of *Eloquent Peasant*, but this would undermine a key argument of Khunanup's, that whereas human judgment is imperfect if not outright corrupt in some cases, divine judgment (as overseen by Thoth) is as objective as the unimpeded physical action of the balance. The solution to the age-old problem of how one finds an honest judge is thus one of biomechanical engineering: in his third petition, Khunanup had already wished that Rensi would simply, literally and anatomically embody the balance:

> Speak not falsehood, for you are great!.
> Be not light, for you are the weighty.
> Speak not falsehood, you are the scales!
> Stray not, you are the standard!
> Look you are the one with the scales;
> if they tilt, then you can tilt.
> Drift not, but steer!,
> rescue with the tiller-rope!
> Seize not, but act against the seizer!
> A selfish great one is not truly great.
> But your tongue is the plummet;
> your heart is the weight;
> your lips are its arms. (*ibid.*: 162–167, B1, lines 191–199)

Again, one can swoon over the author's metaphorical prowess while missing how Egyptians articulated a weighty human-thing relationship. *Eloquent Peasant* is a sophisticated work that both praises and protests the political system (Jeffers 2013); it practices a form of entrapment, using Khunanup's own forceful rhetoric to ultimately and tacitly demonstrate the king's justness (Parkinson 2000; El Nabolsy 2020). It is intensely liminal in the Turnerian sense, allowing a temporary inversion of the social order only to have *structure* reassert itself (Turner 1969: 176). Here the text takes us past entanglement into inter-penetration or something more like the subject-object fluidity of Buddhism, or into the sensibility of the tomb-sculptor who fashioned the

Figure 4.3. Woman as scale weighing metal, in Dynasty 6 Tomb of Kairer, Saqqara, Egypt (Lauer 1976, pl. 68).

idiomatic if not unique image in Ka-irer's tomb wherein a small woman proclaims 'I will act as a balance' while doing precisely that (J. Quack, pers. comm. 2020)[1] (Fig. 4.3).

Like Khunanup's petitions, the image and hieroglyphic caption suggests the Egyptian wish for true embodiment of the impartial, material perfection of the scale, that thing which could establish *ma'at* in all its forms (truth, order, justice) or simply weigh some metal with impartiality.

Material agency may also lurk within the Homeric *psychostasis*. We often read how Hector's fate was determined by Zeus, and yet the text arguably leaves the matter cloudy:

> then the Father lifted on high his golden scales, [210] and set therein two fates of grievous death, one for Achilles, and one for horse-taming Hector; then he grasped the balance by the midst and raised it; and down sank the day of doom of Hector, and departed unto Hades. (Homer, *Iliad*, 22, transl. Murray 1924)

Immediately following this scene, and with no word or act from Zeus, Apollo abandons Hector, and Athena sets the determination into motion; later, Hector is dragged dead behind a chariot. So, who or what killed the Trojan hero: Zeus, his Scale of Fates, Achilles, Athena, poor life choices? Causation here may be intentionally elusive.

Regarding any commercial transaction involving the balance in the physical marketplace, one can thus fairly ask who or what is doing the weighing. Like Zeus, the merchant in his precarious liminal status would rather leave the fraught determination to an external agent or at least not shoulder the entire blame. At least three actors share in the agency: the merchant, the god referenced (explicitly or not), and the balance (including the weights, about which there are no separate textual meditations). Cognitive theory suggests a fourth actor was present – whoever is witnessing the weighing. This concerns enchantment, magical thinking generally, and how a piece of merchant's equipment could embody economic logic while becoming an enduring symbol for justice.

The balance acts: Magical thinking and the ideal economic machine

Pre-enlightenment societies were suffused with magical thinking, just as apparently are post-enlightenment ones (Black 2020). Magical thinkers believe that 'an object, action or circumstance not logically related to a course of events can influence its outcome' (Valdesolo 2010). Cognitive theory informs us that magical thinking soothes anxious minds by removing coincidence, probability, and ambiguity; everything can be blamed on someone or something with satisfying precision (Kajfosz 2008: 365). Ancient magical thinkers believed the sun-god would reward fair use of one's balance-pan weights and punish those who did not, as in the fragmentary Middle Assyrian *Hymn to Shamash:*

> He who [commits] fra[ud] as he holds the ba]lances, Who switches weights, who lowers the [ ], (His) profits are illusory, and he lo[ses the capital] The one who is honest in holding the balance, [ ] plenty of [ ], Whatever (he weighs) will be given to him in plenty [ ]. (Foster 1993: 540, lines 107–111)

Others believed that the moon-god Thoth would do likewise, in the Ramesside *Instructions of Amenemope*:

> Where is a god as great as Thoth, who invented these things and made them? Do not make for yourself deficient weights They are rich in grief through the might of god. (Lichtheim 2006:156–157; *cf*. Proverbs 11:1 and 16:11)

In commercial transactions there was the rational calculus of the merchant – the knowledge of what things cost and where, how much needed to be sold to make a profit, and what combination of weights to place on the balance-pans. Then there was the expertise required to appear just while practicing a capitalist mode of accumulation. This routine operation of weighing in the public space of the market was arguably part measurement and part performance. On one side was the merchant and his skill; on the other was an audience of customers, peers, and onlookers and their attitudes; in the margin was the balance, a *transitional object* gently bridging the social distance between them. What exactly was required to make this a successful performance, *i.e.* one that reaffirmed various conceptions of balance and fairness?

Gell's (1992; 1998) seminal and anthropological theory of art, which some have called a theory of object agency (Derlon and Jeudy-Ballini 2010), explained how certain objects enchant by abducting human attention. The theory also bridges two seemingly separate realms of behavior – ritual magic and technology. Art objects that appear to transubstantiate material cast a spell of wonder on their audience, endowing the object with a magic power that baffles the non-artist who cannot imagine how else it was made. Gell's example *par excellence* was the carved canoe prows of the Trobriand Islands. Bronze Age comparanda, such as Tutankhamun's funerary mask or Hammurabi's law stele, transubstantiate flesh into gold and stone. Another kind of transubstantiation, less artistic but no less technical, took place in the balance. Setting aside the transubstantiation of mythical *psychostases*, the everyday, earthly scale reproduced hidden equivalencies between silver and many things: gold, copper, grain, animals, labor, people. Considered as one of Gell's art objects, the balance 'mediates between two beings, and therefore creates a social relation between them, which in turn provides a channel for further social relations and influences' (1992: 52). For Gell the durative mediation is not the craftsman's but the resulting halo-effect or social affect generated by the appreciation for that technical difficulty after the fact (and without knowledge) of material creation. After the merchant places the weights and the weighed, the balance could be seen from a magical perspective as acting on its own.

How the balance could have achieved its halo-effect is necessarily different from how war canoes or Tutankhamun's mask did. Scales were not wondrous creations crafted from exotic materials necessarily, and as machines they were models of simple elegance despite the considerable technical skill to both manufacture and use them convincingly in a commercial context. The scale's only moving part, the beam, was made to precise tolerances and could determine equivalencies more rapidly and far more precisely than a person using their unassisted judgment (Büttner 2017). Interpreting the scale's movement was another matter, a hidden mental process based in rationality and learning (Michailidou 2010; Rahmstorf 2010; Monroe 2009: 48–56, 127). In terms of technical difficulty those imposing canoes might pale next to the hidden mathematical knowledge of the merchant who could break down talents into minas and shekels, produce attractive stone and metal weights representing these abstractions, and moreover transpose values among various local standards. The customer did not witness the merchant studying and copying tables of weight units and divisions, as in the Akkadian tablet RS 20.014 from Ugarit, or making the calculation given in Ugaritic tablet RS varia 13: '7 talents of wool in the talent of Ashdod; and in the talent of Ugarit (that is) 5 talents (and) 1800 shekels' (Monroe 2009: 55). These were technical skills hidden from the uninitiated who only saw the seemingly magical result. I do not suggest that mathematical exercises alone would have generated a halo-effect capable of mass enchantment and social influence; the real magic of the scale was made in the middle ground between a cognitive demand (justice or fairness) and a socially constructed homology (a divinely overseen machine) empowered to satisfy it.

Does Gell's theory account for how justice became so attached to a technology that functioned in daily, profane use? If one shifts into magical thinking, it becomes more plausible. One must project that the true object being crafted is not the war canoe, but the victory it brings; not the fleshy features of the eternally golden mask, but the eternal life it promises; not the equivalence between chunks of silver and a stone weight, but a more equitable social existence. Hammurabi's stele of laws can of course be read as an attempt to engineer equity through a similar logic (Fig. 4.3, above); it makes a powerful visual and textual argument that he was carrying out justice with the aid and oversight of Shamash, with myriad legal examples below (Roth 1997: 71–76). But the work is focused ultimately on Hammurabi, and its limited visibility or access, and lack of broad or lasting reproduction suggests a minimal halo-effect during its time. An example of a more successful halo-effect of justice is the Statue of Liberty, a monumental, inscribed statue that is reproduced (at various sizes and price points) on an almost ridiculous scale. Like the Hammurabi stele, the statue makes a case for the state providing social justice, but it focuses on an anthropomorphized idea rather than a living person, and it promises justice to a global audience rather than specifically enumerated social classes. Its halo of sun rays and liminal location at a portal into a 'new world' only help in generating the desired effect. Like Hammurabi's rulership, the reality of American democracy fails to live up to the embodied ideal, especially of late. Regardless, what matters here is not the actual but 'imagined capacity' or *sentiment* of such objects.

Adam T. Smith (2015) weaves this imagined capacity into a triad of concepts that together constitute the dimensions of the human-thing relationship: Sensibility, Sense, and Sentiment. Sensibility here connotes physicality, including material properties such as whether a thing can be melted, re-formed, burned, etc. Sense is the domain of meaning and signification, *i.e.* how humans interact with things and make sense of them; weights and balances possess sense in that they are deeply involved in how humans place value on things, decide how they will be exchanged, commodified, capitalized, etc. Sentiment, finally, is the 'magical "halo" that surrounds certain things, embedding "the capacities of things within the objects themselves rather than within our senses"' (*ibid.*: 14). This hybrid agency of human-thing interaction draws from Hodder's entanglement and entrapment (2012) and Gell's enchantment (1992), which itself depends on technology. Smith's concern is how sovereigns use material things to manufacture authority, power, and sociopolitical reproduction, and how these resultant *political machines* then wield their own agency in human-thing interactions that outlast their design and manufacture. One can build on this concept by considering other assemblages, for example those used by merchants rather than princes that arguably constitute *ideological machines* wherein the logic of design is moral-economical rather than political, while exhibiting the same dynamics of sense, sensibility and sentiment. The locus of reproduction would also differ from Smith's subjects, being in the world of the market rather than the monumental. In sum, the daily repeated performance of equitable commercial outcomes with the balance, sanctioned by the overseeing gods, would reproduce a metaphysical halo-effect of social justice. Understanding more fully how this capacity might be generated by human-thing interaction requires a last look at magical thinking. or more instrumentally, theories of magic.

It is not obvious that a magical halo would ever surround objects as mundane as weights or scales. Yet once one steps into the liminal space of the merchant, it is practically inevitable. Echoing aspects of Eliade's theory of camouflage (1959), Sorensen's (2006) *Cognitive Theory of Magic* recognizes that magic requires a space where the sacred and profane may combine. Ancient commercial transactions were ritualized by injecting the sacred (*e.g.*, Shamash, Thoth, Yahweh) into an ostensibly mundane yet liminally disturbed and anxious space. Part of the effectiveness of this ritual intervention may be understood again as performance, like the theatrical magic practiced by professional magician-entertainers. Drawing substantially from Gendler (2008), Leddington (2016) argues against the common misconception that theatrical magic is simply suspension of disbelief. Cognitive dissonance, or bafflement – 'my god, how is she doing that?!' – is a crucial ingredient for successful, enjoyable magic. Key to this is Gendler's *alief*, defined as:

> a mental state with associatively linked content that is representational, affective and behavioral, and that is activated – consciously or nonconsciously – by features of the subject's internal or ambient environment. (quoted in Leddington 2016, 257)

Put another way, the magician creates an emotional, sentimental belief in the magic rather than an intellectual one; indeed, the intellect is at odds with the belief. Theatrical magic invites us to believe something, coerces us into believing it, and ultimately denies proof of it (Leddington 2016, 260). This magical process is intended to leave one excited, entertained, and baffled. It also creates an illusion of power that confers actual, material benefits on the magician.

This understanding of theatrical magic adds an important component to what can be constructed as the *sentimentality* of the ancient balance, its imagined efficacy and its agentive potential to transform social life. As the essential instrument of the marketplace, the balance should therefore infuse our sense of Bronze Age economic logics with magic. If magic is a theatrical depiction of impossible events, what then was the equivalence between barley and silver – or the universal justice articulated by Hammurabi and the *Eloquent Peasant* – other than well-performed promises lacking rational proof? The ancient merchant's balance was an enchanting technology designed to keep its user wealthy and its audience believing if ultimately baffled. A halo-effect of sentiment may moreover explain how this mundane commercial device became an ideological machine, silently reproducing its moral-economic logic from the Bronze Age until the unbalanced present.

Acknowledgements

Special thanks to the organizers and participants of the TOPOI Workshop, *Physics and metaphysics of the balance*, held Oct. 5–7, 2017 at TOPOI Haus, Berlin, where many of these ideas were first presented.

Notes

1. 'The text to the left of the woman (from her perspective) says "I will act as a balance". The one on the right is a bit less certain in its meaning, but probably "I will be in balance". It could actually, if attributed to the man, also be an imperative "be in balance!". To me, especially the first text makes it clear that the woman is speaking herself, so she has to be human, not just scale in the shape of a woman.'

Bibliography

Alberti, M.E., Ascalone, E. and Peyronel, L. (eds) (2006). *Weights in Context: Bronze Age weighing systems of Eastern Mediterranean. Chronology, typology, material and archaeological contexts. Proceedings of the International Colloquium Rome 22nd–24th November 2004.* Roma: Studi i Materiali 13.

Alster, B. (1997). *Proverbs of Ancient Sumer: The World's earliest proverb collections.* Bethesda MD: CDL Press.

Beckman, G. (1996). *Hittite Diplomatic Texts.* Atlanta GA: Scholars Press.

Beckman, G., Bryce, T. and Cline, E. (2011). *The Ahhiyawa Texts.* Atlanta GA: Society of Biblical Literature.

Bissonnette, J.-F. (2016). From the moral to the neural: Brain scans, decision-making, and the problematization of economic (ir)rationality. *Journal of Cultural Economy* 9(4), 364–381 [https://doi.org/10.1080/17530350.2016.1181097]

Black, M. (2020). *A Demon-Haunted Land: Witches, wonder doctors, and the ghosts of the past in post-WWII Germany.* New York: Metropolitan Books.

Bordreuil, E. (2006). Preliminary considerations for a typology of the weights of the Late Bronze Age discovered at Ras-Shamra-Ugarit. Archaeological and textual data. In: Alberti *et al.* (eds) 2006, 203–232.

Broodbank, C. (2013). *The Making of the Middle Sea: A history of the Mediterranean from the beginning to the emergence of the Classical World.* New York: Oxford University Press.

Büttner J. (2017). Modern physics of ancient balances. Unpublished lecture in the Workshop, *Physics and metaphysics of the balance*, Oct. 5–7, 2017, TOPOI Haus, Berlin.

Cline, E. (2015). *1177 BC: The year civilization collapsed.* Princeton NJ: Princeton University Press.

Davies, N. de G. and Faulkner, R.O. (1947). A Syrian trading venture to Egypt. *Journal of Egyptian Archaeology* 33, 40–46.

Derlon, B. and Jeudy-Ballini, M. (2010). The theory of enchantment and the enchantment of theory: The art of Alfred Gell. *Oceania* 80(2), 129–142.

El Nabolsy, Z. (2020). Using the concepts of hermeneutical injustice and ideology to explain the stability of Ancient Egypt during the Middle Kingdom. *Journal of Historical Sociology* 33(3), 345–70 [https://doi.org/10.1111/johs.12287]

Eliade, M. (1959). *Cosmos and History: The Myth of the Eternal Return.* New York: Harper & Brothers.

Evers, H.-D. (1994). The trader's dilemma: a theory of the social transformation of markets and society. In: Evers, H.-D. and Schrader, H. (eds) *The Moral Economy of Trade: Ethnicity and developing markets.* New York & London: Routledge, 7–14.

Finkelstein, J.J. (1961). Ammiṣaduqa's edict and the Babylonian 'Law Codes'. *Journal of Cuneiform Studies* 15(3), 91–104.

Foster, B.R. (1993). *Before the Muses. An Anthology of Akkadian Literature. Vol. 2. Mature, Late*. Bethesda MD: CDL Press.
Gell, A. (1992). The technology of enchantment and the enchantment of technology. In: Coote, J. and Shelton, A. (eds) *Anthropology, Art and Aesthetic*. Oxford: Clarendon Press, 40–63.
Gell, A. (1998). *Art and Agency. An Anthropological Theory*. Oxford: Clarendon Press.
Gendler, T.S. (2008). Alief and belief. *Journal of Philosophy* 105, 634–663.
Graziano, M. (2019). Mind/brain and economic behaviour: For a naturalized economics. *Axiomathes* 29, 237–264, [https://doi.org/10.1007/s10516-018-9404-4]
Helms, M. (1988). *Ulysses' Sail: An ethnographic odyssey of power, knowledge, and geographical distance*. Princeton NJ: Princeton University Press.
Henrich, J., Boyd, R., Bowles, S., Camerer, C., Gintis, H. and McElreath, R. (2001). In search of Homo economicus: Behavioral experiments in 15 small-scale societies. *American Economic Review* 91(2), 73–78.
Hodder, I. (2012). *Entangled: An archaeology of the relationships between humans and things*. Malden MA, Wiley-Blackwell.
Jeffers, C. (2013). Embodying justice in Ancient Egypt: *The Tale of the Eloquent Peasant* as a classic tale of political philosophy. *British Journal for the History of Philosophy* 21(3), 421–442 [http://dx.doi.org/10.1080/09608788.2013.771609]
Kahneman, D. (1994). New challenges to the rationality assumption. *Journal of Institutional and Theoretical Economics* 150(1), 18–36.
Kajfosz, J. (2008). Magic, categorization and folk metaphysics. Towards cognitive theory of magic. *Český lid* 95(4), 355–368. [http://www.jstor.org/stable/42640191]
Knapp, A.B. (2012). Matter of fact: transcultural contacts in the Late Bronze Age Eastern Mediterranean. In: Maran and Stockhammer (eds) 2012, 32–50.
Knapp, A.B. (2016). Afterword: identity… and things. In: Pierce, E., Russell, A., Maldonado, A. and Campbell, L. (eds) *Creating Material Worlds. The Uses of Identity in Archaeology*. Oxford & Philadelphia: Oxbow Books, 241–246.
Kristiansen, K. and Larsson, T.B. (2005). *The Rise of Bronze Age Society: Travels, transmissions and transformations*. Cambridge and New York: Cambridge University Press.
Larsen, M.T. (2015). *Ancient Kanesh: A merchant colony in Bronze Age Anatolia*. New York: Cambridge University Press.
Latour, B. (1991). *We Have Never Been Modern*. Cambridge MA: Harvard University Press.
Lauer, J.-P. (1976) *Saqqara. The Royal Cemetery of Memphis*. New York: Scribner.
Leddington, J. (2016). The experience of magic. *Journal of Aesthetics and Art Criticism* 74(3), 253–264
Lichtheim, M. (2006). *Ancient Egyptian Literature. Volume IL The New Kingdom*. Berkeley CA: University of California Press.
Malkin, I. (2011). *A Small Creek World: Networks in the Ancient Mediterranean*. New York: Oxford University Press.
Maran, J. and Stockhammer, P.W. (eds) (2012). *Materiality and Social Practice: Transformative capacities of intercultural encounters*. Oxford: Oxbow Books.
Michailidou, A. (2010). Measuring by weight in the Late Bronze Age Aegean: The people behind the measuring tools. In: Morely, I. and Renfrew, C. (eds) *The Archaeology of Measurement. Comprehending Heaven, Earth and Time in Ancient Societies*. Cambridge: Cambridge University Press, 71–87.
Monroe, C. (2009). *Scales of Fate. Trade, Tradition, and Transformation in the Eastern Mediterranean, ca. 1350–1175 BCE*. Munster: Alter OrientundAltes Testament 357.
Monroe, C. (2011). From luxuries to anxieties: A liminal view of the Late Bronze Age world-system. In: Wilkinson, T., Sherratt, S. and Bennet, J. (eds) *Interweaving Worlds: Systemic interaction in Eurasia 7th to 1st Millennia BC*. Oxford: Oxbow Books, 87–99.
Monroe, C. (2015). 'Tangled up in blue': Material and immaterial relations of exchange in the Late Bronze Age world. In: Howe, T. (ed.) *Traders in the Ancient Mediterranean*. Chicago: Publications of the Association of Ancient Historians 11,. 7–46.

Murray, A.T. (1924). *The Iliad*, translation from http://data.perseus.org/citations/urn:cts:greek-Lit:tlg0012.tlg001.perseus-eng1:22.177-22.223

Osnos, E. (2017). On the brink with North Korea. *New Yorker* 18 September17 [https://www.newyorker.com/magazine/2017/09/18/the-risk-of-nuclear-war-with-north-korea]

Parkinson, R.B. (2000). Imposing words: The entrapment of language in the *Tale of the Eloquent Peasant. Lingua Aegyptia* 8, 27–51.

Parkinson, R.B. (2012). *The Tale of the Eloquent Peasant: A reader's commentary*. Hamburg: Widmaier.

Portelli, S.J. (2014). Probablistic risk, neuroeconomic ambiguity, and Keyesian uncertainty. *Journal of Post Keynesian Economics* 36(1), 3–14.

Pulak, C. (2000). The balance weights from the Late Bronze Age shipwreck at Uluburun. In: Pare, C. (ed.) *Metals Make the World Go Round: Supply and circulation of metals in Bronze Age Europe*. Oxford: Oxbow Books, 247–266.

Pulak, C. (2006). The balance weights from Uluburun and Cape Geldonya. In: Alberti *et al.* (eds) 2006, 47–48.

Pulak, C. (2008). The Uluburun shipwreck and Late Bronze Age Trade. In: Aruz, J., Benzel, K. and Evans, J.M. (eds) *Beyond Babylon: Art, trade, and diplomacy in the second millennium BC*. New York: Metropolitan Museum of Art, 289–305.

Rahmstorf, L. (2010). The concept of weighing during the Bronze Age in the Aegean, the Near East and Europe. In: Morely, I. and Renfrew, C. (eds) *The Archaeology of Measurement. Comprehending Heaven, Earth and Time in Ancient Societies*. Cambridge: Cambridge University Press, 88–108.

Ray, H.R. (2003). *The Archaeology of Seafaring in Ancient South Asia*. Cambridge: Cambridge University Press.

Reuter, M. and Montag, C. (eds) (2016). *Neuroeconomics. Studies in Neuroscience, Psychology and Behavioral Economics*. Berlin-Heidelberg: Springer

Roth, M.T. (1997). *Law Collections from Mesopotamia and Asia Minor* (2nd edition). Atlanta GA: Scholars Press.

Schloen, J.D. (2001). *The House of the Father as Fact and Symbol: Patrimonialism in Ugarit and the Ancient Near East*. Winona Lake, IN: Studies in the Archaeology and History of the Levant 2.

Schumpeter, J.A. (1994). *Capitalism, Socialism and Democracy*. London: Routledge.

Schwemer, D. (2015). Hittite prayers to the sun-god for appeasing an angry personal god. A critical edition of *CTH* 372–74. *Orbis Biblicus et Orientalis* 273, 349–393.

Shepler, J. (2020). Einstein's Compass, available at [https://www.johnshepler.com/articles/einstein.html]

Smith, A.T. (2015). *The Political Machine: Assembling Sovereignty in the Bronze Age Caucasus*. Princeton NJ: Princeton University Press.

Sørensen, J. (2006). *A Cognitive Theory of Magic*. Lanham MD: Altamira Press.

Turner, V. (1969). *The Ritual Process: Structure and Antistructure*. Chicago: University of Chicago Press.

Turner, V. (1974). *Dramas, Fields, and Metaphors*. Ithaca NY: Cornell University Press.

Valdesolo, P. (2010). Why 'magical thinking' works for some people [https://www.scientificamerican.com/article/superstitions-can-make-you/]

Van de Mieroop, M. (2007). *A History of the Ancient Near East ca. 3000–323 BC* (2nd edition) Malden MA: Blackwell.

Warburton, D. (2016). *The Fundamentals of Economics. Lessons from the Bronze Age Near East*. Grand-Saconnex: Civilisations du Proche-Orient Serie IV, Histoire-Essais 3.

Westerdahl, C. (2005). Seal on land, elk at sea: notes on and applications of the ritual landscape at the seaboard. *International Journal of Nautical Archaeology* 34(1), 2–23.

Chapter 5

Markets, efflorescence, and political economy in the Ancient Mediterranean and the Ancient Near East[1]

Reinhard Pirngruber

Introduction: The ancient economy and new-institutional economics

The last 15 years or so have seen a marked revival of studies on the economy of the Classical World, thus Ancient Greece and Rome. As a corollary of this renewed interest, a novel approach predicated on the research paradigms of the New Institutional Economics (NIE), associated mainly with the work of Douglass C. North, became increasingly prominent. Indeed, the monumental *Cambridge Economic History of the Greco-Roman World* (Scheidel *et al.* 2007) expressly aims at connecting with North's two-pronged focus on structure and performance, and lays out a research agenda for economic historians of antiquity:

> We see the main challenges facing Greco-Roman economic historians in the early twenty-first century as being (i) to find ways to document performance more accurately; (ii) to build on twentieth-century advances in understanding institutions and ideology by clarifying the relationships between structures and performance; and (iii) to pursue comparative analyses of why the Greco-Roman economy broke down. (Scheidel *et al.* 2007: 7)[2]

Scholars across the world quickly followed suit, and the number of journal articles, monographs, and conference volumes on the 'Ancient Economy' referring explicitly to the New Institutional Economics has multiplied in the last decade (recent examples include Morris 2004; Ober 2010; 2014; Lyttkens 2013; Bresson 2014; 2016; Verboven 2015; Droß-Krüpe *et al.* 2016; Terpstra 2019). Of the three key issues listed in the introduction to the *Cambridge Economic History of the Greco-Roman World*, the second point has so far met with the biggest responses; nowhere more so than in the study of the economy of the Greek world roughly between the Cleisthenic reforms in 508 and the rise of Macedon in the third quarter of the 4th century . One core assumption shared by virtually all historians analysing the economy of this period through the lenses of NIE is their insistence that the emerging markets that underpin the economic growth leading to unprecedented welfare were enabled by the political structure of the period characterized by free and independent *poleis* (city-states). Hence, they posit a causal relationship between market economy, economic growth, and civic constitutionalism. The most explicit formulation of this stance is found in Josiah Ober's monograph on *The Rise and Fall of Ancient Greece*, who postulates a 'sustained economic growth ... made possible by a distinctive approach to politics' (Ober 2015: 30–31). An important corollary this line of reasoning is that its explanatory power is confined to Ancient Greece. Alain Bresson (2016: 103–104) thus points out 'fundamental difference between the world of the kingdoms (of the Ancient Near East, RP) and what was the civic world in the Greek manner' which according to him is precisely the 'role [that] was played by the allocation of goods through the intermediary of the market'; the economy of the Near East being characterized by a system that was largely tributary in nature.

Yet (not so) recent research economic structures Babylonia during the 1st millennium has demonstrated that this notion of the Ancient Near Eastern economy is fundamentally flawed. In particular, the outdated model of a redistributive economy with concomitant little scope for the market as mode of exchange has been thoroughly dismantled. A new research paradigm posits that 'growing urban population prompted agrarian change, stimulated the development of markets and money-based exchange, and allowed increasing economic specialisation and division of labour' (Jursa 2010: 799) during the 'long 6th century', *i.e.* the period between the rise of the Neo-Babylonian dynasty and the abortive revolts in the second year of the Achaemenid king Xerxes (484), which brought about significant changes in the country's socio-economic framework (on this watershed, see Waerzeggers (2003–2004), and now the contributions in Waerzeggers and Seire (2018)). Also, for later centuries, the period of Seleucid and Parthian supremacy over Babylonia (late 4th–1st century), the case for a significant role for the market in the exchange of staple goods (such as barley, dates, and wool) has been made on the basis of thousands of commodity price observations contained in the so-called 'Astronomical Diaries' (Pirngruber 2017).

However, contrary to the study of the Ancient Greek and Roman economies, the impact of the NIE research model has been much smaller for the period of efflorescence in Babylonia during the 'long 6th century'. Additionally, the few contributions that explicitly refer to the NIE address the perceived shortcoming of the Ancient Near Eastern economy in the longer run (and hence are leaning towards the third point listed in the introduction to the *Cambridge Economic History of the Greco-Roman World*). Michael Kozuh (2015: 86–98), for example, points to state, or rather crown, interventionism as one reason of economic instability and inefficiency, while Laetitia Graslin-Thomé (2016) points to an 'institutional standstill' hampering private engagement in long-distance trade, which thus remained firmly in the hand of big institutional players, *i.e.* crown and temple. Because of these different historiographic perspectives, we find two very different and neatly separated narratives dominating the contemporary discourses on the Greek and Ancient Near Eastern economies around the middle of the 1st millennium.[3] On the one hand, a bottom-up approach to the Ancient Greek economy attributes Greek wealth to 'uncounted individual choices' (Ober 2015: 104) enabled by an institutional framework guaranteeing rule egalitarianism and protection from arbitrary (state) action while at the same time fostering competitive innovation.[4] This radically new framework found its fitting expression in the institution of the Greek *polis* (Bresson 2014: 51). On the other hand, Babylonian economic growth is usually described in a top-down fashion; as a fortuitous juxtaposition of impersonal forces, such as demographic growth after an extended period of crisis, and spill-overs from a strong state, putting into circulation some of the booty gained in the course of successful military campaigns.[5] The role of demographic growth in the respective models is suggestive in this regard: while for Ancient Near Eastern historians it plays the role of a catalyst enabling economic growth (see the quote of M. Jursa in the preceding endnote), for Greek historians it is either phrased neutrally as concomitant factor (Lyttkens 2013: 27) or the focus is shifted to the capacity of the Greek economy to feed an expanding population at rising levels at consumption, which then is taken to be one key indicator of economic growth (Ober 2010: 249–251; 2015: 71–100; Bresson 2014: 48–50). However, the observed increases in population are usually not mentioned among the causal dynamics spurring economic growth.

In what follows, I aim to demonstrate that the seemingly irreconcilable divide between 'Greek democratic wealth' and 'Babylonian spoils-of-empire' is rather a result of the narratives offered than an incontestable historical datum. This is of course not to argue for an essential sameness (nor even similarity) of the respective institutional arrangements – which would be a patently absurd undertaking – and nor do I wish to make a case for a redimensioning of the observed levels of wealth. Rather, it is my contention that the impact of institutions on efflorescence has not only been vastly overstated in recent accounts of the Greek economy. It is even possible, as I hope to show, to provide an account of Babylonian economic growth and welfare during the long 6th century based on the very same premises that are offered by the current NIE paradigm for Greece. As a consequence, the factors proffered by this strand of literature as drivers of economic growth are revealed as a rather arbitrary selection of social and political phenomena, with little explanatory power for the question of economic growth. This result leads me to reconsider the role of natural constraints, in particular geographic factors, which have been relegated in the current models of economic growth to an ancillary role. I will also take a brief look at the historiographic traditions on socioeconomic developments in the respective disciplines of Classical Studies and Assyriology, as they are part and parcel of the currently prevailing dichotomy.

An NIE perspective on Babylonia during the long 6th century

Remarkable extensive growth took place ...

It is uncontested today that the 'long 6th century' constitutes a period of efflorescence in Babylonia, enabled by rising *per capita* output. Not only saw the first half of the 6th century an increase in the total area under cultivation, it was also the case the agricultural production intensified and became increasingly reliant on market exchange – to the point that it is now customary to speak of cash-crop production. This pattern applies to the cities' main temples, large institutional households, across Babylonia.

The best attested case is the Ebabbar temple in the northern Babylonian town of Sippar, where a shift from extensive cereal farming to intensive date horticulture is in evidence starting already at the turn from the 7th to the 6th century (Jursa 2010: 355–360, 576–594). Additionally, hitherto undeveloped lands in the town's hinterland were brought under cultivation. The temple sold its significant surplus in dates on the market, often to large-scale traders who would then deal the dates at retail. The silver thus earned was fed back into the economy mainly via two avenues of expenditure, both of which served to further stimulate demand and ultimately economic growth. First, the temple had to pay (silver) wages for hired workers employed in the crown's large-scale building projects, to which the temples were obliged to contribute (and for which its own dependents, the temple serfs (*širkus*) were not sufficient in number).[6] Second, numerous documents attest to the acquisition of goods, which the temple did not produce itself, including various agricultural produces (sesame, barley) sacrificial animals (sheep, cattle) as well as prestige goods imported by long-distances traders (Jursa 2010: 514–525 for an overview). Another well-explored example is the Eanna temple in Uruk in southern Babylonia, who owned large flocks of sheeps (and, to a significantly lesser extent, goats) and sold the surplus wool for silver (Kleber 2008, 237–246; Kleber in Jursa 2010, 595–623).[7] The most frequently attested transaction type attested were retails sales, which the temple itself engaged in. More important as regards volume, however, were large-scale sales to traders servicing the palace and/or provincial governors; about two-thirds of the temple's silver income was generated from these transactions.

One well-explored corollary of this period of economic growth is an unprecedented rise in welfare levels for non-elite citizens. In terms of the wheat wage (*i.e.* an unskilled labourers daily income in terms of a society's staple grain), Babylonia was roughly at the same levels of Athens in the fourth century and both in turn at the high end for pre-industrial societies (Jursa 2010, 811–816; Scheidel 2010).[8]

... based on a highly favourable global institutional framework ...

Key to this development was an essentially stable and peaceful political environment following the establishment of the Chaldean dynasty by Nabopolassar in 626, and the annihilation of the Assyrian Empire and the incorporation of its remnants soon thereafter. Two aspects are central for the economic development during the ensuing long 6th century. Babylonia was spared incursions or internal military conflict on a major scale for about a century and a half. The conquest of Babylonia by Cyrus II and the overthrow of the last Chaldean king Nabonidus was rather swift and did not cause major destructions in cities and countryside nor did it lead to a rupture in the country's social and economic institutions.[9] As stated in note 4, it was only in the early 5th century, after abortive revolts against Persian rule in the second regnal year of Xerxes that a major structural break can be ascertained.

Moreover, Babylon became the centre of gravity of an empire spanning large swathes of the Ancient Middle East, from the shores of the Eastern Mediterranean to the Zagros mountain range and, after the Persian conquest, beyond. This central position, which was only gradually abandoned after the Achaemenid conquest – note that the city was one of the four capital cities of the Achaemenid Empire, besides Ecbatana, Persepolis, and Susa – meant a constant influx of the 'spoils of empire'. These included most importantly silver and other precious metals in form of war booty and later tribute and taxes, as well as labour power in form of forced resettlements to the imperial core (see most recently Levavi 2020).

State spending on a large scale complemented these fortuitous political circumstances. Thus, the crown not only initiated and at least indirectly contributed to prestige buildings such as palaces and temple renovations, but also provided funding for the country's agricultural infrastructure. Of particular importance was the canal network; an emblematic undertaking was the digging of the 'royal canal' (*nār šarri*) connecting Euphrates and Tigris rivers in northern Babylonia. The expansion of horticulture in the Sippar region, for example, proceeded precisely along these new waterways. Not only were they indispensable in providing a key means of production in an agricultural regime based on irrigation, but they also facilitated the economic integration of the wider region. The increasingly dense network of canals was employed as arteries of transport, enabling the movement of bulky goods including staple foods such as barley and dates over longer distances at reasonable expenses (Weszeli in Jursa 2010: 140–152; on the Ebabbar temple's agricultural holdings along the *nār šarri*, see Jursa 2010: 326–334).

Lastly, 'a fundamentally coherent and rationally and equitably applied rule of law' fostered economic growth from within (Magdalene *et al.* 2019: 327).[10] This included a rather strong position of local officials (often the chief temple administrator, *šatammu*) and institutions such as the city assembly (*puhru*) vis-á-vis the crown. This favourable power balance had its roots in the troubled period in the later 8th century, when the Assyrian king struggled to assert control over the south and the success of counter-kings such as Marduk-apla-iddina II (Merodach-baladan) provided cities with considerable leverage to obtain concessions from Assur (Barjamović 2004; Pirngruber 2015). The reach of the law pervaded even the sphere of religious and social identity. As argued by C. Waerzeggers, it was the *legal* possession of the priestly title (Waerzeggers 2010: 34–37; she also emphasizes the importance of royal protection of this title) that defined membership in the temple community (*kiništu*) from whose ranks the highest local officials such as the *šatammu* were recruited.

Thousands of business records, including promissory note, sales contracts, rental agreements, etc., attest to a sophisticated legal framework guaranteeing a smooth flow of economic transactions of diverse nature.[11] One thing that stands out is a disappearance of methods such as river ordeals so prominent in earlier periods (as documented *e.g.* in the Laws of Hammurapi), a reduced role of increasingly standardized oaths, which disappear from contract law, and a greater reliance of 'rational' evidence and argumentation. In cases of contested ownership or status, it became customary to produce the pertinent records as proof of lawful title, while during the investigation of criminal cases the questioning (*maš'altu*) of litigants, the recording of witnesses' statements and the exhibition of tangible proofs were routine.

... division of labor, extensive trade, radical improvements in financial and contracting practices ...

These legal innovations extended likewise to the sphere of business and trade. Business records from the period contain a plethora of more-or-less standardized formulas specifying rights and obligations of trade partners. Of particular relevance as regards the protection of property rights is a joint liability clause in which multiple debtors hold each other accountable for repayment (or multiple sellers for legal integrity of the object of sale), which emerges besides guarantee clauses of single sellers/debtors. Also strengthening the creditor's position is the occasional right-of-disposal clause which specifies precedence of the claims of current creditor over eventual other claims incurred by the debtor; as were pledges (*maškānu*) and warrantors who would assume the debt stipulated. Also, eventual previous obligations of a debtor were often explicitly excluded from the present arrangement. In some instances, a contract concludes by noting that both parties to the contract received a copy thereof, maybe for the case of future contestations. Moreover, the long 6th century also saw the emergence of new contract types, most notably *harrānu* ventures. This contract type, similar to medieval *commendas*, allowed for the pooling of the financial resources of several investors, which then put at the disposal of a trading agent for the purpose of a trading expedition or similar (Lanz 1976; Jursa 2010, 208–214).

These legal standards are present throughout Babylonia, in different archives from different cities. Below, I shall quote pertinent passages from the archive of Iššar-tarībi, a small-scale merchant from Sippar, for the purpose of illustration:[12]

- (The seller) Mannu-kî-Banītu guarantees that the donkey is free of prior claims.
- (Of two debtors) guarantees for the other, whoever is available will repay the silver.
- (Two investors put together funding) for the purpose of a *harrānu*. Everything they earn in town and countryside from aforementioned 2½ minas of silver, they will have an equal share in the profit from the seed capital. Each (of the partners) took one copy (of the contract).
- Zabdīya, his son is held as a pledge for the aforementioned 15 shekels silver
- Guarantor for the aforementioned 1½ minas and 4 shekels of *nuhhutu*-silver with 1/8th alloy, without *ginnu*-mark, is A, son of B

The final example brings us to another point, which is the unprecedentedly varied terminology for silver in the long 6th century. Some of the expressions encountered, such as the *ginnu*-mark just mentioned were guarantees for the quality of the silver; the specification of 1/8th alloy means a degree of fineness of 87.5% (Jursa 2010: 474–490).[13] Another key difference to earlier periods was the availability of silver. Not only was a much larger quantity of silver current in Babylonia, and hence its value rather low compared to the commodities it bought, which is reflected in a lower price level. Silver was also more ubiquitous in transactions and in smallest denominations: the *hallūru* ('chickpea') of 1/40 of a shekel (itself 8.33 g) mentioned in several texts is surpassed by archaeologically attested weights of even 1/60 of a shekel (Jursa 2010: 479).[14] The tiny fractions attested are an important indication of another key element the functioning of market-based exchange, and one that is often underrated because not explicit in the sources, namely trust in the institutional framework. It was too impractical (and costly) to control the weight of the money exchanged during each transaction. Money users thus partly relied on visual and haptic judgement based on experience, but they also had to feel confident that these pieces would be accepted in further transactions (and that irregularities in weight would cancel themselves out eventually). This is no yet fiduciary money – *i.e.*, money whose value is purely the result of social conventions – but it is clear that the economy was greased by a monetary system, which imposed on economic actors denominations the value of which they could not validate on the spot in person.

In addition to scrupulous qualifications for and quantifications of silver (and other, less specific expressions such *kaspu ša nadāni u mahīri*, 'silver commonly used for transactions'), it is remarkable that also capacity measures and weights were uniform throughout the period. For staple goods such as barley and dates a system with a basis of one *qû*, roughly equivalent to one metric litre was used; the largest denomination being a *kurru* of 180 litres.

Information on prices was public. In addition to the meticulous recordings in the Astronomical Diaries of the price equivalents of six standardised basic commodities (including barley, dates, and wool), there is evidence in epistolographic material that economic actors, private as well as institutional monitored price developments.[15] Most impressively, a fragmentary letter from the Eanna temple in Uruk tracks price differences in northern Babylonia: the cities of Babylon, Borsippa, Sippar and Opis are mentioned.[16] A final aspect to mentioned here were the (for pre-industrial societies) low interest rates, hovering around (and often below, especially during the reigns of Nabopolassar and Nechadnezzar II) the customary 20% *per annum* (Jursa 2010: 490–499). The high level of standardization and the public nature of central information are synonymous with low transaction costs.

These favorable developments brought with themselves increased possibilities for traders. At one end of the scale, the temples purchased large quantities of luxurious items from overland trade with the Levantine coast – purple and others dyes as well as dyed fabrics, copper and iron, alaun – from independent traders whom they provided with seed capital (Graslin-Thomé 2009: 36–55). On the other end, even small-scale businessmen like Iššar-tarībi, mentioned above, were able to draw profit from the imperial infrastructure by expanding the horizon of their business. Iššar-tarībi, who had a stake in trades as diverse as brewing and the manufacture of military caps, was not only active in his hometown of Sippar and its surroundings. He is also attested as doing business as far as Humadēšu, beyond the Zagros mountains, close to the Persian heartland, where Babylonia traders actively sought to establish contacts with Iranian merchants (Pirngruber 2020: 169). The career of Iššar-tarībi is important as it shows that it was possible for traders during the 6th century to achieve prosperity without any kind of institutional affiliation; he had no ties to his city's temple-centred elite, which tended to cut itself off from their surroundings – indeed, it is likely that Iššar-tarībi himself was an immigrant from Assyria.[17] It is also clear that he was by no means an exceptional person and more private archives of traders with a similar scope (and sometimes different portfolios) have come down to us. The onomastics of these people firmly demonstrate that imperial wealth was not restricted to Babylonians (as already was the case with Iššar-tarībi); in particular, persons with West Semitics names, including Judeans, were frequent actors in overland trade.[18]

The final point to be raised here is the increased division of labor. The majority of texts from an institutional setting refers to hired unskilled laborers (*agrus*), whose tasks included such onerous activities as brick making and canal digging, and to the temple's textile manufacture in the case of the Eanna temple. Additionally, a broad variety of remunerated activities, ranking from part-time activities to permanent occupations is in evidence. Among the latter, three dozen (!) apprenticeship contracts stand out, with either children or more often slaves being handed over to a master in order to learn a trade (Hackl in Jursa 2010: 700–725). Attested professions included baker, carpenter, and goldsmith, and the duration varied from 12 months to eight years. The master received a compensation for his effort, often silver and/or the labor power after the finished apprenticeship for a period, but was liable for penalty payment in the case of negligence. Attested part-time jobs included services spanning from mercenary to laundry work and wet nursing. Hence, as is also the case for the temples' textile workshops, women could and did participate in extra-domestic labor, supplementing their family's income (Joannès 2008).

Historiographies of economic developments in Athens and Babylon

Arbitrariness of discourse?

As the preceding pages have shown, it is very well possible to couch the economic history of Babylonia during the long 6th century – a story of growth and rising prosperity – exclusively in terms of the New Institutional Economics. Indeed, the subheadings above are a quote from Alain Bresson summarizing his account of the Greek economy in the Classical period.[19] His main factors supposedly underlying economic growth in Greece during the 5th century can be applied one by one to explain developments in Babylonia about a century earlier. This has several important consequences. Most obviously, it is time to discard assessments of the Ancient Near East as a world that can be set aside from any debate on elements of market economies, and the prosperity these brought about, in the Ancient world. More importantly, however, it is the model of economic development proffered by Bresson, Ober and other proponents of the NIE that is called into question by the parallelism of phenomena elaborated in the preceding section.[20] Ober particularly insists on the explanatory power of the institutional framework as main (and even sole) driver of economic growth and rising levels of well-being. According to him, 'the solution to the puzzle of Greek economic exceptionalism is political exceptionalism' (Ober 2015: 103; for similar quotes see endnote 4). Yet, the same phenomena are clearly in evidence in Babylonia – investment in human capital in form of apprenticeship contracts; legal protection of property rights and elaborate dispute resolution procedures; a stable institutional framework guaranteeing the quality of currency as well as weights and standards. Not much remains, then, of the alleged 'Greek exceptionalism'. The same holds true for the political sphere, and it is easily possible to come up with a narrative of economic growth in Classical Athens under the title of Jursa (2014a), *viz.* 'economic growth in times of empire.'

Athens – economic growth in times of empire?

Turning the tables, such a narrative could place emphasis on Athens' role as the heart of an empire, the Delian League. The spoils of empire included both substantial tribute payment from allies (note that *phoros* is the same term employed for payments exacted by the Achaemenid kings from their vassals in Greek historiography) as well as war booty, both silver (capital) and slaves (labor power). Resistance among the allies or refusals to join the league were met with severe acts of reprisals, as the annihilation of the male population of the island of Melos and the sale into slavery of its women and children demonstrates (on the fate of Melos, see Tritle 2010: 132–136). All of this can be easily illustrated with a few quotes from Thucydides:

> Now was the time that the office of *Hellenotamiai* ('Treasurers for Hellas') was first instituted by the Athenians. These officers received the tribute (*phoros*), as the money contributed was called. The tribute was first fixed at four hundred and sixty talents. (*Thuc* I 96.2)[21]

> First the Athenians besieged and captured Eion on the Strymon from the Medes, and made slaves of the inhabitants, being under the command of Cimon, son of Miltiades. Next they enslaved Scyros the island in the Aegean, containing a Dolopian population, and colonized it themselves. (*Thuc.* I 98.1–2)

> Of all the causes of defection, that connected with arrears of tribute and vessels, and with failure of service, was the chief; for the Athenians were very severe and exacting. (*Thuc.* I 99.1)

In addition to its income from military activity (tribute and booty), the discovery of large deposits in the silver mines of Laurion in southern Attica – which were in turn exploited by slave laborers – was a happy windfall for the nascent empire. Lavish state spending fed the spoils of empire back into circulation. Athens spent its income heavily on military resources (*e.g.*, Pritchard 2012), in particular the fleet, which was the cornerstone in the league's aggressive and expansionist policies, and on the upkeep of its military defences, such as the imposing walls connecting the city to its harbour in the Piraeus:

> they have stuffed the city with harbors and arsenals and walls and tribute and suchlike trash. (Plato, *Gorgias* 519a)

Finally, the state financed a large-scale building programme of purely ideological nature, aimed at celebrating Athens' imperial glory. The reference here is of course to the expansion of the acropolis under Pericles and the construction of the Parthenon with the statue of the city-goddess Athena holding Nike, deified victory, in her outstretched hand.

Selective readings

While the preceding lines are deliberately hyperbolic and lopsided (though not more than the generic assessments of the Near East quoted in the introduction), they still reflect an approach that is not uncommon among classicists.[22] The violent nature and expansionist aims of the Athenian empire are acknowledged without difficulty, as are the economic gains the city derived therefrom. Some scholars even suggest that Athens' imperial politics were from the outset designed to serve economic goals (Kallet 2013; namely, control of trade routes rather than plunder). Present NIE research, on the other hand, not only downplays the role of state agency, but also and especially sidesteps uncomfortable aspects thereof that sit rather ill with the rose-tinged world of stable institutional frameworks and low transaction costs. Hence, the Athenian Empire's beneficial inner-Greek politics – security, protection of economic interests, access to a common market, etc. – 'encouraged *rational submission to imperial rule*' (Ober 2015: 201, my italics). The rhetoric employed thereby sometimes borders on the cynical; for example, when Ober writes about the benefits of empire for Athens' lower social classes, who would benefit from 'agricultural land (that) was confiscated from a subject state that had failed fully to grasp the *rationality of acquiescence*' (Ober 2015: 204; my italics). This phrase says less about Athenian policies towards defeated states or the experience of those driven from their land, sold into slavery or killed to provide a terrifying example for potential future defectors, than it does about the mind-set of its author, who seem to embrace the idea of an Athenian Manifest Destiny of sorts. Hence, when Philipp II conquered the Greek World, 'the great states of Greece fell to a *predatory* empire' and likewise, Achaemenid Persia is a 'predatory' empire (Ober 2015: 6 and 10, respectively; my italics), but failure to submit to Athenian imperialism is poor judgement on part of the vanquished.

Excursus – The academic East–West divide

This clear-cut division between Classical Antiquity and the Ancient Near East that is in evidence in contemporary scholarship harkens back at least to the work of Moses Finley, who famously insisted on a fundamental otherness of the east and its economic structures. The latter were 'dominated by large palace- or temple complexes, who owned the greater part of the arable ... and organized the economic ... life of the society through a single complicated, bureaucratic, record-keeping operation' (Finlay 1999: 29).[23] Such a statement reflects quite well the state of our knowledge in 1973 (when *The Ancient Economy* was first published), yet it is surprising, and disappointing, to see that Finley's successors still cling to this, by now, obsolete conception. To be clear, Finley was right in pointing out a fundamental difference in the social organisation of Ancient Near Eastern cities and the Greek *polis*. It is the impact on economic performance NIE influenced research attributes to the peculiar social structure as well as the alleged absence of markets structures in the ancient near East that I would like to dispute.

On the other side of the divide, scholars of the Ancient Near East have been slow to accept the presence of market elements in Mesopotamia. This is in large part the legacy of Karl Polanyi, whose ideas about the 'marketless society' were the most influential theoretical approach to the study of the Ancient Near Eastern economy on the second half of the 20th century AD. Still today, although his hypotheses are largely superseded, he serves as obligatory reference point in prefaces and introductory chapters in most works of aspects of the Babylonian economy.[24] At the same time, with the exception of Old Assyrian studies, the focus of scholarship has been on economic activities of the large institutional households, rather than on private business. This was only in part a result of the nature of the extant sources, which often originated precisely in these institutional households (*e.g.* during the Ur III period *c.* 2050, which also yielded an unusually high number of cuneiform records), but equally of the often implicit framework against which these texts have been interpreted.[25]

Conclusion: Markets in Athens and Babylon

Commonalities

It should be clear by now that theses of Greek economic exceptionalism, which explain economic growth and rising levels of welfare almost solely by reference to the institutional framework, lack a defendable base. Research beyond the boundaries of the disciplines of Assyriology and Ancient History seems to concur. Bas van Bavel's (2016) monograph on cases of pre-industrial market economies shows that they are a recurring phenomenon in world history, discussing cases as diverse as early Islamic Iraq, late medieval Italy, and the Netherlands during the 'Golden Age'. In his view, Babylon is a 'possible' case of a market economy, while Athens is even relegated to the rank of a 'questionable' instance (van Bavel 2016: 31–32, 35 table 1.2).[26]

Let us, then, briefly outline a scenario in a comparative perspective assuming that the observed shared features that underlay and sustained the observed increase in production and wealth in both cases are not coincidental. On the macro-level, the beginning of both growth spurts was contemporary to the onset of extended periods of demographic growth and concomitant rising urbanisation. On the level of the *histoire événementielle*, it was marked by a favourable political framework that saw Athens and Babylon as the centres of larger entities, the Delian League, which developed towards a tributary empire, and the Neo-Babylonian and later Achaemenid Empire respectively. This situation was the pre-condition for capital accumulation on a large scale and subsequent government spending, which still in the modern world are key drivers of economic growth. This is best exemplified by the case of contemporary China, where the impact of these factors on economic growth by far outweighs modernization and adaptation of the legal and institutional framework (Yueh 2013).[27]

The effect of government spending can be illustrated by the frenzied building programmes undertaken during the imperial heyday of both Athens and Babylonia. Similar to what has been said above about Nebuchadnezzar II's building activity in Babylon, Pericles' programme yielded 'material benefits for many poorer citizens because it offered countless opportunities for employment for skilled and unskilled workers alike and supported contractors supplying raw materials' (Martin 2016: 170).[28] Armed forces were similarly a significant expense in the case of Athens, as well as an potential source of income for the lower classes (*e.g.* as rower in the navy, see Ober 2015: 169). Evidence for the Neo-Babylonian Empire's military organisation is sparse and indirect. However, we not only know that the Nabopolassar and his successors were frequently on campaign, but also the nomenclature of the Babylonian tax system is indicative of a system rooted in the performance of military service (which in times of peace was converted to generic labor service). A text from the archive of Iššar-tarībi nicely illustrates the effect of this system: rather than performing the obligation of the 'royal soldier' (*ṣab šarri*) themselves, Iššar-tarībi and his brother preferred to pay a third person who would discharge their duty (Pirngruber 2020, text 2; the tax system is discussed in detail in Jursa 2009). A larger amount of specie in circulation, distributed among a greater number of individuals, resulted in rising consumption and stimulated productivity, in what Jursa (2014a) called a 'positive feedback cycle'.

A third commonality is the presence of an institutional framework conducive to further growth by guaranteeing a degree of legal stability and lowering transaction costs. While not the catalyst of growth it was made out to be by recent NIE inspired research, nor unique to the Greek experience, it undeniably contributed to the observed developments that raised standards of livings to unprecedented heights. Two clarifications are maybe in order here: first, it should go without saying that I do not wish to argue for an essential sameness of the institutional arrangements in Athens and Babylonia. Yet, there is a notable comparability in the general direction of the latter – towards protection of property rights and of creditors, towards an increased role of contractual provisions rather than the use of force, and towards rational procedure. Such elements are present in any case of emergent market economies (or, phrased more cautiously, any economic system with a significant scope for the market as mode of economic integration), but neither are they the only nor the most important vector. Secondly, under different political superstructures, the long-term (economic, but also social and political) effects of the respective institutional frameworks may vary to a considerable degree and lead over time to fundamentally different outcomes.

Differences

While this contribution so far has focused on parallel developments and similarities, I will now turn to important differences between Athens and Babylon in the respective economic structures, and how these may have influenced productivity and market performance. A first aspect is the organisation of labour relations and the role of slavery. Deportations and forced resettlement were the central slaving practices in the Ancient Near East, often not considered as such.[29] Communities of deportees were settled at some distance to the cities, where they were allotted agricultural holdings, which they were to work in exchange for taxes (in form of produce these lands yielded) and labour services; a well-known case being the Judean community near Āl-Yāhūdu in south-central Babylonia (Waerzeggers 2015). In Athens, one the other hand, slave labor was exploited to a much higher extent in activities generating higher cash value – more productive purposes, in economists' parlance. First and foremost, the arduous and dangerous work in the silver mines comes to mind here, which 'comes very near to being a monopoly of slaves' (Finley 1999: 72). In addition, employment in various crafts in *ergasteria* – translated occasionally as 'sweatshops' – played a more important role compared to Babylon.[30] In agriculture, sharecropping arrangements prevailing in Babylonia may have been less conducive to producing maximum possible output compared to the deployment of slave labor on a large scale.

A second aspect wherein Athens and Babylon differ significantly is geography and geographic constraints. The Neo-Babylonian and Achaemenid Empires were large territorial entities, incorporating large stretches of the Ancient Middle East, stretching from the eastern shores of the Mediterranean to (and including, in the case of the Achaemenids) the Iranian highlands. Yet, Babylon, the imperial core, is a comparatively self-contained region, delineated to west and east by Euphrates and Tigris, beyond which the Syrian Desert and the Zagros mountain range are natural barriers to trade. This does not mean that long-distance trade did not take place, but is was confined to high-value, low-bulk commodities. For staple goods such as grain, overland transport costs made trading prospects beyond the reaches of Babylonia's network of canals unlikely (Pirngruber 2017: 214). Additionally, the high degree of centralisation in Babylonia also meant that trade flows were directed almost exclusively towards the capital city, leading to a stronger concentration of wealth (Jursa 2010: 73–80).

Athens' geostrategic location as a tributary empire was precisely the other way around. Excluding colonies, the city's territory comprised its hinterland and large parts of Attica, but little territory beyond that. Conversely, Athens was integrated into the enormous economically integrated region that is the Mediterranean, with the possibility to important grain from regions as distant as the Black Sea, Egypt and Cyrene, and Sicily.[31] These different sources of grain supply provided Athens with a safeguard in the case of harvest failure in Attica – a buffer that was not available to Babylon, which depended for its harvest crucially on a single source: the river level of the Euphrates, which was decided by the amount of winter precipitation in the Anatolian mountains. Together with a strong political position, it also ensured a rather predictable level of supply, thus fostering regional specialisation in non-food producing activities, which in turn stimulated both demand for grain in the interior, and exports for foreign trade.

The consequences of this divergent structure of the two economic regions under discussion – multipolarity in the Mediterranean and a single dominant centre in the Ancient Near East – can also be formalized. As Földvari *et al.* (2011) have shown, price volatility, a common indicator of market efficiency, which is the capacity of markets to adjust to supply or demand shocks is much lower in a balanced system of centres with roughly equal power. Athens' integration into the Mediterranean world proves thus to be one key advantage in the long run, with beneficial impacts on its economy also after the short period of imperial glory.[32]

Notes

1. This contribution has been long in the making. A preliminary version was presented at the international workshop *Economic Growth in Antiquity* (FU Berlin, 18–21 November 2016) organized by Prof. D. Warburton under the auspices of the TOPOI Excellence cluster. All dates are BC.
2. Early in their introduction to the *Cambridge Economic History of the Greco-Roman World*, we find an extensive quote of D. North describing the purpose of economic history as elucidating an economy's structure and performance. Relevant works include North (1990) and (2005).
3. One reason to focus on these two eras/regions is their inclusion in the monumental *Cambridge History of Capitalism* (Neal and Williamson 2014), the first two chapters of which concern Babylonia during the Chaldean and Achaemenid dynasties on the one hand (Jursa 2014a), and Classical Greece, and in particular Athens, on the other (Bresson 2014).
4. 'Rules protecting individuals from exploitation, and subsequent individual choices to invest in human and social capital, led to the emergence of a vibrant market-based economy', as Ober (2015: 112) puts it succinctly. See also Ober (2010: 266–267): 'the answer to why Greece *outperformed* other premodern societies is best sought in distinctive Greek institutions ... egalitarian rules and institutional innovation' (my italics).
5. See *e.g.* Jursa (2014a: 31): 'Profiting from state-controlled investment in the agrarian infrastructure and generally lavish state spending, population growth and a concomitant process of urbanization set in motion (and were in turn sustained by) a positive feedback cycle in the economy. This led to an increase in demand and to an increase in aggregate as well as per capita production. Urbanization allowed an increasing division of labor and economic specialization, and thus led to higher productivity'.

6. Note that the system of taxation in the Neo-Babylonian and Achaemenid periods was geared strongly towards the mobilization of labor for its building projects, such as the construction of Nebuchadnezzar's North Palace in Babylon; for a detailed case study of the latter see Beaulieu (2005).
7. She gives an estimate of an annual wool production in the range between 75 and 112.5 metric tons of wool (*ibid.*: 595) which corresponds to a minimum estimate of 700 kg of silver annually (reckoning with the average price of 1.4 shekels per 5 minas of silver).
8. For a similar result see Pirngruber (2016) with an attempt to gauge prosperity by means of the welfare ratio measuring the ratio of income and a consumption basket.
9. Beaulieu (2018: 219–254) provides a concise political history of Babylonia under the Neo-Babylonian and Achaemenid dynasties; see also Jursa (2007) on the transition years. Pirngruber (2018) argues for a stronger impact of the Persian conquest, which continued a trend towards increasing state pressure already evident in the mid-6th century.
10. See similarly Jursa (2014b:196), who speaks of a 'stable legal system that protected property rights and business interests.'
11. Jursa 2005 provides an overview of the extant material, including an introduction to the most common text types. The legal framework of the long sixth century is discussed, *e.g.* in Oelsner *et al.* (2003) and Magdalene *et al.* (2019: especially 303–332).
12. Pirngruber (2020: quotes from texts 7, 10, 21, 23 and 22 (in this order). The same and more provisions are likewise in evidence in larger archives; see Jursa (2005) for an exhaustive list of archives from 1st millennium Babylonia with short description of archive contents. The best-known example is the archive of the Egibi family from Babylon, a family of entrepreneurs specializing in (regional) trade in agricultural products and date gardening who acquired considerable wealth in the later Neo-Babylonian and Achaemenid periods. The exceptionally large archive comprising *c.* 1700 tablets is briefly described in Jursa (2005: 65–66 (sub 7.1.2.4), with additional literature).
13. Jursa discards the earlier hypothesis according to which *ginnu* refers to Croesids and *sigloi*. The adjective *nuhhutu* in the example above maybe refers to *Hacksilber* (cut up silver), (*ibid.*: 479) rather than to a specific quality.
14. See Jursa (2018) for the application of the concept of 'deep monetisation' for 6th century Babylonia.
15. The Astronomical Diaries were analysed in depth in Pirngruber (2017, with references to earlier literature). The extant tablets span mainly the 4th–1st centuries, but the genre is said to have had its beginnings during the reign of King Nabonassar in the mid-8th century. The earliest extant tablet with price data dates to 568/7, which is year 37 of the reign of Nebuchadnezzar II.
16. The still unpublished letter is inventoried at the Vorderasiatisches Museum (Berlin) under the museum number W 3381z; Kleber (2012: 229) provides a translation and a contextualisation of the text. See also Pirngruber (2017: 32–33) for this and similar texts.
17. For a detailed account of Iššar-tarībi's business, see Pirngruber (2020). The isolationist tendencies of the old-established highest echelons of Babylonian cities are described in Still (2019: 27–63) on the basis of their marriage patterns.
18. Alstola (2017; 2019: 79–101) on Judeans and 237–250 on a group of persons from Neirab in modern-day Syria. For a detailed overview of trade according to Babylonian archives, see Jursa (2010: 214–228).
19. Bresson (2014: 48): 'remarkable extensive growth took place, based on a highly favourable global institutional framework, division of labor, extensive trade, radical improvements in financial and contracting practices'.
20. B. Graziosi also expressed unease about Ober's discourse from the perspective of a cultural historian in a review of his book in the *Times Literary Supplement* (19.08.2015), in particular about his

emphasis on risen wealth levels as central achievement of the Greeks. For a review of Bresson (2016) taking issue with his cut-and-dried East–West dichotomy, see Van der Spek (2017).

21. All Greek translations are from http://www.perseus.tufts.edu/.
22. *E.g.*, Pébarthe (2008), Pritchard (2012) and the Pericles biography (Azoulay 2014, 51–61; who even speaks of 'the enslavement of its (*i.e.*, the Athenian *demos*', RP) allies within the framework of the Delian League'; for an opposing view more sympathetic with Athens, see Martin (2016: 153–154)). Harrison (2010: 516) speaks of 'limitless ambition and unabashed pride' on the part of the Athenians.
23. See Launaro (2016) for an appreciation of Finley's work on the ancient economy and its ongoing relevance.
24. *E.g.* Jursa (2010: 19–21). On Polanyi's work and lasting influence, see the essays in Clancier (*et al.* eds 2005: in particular the chapter by J. Renger for an illustrative example of 'Polanyian scholarship').
25. A still useful overview, and exceptional in its explicitly theoretical reflections, is Van de Mieroop (1999, 105–135), who endorses a substantivist approach, emphasizing the embeddedness of the economy in society and a reduced scope for markets. While he postulates that most scholars follow modernist assumptions, his discussion shows that substantivist (*i.e.* scholars influenced by Polanyi and Max Weber, such as J. Renger) and (Neo-)Marxist models (I. Diakonoff, M. Liverani, C. Zacccagnini), were much more influential current over the last 50 years.
26. His focus is on factor markets – hence, markets for land, labour and capital – rather than commodity markets, which are qualitatively on a different level; see Jursa (2014b) for factor markets in Babylonia. Van Bavel's central hypothesis is that market economies carry the seed of their decline in them because wealth accumulation by new market elites and rising inequality translate inevitably into political power, ultimately eroding the institutional foundations of a market. This fits very well with the reading of the socio-economic dynamics evident in the Murašû archive in Pirngruber (2017: 65–66 *et passim*). Overall, however, this scenario is hard to prove in antiquity because of comparatively rapid political turnovers.
27. *e.g.* 319: 'Investment and capital accumulation have been the most important component of China's growth'.
28. Martin also compares Pericles' building programme with F.D. Roosevelt's New Deal; see in general also Martin 2016: 166–170). Similarly Azoulay (2014, 76–80).
29. Rather than analysing slavery in terms of a legal relationship between owner and property, or similar, a historical approach advocated i.a. by Joseph Miller defines slaving as 'appropriation of human resources external to given historical contexts ... for internal purposes'. (Miller 2012: 37).
30. See Lewis (2018: 176–179). While occupation of slaves as craftsmen is known, the presence of structures akin to *ergasteria* has never been pondered, with the possible exception of temple workshops (for which in turn there is no evidence for the employment of privately owned slaves).
31. Bresson (2016: 79) remarks that it was the 'permanent free supply of free energy provided by wind that constitutes the true "secret hero" in of the growth of the economy in the ancient Mediterranean world'. He provides a detailed discussion on Athens' provisions with grain by regional and long-distance trade in the Greek world: *ibid.*: 402–414.
32. Ober (2010: 275–277), has rightly observed the fragmentation prevailing in the Mediterranean fuelled competition among states and may have spurred institutional innovations. Yet, in practice, it was more often the *realpolitik* of regional hegemons that decided the course of action for most poleis.

Bibliography

Alstola, T. (2017). Judean Merchants in Babylonia and their participation in long-distance trade. *Die Welt des Orients* 47, 25–51

Alstola, T. (2019). *Judeans in Babylonia. A Study of Deportees in the Sixth and Fifth Centuries BCE*. Leiden and Boston MA: Culture and History of the Ancient Near East 109

Azoulay, V. (2014) *Pericles of Athens*. Princeton NJ, Princeton University Press.

Barjamović, G. (2004). Civic institutions and self-government in Southern Mesopotamia in the mid-first millennium BC. In: Dercksen, J.G. (ed.) *Assyria and beyond. Studies Presented to Mogens Trolle Larsen*. Leiden: PIHANS AQ: please give in full 100, 47–98.

Beaulieu, P.-A. (2005). Eanna's contribution to the construction of the North Palace at Babylon. In: Baker, H. and Jursa, M. (eds) *Approaching the Babylonian Economy. Proceedings of the START Project Symposium Held in Vienna, 1-3 July 2004*. Münster: Alter Orient und Altes Testament 330, 45–73.

Beaulieu, P.-A. (2018). *A History of Babylon 2200 BC-AD 75*. Chichester: Blackwell History of the Ancient World.

Bresson, A. (2014). Capitalism and the Ancient Greek economy. In: Neal and Williamson (eds) 2014, 43–74.

Bresson, A. (2016). *The Making of the Ancient Greek Economy. Institutions, Markets and, Growth in the City-States*. Oxford and Princeton NJ: Princeton University Press

Clancier, P., Joannès, F., Rouillard, P. and Tenu, A. (eds) (2005). *Autour de Polanyi. Vocabulaires, théories et modalités des échanges*. Paris: De Boccard.

Droß-Krüpe, K., Föllinger, S. and Ruffing, K. (eds) (2016). *Antike Wirtschaft und ihre kulturelle Prägung - The Cultural Shaping of the Ancient Economy*. Wiesbaden: Philippika – Altertumskundliche Abhandlungen.

Finley, M.I. (1999). *The Ancient Economy* (updated edition with a new foreword by I. Morris). Berkeley CA: University of California Press

Földvári, P., Van Leeuwen, B. and Van Zanden, J.L. (2011). Long-run patterns in market efficiency and the genesis of the market economy: Markets around the Mediterranean from Nebuchadnezzar to Napoleon (580 BC and 1800 AD). *C.E.P.R. Discussion Papers 8521*. [https://econpapers.repec.org/paper/cprceprdp/8521.htm]

Graslin-Thomé, L. (2009). *Les échanges à longue distance en Mésopotamie au Ier millénaire. Une approche économique*. Paris: Orient et Méditerranée 5.

Graslin-Thomé, L. (2016). Long-distance trade in Neo-Babylonian Mesopotamia: The effects of institutional changes. In: Moreno Garcia, J.C. (ed.) *Dynamics of Production in the Ancient Near East, 1300-500 BC*. Oxford: Oxbow Books, 167–186

Harrison, T. (2010). The Greek World, 478–432. In Kinzl, K. (ed.) *A Companion to the Classical Greek World*. Chichester: Blackwells Companions to the Ancient World, 509–525.

Joannès, F. (2008). Place et rôle des femmes dans le personnel des grands organismes néobabyloniens. In: Briant, P., Henkelman, W. and Stolper, M. (eds) *L'archive des fortifications de Persépolis. État des questions et perspectives de recherché*. Paris: Persika 12, 465–480.

Jursa, M. (2005). *Neo-Babylonian Legal and Administrative Documents. Typology, Contents and Archives*. Münster: Guides to the Mesopotamian Textual Records 1.

Jursa, M. (2007). The transition of Babylonia from the Neo-Babylonian Empire to Achaemenid rule. In: Crawford, H. (ed.) *Regime Change in the Ancient Near East and Egypt: From Sargon of Agade to Saddam Hussein*. Oxford: Proceedings of the British Academy 136, 73–94.

Jursa, M. (2009). On aspects of taxation in Achaemenid Babylonia: new evidence from Borsippa. With contributions by C. Waerzeggers. In: Briant, P. and Chauveau, M. (eds) *Organisation des pouvoirs et contacts culturels dans les pays de l'empire achéménide*. Persika Paris: 14, 237–269.

Jursa, M. (2010). *Aspects of the Economic History of Babylonia in the First Millennium BC. Economic Geography, Economic Mentalities, Agriculture, the Use of Money and the Problem of Economic Growth.* With contributions by J. Hackl, B. Janković, K. Kleber, E.E. Payne, C. Waerzeggers and M. Weszeli. Münster: Alter Orient und Altes Testament 377.

Jursa, M. (2014a). Babylonia in the first millennium BCE – economic growth in times of empire. In: Neal and Williamson (eds) 2014, 24–42.

Jursa, M. (2014b). On the existence of factor markets in Babylonia from the long sixth century to the end of Achaemenid rule. *Journal of the Economic and Social History of the Orient* 57(2), 173–202.

Jursa, M. (2018). The first millennium BC. In: Van der Spek, R.J. and Van Leeuwen, B. (eds) *Money, Currency and Crisis. In Search of Trust, 2000 BC to AD 2000.* London and New York: Routledge Explorations in Economic History 80, 116–121.

Kallet, L. (2013). The origins of the Athenian economic *arche*. *Journal of Hellenic Studies* 133, 43–60.

Kleber, K. (2008). *Temple und Palast. Die Beziehungen zwischen dem König und dem Eanna-Tempel im spätbabylonischen Uruk.* Münster: Alter Orient und Altes Testament 358.

Kleber, K. (2012). Famine in Babylonia. A microhistorical approach to an agricultural crisis in 528–526 BC. *Zeitschrift für Assyriologie* 102, 219–44.

Kozuh, M. (2015). A hand anything but hidden: institution and markets in first millennium BCE Mesopotamia. In: Howe, T. (ed.) *Traders in the Ancient Mediterranean.* Chicago: Publications of the Association of Ancient Historians 11, 73–100.

Lanz, H. (1976). *Die neubabylonischen ḫarrânu Geschäfsunternehmen.* Berlin: Münchner Universitätsschriften – Juristische Fakultät – Abhandlungen zur rechtswissenschaftlichen Grundlagenforschung Band 18.

Launaro, A. (2016). Finley and the Ancient Economy. In: Jew, D., Osborne, R. and Scott, M. (eds) *M.I. Finley. An Ancient Historian and his Impact.* Cambridge: Cambridge Classical Studies, 227–249.

Levavi, Y. (2020). The Neo-Babylonian empire: the imperial periphery as seen from the centre. *Journal of Ancient Near Eastern History* 7(1), 59–84.

Lewis, D.M. (2018). *Greek Slave Systems in their Eastern Mediterranean Context, c. 800–146 BC.* Oxford: Oxford University Press.

Lyttkens, C.H. (2013). *Economic Analysis of Institutional Change in ancient Greece: Politics, taxation and rational behavior.* London and New York: Routledge Explorations in Economic History 58.

Magdalene, F.R., Wunsch, C. and Wells, B. (2019). *Fault, Responsibility, and Administrative Law in Late Babylonian Legal Texts.* University Park, PA: Mesopotamian Civilizations 23.

Martin, T.R. (2016). *Pericles. A Biography in Context.* Cambridge: Cambridge University Press.

Miller, J.C. (2012). *The Problem of Slavery as History: A global approach.* New Haven CT: Yale University Press.

Morris, I. (2004). Economic growth in Ancient Greece. *Journal of Institutional and Theoretical Economics* 160, 709–742.

Neal, L. and Williamson, J.G. (eds) (2014). *The Cambridge History of Capitalism Volume I. The Rise of Capitalism: From Ancient Origins to 1848.* Cambridge: Cambridge University Press.

North, D.C. (1990). *Institutions, Institutional Change and Economic Performance.* Cambridge: Cambridge University Press.

North, D.C. (2005). *Understanding the Process of Economic Change.* Oxford and Princeton NJ: Princeton University Press.

Ober, J. (2010). Wealthy Hellas. *Transaction of the American Philological Association* 140(2), 241–260.

Ober, J. (2015). *The Rise and Fall of Ancient Greece.* Oxford and Princeton NJ: Princeton University Press.

Oelsner, J., Wells, B. and Wunsch, C. (2003). The Neo-Babylonian period. In: Westbrook, R. (ed.) *A History of Ancient Near Eastern Law.* Leiden: Handbuch der Orientalistik I(72), 1–2, 911–974.

Pébarthe, C. (2008). Quand Athènes dominait le monde grec: l'empire oublié (477–404). In: Hurlet, F. (ed.) *Les Empires aux époques antique et médiévale. Études comparées.* Rennes: Presses Universitaires de Rennes, 33–55.

Pirngruber, R. (2015). *šulmu iâši libbaka lu ṭābka* – The interaction between the Neo-Assyrian king and the outside world. In: Rollinger, R. and van Dongen, E. (eds) *Mesopotamia in the Ancient World: Impact, continuities, parallels*. Münster: Mellamu Symposia 7, 317–329.

Pirngruber, R. (2016). The value of silver: Wages as guides to the standard of living in first millennium BC Babylonia. In: Pirngruber, R. and Kleber, K. (eds) *Silver, Money and Credit. A Tribute to Robartus J. van der Spek on the Occasion of his 65th Birthday on 18th September 2014*. Leiden: PIHANS AQ: please give in full 128, 107–118.

Pirngruber, R. (2017). *The Economy of Late Achaemenid and Seleucid Babylonia*. Cambridge: Cambridge University Press.

Pirngruber, R. (2018). Towards a framework for interpreting social and economic change in Babylonia during the long 6th century BCE. In: Waerzeggers and Seire (eds) 2018, 19–33.

Pirngruber, R. (2020). Minor archives from first millennium BCE Babylonia: the archive of Iššar-tarībi from Sippar. *Journal of Cuneiform Studies* 72, 165–198.

Pritchard, D. (2012). Costing festivals and war. Spending priories of the Athenian democracy. *Historia - Zeitschrift für Alte Geschichte* 61(1), 18–65.

Scheidel, W (2010). Real wages in early economies: Evidence for living standards from 1800 BCE to 1300 CE. *Journal of the Economic and Social History of the Orient* 53, 425–462.

Scheidel, W., Morris, I. and Saller, R. (eds) (2007). *The Cambridge Economic History of the Greco-Roman World*. Cambridge: Cambridge University Press.

Still, B.J.F. (2019). *The Social World of the Babylonian Priest*. Leiden and Boston MA: Culture and History of the Ancient Near East 103.

Terpstra, T. (2019). *Trade in the Ancient Mediterranean. Private Order and Public Institutions*. Princeton NJ: Princeton University Press.

Tritle, L.A. (2010). *A New History of the Peloponnesian War*. Chichester: Wiley.

Van Bavel, B. (2016). *The Invisible Hand? How Market Economies Have Emerged and Declined since AD 500*. Oxford: Oxford University Press

Van de Mieroop, M. (1999). *Cuneiform Texts and the Writing of History*. London and New York: Routledge.

Van der Spek, R.J. (2017). Review of Alain Bresson, *The Making of the Ancient Greek Economy. Institutions, Markets, and Growth in the City-States*. *Journal of Economic History* 77(2), 601–604.

Verboven, K. (2015). The knights who say NIE. Can neo-institutional economics live up to its expectation in ancient history research? In: Erdkamp, P. and Verboven, K. (eds) *Structure and Performance in the Roman Economy. Models, Methods and Case Studies*. Brussels: Collection Latomus 350, 33–57.

Waerzeggers, C. (2003–2004). The Babylonian revolts against Xerxes and the 'end of archives'. *Archiv für Orientforschung* 50, 150–173.

Waerzeggers, C. (2010). *The Ezida Temple of Borsippa. Prieshood, Cult, Archives*. Leiden: Achaemenid History 15.

Waerzeggers, C. (2015). Review article of Laurie E. Pearce and Cornelia Wunsch, *Documents of Judean Exiles and West Semites in Babylonia in the Collection of David Sofer*. *STRATA* 33, 179–194.

Waerzeggers, C and Seire, M. (eds) (2018). *Xerxes and Babylonia. The Cuneiform Evidence*. Leuven, Paris, Bristol CT: Orientalia Lovaniensia Analecta 277.

Yueh, L. (2013). *China's Growth: The making of an economic superpower*. Oxford: Oxford University Press.

Chapter 6

Peasants, rural economy, and cash crops in medieval Islam

Bethany J. Walker

Introduction: Debunking myths

A common theme in the historical and archaeological literature on the medieval Arab world is the economic isolation of rural communities. According to this image, villages were largely self-sufficient, were not integrated into regional or international markets, and relied on barter exchange for their daily transactions. While many examples of small-scale communities can be found that fit this scenario, even more bear no resemblance to it. Ottomanists are increasingly identifying ways in which rural farmers throughout the Ottomans' domains gained knowledge of markets, making decisions about land use guided by emerging economic opportunities and their own social networks (Sutton 2000; Forbes 2007; Given 2017; Shopov 2020). We are increasingly coming to appreciate how true this was of earlier centuries. The Mamluk era (1250–1516 CE) is particularly rich in documentary sources, through which one can gain a glimpse into the world of rural, medieval exchange. What emerges from these texts is that villages in the Arab world were far from isolated socially, economically, or politically: they were tightly networked through local Sharīʿa (Islamic law) courts and a rich variety of local and regional markets. These markets functioned largely through monetarized exchange.

While the urban centers, such as Cairo, Damascus, and Jerusalem, were serviced by large and well-staffed law courts, many peasants made use of smaller courts closer to home to get legal advice; register marriages, divorces, and inheritance; file complaints against neighbors and government officials, which they did with surprising frequency; and buy, sell, and endow property. This legal network was one factor in the frequent travel of people from one village and town to another. To use the Transjordan, with which the author is most familiar, as an example, all the major towns and many villages had their own *qāḍī* (judge): the castle towns of Kerak, Shobak, and Ajlun; the smaller district capitals of Salṭ, Amman, and Ḥisbān; and smaller villages, such as Marw (located north of Irbid), to name a few. Other villages appear to have been serviced by itinerant judges, who, like the circuit courts of early America, moved from place to place, providing legal services to each settlement in turn. On rural estates (*iqṭāʿt*), the land manager (*mutawalli*) dispensed justice, intervening in disputes between peasants over issues ranging from access to water and land to physical attacks on one another. Land on both sides of the Jordan River regularly exchanged hands, and much of this activity was registered in the Jerusalem courts. The Ottoman archives of the Jerusalem Sharīʿa court include many documents registering the sale and purchase of farmland in the Jerusalem area to people in the Transjordan. While I have found one reference to a local judge selling his own land, most of the buying and selling in this manner in the 16th century appears to have been done by villagers of no particular status (Walker 2011: 181–186).

The courts clearly supported the business of doing business, particularly as related to real estate. The rural communities of southern Syria (Bilād al-Shām) made use of a wide variety of markets (*sūqs*), large and small, through which they exchanged with other villages, Bedouin populations, and larger towns, and came to acquire goods from further afield. These included year-round, weekly village markets (*aswāq shaʿiba*), seasonal markets (*aswāq mawsimiyya*) open during pilgrimage season, and urban markets operating on a daily basis (Walker 2011: 38–40; Al Shqour 2019). Certain villages were renown for specific produce: to cite a few from Jordan, Umm Qeis for its olives and pomegranates, Ḥisbān and other villages on the Madaba Plains for their wheat and walnuts; the communities living in the shadow of Kerak Castle for their wheat and cheese; the villages of the Jordan Valley for their fruits, vegetables, and sugar cane (Walker 2007: 120). With such localized specialization, people came to rely on the village markets to gain access to a wider variety of produce, meat, and animal by-products. With the Ottoman annexation of Syria, a new tax (the *bāj bazār*) was levied on the urban marketplaces. Here cereals were bought and sold by professional grain brokers, who also did business at the threshing floors (Ibn Ṭawq, cited in Wollina 2012: 221; Ibn Ḥijjī, cited in Walker *et al.* 2017b: 181–182). The village markets were taxed by the Ottomans at a lower rate, the revenues assigned to the provincial governor. Among the largest markets in 16th century Transjordan were those of the villages of Ḥubrāṣ and Irbid (in the North) and Salṭ (central plains), the castle towns of Ajlun and Kerak, and the customs house and port at Aqaba (Walker 2011: 60).

Such an extensive network and diversity of rural markets necessitated a form of exchange that went beyond basic barter. The rural economy relied on both barter (which leaves neither a textual nor, arguably, an archaeological trace) and coinage. Gold (*dinārs*) and silver (*dirhams*) coins were used for paying taxes (though some agricultural commodities, such as grains, were paid in kind), paying soldier's wages, and buying land. However, what drove the rural economy was the humble copper coin (s. *fils*/pl. *fulūs*) – the currency of daily exchange in the local marketplace. It is generally recognized as the numismatic marker of economic growth (Heidemann 2009; 2015). Both Mamluk and Ottoman era *dirhams* and *fulūs* have been recovered during archaeological excavations of rural sites in Greater Syria. Dirham hoards have been found at many sites in Jordan – including villages – and have been associated with hoarding during a time of political or economic trouble (Schultz 2018), or the personal goods of a resident merchant (Walker 2018). On the other hand, copper coins – the small-change of the household – dominate the numismatic assemblages at archaeological sites (Schultz forthcoming). Tall Ḥisbān has produced one hoard of over 60 13th century silver coins, but hundreds of individual copper coins of the Mamluk period (Walker *et al.* 2017a, 511 and 518–518; Schultz 2018). The 16th century levels at Khirbet Beit Mazmīl have yielded dozens of piles of *mangīrs*, the heavy copper coins in widest circulation at the time in Jerusalem (Walker and Dolinka 2020, 217–219). These were tucked away in corners of rooms and appear to have been carried around in small cloth bags (coin purses?). So many copper coins at village sites bears witness to active financial exchange in local markets.

Against this backdrop of rural economic structure, the following essay explores the ways in which the residents of small-scale communities gained entrance into agricultural markets and actively participated in cash crop production. It focuses on the late medieval and early modern period, namely the eras of the Mamluk (1250–1516)[1] and Ottoman Sultanates (1516–1918, in the Arab world), in the lands of southern Syria (modern Israel and Jordan). Combining historical and archaeological methods, it then highlights lessons learned about the rural economy from two Mamluk-era villages: Beit Mazmīl in the Jerusalem hinterland and Ḥisbān on the Madaba Plains of central Jordan.

A moment in time

Managing and farming the iqṭāʿt

Erroneously equated with the fief of medieval Europe, the most widespread form of land tenure in the medieval Islamic world – the *iqṭāʿ* – can be traced back to the Seljuk period. It was a grant of the tax revenues (generally of land) to an officer or official, in lieu of a cash salary, and became the financial foundations of the Mamluk military apparatus.[2] Private property in the agricultural sphere existed, but was minimal, and by the Mamluk period was generally limited to fields of limited dimensions, gardens, and orchards, or, as was more generally the case, only the produce from them. As the official 'owner' of most agriculture land, the state maintained, for a time, rigid regulations for land tenure and exchange.

The day-to-day management of the *iqtaʿāt*, however, was of little interest to the sultans in Cairo, so long as revenues were carefully recorded and taxes collected. The *muqṭāʿ*s to whom were assigned the tax revenues of these estates, visited their *iqṭāʿ*s on occasion, and may have resided in them for short periods during the harvest, but most did not live there year-round; military officers were otherwise resident in garrisons or urban houses, or traveling on military campaigns. On the other hand, the narrative sources lead us to believe that other officials acting on behalf of the *muqṭāʿ*, such as the *wakīl* (estate manager), spent the most time on the estates and had the most direct contact with local peasants. Other officials were recruited locally, such as the *khawlī* (overseer), who had good knowledge about local cultivation and practice, and the *shaykh al-balad*, a village notable. The latter was a peasant himself and acted as a mediator between the heads of the village's families, was physically present at the time land was assigned for cultivation (during rotation of fields), reported on the agricultural conditions of the village during cadastral surveys, and gathered barley (as a tax in kind) for the governor as fodder (to feed the horses of the army) (Tsugitaka 2007; Walker *et al.* 2017b, 177). The *shaykh* was paid for these services through revenues from *rizaq* lands (lands allotted by the sultan from the Treasury, as a form of wage) (Michel 1996). Neither the state nor its officials, however, interfered in cultivation or dictated cropping on these lands.[3] These decisions were left to the peasants themselves.

A more detailed picture of the mechanics of ground preparation, planting, and harvesting can be found in the medieval Arabic agrarian treatises (*filāḥa* manuals) that circulated in Iraq and Spain from the 10th century, and then in Egypt, Yemen, and Syria. They gained in popularity with the ruling and urban elites in the late Mamluk and Ottoman periods, when many were copied and sent to imperial libraries (Shopov 2016). They are rich sources of information about soils and water conditions, what crops are best planted under different conditions, and even technical issues such as soil enrichment through manuring and how to prune fruit trees. There is growing scholarly interest today in these manuals, as well as intensive debate about their ultimate function and readership. The earliest Arabic manuals were compendiums of knowledge: encyclopaedic translations of works from Greek and Persian. By the 15th century, however, new manuals appeared in Syria, penned by gentlemen farmers, the majority of whom were clerics (the *ulama*) who came to control the revenues of agricultural land as managers of rural endowments. The authors of some of these manuals note that they have acquired their knowledge about land, crops, soils, and watering conditions through personal experience or watching farmers in the fields (Shopov 2016).[4] Occasionally, Syrian chroniclers of the period also flaunt, with some pride, their personal knowledge of villages, villagers, and farmland (Ibn Ṭawq 2000–2007; Wollina 2012). Market conditions would have been of vital interest to them, as their salaries depended on turning profits from yield. It is not yet clear, however, how they came to know the business side of agriculture. The Damascene historian Ibn Ḥijjī was a keen observer of the fluctuating prices of local foodstuffs (Ibn Ḥijjī 2003; Walker 2011, 61). In his case, his knowledge was acquired through family connections and correspondence.[5]

Daily decision-making in the cultivation and care of crops, however, was securely in the hands of the peasants themselves. The archaeological and botanical records offer the best source of information on cultivation strategies; from them we obtain the physical residue of agricultural practices, from socially and culturally meaningful spatial contexts (Walker *et al.* 2017b). Interpreting this record is, however, fraught with challenges. Much of the debate about peasant decision-making in archaeological circles centers on to what degree practices were risk-buffering and to what degree market-oriented. The resilience of peasants as food-producers must have been the result of a balance of both.

Peasants (*fallāḥīn*) had to weigh their options carefully, to avoid risk and at the same time turn a profit when market conditions allowed. To cite one example, mixed cereal cultivation, as a form of crop diversification, has been historically, as today, adopted as a risk management strategy. The seeds of different cereals are frequently sown together, and in many countries in the Middle East today, a variety of different wheats and barleys are grown simultaneously, in different fields. The ratio between hulled barley and naked wheat has been recently cited as one way to differentiate between subsistence and market-oriented production (Marston 2011). Barley, for example, is a drought-resistant, 'hearty' cereal; its hulled variety makes it best suited for long-time storage, because of its resistance to spoiling. Durum ('hard' or 'naked') wheat is free-threshing; by losing its loose-fitting husk during threshing, it is of lighter weight (and less expensive) for long-distance transport, making it well suited for export to distant markets (Heinrich 2017). A village that cultivated more durum wheat than hulled barley, according to this argument, produced primarily for the market. Likewise, although agricultural intensification could be a response to different pressures, it is usually associated with market-production. Archaeobotanical evidence of intensification in the cereal sector includes irrigation of high-value cereals, identified through the irrigation signals of wheat phytoliths (Laparidou and Rosen 2015). By-products from cereal production (such as straw for stabling and construction material) and animal husbandry (dung for fertilizer) also had a market value, as documented in the *filāḥa* treatises and administrative manuals (Varisco 2012; Ibn Mammātī, as cited in Walker *et al.* 2017a, 178). Archaeologists, botanists, and soil scientists have developed a range of field and lab techniques for identifying these practices at archaeological sites and in ancient agricultural fields (Portillo and Albert 2011; Lauer *et al.* 2014).

Land for sale

As long as most agricultural land remained tied up in *iqṭāʿāt*, cultivation continued relatively unchanged in most sectors of the agrarian economy. The most notable changes in land use in the pre-modern Arab world – the development of market agriculture, the large-scale cultivation of cash crops (cotton, tobacco, olives for soap, wheat for export), and the emergence of urban gardening – were made possible by a collusion of fiscal and legal developments in the 14th through 16th centuries. These included the liquidation and privatization of state lands, the 'waqfization' of the countryside, new forms of land leasing and exchange (*ijār* and *istabdāl*), and access (though limited) to credit through the 'cash *waqf*' (al-Sabagh 2014). Credit, unfortunately, quickly led to peasant debt: rural indebtedness had become a chronic problem by the 16th century, as the confirmation (*tathbīt*) of debt liability was frequently registered then in the Jerusalem courts (Walker 2011: 185–186).

It was inevitable that the medieval *muqṭāᶜ*s would try to convert their temporary right to collect taxes from agricultural land into permanent tenure of the land itself. *Iqṭāᶜ* land and royal lands were gradually transformed into private property (*milk*) from the fourteenth century through two means: 1) low-cost rental (*istijār*) of land from the state by amirs, and 2) purchase of land directly from the Treasury. Over time, increasingly more state land was sold by the imperial Treasury, not only to amirs and clerics, but to anyone who had the ready cash for such purposes. In an effort to protect property purchased from the Treasury from future confiscation, and as a tax shelter, the new owners frequently endowed the property through a system called *waqf*, where title to income producing property was given to God or to a foundation (usually family run), and the revenues earmarked for charitable purposes (or for the financial support of the family) in perpetuity. In this way, large parts of the countryside in Syria and Egypt fell out of government control; it has been calculated that by the time of the Ottoman conquest (1517), some 90% of Egypt's agricultural land, for example, was tied up in endowments and could not be taxed (Abu Ghazi 2000: 66).

The collapse of the *iqṭāᶜ* system that resulted, while undermining the financial foundations of the Mamluk state (Fig 6.1), not only financially benefitted some sectors of the political and legal elites, but also created new opportunities for peasant entrepreneurs. The latter generally purchased small plots of land, with a preference for gardens and orchards (or lands which could be converted to such use).[6] Some were irrigated, though not all. With their newly gained wealth, some peasants and village notables built small mosques for their villages or renovated old ones, creating endowments for their upkeep. Other lands were transformed into family endowments, to provide income for future generations (Walker 2011 for examples).

The privatization of former state lands and their subsequent endowment (from the 14th century), the eventual leasing of these endowed lands (in the late Mamluk and early Ottoman periods), and the growing popularity of endowment-based mortgages and more ready access to credit (from the 16th century on) are important factors behind changes in land tenure over time. Each stage of development resulted in observable changes in, literally, the 'lay of the land', with the construction of terraces, planned soil enrichment, expansion of irrigation systems, and, central to this paper, types of crops cultivated. These methods of intensification of agricultural production were primarily market-driven. While this remains an area of debate, these practices do not appear to have been adopted in response to demographic growth or merely as a risk-buffering strategy by peasants concerned with subsistence.

A tale of two villages

Comparison of two contemporary villages in the highlands of southern Bilād al-Shām reveals ways in which these changes in land tenure and use played out in small-scale communities. In both cases markets were central forces behind decisions on what to cultivate and how. The physical remains of a farmstead associated with the village of

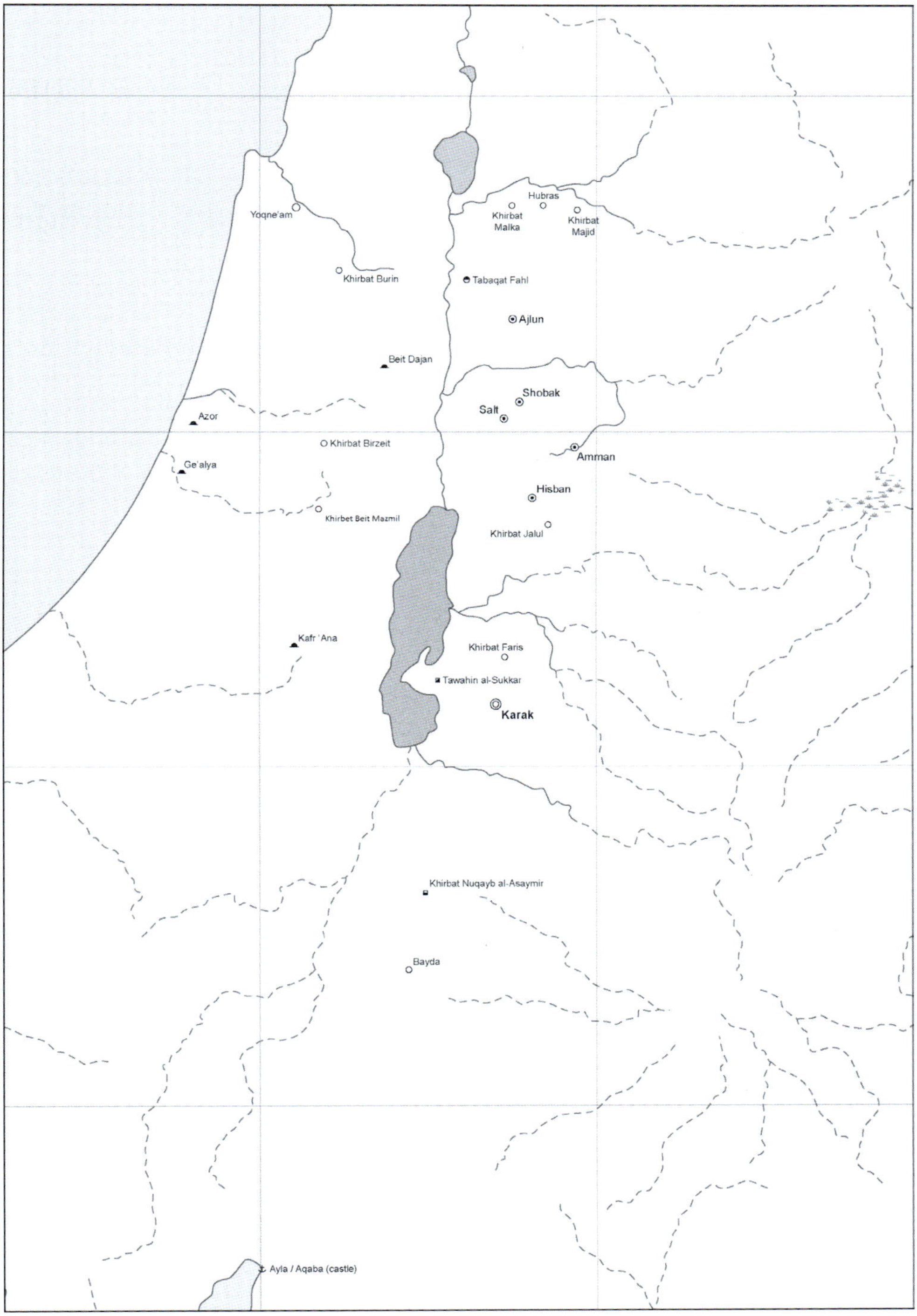

Figure 6.1. Map of Mamluk-era sites in Southern Syria (courtesy Martin Grosch, Berlin).

Beit Mazmīl and the Mamluk-era Citadel and village of Ḥisbān have been the focus of archaeological excavations by the author for many years. The archaeological sites of Khirbet Beit Mazmīl and Tall Ḥisbān are located in the central Palestinian highlands (outskirts of Jerusalem) and the Madaba Plains of Jordan, respectively. The hilltop sites are only about 50 km from each other, as the crow flies. Jerusalem is, moreover, visible from Ḥisbān. When standing on the summit of Ḥisbān's tell, one can see the lights of Jerusalem in the early morning light; when skies are clear, the rising sun is also reflected off the Dome of the Rock.

The villagers of the Jerusalem area and those of Ḥisbān participated in the same network of 'farmers' markets' and legal courts in the Mamluk period. Villagers regularly traveled between Ḥisbān and Jerusalem to buy and sell land, produce, and animals, and to use the services of the local Sharīʿah courts, taking the well-worn road that passed by Jericho. Though frequently traveled, the road was not always safe, however. One document (no. 30) in the Ḥaram archive describes an attack in Jericho on peasants travelling from the Jerusalem village of al-Quṣūr in 795H/1393 CE. They were en route to the Ḥisbān market to sell *zabīb* (raisins), *hub rummān* (pomegranate seeds), and other produce. Their sheikh, traveling with then, was killed (Müller 2017).[7] The real estate business also brought Ḥisbānīs to Jerusalem. Another document (no. 629) in the same archive records the lease in 796H/1394 CE of land located outside Jerusalem – a date, grape, and almond grove and part of land endowed for a *madrasa* – by a sheikh from Ḥisbān, who was the supervisor of several rural endowments in the Jerusalem hinterland (Walker 2011: 170).

The following distils data relevant to market production based on years of archaeological fieldwork, ongoing analysis of botanical remains, and a preliminary reading of medieval Arabic and Ottoman Turkish texts most relevant to the study of land use. The most important written sources for the 14th–16th centuries are a series of endowment documents, tax registers, and court documents, which collectively describe how changes in land tenure in time related to changes in land use. In combination with the archaeological record, they shed light on the ways in which peasant decision-making was, at least in part, market-driven in this period. *Waqfiyyāt* (endowment registers) – though difficult to find in the Egyptian, Syrian, and Turkish archives – are rich in details about the income producing properties (the *mawqūf ʿalayhi*), both urban and rural, which financially supported both charitable and family foundations. Perhaps because they appear later in the document, the lists of the supporting rural properties tend to be overlooked and have not attracted the scholarly attention they deserve. If one has the patience to read them to their end, one finds descriptions (though brief) of village houses, roads, cisterns and wells, and, most importantly, fields, orchards, gardens, and occasionally the crops that were planted there. Ottoman tax registers for the Transjordan have been identified only for the 16th century (al-Bakhit and Hmoud 1989: 1991; for others see Walker 2011)[8]; for Jerusalem only the 16th century series has been published (al-Bakhit and al-Sawariyyah 2005).

They are priceless resources for their descriptions of crops and levels of production, as well as markets. For the Jerusalem area, we are fortunate that a 300 year series of Ottoman era court registers (*sijillāt*) have been preserved in the Turkish archives; part of this series has been published in the form of images of the manuscripts and summaries in Arabic of their contents (Rabāyiᶜah 2010–2018). Others, in microfilm form, can be found at the University of Jordan (al-Bakhit *et al.* 1991). The village of Beit Mazmīl figures prominently in them. These documents include registration of land sales, which record in detail the location and size of cultivated fields, orchards, and gardens, their cropping, land prices, and names of buyers and sellers. Such a high-resolution series of economic and legal documents is rare for the medieval and post-medieval Arab world. In combination with archaeological and botanical analysis, it provides a unique opportunity to study the ways in which agricultural production in small-scale communities changed over time.

Village of Beit Mazmīl

The so-called 'Maghribi waqf' of Jerusalem is one of the longest lived, and most contested, endowments of the Mamluk period. The *waqf* actually consists of several endowments that span hundreds of years. The most extensive of them is the 14th century endowment in honor of the Maghribi Sufi Abu Madyan Shu'ayb, who died in Tlemcen (Algeria) in 594H/1197 CE. The landscape of the region at the time was devoted to a combination of terraced fields of fruit orchards and olive groves and open fields for cereals but had suffered from neglect following the collapse of the Crusader state (and the monasteries that controlled much of this land). The Mamluk era *waqf* was meant to promote revival of these lands, in order to create revenues to support a *zāwiya* (religious school) in Jerusalem and for Maghribi pilgrims visiting the Holy City (Massignon 1951; 1953; Weigert 1990). Beit Mazmīl marked the easternmost border of this endowed area.

According to the Ottoman tax registers, we learn much about the growth of this place in the decades after the Ottoman conquest. During the early years of Ottoman control, Beit Mazmīl was a small community, with three households and three 'bachelors' (single men), according to the register (*defter*) of 932–934/1526–1528 (al-Bakhīt and al-Sawariyyah 2005). Its land was cropped in cereals: wheat and barley (surprisingly, there is no mention of 'summer crops', such as fruits and vegetables, among the taxed products.) By the end of the century it had grown ten-fold in population. Beit Mazmīl appears to have grown into a village over the course of the Ottoman centuries, as is attested by references to the site in Ottoman mandates and edicts (Walker and Dolinka 2020).

The development of the village's farmland from the 16th–18th centuries can be traced in some detail from the Jerusalem Sharīᶜa court *sijillāt*. At this time, land became available through purchase and lease, and much of the land exchanged in this fashion was cultivated in orchards. While the defter series records such exchanges for a 300 year period, we cite only a few examples. In one court document dated to 996/1588, a sheikh from what was then called the village (*qaryah*) of Beit Mazmīl bought 12 shares of land planted with olive trees, grape vines, and fig trees for eight Syrian Sultanis (gold coins) from another resident of the same village.[9] The same register documents other land purchases by the same man that year: they were all shares in orchards. This year, as well, one of the Maghribi sheikhs sold a share in the fruit produced by an orchard to a resident of the village of Beit Mazmīl. The seller was likely involved in the management of the *waqf*, as the commodity sold – a share in the fruit produced by an orchard – was grown on land that belonged to the endowment. The buyer lived in Beit Mazmīl.[10] In a third record dated two years later, the Jerusalem court judge approved the establishment of a tax farm created from the revenues of the village of Beit Mazmīl, which at the time is said to belong to the Khalīl (Hebron) endowment.[11] The property in question was one-third of the yield of both winter (cereals) and summer (fruit and vegetables) crops, which would financially benefit the descendants of three of the villagers. Over the course of a century tax farming became commonplace, providing another method of land exchange. We have numerous examples in the *sijillāt*, as well, of mortgages secured by the endowment and what appear to be cash *waqf*s (a financial innovation of the 16th century).

What followed was a bit of a real estate 'boom', with orchards in the lands surrounding Beit Mazmīl, shares in orchards, and shares in the produce from these orchards (all different commodities) regularly changing hands. The base of people participating in these exchanges expanded beyond the local clerics and village sheikhs – who had the financial means, political connections, and, apparently, enough market knowledge to buy and sell real estate – to include other villagers and their kin. By the 17th century, the village was surrounded by countless vineyards, olive groves, and orchards of figs, apples, and quince.[12] The land still technically belonged to the Maghribi endowment, but had been leased and released so many times, and sold off through extra-judicial means, that much of the agricultural land between Jerusalem and Ein Kerem was privatized, once again, by the 17th century.[13] The land exchanged in this period tended to be small plots of land, or shares in the same; many of the same people bought multiple, scattered plots, often in quick succession.

The archaeological site of Khirbet Beit Mazmīl is a 2.8 dunam (0.28 ha) walled farming complex in Jerusalem's agricultural hinterland that was once part of a much larger terraced landscape devoted to intensive cultivation of fruit trees (Figs 6.2 and 6.3). It is the best-preserved medieval rural site in the immediate outskirts of Jerusalem, and has been occupied, reused, and remodeled more or less continuously since the Late Byzantine period, though its standing remains date mainly to the Mamluk and Ottoman eras. Khirbet (the 'ruins of') Beit Mazmīl ('the House of the Flute') was the name given to the complex in the 19th and early 20th century by local people. We do not know the historical name of this small archaeological site. It was likely a satellite settlement – an off-shoot ('daughter') village or seasonal farmstead – of the Arab village of Beit Mazmīl, located until 1967 1 km to the south of the site. Perched on the summit of the highest hill in the Jerusalem Municipality, and located 7 km

Figure 6.2. Khirbet Beit Mazmīl - entrance to the site (photo by author).

southwest of the New Gate of Jerusalem's Old City, Khirbet Beit Mazmīl commands a view to the Old City, Hebron, and the village of Ein Karem. It sat astride the main Christian pilgrim's route between Jerusalem and Ein Karem in the Crusader and Middle Islamic periods.

The *khirbeh* was first excavated by the Israel Antiquities Authority in 2013 and 2014 as a salvage project proceeding construction of an apartment complex and school. In 2015 I was invited to begin a scientific excavation of what was left of the site - the northern half, with standing remains of a large drystone complex hidden in an almond orchard. Two years later the project expanded to include a study of the larger agricultural landscape around the site, to identify ancient terraces, date them, and determine what was originally grown there. The field project expanded in 2017 to include a hinterland component, centered on the excavation and dating of relic agricultural terraces, to reconstruct the development of cultivated fields historically tied to the village of Beit Mazmīl, The Medieval Jerusalem Hinterland Project continued for two more seasons and is now in final publication stage.[14]

Khirbet Beit Mazmīl is, in fact, a superposition of one farmstead on top of another, the built complexes occupied in three different phases: late Mamluk (13th–early 16th centuries, height in 15th century), early Ottoman (late 16th–17th centuries), and Middle–Late Ottoman and British Mandate (late 18th–early 20th centuries). The site's

Figure 6.3. Plan of Khirbet Beit Mazmīl and occupational phasing (phasing by Dr Nicoló Pini, University of Leiden; based on original plans by Slava Pirsky).

physical and functional development over the course of this period can be related to the increasingly market-orientation of agricultural production in the Jerusalem region. I will summarize briefly the results of these five seasons of excavation most relevant to this paper.

The earliest extant complex was built directly on bedrock after having demolished earlier buildings but re-using the wall stubs of some Crusader and Byzantine era structures and a Roman era water system. At the bottom of the hill are the remains of 'outbuildings', which included stables, industrial areas, and storage facilities (Storchan and Dolinka 2014). The recovery here of weapon fragments, horse gear, and, most importantly, glazed pottery with formal militarized inscriptions (Walker in press), suggests that this was a Mamluk amiral estate of the 13th–15th centuries, possibly the residence of an estate manager. The main residence was on the summit of the hill: it was once a monumental complex, comprising at least two buildings, the northernmost constructed with cross-vaults. The North Building included a small industrial facility, tentatively identified as a *madbasa* (date honey press) and various storage facilities. In the South Building were smaller living quarters with kitchens. Such amiral *quṣūr* (fortified rural estates) were a familiar site in the Jerusalem hinterland in the 14th century, perched atop the hills that surrounded the city (al-ʾUlaymī 1999: 81–83). This estate was abandoned, probably for several decades, after the Ottoman conquest.

In the late 16th century portions of this monumental building were re-occupied, its spaces subdivided into what appear to be separate domestic units of similar dimensions and layout. The walls and floors were heavily, and repeatedly, plastered, flagstone floors were laid, and ṭabuns (ovens) were built into the corners of many rooms. The small subdivisions were built on different levels, with stairs leading from one level to the next. What is not clear is whether these domestic units were housing for an extended family, or whether each unit was rented space (for which we have parallels in this period.) The former Mamluk estate was clearly transformed in the Early Ottoman period into a family home. Bags of small change (the heavy copper *mangīrs* described above) were recovered from the corners of rooms; baby's rattles, numerous smoking pipes (*chibouks*), glass bracelets and kohl kits, and fragments of metal knives and other tools speak to occupation of the house by a large family unit (or several smaller ones). Occupation of the farmstead peaked in the 17th century – the period of the big 'real estate boom' documented in the Ottoman *sijills.*

The farmstead was then abandoned – under what conditions we do not yet know – and part of the superstructure of the medieval vaulted buildings collapsed. The complex was re-occupied at some point in Late Ottoman period (the late 18th or early 19th centuries). The partially dilapidated structures were repaired, and a large, walled farmstead of irregular form and drystone construction was built, incorporating the structurally sound walls and vaults of the Late Mamluk complex. Small agricultural watch towers (*mantarahs/shomerahs*)[15] and a perimeter wall were constructed around the entire complex. Soil (and rubble) were brought in to fill the spaces between the medieval buildings and create a level space for a courtyard and garden. The slopes of the hill were then terraced and cultivated. The new farmstead was of the *eʿzbeh* (a seasonally inhabited family farm) form that was once widespread in the central Palestinian highlands, supporting cultivation of terraced olive groves and vineyards. An earthquake in the 1920s did severe structural damage to this farmstead and its residents left. Years later the ruins were converted to a terraced garden, the site transformed into an almond and pomegranate orchard. Though heavily overgrown at the time, this was the tranquil scene that greeted us when we began fieldwork there in 2015 (Walker and Dolinka 2020).

Fortunately for us, not only the architecture, but also the remains of cultivated plants and food have been preserved at Khirbet Beit Mazmīl and its cultivated fields, providing evidence 'on the ground' of planting practices. In conjunction with the archaeological excavations, joint sampling of soils from stratified and culturally significant deposits (such as *tabuns* and other cooking areas, floors, refuse pits, storage installations, and relic agricultural terraces) were done for macrobotanical, phytolith, pollen, and zooarchaeological analysis. The goal has been to reconstruct what kinds of foods were not only consumed (and then discarded), but also processed on-site (either for local consumption or to prepare for transportation to markets) or used for purposes other than human consumption (to make floors or tabuns or use as fuel). While this analysis is far from complete, some general trends can be identified. The main economic plants in the late Mamluk period were cereals (both wheat and barley, in different varieties) and date palms. This reliance on these three crops continues through the early Ottoman period. The diet was heavy in cereal (namely hard, or durum, wheat and hulled barley) consumption, and supplemented with pulses (lentils, peas, and bitter vetch), spices (such as cumin), and a wide range of summer crops (olives, grapes, carobs, figs). Some processing of the cereals took place indoors. There is extensive evidence for the on-site production of olive oil as numerous fragmented olive stones (suggesting crushing, rather than consumption, of olives) and press cakes have been identified. Meat consumption was based almost entirely on sheep (mutton) and goat. Reeds, olive waste, and dung were used as fuel, while reeds and palm leaves may have also been used as construction material.[16]

The botanical record suggests changes in cultivation strategy during the Ottoman period. Agricultural production became increasingly diversified, with a balance of cereal and orchard-based cultivation. The choice of specific crops, however, seems to have been largely driven by market opportunities. Emmer (soft or 'bread') wheat was not cultivated or consumed. Instead, durum (hard) wheat and hulled barley were. Durum wheat was best suited for long distance transport, and hulled barley for long term storage and local consumption. This kind of cereal cultivation was a regional pattern, which has been carefully reconstructed at Tall Ḥisbān, discussed in the following section. As for the non-cereal component of the diet, the household at Khirbet Beit Mazmīl had access to a surprising variety of fruits and vegetables, including lentils, bitter vetch, the common peas, olives, grapes, and figs.[17] Meat preferences, as well, seem to have changed over time: chicken came to occupy a more important part of the diet than mutton in the 16th–18th centuries, though consumption of sheep and goat did not disappear. The gradual shift to a chicken-based diet may be related to the influence of urban kitchen culture in the 16th century, demonstrating closer social and economic ties to Jerusalem.[18] While a range of factors would have come to play in the decision to cultivate crops and raise animals in this manner, the economic incentives presented by the growing rural real estate market, as described above, must be considered.

Farmsteads, of course, do not operate in a vacuum. They are only one component of a larger agricultural landscape. In an effort to document changes in land use and landscape development contemporary with these phases of occupation at Khirbet Beit Mazmīl, study of the relic agricultural terraces in the site's vicinity began in 2017.[19] The study area was defined by the texts themselves: land that was associated with the Maghribi endowment and the location of fields described in the Ottoman *sijills* as belonging to the village of Beit Mazmīl. Soils from the terrace remains were dated by OSL (optically stimulated luminescence), a laboratory technique which dates the last time the quartz in the soils was exposed to light. Fieldwork by Tel Aviv University prior to our current project suggested that the most active period of terrace construction in the highlands west of Jerusalem was in the Late Mamluk and Early Ottoman periods, and that development of farmland through terracing was a phenomenon of the last 800 years (Gadot *et al.* 2016). Fieldwork in the immediate vicinity of Khirbet Beit Mazmīl since 2017 has documented a further development: fields terraced in this period were subsequently partitioned into smaller plots by field walls in the 17th–19th centuries (Walker *et al.* 2020). This history of terrace-building complements the process suggested by the botanical record and court registers: privatization and endowment of land in the Late Mamluk period, followed by development of farmland and agricultural intensification for market production, and an active sale of ever-smaller plots of orchard land over time.[20]

The ruins of Khirbet Beit Mazmīl present a vivid picture of life in a rural community during the transition from Mamluk to Ottoman rule. The transformation of site from an agricultural estate to a small family farm and then a walled *eʿzbah* is mirrored by investments in the nearby cultivated fields. The farmstead thus developed in tandem with its farmland, both responding to the opportunities offered by privatization of land and the emergence of market agriculture in the Jerusalem hinterland. The high chronological resolution and tightly integrated data sets offered by the stratigraphic sequence at the *khirbeh*, the richly preserved botanical remains, the detailed and long series of court and tax records, and the OSL-dating of soils from the terraces – a rare combination for historians and archaeologists – have made it possible to document these changes over time in detail.

Village of Ḥisbān

Tall Ḥisbān is an 8 hectare multi-period site in the Madaba Plains of central Jordan. This plateau was the granary of empires for centuries and remains today a center of cereal production (Figs 6.4 and 6.5). In the Mamluk period, the village of Ḥisbān was strategically located on the pigeon route (for postal communication) and just off the pilgrimage route from Cairo to Damascus. The site has been subject to scientific excavations by American teams since 1968.[21] A modest, Mamluk period Citadel occupies the summit

Figure 6.4. Tall Ḥisbān and the wheat fields of the Madaba Plains (courtesy Prof. Dave Sherwinn, Andrews University).

of the tell, which is surrounded at its base by a densely settled village, comprised of clusters of one-room farmhouses with shared courtyards and cisterns. Medieval Ḥisbān reached political and social prominence in the 14th century, when it was promoted in administrative status to a district capital and a small garrison posted there during the third reign of the Sultan al-Nāṣir Muḥammad (1310–1340). State investment helped to 'urbanize' the village, which grew rapidly in size, if not complexity, in a short period of time. Its *sūq* (market) served a large area of the Transjordan central highlands, commanding 300 other villages on the Madaba Plains (Khalīl al-Zāhirī in Walker 2011, 71 note 146) and serving as an important regional market entrepôt. Ḥisbān also came to be a center of legal training; in the Ayyubid period a *madrasa* (Islamic law school) was built there, over the course of Mamluk rule, scholars trained there went on to make successful legal careers throughout Syria and Egypt. The village (or 'town' as it was called in the later 14th century) had its own Sharīʿa court and judge (*qāḍī*) and maintained close relations with the legal establishment in Damascus (Walker 2014).

An earthquake decades later was the apparent catalyst for the transfer of the garrison to Amman, eventually along with the marketplace, legal court, and part of the local population. The village shrank in size and was very slowly abandoned for full-time occupation by the 16th century, with only sporadic and seasonal occupation of its ruins until the Tanzimat era, when the modern village was established a half kilometer to the south of the tell. As the excavations at this site have been heavily published during the last five decades, and its medieval agriculture has been recently a focus of intensive research, I summarize here very briefly the most relevant results, citing the published reports.

Ḥisbān's participation in interregional markets was always based on its cereal production, though the specifics of this production changed over time.[22] Recent botanical analysis at the archaeological site has documented the most important developments in this regard in the 14th century: diversification of cereal production (2-rowed hulled barley, hard wheat, bread wheat, and emmer wheat) and intensification of production of wheat, in particular, through irrigation (Laparidou and Rosen 2015; Walker *et al.* 2017b).[23] Such patterns of cultivation, as noted above, can be associated with a cautious balance between market production and risk buffering. These are decisions that were more likely made by the cultivators themselves than by any state imperative or

Figure 6.5. Aerial photo of Tall Ḥisbān (courtesy APAAME: Aerial Photographic Archive for Archaeology in the Middle East. APAAME_20090930_MJN-50 © Michael John Neville).

policy. Even the economic pressure of taxation would not account for the selection of specific cereals we see in the archaeological record at this site.

As for scale of production, though difficult to quantify, it is suggested by the size and number of storage facilities and data culled from tax registers (which unfortunately do not differentiate between different species of cereals, noting only wheat and barley as taxable commodities). Cereal production was the most important taxable commodity at this village in the early 16th century (al-Bakhit and Hmoud 1989). By the century's end, however, no-one lived in the village, although it (*i.e.* pastoralists living nearby) continued to pay a tax on livestock (Hütteroth and Abdulfattah 1977; al-Bakhit and Hmoud 1991). As for storage, it is likely that in the Mamluk period, most grains were kept, for longer periods of time, in repurposed (and replastered) cisterns and caves, which are plentiful at Ḥisbān and in the region. In the Ottoman era, built structures were the norm: tower-like *shuna*s, *qaṣr*s (walled, family-run agricultural estates); the arch-and-grain bin houses (McQuitty and Lenzen 1989); and, inside individual houses, the bin-shaped *qiwāra*. Large quantities of grain were stored in the *quṣūr* of the Wadi Ḥisbān in the 18th and 19th centuries (Prag 1991). With the 'grain boom' of the mid-19th century, many villages in the Transjordan began to cultivate cereals for transport to Palestinian ports and export to the West (Walker *et al.* 2011). In the Tanzimat era, the cereal fields of the Madaba Plains were revived, frequently by Palestinian absentee landowners who purchased and registered land; the 'Nabulsi *qaṣr*' located a kilometer south of Tall Ḥisbān is a stark architectural reminder of those days (Carroll *et al.* 2006; Carroll 2008). At each of these stages either local farmers or foreign entrepreneurs seized market opportunities and intensified cereal production in the village.

Conclusions

The emerging pictures of the Mazmīl farmstead in its larger cultivated landscape and the evidence of agricultural production at the village of Ḥisbān further suggest a process by which at least this region of southern Syria developed agriculturally over the course of the later historical periods. Land tenure and land use cannot be separated from one another; they are part of the same socioeconomic system that characterized rural life from the 14th century. The 16th century stands as the turning point in the relationship between local communities and the large-scale commercialization of agriculture. The foundations for these changes, however, were laid in the late Mamluk period, with the growing opportunities provided to villagers to buy and sell farmland.

Notes

1. The Mamluk Sultanate was a Muslim state led by former military slaves, which controlled much of the eastern Mediterranean from the collapse of the Crusader states until the Ottoman conquest. The political capital was Cairo.

2. The difference between a fief and an *iqṭāᶜ* is beyond the scope of this essay. Its most salient features are that, by the Mamluk period, they often tended to be shares of a property (parts of fields, parts of a village) and they could not be bequeathed to the military officer's progeny.
3. The one notable exception in the Mamuk period were sugar plantations, where everything from crop selection, crop rotation, water use, and labor organization was dictated by the state. Lands devoted to the cultivation of sugar cane generally remained the private lands of the sultans or amiral *iqṭāᶜs*.
4. Among the most relevant manuscripts in this regard (all unpublished) are al-Tamān Tamrī's (d. 1395) *Kitāb al-falāḥa al-muntakhaba*, and al-Ghazzī al-ᶜĀmirī's (d. 1528) *Jāmi' farā'id al-milāḥa fī jawāmi' fawā'id al-falāḥa* (www.filaha.org). These two manuscripts are currently under study and being edited and published by the Research Group 'Agriculture and the Making of Sciences' at the Max Planck Institute in Berlin, of which I am a participant.
5. We do not know, moreover, to what degree the peasants themselves had knowledge of market conditions; ethnographic accounts of the 19th and early 20th centuries merely provide a glimpse of information sharing in rural communities (Walker 2007).
6. This kind of investment followed a practice long established in the Islamic world, where lands developed by the cultivator fell under his tenure and could be bequeathed, leased, sold, and endowed. Gardens and orchards, in particular, required considerable efforts in soil enrichment, terracing, irrigation, and pruning.
7. I am grateful to Prof. Yossi Rapoport of Queen Mary College, University of London for bringing this reference to my attention.
8. As a result of Tanzimat-era legislation, land was again registered by the state for tax purposes in the late 19th century. The earliest registers for Transjordan are from the Irbid region and date to 1876 (Lucke *et al.* 2012, 108).
9. 67 Sicil Mahkemetul Kudus Resimleri, p. 247, doc. #2 (Islam Arastirmalari Merkezi Kutuphanesi, Istanbul). I want to thank Dr Munther al-Sabagh (University of California-Santa Barbara) for guiding me to this archive. Catalogues of many of the sijjilāt, but not all of them, have been published in Arabic in Rabāyi'ah, *Sijillāt Maḥkamat al-Quds al-Sharᶜīyah*. A complete set can also be found in the Microfilm Archive of the University of Jordan in Amman. AQ: not in bilbiography
10. 67 Sicil Mahkemetul Kudus Resimleri, p. 331, doc. #2 (Islam Arastirmalari Merkezi Kutuphanesi, Istanbul).
11. 67 Sicil Mahkemetul Kudus Resimleri, p. 44, doc. #4, 998H/1590 CE (Islam Arastirmalari Merkezi Kutuphanesi, Istanbul).
12. Sijillāt Mahkamat al-Quds al-Sharᶜīyah, doc. # 55, 1065 H/1654 CE (National Library, Givat Ram, Jerusalem). Prof. Yehoshua Frenkel (Emeritus, University of Haifa), was kind enough to direct me to this resource, accessible only in person in Jerusalem.
13. The legal status of the old Mamluk-era *waqf* was disputed over the course of the Ottoman era and during the period of the British Mandate, as documented clearly by a series of decrees and legal complaints.
14. The excavations in 2015, 2017, and 2018 were co-directed by the author and Dr Benajmin Dolinka (formerly of the Israel Antiquities Authority), and in 2019 by the author and Omer Zeᶜevi (then at Tel Aviv University). We gratefully acknowledge the generous financial sponsorship of the Barakat Trust (2015 field season), Palestine Exploration Fund (2015), Deutscher Verein zur Erforschung Palästinas (2015), and the German-Israeli Foundation for Scientific Research and Development (2017–2019).
15. These were not defensive. The hills of the Palestinian highlands were once covered with terraced vineyards and olive groves, interspersed with small watch towers that were used to guard the fields during harvest time against theft.

16. Presentations by Dr Sofia Laparidou and Ms Annette Hansen, 'The Medieval Jerusalem Hinterland Project Final Workshop', Bonn, 17 August 2019.
17. Hansen, project files. Macrobotanical remains of carob and roses may be contamination from more modern levels.
18. Cooking manuals from contemporary Damascus include more recipes for chicken-based dishes (Wollina 2012: 156–170). On the role of chicken in the Cairene diet of the Mamluk period, see Lewicka (2011) and Levanoni (2005).
19. The terrace component of the project was led by Yuval Gadot of Tel Aviv University and builds on his 'The Formation of Terraced Landscapes in the Judean Highlands' project, funded by the Israel Science Foundation.
20. The botanical remains from the terrace soils are still being processed and studied.
21. Tall Ḥisbān has been subject to excavations since 1968 by Andrews University of Michigan, USA. Excavations today are directed by the author, as part of the larger Hisban Cultural Heritage Project, under the senior direction of Øystein S. Labianca of Andrews University. A full bibliography of project publications since 1968 can be found at www.madaplains.org/hisban and https://www.mamluk.uni-bonn.de/islamic-archaeology/field-projects/tall-hisban.
22. The farmers of medieval Ḥisbān did not only cultivate cereals. Their gardens and walnut groves were also regionally renown, but were marketed closer to home (Walker 2011: 61).
23. The soils sampled for this analysis were taken from cereal processing spaces, the Citadel storeroom.

Bibliography

Primary sources

al-Bakhit, M.ᶜA. and N.R. Hmoud (eds) (1989). *The Detailed Defter of Liwāʾ ᶜAjlūn: Tapu Defteri No. 970.* Amman: University of Jordan (in Turkish with Arabic commentary.)

al-Bakhit, M.ᶜA. and N.R. Hmoud (eds) (1991). *The Detailed Defter of Liwāʾ ᶜAjlūn: Tapu Defteri No. 185, Ankara 1005 AH/1596 AD.* Amman: University of Jordan (in Turkish with Arabic commentary.)

al-Bakhit, M.ᶜA., N.R. Hmoud, and A.ᶜA. Khuraysāt (eds) (1991). *Al-Quds al-Sharīf: Wathāʾiquhā wa-Sijillātuhā waMakhṭūṭātuhā al-Muṣawwarah fī Markaz al-Wathāʾiq wa-al-Makhṭūṭāt fī al-Jāmiᶜah al-Urduniyyah (936 H/1529 M–1404 H/1984 M).* Amman: Centre for Archives and Manuscripts, University of Jordan.

al-Bakhiṭ, M.ᶜA. and N.R. al-Sawariyyah (eds) (2005). *The Detailed Defter of the Liwaʾ of Noble Jerusalem. Vols. 1-6: Tapu Defterleri No. 427 (932–934 A.H./1525–26–1527–28), 131 (932–938/1525–1531–2), 1015 (945/1538–9), 289 (961/1553–4), 516 (976/1562), and 515 (1005/1596–7).* Amman/London: al-Furqān.

Ibn Ḥijjī, Shihāb al-Dīn Abī al-ᶜAbbās Aḥmad al-Saᶜīdī al-Ḥisbānī al- Dimashqī (2003). *Tārīkh Ibn Ḥijjī: Ḥawādith wa-Wafayāt 796–815 H.*, ed. A. al-Kundarī. Beirut: Dār Ibn Ḥazm.

Ibn Ṭawq, Shihāb al-Dīn Aḥmad (2000–2007). *Yawmiyyāt Shihāb al-Dīn Aḥmad b. Ṭawq, 834–915 H/1430–1509 M, vols. 1–4.* ed. J. Al-Muhajir (Damascus: Institut Français d'Études Arabes de Damas).

Massignon, L. (1951). Documents sur certains waqfs des lieux saints de l'Islam: principalement sur le waqf Tamimi à Hébron et sur le waqf tlemcénien Abû Madyan à Jérusalem. *Revue Études Islamiques* 1951: 73–120.

Massignon, L. (1953). Documents sur certains waqfs des lieux saints de l'Islam: principalement sur le waqf Tamimi à Hébron et sur le waqf tlemcénien Abû Madyan à Jérusalem. (Additions et corrections à Rev. Et. Isl., 1951, pp. 73–120). *Revue Études Islamiques*1953: 39–42.

Sijillāt Maḥkamat al-Quds al-Shar'īyah
Rabāyi'ah, I. (ed.) (2010–2018) 12 vols. Istanbul: IRCICA.

al-ᶜUlaymī, Mujīr al-Dīn (1999). *al-Uns al-Jalīl bi-Tārīkh al-Quds wa-Khalīl*, ed. M.ᶜA. al-Kaᶜābinat. Amman: Maktabat Dandīs.

Secondary sources

Abu Ghazi, ʿI. (2000). *Taṭawwur al-Ḥiyāzah al-Zirāʿiyyah fī Miṣr Zaman al-Mamālīk al-Jarākisah: Dirāsah fī Bayʿ Amlāk Bayt al-Māl.* Cairo: ʿAyn lil-Dirāsāt wa-al-Buḥūth al-Insāniyyah wa-al-Ijtmāʿiyyah.

Al Shqour, R.S. (2019). *The Aqabah Khans and the Origin of Khans in Jordan: An archaeological approach*, Piscataway NJ: Giorgas Press.

Carroll, L. (2008). Sowing the seeds of modernity on the Ottoman frontier: Agricultural investment and the formation of large farms in nineteenth-century Transjordan. *Archaeologies* 4, 233–249.

Carroll L., Fenner, A. and LaBianca, Ø.S. (2006). The Ottoman Qasr at Hisban: Architecture, reform, and new social relations. *Near Eastern Archaeology* 69(/3–4), 138–145.

Forbes, H. (2007). Early Modern Greece: Liquid landscapes and fluid populations. In: David, S. and Davies, J. (eds) *Between Venice and Istanbul: Colonial landscape in Early Modern Greece*. Princeton NJ: Princeton University Press, 111–135.

Gadot, Y., Davidovich, U., Avni, G., Avni, Y., Piasetzky, M., Faershtein, G., Golan, D. and Porat, N. (2016). The Ffrmation of a Mediterranean terraced landscape: Mount Eitan, Judean highlands, Israel. *Journal of Archaeological Science Report* 6, 397–417.

Given, M. (2017). Global peasant, local elite: Mobility and interaction in Ottoman Cyprus. *Journal of Islamic Archaeology* 4(1), 1–21.

Heidemann, S. (2009). Economic growth and currency in Ayyubid Palestone. In: Hillenbrand, R. and Auld, S. *Ayyubid Jerusalem: The Holy City in Context 1187-1250*. London: Altajir Trust, 276–300.

Heidemann, S. (2015). How to measure economic growth in the Middle East? A framework of inquiry for the Middle Islamic period. In: Talmon-Heller, D. and Cytryn-Silverman, K. (eds) *Material Evidence and Narrative Sources: Interdisciplinary studies of the history of the Middle East*. Leiden: Brill, 30–57.

Heinrich, F.B.J. (2017). Modelling crop-selection in Roman Italy: The Economics of agricultural decision making in a globalizing economy. In de Haas, T. and Tol, G.W. (eds) *Rural Communities in a Globalizing Economy: New perspectives on the economic integration of Roman Italy*. Leiden: Brill, 141–169.

Hütteroth, W.-D. and Abdulfattah, K. (1977). *Historical Geography of Palestine, Transjordan and Southern Syria in the Late 16th Century.* Erlangen: Fränkischen Geographischen Gesellschaft.

Laparidou, S. and Rosen, A. (2015). Intensification of production in medieval Islamic Jordan and its ecological impact: Towns of the Anthropocene. *The Holocene* 25(10), 1685–1697.

Levanoni, A. (2005). Food and cooking during the Mamluk Era: Social and political implications. *Mamluk Studies Review* 9(2), 201–222.

Lewicka, P.S. (2011). *Food and Foodways of the Medieval Cairenes: Aspects of life in an Islamic metropolis of the eastern Mediterranean*, Leiden: Brill.

Lucke, B., Shunnaq, M., Walker, B.J., Shiyab, A., al-Muheisen, Z., al-Sababha, H., Bäumler, R. and Schmidt, M. (2012). Questioning Transjordan's historic desertification: A critical review of the paradigm of 'empty lands'. *Levant* 44(1), 100–126.

Lauer, F., Prost, K., Gerlach, R., Pätzold, S., Wolf, M., Urmersbach, S., Lehndorff. E., Eckmeier, E. and Amelung, W. (2014). Organic fertilization and sufficient nutrient status in prehistoric agriculture? – Indications from multi-proxy analyses of archaeological topsoil relicts, *PLOS One* 9/9: e106244 [https://doi.org/10.1371/journal.pone.106244]

Marston, J.M. (2011). Archaeological markers of agricultural risk management. *Journal of Anthropological Archaeology* 30(2), 190–205.

McQuitty, A. and Lenzen C.J. (1989). An architectural study of the Irbid Region with particular reference to a building in Irbid. *Levant* 21, 119–128.

Michel, N. (1996). Les *rizaq iḥbāsiyyah,* terres agricoles en mainmorte dans l'Egypte mamelouke et ottomane: Etude sur les *Dafātir al-Aḥbās* ottomans. *Annales islamologiques* 30, 105–98.

Müller, C. (2017). Crimes without criminals? Legal documents on 14th-century injury and homocide from the Ḥaram al-Šarīf-collection in Jerusalem. In: van Berkel, M., Buskens, L. and Sijpesteijn,

P. (eds) *Legal Documents as Sources for the History of Muslim Societies: Studies in honour of Rudolph Peters*. Leiden: Brill, 129–179.

Portillo, M. and Albert, R.M. (2011). Husbandry practices and livestock dung at the Numidian site of Althiburos (el Médéina, Kef Governorate, northern Tunisia): the phytolith and spherulite evidence. *Journal of Archaeological Science* 38(12), 3224–3233.

Prag, K. (1991). A walk in the Wadi Hesban. *Palestine Exploration Quarterly* 123, 48–61.

al-Sabagh, Munther H. (2014). Before Banks: Credit, society, and law in sixteenth-century Palestine and Syria. Unpublished Ph.D thesis, University of California-Santa Barbara.

Schultz, W.C. (2018). Re-excavating the excavated: Analyzing Mamluk dirham hoards from Jordan via their published reports, and why that is worth doing. In: Callagher, B. and D'Ottone Rambach, A. (eds) *Proceedings of the 5th Simone Assemani Symposium on Islamic Coins, Rome, 29–30 September 2017*. Trieste: EVT Edizioni Università di Trieste, 213–226.

Schultz, W.C. (forthcoming). Coins where there were no mints: MamlukcCoins from Jordanian archaeological sites. In: Bauden, F. (ed.) *Proceedings of the Second Conference of the School of Mamluk Studies, 2015*. Leiden: Brill.

Shopov, A. (2016). Between the Pen and the Fields: Books on farming, changing land regimes, and urban agriculture in the Ottoman Eastern Mediterranean ca. 1500–1700. Unpublished Ph.D thesis, Harvard University.

Shopov, A. (2020). The vernacularization of sixteenth-century Ottoman agricultural science in its economic context. In: Walker, B.J. and al-Ghouz, A. (eds) *Living with Nature and Things: Contributions to a new social history of the Middle Islamic periods*. Bonn: V&R Press, 639–681.

Storchan, B. and Dolinka, B. (2014). Jerusalem, Bayit Va-Gan, *Hadashot Arkheologiyot* 126. [https://hadashot-esi.org.il/report_detail_eng.aspx?id=11622&mag_id=121].

Sutton, S.B. (2000). Liquid landscapes: Demographic transitions in the Ermionidha. In: Sutton, S. (ed.) *Contingent Countryside: Settlement, economy, and land use in the southern Argolid since 1700*. Stanford CA: Stanford University Press, 84–106.

Tsugitaka S. (1997). *State and Rural Society in Medieval Islam: Sultans, Muqtaʿs and Fallahun*, Leiden: Brill.

Varisco, D. (2012). *Zibla* and *zirāʿa*: Coming to terms with manure in Arab agriculture. In: Jones, R. (ed.) *Manure Matters: Historical, archaeological, and ethnographic perspectives*. Farnham: Ashgate, 131–145.

Walker, B.J. (2007). Regional markets and their impact on agriculture in Mamluk and Ottoman Transjordan. In: van der Steen, E. and Saidel, B. (eds), *On the Fringe of Society: Archaeological and ethnoarchaeological perspectives on pastoral and agricultural societies*. Oxford: British Archaeological Report S1657, 117–125.

Walker, B.J. (2011). *Jordan in the Late Middle Ages: Transformation of the Mamluk frontier*. Chicago IL: Middle East Documentation Center, University of Chicago.

Walker, B.J. (2014). Mobility and migration in Mamluk Syria: The dynamism of villagers 'on the move'. In: Conermann, S. (ed.) *Proceedings of the Conference 'Everything is on the Move: The "Mamluk Empire" as a node in (trans-) regional networks'*. Bonn: V&R Press, 324–348.

Walker, B.J. (2018). Settlement abandonment and site formation processes: Case studies from Late Islamic Syria. In: Ritter, M. and Guidetti, M. (eds) *Proceedings of the Tenth International Conference on the Archaeology of the Ancient Near East, 2016*. Wiesbaden: Harrossowitz, 681–694.

Walker, B.J. (in press). Made on order for the Amir: What *was* the function of Mamluk 'Barracks Wares?'. In: Vroom, J. (ed.) *Material Entanglements in the Islamic World: New approaches to Islamic archaeology & ceramics*. Tournhout: Brepols.

Walker, B.J. and Dolinka, B. (2020). *Ḫirbet Bēt Mazmīl*, Investigations of Medieval Jerusalem's Hinterland: Interim Report on the 2015 and 2017 Field Seasons. *Zeitschrift der Deutschen Palaestina-Verein* 136(2), 191–234.

Walker, B.J., Bates, R., Hudon, J. and LaBianca, Ø.S. (2017a). Tall Hisban 2013 and 2014 excavation seasons: Exploration of the Medieval village and long-term water systems. *Annual of the Department of Antiquities of Jordan* 58, 483–523.

Walker, B.J., Laparidou, S., Hansen, A. and Corbino, C. (2017b). Did the Mamluks have an environmental sense? Natural resource management in Syrian villages. *Mamluk Studies Review* 20, 167–245.

Walker, B.J., Gadot, Y., Elgart-Sharon, Y. and Zeᶜevi, O. (2020). Agricultural terracing and rural revival in late medieval Palestine. In: Korn, L. and Heidenreich, A. (eds) *Proceedings of the 11th International Congress on the Archaeology of the Ancient Near East*, vol. 2. Wiesbaden: Harrossowitz, 651–661.

Walker, B.J., Shunnaq, M., Byers, D., al-Bataineh, M., Laparidou, S., Lucke, B. and Shiyab, A. (2011). Northern Jordan Project 2010: the al-Turra Survey. *Annual of the Department of Antiquities of Jordan* 55, 509–536.

Weigert, G. (1990). A Maghribi religious endowment in fourteenth-century Jerusalem: On Abū Madyan al-Maghribī's endowment in Jerusalem. *Cathedra* 58, 25–34 [in Hebrew].

Wollina, T. (2012). *Zwanzig Jahre Alltag: Lens-, Welt- und Selbstbild im Journal des Aḥmad Ibn Ṭawq*, Bonn: V&R Press.

Chapter 7

Markets in the shadows, trade diasporas, and self-organizing trading/smuggling networks

J.B. Owens

For David R. Ringrose (1938–2020), outstanding economic historian, mentor, and friend.

Murder in Almansa

I doubt that during the first few years after Philip II of Habsburg established his Household and Court in Madrid, any royal official had fled there from the Kingdom of Murcia to tell a tale more lurid than the one narrated by Juan Catalán. Catalán, originally from Navarre, had served 14 years as a mounted royal border guard along Castile's frontiers from France to Murcia. While Castile and the Kingdom of Valencia shared a monarch, they were separate countries and customs posts, known as dry ports, dotted the border Catalán patrolled at the time (Lapeyre 1981). When, in the late summer or early fall of 1564, he and his partner, Francisco Martínez, encountered a group of smugglers within the jurisdiction of the Castilian town of Almansa on the road to the Kingdom of Valencia, Martínez was murdered, leaving his wife, Juana de Talavera and minor children, and Catalán was wounded so badly that he almost died. Because the criminals threatened Catalán and his family if he made further reports to the Crown, he escaped west to Madrid. Numerous times before this violent event, Catalán had informed the royal Treasury's accountants (*contaduría mayor*) about the extensive smuggling by armed groups of items whose export to Valencia was prohibited but where they brought higher prices. He felt that, after those in Madrid did nothing in response, someone leaked information about his denunciations to criminals along the border with the Kingdom of Valencia, which jeopardized the guards' safety. We cannot evaluate this claim because we possess few details about the attack. The criminal trial transcripts no longer exist. From subsequent official correspondence we do know that Antón Hernández the Younger stabbed Catalán while Martín Rey and several others murdered Martínez, but these men likely worked for much more important economic and political leaders of Castilian border communities (Sello, f. 609, Madrid, 15 February 1565; f. 591, Madrid, 22 February 1565; f. 578, Madrid, 29 January 1566). In studies of criminal gangs one often reads that members of the group should avoid any friction with judicial officials which would trigger unwanted scrutiny. An armed confrontation resulting in a murder would certainly have constituted an extreme example of 'friction' (for example, Venkatesh 2008: 118). The consequences would have exceeded anything the gang leaders might have expected.

Catalán managed to present a petition directly to King Philip II, in which he explained what had happened (Estado, leg. 145, f. 53). The border guard described for the King various smuggling operations which extended from the Marquisate of Moya in the north to the southern end of the Marquisate of Villena in the kingdom of Murcia. In addition to providing information about his own situation, Catalán offered detailed descriptions about how smugglers worked and who at Court held the documents produced by earlier investigations. Thus, when a commissioned investigating judge began his work, he already possessed a useful list of people to arrest and question. In his account Catalán made clear the degree to which local officials and royal justices had been unreliable servants of the Crown. The leaders of the various smuggling networks on the Castile–Valencia border were generally wealthy livestock owners who sometimes held office as councilmen (*regidores*) of their frontier municipalities. In order to initiate a vigorous investigation, Catalán recommended that Philip commission a relatively new *corregidor* (royal high commissioner) of the towns of Requena and Utiel, also on the border and just north of the Marquisate of Villena and the Kingdom of Murcia, because it appeared that he could not be corrupted. Appropriately, his name was Dr Valencia.

Dr Valencia's investigation

Philip perhaps felt that the smuggling story possessed more complications than the diligent Catalán realized. At the time, the king worried about how easily heretical books entered the peninsula through ports along the coast of his domains of the Crown of Aragon (Kamen 1997: 105). In addition to the standard commission to Dr Valencia as the investigating judge, the king sent him a personal letter, indicating that Francisco de Eraso, functioning as Philip's private secretary, would inform him in more detail about what he was to do. Philip emphasized two points. First, he ordered Dr Valencia to advise him about the course of his investigation, sending his dispatches through Eraso. Second, everything had to be done secretly. In other words, Philip bypassed both the Council of the Treasury, which had jurisdiction over the customs houses in the dry ports, and the Council of Castile, which had direct jurisdiction over the large royal lordship of the Marquisate of Villena and over Dr Valencia as its corregidor for Requena and Utiel. Because these councils were excluded from receiving documents from Dr Valencia, many of his reports to Philip and Eraso survived even though most of the trial transcripts have been lost. Eraso had to store the reports, and he simply stuffed them into his own files. Because he was also secretary of the Council of State (*Estado*), Dr Valencia's reports and the responses ended up in that section of the Archivo

General de Simancas. Owens (2005b) describes the smuggling and Dr Valencia's investigation of it.

One must not underestimate the difficult task Dr Valencia accepted. Initially, the smuggling and other criminal activity appeared to center in municipalities in the eastern part of the Marquisate of Villena, a huge seigneury (over 15,000 km^2), which the Crown had absorbed in the late 15th century (Torres Fontes 1953). The marquisate was territorially split between the southeastern Kingdom of Murcia (over 22,000 km^2) and the Bishopric of Cuenca to the north (Fig. 7.1). Because the area was quite rural, Dr Valencia traveled a lot in pursuit of leads. He did not have to torture anyone. Merchants usually traveled with account books, contracts, and perhaps correspondence books. In terms of the local smugglers along the border, they stored their archives at home. Furthermore, when Dr Valencia convicted someone, he could seize the property smuggled, level fines, and send the miscreant into exile. The relevant laws divided the value obtained in the judgement three ways: a third to the Crown, a third to the sentencing judge, and a third to the person who denounced the crime (NR, Book VI, Title 18: 'Of things prohibited to take from the Kingdom, and brought into it ...').

To give some idea of the relative population size of some of the border municipalities, I offer these minimums (derived from Chacón Jiménez 2000): the two seigneurial towns were the smallest (Carcelén, perhaps a population of 100; Montealegre, 225); the smallest of the towns of the Marquisate of Villena sat at the north and south ends of the border (Ves, about 450 people; Sax, 500); Albacete with 4250 residents was the largest of the core municipalities; the cities of Chinchilla and Villena housed 2600 and 2500 respectively; Yecla, the dry port for wool exports, had 1800; and Almansa, where this story began, added about 2100 to the area. All were small; however, the cities of the south of the Kingdom of Murcia could not be considered huge. Murcia's population was about 11,500 residents, of which 1000 lived in the villages of its large jurisdiction. The port of Cartagena, through which much wool was exported to Genoa and Milan, only had a population about 2000, which in conjunction with the small rural population along the Kingdom of Murcia's coast, made it difficult to protect the area from Muslim raiders, who came mostly to capture people for the North African slave market. Because Cartagena had characteristics like those of Mahon in the Balearic Islands, its vulnerability was exposed in 1535 when a Muslim fleet penetrated the harbor of Mahon and sacked the city over a period of days (Pardo Molero 2010; Jiménez Zamora 2016).

Although Dr Valencia concentrated most of his arrests in the core municipalities of Almansa, Chinchilla, and Villena, he suddenly arrived in the city of Cuenca, a major cloth manufacturing center and a crucial market for raw wool because of its proximity to the major eastern livestock trails (past Logroño, Soria, Molina, and Tragacete) for transhumance of Merino sheep and to the province's own large flocks (Lemeunier 1977). There, the judge tried to arrest Juan Pedro de Anón, a resident merchant (a *vecino* or local citizen) from Milan, who was one of the major wool exporters in the 1560s (on Cuenca's Milanese merchants, see Owens 2011b). Anón fled through a secret

Figure 7.1. The smuggling frontier in the 16th century.

rear door in his house, which he shared with several other Milanese merchants, to the offices of the local Inquisition tribunal, and he created a jurisdictional conflict between the Church court and the royal judge when he claimed to be a lay associate (*familiar*) of the 'Holy Office', for Tragacete rather than for the city of Cuenca. Anón had done much the same thing two years earlier when another judge had tried to arrest him for smuggling precious metals from Castile. As a rule, the Inquisition defended its privilege, felt necessary for its image of superior authority, to try all offenses involving its officials. However, in June 1566, the Supreme Council of the Inquisition in Madrid ordered Cuenca's inquisitors to surrender jurisdiction to the investigating royal judge and to send him any relevant documents in their possession.

In addition to investigations in Cuenca, Dr Valencia wished to pursue his work in Toledo, based on the men from the city he had convicted on the border. In this chapter, I will concentrate on the evidence about Toledo. The city had a population of about 60,000, making it far larger than either Cuenca or Murcia (Montemayor 1996). However, he increasingly faced resistance from Madrid. In part, that was because representatives from some border municipalities sought relief from the Council of Castile, which ordered Dr Valencia back to Requena and to turn in the trial transcripts and documents he had collected. This effort increased when Borsio Cabitelo, Juan Pedro de Anón's business partner, both from Philip's Duchy of Milan (Cremona and Milan respectively), and Payo Sotelo, a notable merchant in Toledo, whom Dr

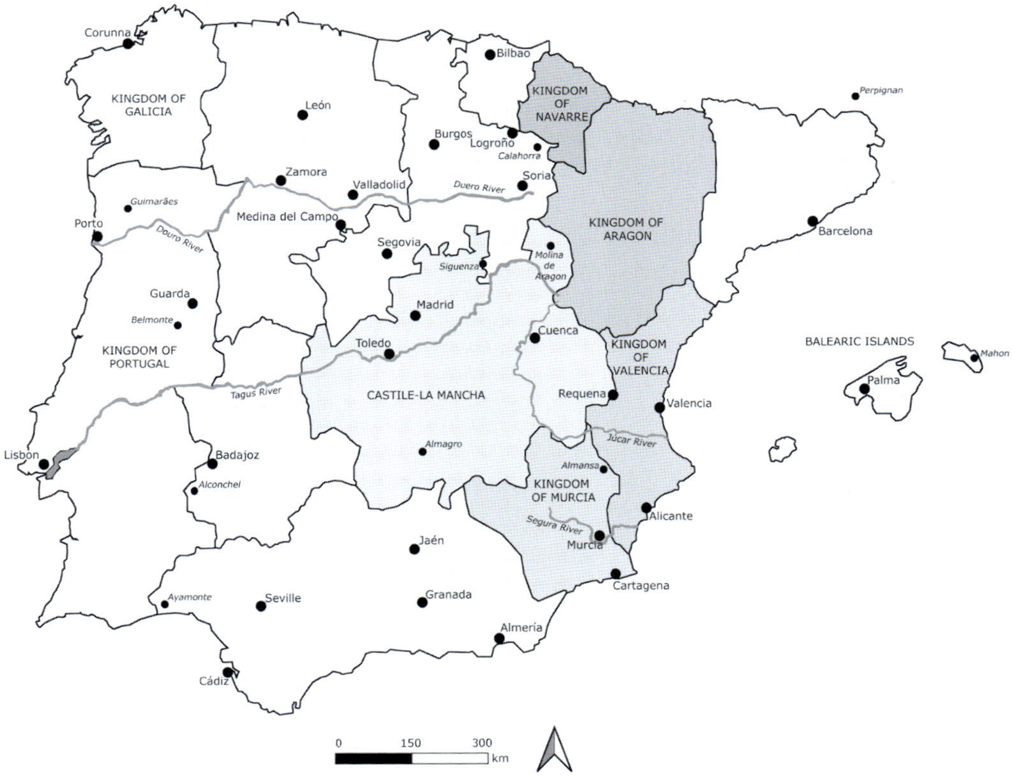

Figure 7.2. The Iberian Peninsula in the early modern period.

Valencia had tried in Almansa, circulated among prominent royal officials in Madrid seeking to stop Dr Valencia from continuing. They did not know that the king stood behind the investigation for which he had commissioned Dr Valencia, which meant that the judge received permission to continue his work in Toledo. He completed his work there just prior to assuming the corregimiento of Jaén and Andújar, which was an important step up because Jaén was one of the cities that sent representatives to the Cortes, Castile's parliamentary body.

Beyond trying and convicting criminals, Dr Valencia's investigation would provide Philip II with a much fuller picture of the administrative and economic reality of eastern Castile. The frontier of the Marquisate of Villena fell within the jurisdiction of a royal judge, who dealt with the export and import of prohibited products, but the arrests by this type of justice normally involved men caught at the border, who lived in the area. Before Dr Valencia had finished his work, he provided the King with a detailed explanation of the involvement in this clandestine commerce of Valencian merchants and of major New Christian merchant general (unlimited) partnerships in the city of Toledo (Martz 2003) and of merchants from Philip's Duchy of Milan (Sella and Capra 1984), the latter based in Cuenca and Toledo. Both cities served as major Castilian financial, marketing, and manufacturing centres. Thus, the work of commissioned royal justices constituted a type of 'information technology' (term used in Torres Fauaz 2013) which played a substantial but often overlooked role in connecting the Crown to life in often distant royal domains.

Despite Dr Valencia's work, we cannot see the narrative as one pitting against each other the forces of law and those of crime. The Crown did not have clean hands from the point of view of many subjects, who were damaged and angered by the often arbitrary and illegal actions of royal authorities acting on specific orders from the king. For example, in 1556, Philip, who had only recently become monarch after the abdication of his father, the Emperor Charles V, ordered his regency government in Valladolid, headed by his sister Juana, the queen-mother of Portugal, to confiscate all of the privately owned bullion arriving in Seville on American fleets. She refused on the grounds that the action was illegal. However, Philip did not care and insisted that the regency carry out the embargo in 1557. In exchange for their seized precious metals, the damaged female and male merchants would receive government bonds (*juros*), which entitled their holders to regular payments from various Crown revenue sources. Of course, the merchants looked forward to the arrival of the fleet so that they could satisfy obligations to others and make investments and purchases for their businesses. The embargo forced the merchants out of any of the factor markets and into a financial market, in a way that threatened Castile's economy with stagnation. The confiscation, therefore, resulted in severe damage to commerce and production (Rodríguez-Salgado 1988: 68–70, 208–213). Throughout the rest of his reign, to his death in 1598, Philip continued his disruptive and likely illegal actions: suspending payments on Crown debts and forcing major debtors, such as Genoese merchants, to accept a reorganization of their compensation on worse terms; and the sales of municipal offices and towns taken from the jurisdictions of the Church and major municipalities and, therefore, off their tax rolls. To control actions seen as arbitrary and damaging to the property and incomes of Castilians, the Cortes forced the Crown near the end of Philip's reign, to accept a contract with the Kingdom, in which the king agreed to controls on royal mandates, in exchange for a one-time expansion of taxation (Fortea Pérez 1990).

Money and factor markets in the shadows

Just a word about money, because the merchant-smugglers moved a great deal of it out of Castile. Values were expressed in two ways – in metallic coins and in money of account. The most valuable coin was the gold *escudo*, which weighed 3.38 g of which 3.10 g were gold. Silver made the global economy run and Castile's silver coin was the *real*, which weighed 3.44 g, of which 3.16 g were silver. There were also copper coins denominated in *maravedíes*. Of course, other coins, minted by other European governments, entered Castile to be exchanged during the four annual fairs of Medina del Campo. To keep track of wealth, merchants and government officials often employed 'money of account'. Their books and contracts frequently show amounts measured in *ducados* and *maravedíes* (mrs; not the copper coins of the same name), which did not normally depreciate in relation to silver. Royal statute established the values of gold and silver. Until 1566, that for the gold *escudo* was 350 mrs and for the silver *real* 34 mrs. A ducado was valued at 11 *reales* and one *mr*. In 1566 the Crown increased the legal value of the gold escudo to 400 mrs because the lower valuation served as a motivation for smugglers (Ulloa 1977: 32–33). In contracts and letters of credit, large amounts were often stated partly in *cuentos*: in 1565, 3000 ducados equalled one cuento and 125,000 mrs.

Merchants usually formed general (unlimited responsibility) partnerships, with a small number of participants, often only two. Among the advantages of this type of partnership over administrative entities and large commercial companies are their ability to respond quickly to small fluctuations in niche markets, such as that for wool, disruption to a transportation route through frontier communities, and changes in more impersonal markets, such as the fairs of Medina del Campo, which would experience serious problems after the Crown suspended debt payments in 1575 (Marcos Martín 2017). Although some benefits might have materialized from larger companies, the cost of co-ordination would likely have exceeded any benefits obtained, thereby raising transaction costs beyond those of small general partnerships (Straub *et al.* 2020). Partnerships of merchant-smugglers participated simultaneously in overlapping factor markets. The major goal of most of the Italian ones was the export of wool to feed cloth production in their homelands. This desire meant that they purchased a great deal of wool, preferring to do so by providing contracts to producers, for which the suppliers sometimes received substantial advances (Phillips and Phillips 1997). Whenever possible, the merchants wanted their commissioned agents to collect the wool in smaller villages, to avoid as much as possible the official oversight that would force them to pay the sales taxes. Juan Pedro de Anón and his brother Francisco got fined, after an adverse judgement against them, for their failure to pay sales taxes for 1563 and 1564 for cattle hides they had obtained in Seville and sold in Cuenca (Cuenca, 10 April 1565; CP0176, ff. 248–248v). These commissioned agents often maintained close relations with the merchant-smugglers. For example, one agent of the Milanese in the Bishopric of Cuenca, Pedro de Alegría, vecino of Pareja, had accepted a contract with the Milanese Juan Pedro de Anón, Julián Castellón, Juan Pablo Dada, and Jusepe Vila, in exchange for the housekeeping work at their residence of his daughter, Juana, who earned money and personal items for her dowry, which her father collected on her behalf at the end of her service on 26 September 1565 (CP0176, ff. 578–578v). All of those who marketed wool participated in a specialized labor market for seasonal wool sorters and washers, who often came from towns farther north. Of course, the market for carters to transport wool and other commodities formed another core part of their networks. One has trouble locating contracts for carters, which makes it likely that these matters did not become subject to documents prepared before a public notary or that the contracts were prepared by notaries outside of Cuenca whose registers have not survived. One finds the same sorts of network operating south of Toledo, where a wool purchasing and export business was managed by Pedro Juan Forniel, a Genoese living in Almagro, east of Ciudad Real, organizing throughout a large area wool collection, preparation, and transportation. Pedro Juan was the brother of Vicencio and Domingo Forniel, Genoese living in Toledo, and a member of their general partnership, for which Pedro Juan maintained factors (permanent agents) to deal with the extensive grazing lands of the region (for example, the elaborate power of attorney, which mentions Montiel, east of Almagro: 22 September 1566; TP01534, ff. 1452–1452v).

Border smugglers would move wool into the Kingdoms of Aragon and Valencia. As the border guard Juan Catalán revealed in his exposé given to the king, some built houses with corrals right on the border. They would bring sheep there to shear, quickly transporting the product into domains of the Crown of Aragon, the Kingdoms of Aragon and Valencia. However, they also acted as suppliers of Valencian demand for meat because they herded the animals to major slaughter centers such as Benaguacil. In addition to smuggling sheep and goats for fleece and meat, the smugglers also supplied contracts in the Kingdom of Valencia for grain. Without some sort of special royal license for these exports, this activity was illegal but responded to substantial demand. Valencia was the largest port along Iberia's east coast, and Alicante was the fastest-growing. The kingdom's hinterland could not supply enough basic products to sustain this exuberant demographic expansion (Salvador Esteban 1972). Moreover, the relevant royal legislation makes it clear that horses, especially foals, were highly desired in the Kingdom of Valencia because certain parts of the Kingdom of Murcia were noted for the quality of their horses. These dodges to escape export prohibitions and customs taxes might also permit producers to escape a tax on their production known as the *diezmo*, literally at least 10% of the value of animals, grain and other products, one-third for the parish, one-third for the bishop and his council (*Cabildo*), and one-third for the royal treasury (Lemeunier 1976).

Permeable borders

Although Dr Valencia assured the king and Eraso that he was uprooting the smuggling to such an extent that the criminal behavior would not return to that area, the borders remained so open that merchant-smugglers and others would continue to exploit the situation. The porous frontier between Castile and the peninsular domains of the Crown of Aragon continued to invite people to dodge the customs posts and the border with Portugal offered the same conditions. How could it be otherwise when few Crown judicial officials worked these borders? The judges of contraband cases had responsibility for large territories, possessing titles such as, for the bishoprics of Salamanca, Zamora, and the Kingdom of Galicia; for the bishoprics of Badajoz and Ciudad Rodrigo; for the bishoprics of Osma, Calahorra, Sigüenza, and Cuenca (Partido de Requena); of the bishoprics of Cartagena, Almería, and the Kingdom of Granada. Historians have done little work on these justices, and I know nothing about the responsibilities of the one covering the southwestern bishoprics. However, Gerónimo de Salamanca, who 'farmed' customs collections along the entire border with Portugal, identified a major center for smuggling, by land and sea: the Marquisate of Ayamonte, whose lord was an influential member of the House of Béjar (Sello, March 1567, f. 976; on these territorial aristocrats, see Owens 2005a). The Archivo General de Simancas section, *Registro General del Sello*, includes many other documents recording the complaints of Alonso de la Fuente y de Andrada, the collector of taxes for the borderlands with the Crown of Aragon, and of Salamanca, who held the same position for the border with Portugal. These men had bid for the collection rights, which guaranteed a fix amount to the Crown, leaving the chief collectors anything above what they bid. The first man was a relative at some degree of some of Toledo's merchant-smugglers, and the second was a member of one of the most prominent merchant families of the northern financial centre of Burgos, who had returned to Castile after almost thirty years in Antwerp (on Salamanca: Casado Alonso 2013: 364–365). Both were experienced enough to provide accurate reports of the smuggling activity in their jurisdictions.

At about the same time, late 1566, a murder exposed just how permeable the Castile-Portugal border was. Because Philip II would not assume the Portuguese crown until 1580–1581, the murder set off a major diplomatic incident. Men from the town of Alconchel, south of Badajoz, crossed the border to kill Juan Lorenzo, the warden of the large castle of Monsaraz in Portugal. To confuse matters further, Alconchel was a seigneurial town of Don Fadrique de Zúñiga, raising the same issues Dr Valencia provoked with investigations in the seigneurial towns of Carcelén and Montealegre in the Kingdom of Murcia. The local lord was upset when Portuguese officials crossed the border to arrest a suspect in Alconchel. The event brought into action the royal councils of Castile and Portugal, acting in the name of their monarchs (Sello, Dec. 1566, f. 344; Feb. 1567, f. 349 & 423; May 1567, f. 595). Nothing impeded those who wished to cross this or any other Castilian border, on land or by sea.

Judicial institutions and the growth of commerce

Despite this messy context for his investigations, Dr Valencia provided a valuable service for researchers who desire to explain the relationship of 'State' institutions to the economic development of a political entity. This chapter's micro-history builds from its limited story of a small number of people toward an improved understanding of the social and cultural environments of 16th century commerce (Revel 1996; Moreno García 2018), although the full account can only be told in a much longer work. In one of his dispatches, Dr Valencia reported that he had jailed more than 70 of the accused in the Almansa fortress, even before he went to Cuenca and Toledo. On the basis of the fragmentary surviving information about his investigation, one can add something to the extended debate about the relationship between judicial institutions, which supposedly reduced risk by defending private property and the terms of contracts, and the economic development of the countries studied (North and Thomas 1973; North 1991; 1995). Clemente (2018) provides a splendid historiographical account of the debates touched off by North's position. Critics of his original position, including eventually North himself, have argued that the 'culture' of a place played an important role in stimulating and refining the role of institutions. A people would not have established effective judicial institutions if they did not have some cultural disposition to think that the 'State' security these institutions promised was desirable. However, economic historians often define the culture favorable to institutional development in unchanging, essentialist terms, which frequently encourages a teleological account. Moreover, proponents of the 'cultural turn' give too little attention to how culture influences human activity. The deficient understandings of culture increasingly play a role in efforts to explain why some country or world region is more successfully developed economically than another. Sometimes, those economists performing comparisons know too little about the country or world region described as backward when compared to the other (for example, Landes 1998).

It is difficult to think of the Kingdom of Castile, or any other jurisdiction in Philip's planetary dynastic agglomeration, which we call the Hispanic Monarchy, as a 'State' in the sense recognized by social scientists writing in the past two centuries. These researchers frequently present the State as a unified entity which, when reified into an actor, possesses adequate *autonomy* and *capacity* to formulate policy and obtain compliance with its will by coercive means, if necessary (Barkey and Parikh 1991). Philip II's suspicion of his own royal councils when he made Dr Valencia's investigation secret testifies to the lack of autonomy from other groups, such as the territorial aristocracy, to formulate policy. The difficulty the Crown faced in obtaining compliance with its orders by various institutions, civil and ecclesiastical, even in Castile when the monarch resided there, demonstrates repeatedly the weakness of royal capacity, which often reduced the king and his officials to negotiations with other groups. Borders were porous everywhere within the Hispanic Monarchy (on the Valencia side of the border, García Martínez 1977; Garés Timor 2015) and with the lands of other governments, such as the Kingdom of Portugal and its vast domains in Africa, Asia, America (Brazil), and the Atlantic Islands. When Philip II became ruler of the Crown of Portugal (as Philip I), the land and sea borders between Iberian Portugal and Castile and the Kingdom of Galicia remained as permeable as before.

Resultant descriptions of 'Spanish culture', asserted in comparisons, frequently contribute to a negative stereotype intended to postulate a general hostility to business and to industrial investment and activity. Caro Baroja (1978) shatters the possibility of any stereotype about 'Spain' by exposing the great variety of cultural expressions during the 16th and 17th centuries. However, he offers no means to explain how a specific cultural perspective might have stimulated human action. In a micro-history of a long dispute between territorial aristocrats and the city of Toledo over private property and a contract, and the Castilian judicial institutions employed to resolve the conflict (1445–1574), Owens (2005a) explains, based on cognitive psychology, how a conjunctural situation could trigger certain aspects of the available 'cultural environment' (taking the term from Alexander 1988) in ways that shaped human understanding and action.

One can find state-like entities within the Hispanic Monarchy, both before and after the addition of Portuguese domains. Cities and towns possessed impressive authority within their population centers and their often vast jurisdictions, which were usually called their *alfoz* or *términos* (Ringrose 1997). In conjunction with ecclesiastical officials, the citizens and other residents of these urban entities dealt, often daily, with institutions that shaped almost all activities. As expressions of political economy, their municipal ordinances contained frameworks and constraints for many human actions, especially in the economic sphere (Martín Gamero 1858; Lemeunier 1982; Lemeunier and Rodríguez Llopis 1983; Corral García 1988; Ladero Quesada 1998; Bejarano Rubio and Molina 1989; Carrilero Martínez 1997; González Arce 2000). Even Inquisition tribunals, which were appointed and supervised by the royal Supreme Council of the Inquisition, usually collaborated with the local authorities in the zones, normally defined by bishoprics, to which inquisitors were posted (Nalle 1992).

Going beyond studies of a single country or a comparison between two of them, economic historians demand attention to the commercial networks that crossed the frontiers of countries and regions. These studies often dissolve possibilities for comparing these geographical entities. Such networks frequently absorbed 'trade diasporas' of specific ethnic groups, who were not content to handle in their home regions products transported to them by merchants from the producing regions. Instead, they established themselves in an important producing region or in a distant market center for desired products, and they developed the knowledge, capital, and relationships necessary to purchase and transport goods. From the perspective of Dr

Valencia's investigation, Genoese and Milanese merchants formed trade diasporas from the Republic of Genoa and Philip II's Duchy of Milan (Lombardy).

Trade diasporas

Curtin (1984) brought to the attention of world historians the importance of trade diasporas, of varying distances, of merchants with a common ethnic background, broadening the historic meaning of 'diaspora', which referred to the dispersal of Jews out of Palestine. Ringrose (2018: 137–148) provides a concise introduction to the trade diasporas of greatest interest to historians: the Multani (Dale 2002; Levi 2007), the Armenians of Julfa (Chaudury 2005; McCabe 2005; Aslanian 2011), the Jews (Israel 2002 for an overview of a much-studied topic), and the Southsea Chinese, sometimes called Overseas Chinese (Chang 1991; Reid 2005; Wills 2011). Roitman (2011) exposes the many ways that one diaspora group, Jews and New Christians of Portuguese origin in Amsterdam, expanded their outlook on possible business associates of other backgrounds and from other countries and, in doing so, possibly transformed their own cultural perspectives and mental models (see also, Studnicki-Gizbert 2009). The numerous publications of Casado Alonso (2003; 2013) remind us that there was a Castilian diaspora to northern Europe, which added to its economic consequences important cultural and political dimensions. Calafat (2011–2012) offers a useful theoretical comment about merchant diasporas and intercultural commerce.

In her exciting book about a general partnership between Jewish merchants in Livorno, Trivellato (2009) uses her subject to expose aspects of 'cross-cultural trade' throughout Europe, the eastern Mediterranean, and the Indian subcontinent. Based on her detailed research, she criticizes many 'trade diaspora' studies, including that of Curtin, for their ahistorical, reductionist discussions of 'culture' (*ibid.*: 16–20). As a guide to future research, she highlights 'three dimensions of the debate about the role of trading diasporas in early modern commerce: the niche specialization of minority groups, the degree of closeness and openness of "ethnic economic networks," and the relation between trading diasporas and state-sponsored commercial organizations' (*ibid.*: 225). Because this chapter deals with 16th century smuggling networks, I cannot say anything about interactions between trading diasporas and any commercial organizations shaped by 'State' licensed trading companies because none existed to connect Castile to other places in the central and western Mediterranean.

Self-organizing networks: What were the organizing nodes in commercial networks?

The overall take-away from Dr Valencia's exposure of the often shadowy efforts of men and women involved in clandestine economic activity is that their networks possessed a much greater ability to adapt to changed conditions, including those resulting from a major disaster, than did the various institutions of the Crown. As we do, these economically active people formed part of a non-linear, non-stationary, complex human system, which was coupled with complex, non-linear, non-stationary natural systems. 'Non-linear' means that human attempts to forecast by creating a cause-and-effect series of events produces limited results. 'Non-stationary' means that even if someone identifies some non-linear sequence, the complex system involves so many interacting components that the perceived sequence might never occur again. Thus, our economic actors expressed their agency within a context of constant uncertainty, not only from massive changes in the human system but also because of the coupling with natural systems. At some level, they recognized that they could not construct their networks according to some ideal plan. Rather, these merchants and producers needed to fashion networks cohesive enough to remain robust and flexible enough to withstand major, unexpected disasters (and opportunities) and adapt to what emerges through an ability to acquire essential information (Doria 1986; Owens 2012b; on 'essential information', Burgin and Cárdenas-García 2020; Cárdenas-García and Ireland 2020). Although it might not be visible to the actors, as their behavior and interactions changed, the overall system altered as well, without necessarily transforming its dynamics. The stability of these dynamics depended on the stability of a small number of critical variables, which are always positioned near instability, sometimes called tipping points. If one or more of these variables moves to instability, the system will enter a 'phase transition', out of which a different system will emerge (Haken 1983; Puu 2003; Mitchell 2009; Owens 2011a; 2012a). The Crown enjoyed only limited adaptability, which is why its policies appeared to bounce rapidly from one crisis to another without lasting success. Moreover, information for Crown institutions often stemmed from the reports of short-term officials, such as specially commissioned judicial investigators, whose vision was clouded by limited familiarity with the situation they confronted and no one could effectively aggregate the information which arrived in Madrid or other centers of administrative activity in the planetary Hispanic Monarchy.

Merchants, on the other hand, possessed the means to alter their interactions and to aggregate information quickly. They belonged to 'communities of practice', which showed the ability to innovate, sometimes through only small changes, to adapt to changing conditions (Wenger 1998; Wenger *et al.* 2002; Hildreth and Kimble 2004; Cox 2005; Gherardi 2012). These 'communities' constituted a setting for the development and maintenance of a specific cultural environment (McClosky 2016; 2017), which shaped the self-organization of merchant networks beyond anything simple calculation would have produced. As Shteynberg and his colleagues have demonstrated (Shteynberg and Galinsky 2011; Shteynberg 2015a; 2015b; 2018; Haj-Mohamadi *et al.* 2018; Shteynberg *et al.* 2014a; 2014b; 2020), the frequent 'shared attention' to common practices intensified emotionally for participants their affiliation, common goal pursuit, and norms. In Toledo, some interactions within the merchant-smuggler group surely took place in arenas of conversation, which have left no documentary trace.

However, we see a matrix for such interactions whenever someone wished to prepare a private document, usually some sort of contract, commission, promissory obligation, or power of attorney. Except in the case of most documents recording the working arrangements of general partnerships (small companies consisting of highly trusted associates), some instructions to agents, and some receipts for the satisfaction of debts, merchants usually recorded documents before a public notary (*escribano público*). Every Castilian municipality had a fixed number of these men who often purchased their positions. Too often, historians attribute to the notary no room to shape the contracts, debt assignments, letters of credit, payment orders, marriage agreements, testaments, or other written material he prepared because they assume that the notary only recorded what the client or clients wanted in the document. Increasingly we see indications that the notary, as an experienced agent, participated in a conversation about what sorts of clause would meet a client's needs. A merchant, female or male, brought to the conversation expertise and information. Moreover, within the list of witnesses, one often sees the names of other merchants, always male, who were present and, therefore, had opportunities to engage in the discussion, perhaps even as the driving force if they were much more experienced than those for whom the notary was preparing the document. Frequently, the names of witnesses included a notary's assistant who would, years later, populate a list of the municipality's notaries. He might also have expertise to offer about what shape a document should have to capture a client's wishes. Merchants frequently authorized incomplete contracts (Macaulay 1963; Tirole 1999; Battigalli and Maggi 2002), including powers of attorney, usually because after discussion, they expected the empowered parties to adjust their behavior according to circumstances which could not be foreseen when creating and signing the contract.

Finally, these conversations often included a *jurado* who could provide additional information and a perspective not available to others involved. Jurados in Toledo served as members of the city's Civic Council (*Ayuntamiento*), representing a specific parish, and many were New Christians (those with Jewish ancestry, which also included many merchants and notaries; Aranda Pérez 1992a; Martz 2003) who were either merchants or relatives of merchants (Aranda Pérez 1992b). Those interested in occupying a council seat considered a *juraduría* less valuable than the other type of seat, a *regimiento* (held by a *regidor*). Because, in 1543, the Crown began expanding civic councils by selling such offices we know the monetary values of the posts. For example, in his final testament of 15 July 1565, jurado Alonso de Herrera left his juraduría in the Parish of San Antolín and San Marcos to his son with wife Teresa de la Fuente, Juan de Herrera, with the responsibility to pay his brother Rodrigo de Herrera 400 ducados for the value of the post. If Juan did not want the office, Rodrigo could have it, paying Juan 400 ducados (TP01530, ff. 172–179v). Although jurados could not vote on most of the proposals dealt with by the Civic Council, which was the privilege of regidores, they acquired valuable information by listening, including to commands and other correspondence from Crown institutions. Moreover, unlike the case of the city of Murcia, which was supposed to follow Toledo's municipal government model, a Toledano jurado would fill one of the two posts as a representative sent to meet with the monarch and his advisors in meetings of the Cortes. The monarch often granted the representatives special benefits, which enhanced the value of holding the office.

For example, holders of council offices could pass their seats to someone else, but only if they lived for 20 days after declaring, in a document before a notary, their wish to do so. The monarch might grant to a Cortes representative a waiver of the 20 day regulation so that he could dispose of his Civic Council office in his will. Furthermore, Toledo's ordinances demanded that jurados oversee many aspects of factor markets involving urban production and the supply of the city, which also provided them with up-to-date information about market values. Ldo. Santa María, jurado and Toledo's attorney, compiled and transcribed the existing ordinances, many dating from the 14th and 15th centuries, in 1562 so that a copy could be sent to jurado Ldo. de Arze, who was at Court. Arze presented the manuscript to the monarch, soliciting his confirmation of the ordinances and his permission to print them (Martín Gamero 1858).

Clearly, the procedure involved expressions of trust among the parties, including the notary. Moreover, the discussion produced an aggregation of information, which benefitted all parties, including those who just stood there and listened, whose names would not be recorded unless they were included among the three witnesses. Many notaries worked from a booth or stall in a public plaza associated with commercial activities. They would go to the home of a client if the desired document was something like a testament for someone near death or an inventory of property within the house. The semi-public nature of notaries' activities meant that information, including that aggregated during the conversation about some document, would be conveyed over time to a larger group than that present at the creation of a document.

Theorists of 'communities of practice' present them as potential sources of innovation in anything produced. Although the research for this chapter is based on too short a timeline to defend the hypothesis, which may require some modelling (McLean and Padgett 2004; Owens and Kantabutra 2020), it is likely that the interactions surrounding the creation of notarized documents produced innovations over time. One can see such changes in the devotional language and charitable grants of testaments, about which a great deal has been written. When an innovation was made, it would have been recorded in the personal manuals of the notary and his assistant, for consultation the next time a similar document was requested. Because of this process, innovations likely crept into the commercial, marriage, and other contracts and documents registered and signed by merchants and their family members, and in the legal texts used to present petitions to the local law courts. In other words, the social networks of merchants had points of contact which offered flexibility of action and the aggregation of information necessary to respond to altered conditions. These frequent meetings and conversations thus allowed the commercial networks of merchant-smugglers to be *self-organizing*, without Crown control, and to manifest behavior founded on common mental models, perspectives, and norms necessary for a dynamic cultural environment always open to alterations and incorporations.

Hawala/Hundi self-organizing networks

One should not be surprised that cooperative, clandestine merchant networks could extend their activities over long distances (Court 2004; Lamikiz 2017). In our time, a system known as a *hawala* or *hundi* manages to remit payments from one country to another without any promissory note and without moving money, and brokers charge the client a much lower commission than a bank or other companies engaged in money transfers. *Hawaladars*, as the service providers are called, exist in many places in the world and most of these brokers are Muslims, although participation is not limited to them. It is likely that this system, or something like it, pre-existed the foundation of Islam. However, one notes the hawala's presence most easily in southwestern and central Asia, the Indian subcontinent, and throughout the Indian Ocean basin, which provides a huge territory for 'a genuine geography of trust' (Herrero Sánchez 2017: 4). Perhaps these *self-organizing networks* become most visible now when they handle remittances from immigrant workers, in London for example, to relatives in their countries of origin, especially if these have weak banking systems. Much of the current literature on the hawala deals with perceived threats because such a network, in which no written records are produced, could provide currency transfers for terrorist organizations or for those avoiding currency exchange rules and taxes (Habib 1971; Ballard 2005; Martin 2009; Ladányi and Kobolka 2014; Lascaux 2015). Based on what we know about the clandestine merchant networks of the 16th century, hawala participants certainly avoid currency and tax regulations.

For example, on 25 November 1565, Juan Zapeña, vecino of Valencia, came to Toledo and granted his power of attorney to Gerónimo de Castro, merchant and vecino of Toledo (and one of the merchant-smugglers tried by Dr Valencia at the border). Zapeña wanted Castro to collect from three Genoese residents of Toledo (Juan Antonio, Jácome, and Esteban Pinelo) 1100 reales de plata castellanos (Castilian silver coins, rather than a money of account) by virtue of a letter of credit issued by Lucian Doria and Jácome Pinelo, Genoese inhabitants of the city of Valencia, on 6 November. Two of the three witnesses were Don Alonso de Pina, vecino of Almansa (tried by Dr Valencia), and Sebastián Gómez, vecino of Valencia (TP01935, f. 289v, notary Luis de Avilés). In theory, this sort of credit should have been settled at one of the four annual fairs of Medina del Campo, which leads one to believe that the parties involved were laundering money and avoiding taxes, possibly tied to goods smuggled earlier from Castile to Valencia without paying any sort of sales or customs tax. A similar power of attorney to Castro had earlier been initiated by Zapeña with another notary but the date was never filled in and the document was left without witnesses and unsigned by the granter. On this occasion, Gerónimo de Castro was not present, suggesting that someone thought it best to wait so that Castro could collect quickly (TP01531, ff. 817–817v, notary Juan Sánchez de Canales). I suspect that on some occasions neither a letter of credit nor the collection would have been recorded in notarized documents, which were open to examination by judicial authorities.

Genoese and Milanese trade diasporas were not closed

Because the trade diasporas of the Genoese and Milanese were not closed (Rodríguez de Gracia 2003; Vela Santamaría 2013–2014; Muñoz Navarro 2015; Crivelli 2017 ; Herrero

Sánchez 2017; Girón Pascual 2018), the interactions with notaries could bring together prominent merchants from Genoa and Milan with Castilian New Christian merchants. For example, on 18 June 1565, the Milanese merchants Juan Ángelo Cernúsculo and Doña Catalina Cernúsculo, husband and wife, and the other member of their general partnership, Doña María de Vitoria, widow of Bernaldino Cernúsculo, met with two of the most important Genoese merchants who were vecinos of Toledo, Francisco Doria and Vicencio de Forniel. The meeting also included one of the city's major New Christian merchants, Luis Hernández de Cuenca (the father of Luis Hernández de Carrión, one of the merchant-smugglers arrested on the border by Dr Valencia), and one of the leaders of the new corporation in Toledo of 17 of the 33 public notaries, Juan Sánchez de Canales. Juan Ángelo and Doña Catalina had been arrested and jailed for debts, some of which may have involved the financing of construction on a fortress in Perpignan, region of Rousillon-Cerdanya, which, at that time, was part of the Crown of Aragon (TP01530, ff. 266–269v). Juan Ángelo issued his obligation to repay a large debt to Pedro Casador, vecino of Barcelona, in two payments at the Medina del Campo fairs of May and October of 1565. The two Genoese and the New Christian agreed as a unified group to be bondsmen guaranteeing Juan Ángelo's payment. In turn, Juan Ángelo and Doña Catalina agreed to hypothecate two *juros* (government bonds), which belonged to her. Although it is not clear to what bonds she referred, she appears to have been one of the merchants given bonds when the Crown confiscated her bullion from the treasure fleet in 1557 (AGS Contaduría de Mercedes, L. 218). In order to pledge the bonds, she explicitly gave up her rights of protection as a woman enumerated by a series of legal sources. Doña María de Vitoria agreed to the same waiver of rights for any claim she might have to the bonds. Finally, Doña Catalina ratified a long oath, declaring that she would never seek to overturn the hypothecate before any ecclesiastical or secular justice. All signed the agreement (TP01529, ff. 1479–1482).

As another example of how tightly woven together these merchants were, in Toledo, on 19 June 1565, Vicencio de Forniel and Juan Espínola, Genoese and inhabitants of Toledo, and New Christian merchants Juan de San Pedro Sotelo and his son, Payo Sotelo (one of Toledo's merchant-smugglers whom Dr Valencia arrested on the border), financed a bail bond for Juan Antonio Pinelo, Genoese, vecino of Toledo. Pinelo had been arrested and jailed by order of the royal council (TP01964, ff. 312–312v). He was one of the more settled Genoese, having married when a widower in 1558 Doña Ana Ortiz de Salazar, a local woman. In August, the same four men would again provide financial backing required by Juan Antonio (TP01964, ff. 415–416). The network also involved Milanese merchants. On 7 July 1565, Juan Antonio sent a power of attorney to Borsio Cabitelo, long-time general partner of Juan Pedro de Anón in Cuenca. Because of the growing importance in commercial and financial affairs of the Court, Cabitelo established a residence in Madrid. Juan Antonio Pinelo asked him to sell some houses he owned there, probably to get funds to confront his legal problems (TP01529, ff. 1507v–1508).

Juan de San Pedro Sotelo was one of the most respected members of the New Christian community, taking on the guardianship of an elderly woman suffering dementia and orphaned children. He employed his expert knowledge of the values of property of all kinds to prepare inventories, and he was often named as a testamentary executor. When Juan Antonio Pinelo died, his sealed testament of 8 June 1565 was opened on 27 August 1566, as was a codicil of 1 August (TP00015, ff. 613/600–615/602; TP01534, ff. 1028–1038v). The document named Juan de San Pedro Sotelo executor, and he carried out the extensive inventory of Juan Antonio's property and its distribution to the widow and Juan Antonio's sons by his first marriage (TP01533, ff. 933–936; TP01921, ff. 575–595v, 617–626v). On 22 October 1566, Sotelo also advised Doña Ana on another delicate matter. Because the widowed Doña Ana was a wealthy woman in full control of her property, she could no longer count on the protection provided by her late husband when he disinherited his son with Doña Ana, Baltasar Pinelo. Her dowry alone amounted to four cuentos, 249,334 mrs. Juan de San Pedro Sotelo witnessed Juan Antonio's declaration (TP00015, ff. 225r/212r-215r, Toledo, 5 April 1566). Baltasar had married in 1564 the daughter of a barber without the consent and against the wishes of his parents, and he abandoned an ecclesiastical benefice which had been arranged for him. Therefore, she granted her power of attorney to a solicitor who was ordered to disinherit Baltasar on her behalf in the law court of the alcalde mayor of Toledo (TP01921, f. 611). Making use of a surviving business letterbook of a Genoese merchant in Genoa, Court (2014; also 2018) illustrates in some detail how an 'errant son' in Sicily could endanger the trusting relationships among merchants on which his father's commercial world depended. In the end, it would be necessary to cut any ties.

Businessmen behaving badly

When one of Toledo's merchants acted badly in his relationship with another, public exposure, rather than simple rumor, might provide the better means of highlighting the matter. However, such exposure would involve bringing into the dispute Crown officials, as happened because of a conflict between Juan Ángelo Cernúsculo, Milanese, and Luis de la Fuente, merchant, both vecinos of Toledo.

In Madrid on 29 December 1564, Ldo. Cespedes de Oviedo, of the council of the monarch and alcalde (judge) of his Household and Court, sent an order (*carta requisitoria*) to Toledo's corregidor, his lieutenant, and any other justices before whom his letter might be presented. Cespedes demanded that the corregidor take the testimony of witnesses in the lawsuit he was adjudicating on appeal between Pedro Hernández, vecino of Seville, who had brought the order to Toledo, and Juan Ángelo Cernúsculo, whom he calls a Genoese (a common error), as cessionary of Luis de la Fuente for a document acknowledging a debt of 79 ducados, guaranteed by certain property held by an unknown bondsman. Cespedes attached a list of questions to be posed to the witnesses presented by Hernández. He also enclosed a simple, unnotarized note acknowledging the payment by Tomé Tenorio, merchant, vecino of both Seville and Toledo, of the payment of the debt in Seville on 12 May 1564, by Hernández in the name of Luis de la Fuente. This interrogatory asked that the witnesses verify the signature of Tenorio and tell what they knew about Luis de la Fuente and the debt. Specifically, they were to comment on the claim that it was public knowledge that Luis de la Fuente had assigned this debt to three or four other people and that he had committed many other deceptive acts, because of which he had left Toledo to hide out in the Kingdom of Valencia (TP01528, ff. 141–143). Marco de Cuellar, municipal judge (*alcalde ordinario*), took the testimony by order of the corregidor, on 3 January 1565, of four men, one explicitly identified as a merchant. Although only a few of the witnesses commented on the general charge about the behavior of Luis de la Fuente, Cuellar did nothing to make the proceedings secret, leaving these men free to discuss the case in public (TP01528, ff. 146–149v).

Local conversation may have led to more serious problems for Luis de la Fuente. From Madrid, on 3 October 1567, the royal council notified Juan de San Pedro Sotelo and his son, Payo Sotelo, that Luis de la Fuente had appealed a judgement against him for a considerable amount of money. The *audiencia* of the Chancillería of Valladolid (a superior appeals court) would hear the appeal and the Sotelos were told to send their solicitor to represent them (Sello, October 1567, leg. 2, f. 565). In Toledo, discussions about this lawsuit and the behavior of Luis de la Fuente may have taken place among relatives. In 1558, Payo Sotelo married Leonor de la Fuente, daughter of jurado Juan de San Pedro de Palma and Elvira de la Torre (TP01502, ff. 1380–1381v). Whatever degree of relationship he may have had with the Sotelos, Luis de la Fuente likely paid a high price for debasing his reputation by acting badly.

However, tales of failures to satisfy their responsibilities could perhaps encompass an entire region in which Toledo's merchant-smugglers organized their commercial networks. At the request of Mosén Martín Merino, vecino of Almansa, on 10 July 1567, the royal council ordered the corregidor or other justices to take up the request for relief (Sello, July 1567, f. 209). Merino had come to Court with a power of attorney and instructions from 12 of Toledo's New Christian merchant-smugglers who had not compensated him adequately for his service. Dr Valencia had convicted them of smuggling money and other things to the Kingdom of Valencia. The 12 included Francisco de Madrid de Herrera, Payo Sotelo, Juan Bautista del Águila, and Gerónimo del Castro. In a commercial world heavily dependent on reputation and trust, a charge of failure to pay one's debts would trouble the ability of Toledo's merchant-smugglers to obtain the cooperation they needed from residents of border towns and cities to smuggle goods.

Collecting financial obligations caused problems among some of these merchant-smugglers and, in one case, the conflict highlighted a possibility for jurisdictional conflicts. On 30 October 1567, the royal council sent an order requested by Payo Sotelo to all ecclesiastical justices. Juan Bautista del Águila, by that time a jurado of Toledo, owed Sotelo 1300 ducados (a money of account), and the time period for repayment had passed. Calculated in silver *reales*, each with 3.16 g of silver, the debt would have been just over 14,338 reales. Sotelo brought a lawsuit against the debtor. Águila was seeking sanctuary in churches and monasteries, with some of his property, to escape his obligation by claiming the ecclesiastical protection from being removed from sacred places. Apparently, Águila had ample property to satisfy the debt. Therefore, the royal council ordered ecclesiastical authorities to expel him, without scandal, so that secular judicial officials could put him in the public jail (Sello, Oct. 1567, f. 633). Sotelo's lawsuit also involved Luis Hurtado, merchant and vecino of Toledo, who solicited from the vicar general of the Archbishop of Toledo (who was confined during his trial by the Inquisition) letters of censure against Sotelo and many others in the royal jurisdiction, which Hurtado wanted announced in all of the churches. He wanted to defame Sotelo, described by his solicitor as a principal person, of much credit, and a good Christian. On 31 October, the royal council ordered the vicar to remit all hearings involving the debt to secular justice and they demanded that all censures and excommunications be sent to the audiencia of the Chancillería of Valladolid (Sello, Oct. 1567, f. 629). The New Christians involved likely found this form of defamation particularly troubling, something to which Águila and Hurtado, as New Christians, should have been sensitive (Martz 2003).

Despite what one might think reading the works of Douglass North's New Institutional History, the presence of a diverse group of economic actors in the commercial networks connecting Castile with Alicante and Valencia, or with Genoa and Milan did not make the Crown's judicial authorities any more important to the merchant-smugglers. The costs of recourse to these authorities, even in the case of fines, would have been a cost of doing business (Gneezy and Rustichini 2000), but it was a cost they would likely have preferred to avoid through negotiation. Overall, these men and women did not rely on Crown institutions of any type to shape their behavior and that of their 'agents'.

Nesting

In fact, the New Christians (of Jewish ancestry) and the Genoese (and the Milanese who were often lumped into this group), besides their desire to escape scrutiny from judicial and other authorities, sought to 'nest' themselves in their human environments by fulfilling their perceived obligations. The Italians frequently converted their names into Castilian. However, more than that, this 'nesting' demanded selling products with equal pricing for all, rather than attempting to maximize each transaction. For example, in the spring of 1565 in Cuenca, the Milanese merchant partners Francisco de Anón, younger brother of Juan Pedro, and Tomás Belo sold woad from Toulouse and cattle hides from the 'Indies', obtained in Seville, for a standard price for each commodity. Moreover, they granted to their customers generous terms for repayment, up to one year (for example, CP0176, ff. 236–236v, 248–248v, 261–261v).

Beginning with a major anti-tax uprising in Toledo in 1449, which transitioned into an assault on Jews and New Christians, certain intellectuals developed a racist ideology. They claimed that conversion to Christianity did nothing to erase the stereotypic faults attributed to all Jews because, despite baptism, their 'blood' carried the corruption (Sicrof 1960; Benito Ruano 1976; Nirenberg 2009; Amrán 2020). By the early 16th century, these racist views dominated Crown official circles, including those of the Inquisition. Just because discriminatory statutes had little impact on Toledo's New Christians (Aranda Pérez 1997) did not mean that viciously racist views were not common among their fellow Christians and could not serve on some occasion as the foundation for violent attacks on them. Nalle (2015) provides a transcription of a song composed by an 'old Christian' jailed by the Inquisition. The text reveals clearly the major reasons for hostility to New Christians, and the 'composition' lumps in the Genoese as equals in evil traits. In the face of this substrate of deep hostility, the possibility of a massacre could not have been far from the nightmares of the denigrated groups, even if the results would not be as horrific as the massacre of 20,000 Chinese in Spanish Manila in 1639 (McCarthy 1970; Kueh 2014).

Women

Women's agency in business

Although the examples often appear scattered, historians have illuminated the presence of businesswomen (for example, Asenjo González 1988; Martín Romera 2009; Establés Susán 2018; Sanz Ayán 2019), including in Milan (Fregulia 2015). When women occupied a position from which they might become the heads of economic enterprises, their families apparently took care to see that they were literate and understood the economic and legal environment in which they would become actors. The results of this education do not show up clearly in the documentation about women's business activities but they are clearer when dealing with an enterprise designed to last a long time, the entailed estate or *mayorazgo* (Clavero 1989; Pérez Picazo 1990). Although the documents establishing such entails provided a detailed succession that favoured males, when there were no male heirs, it fell to a female heir to administer the jurisdiction and property listed in the foundation document. Sometimes, as in the case of the small lordship of Albudeite, 26 km from the city of Murcia, women maintained the entail over a relatively long period of time, either because they did not remarry or their second husband turned out to be incompetent, forcing his wife to oversee affairs in defence of the interests of minor children from the first marriage (Méndez Apenela 2009). Once a woman was widowed, she could administer her affairs without relying on a male to license her agency (Bouzada Gil 1997; Birriel Salcedo 2008; García-Prieto 2016; Marchant Rivera and Barco Cebrián 2017). Although I have found no study of Spanish women's involvement in clandestine economic activities, Montenach (2020) has produced a rich body of work on French female smugglers from the late 17th century until the Revolution.

Apparently, Dr Valencia never grasped that women participated in the clandestine economic activities for which he arrested males. However, in the documents identified in Toledo as a result of searching for the male merchant-smugglers, women can be seen interacting economically with them. For example, Dr Valencia tried Francisco de Madrid y de Herrera, one of the smugglers from Toledo who was arrested on the frontier. On 30 January 1566, María de San Pedro, the widow of Martín Alonso de Madrid, appeared in the court of Diego Ortiz de Ángulo, a municipal justice (*alcalde ordinario*) of Toledo. She wished to take advantage of a provision of the general partnership that had existed between her late husband and Francisco de Madrid y de Herrera, his brother, and with Juan Bautista de Herrera, the son of Francisco. When their company was established, the parties agreed that if one of the men were to die, his widow could become part of the company, if she wished. As usually happened, the three merchants did not register with a notary the formation of their general partnership. However, they prepared a document for themselves in which they included the clause about surviving widows. The partners agreed that the company would last for four years. The notary included this unregistered document, agreed to on 22 May 1565 and ratified on 9 October 1565, when Martín Alonso de Madrid was alive to sign it, as an appendix to the record of the proceedings before the municipal justice (TP01532, ff. 520–522v).

Two things should be noted. First, María de San Pedro represented herself without the assistance of any man and the justice accepted this representation. Second, the three original partners thought any of their wives had the background necessary to assume a partnership in the company. Before the justice, María de San Pedro accepted partnership in the company which, she said, would be a great benefit to her minor children, for whom she asked to be declared guardian, and to her. She offered to provide testimony to support her request. On her behalf, three businessmen (Diego de Palma, Gonzalo de la Palma, and Juan de San Pedro Sotelo, father of Payo Sotelo, one of those arrested by Dr Valencia, all vecinos of Toledo) gave their testimony under oath to acknowledge her guardianship of her minor children with Martín Alonso and the deal among the company's three partners to permit entrance into the partnership of any of their widows. Although there was nothing unusual about her request to serve as the guardian of her minor children, no-one who participated in the proceedings found anything unusual about having a woman join an existing general partnership company. On 6 February, the justice granted the two petitions of María de San Pedro (TP01532, ff. 515–517). On the same day, Francisco de Madrid y de Herrera and Juan Bautista de Herrera accepted María de San Pedro as a partner, waving explicitly the laws which might have prevented her participation because she was a woman (TP01532, ff. 518–519).

Marriage contracts and wives: dowry, arras; protection of part of the capital in marriage in the face of the bankruptcy or the seizure of a husband's property due to a criminal charge

Historians often consider the dowry and groom's *arras* (pledge to the bride) payments in a marriage contract as a means to secure a socially acceptable husband or perhaps as something done to elevate the social status of the bride's family. However, merchants' families clearly considered such expenditures as a component of their economic strategies, especially if they were smugglers. Although the husband would administer these resources, they belonged ultimately to the wife, who could protect from creditors and judicial institutions, including the Inquisition, her interest, and those of her minor children in the event of a disaster (Sperling 2004).

Of course, some marriages arranged by a merchant family might involve an obvious attempt to secure a higher social status. One example of this kind involves the marriage of Don Pedro Bazán to Doña Petronila de la Fuente. Although Bazán does not appear wealthy, he held an *encomienda* (jurisdiction for his maintenance) of the Military Order of Santiago, which required of those admitted to membership that they be of 'pure blood' (not descended from any Jewish or Muslim ancestor) and be free of any commercial background (Salazar Acha 2013). For a family of New Christians, such as that of Doña Petronila, a marriage to someone who wore the tunic of Santiago clearly took all of them a step away from their ancestry. However, Don Pedro's *encomienda* consisted entirely of places in the Kingdoms of Aragon and Valencia, perhaps useful bases for smugglers moving goods through those polities.

To obtain these benefits of increased status and useful smuggling bases, the De la Fuente family combined resources on 2 May 1565. This group effort included Doña Petronila's parents, Pedro de la Fuente and Teresa de la Fuente, and her brothers Ldo. Hernán Pérez de la Fuente (a future *regidor* of Toledo), Diego Pérez de la Fuente, and Francisco de la Fuente. Another brother, Rodrigo de la Fuente, had married and was no longer subordinated to paternal authority. Juan de la Fuente, the arrested smuggler, was not mentioned. As a collective entity, all the named De la Fuentes agreed to pay a huge dowry, some of which Doña Petronila would use to unencumber Don Pedro's entail of sizable accumulated debts. Don Pedro pledged a decent amount to his bride, some of which would come from financial gains made in coming years. Don Hernando de Bazán, a cathedral canon in Toledo and Don Pedro's brother or father, would sustain Don Pedro's commitment to the agreement, and because the cathedral chapter limited its membership to those of 'pure blood', the De la Fuente family gained more support for their emergence from New Christian status (TP01529, ff. 782–787, 1047–1054v; TP01530, ff. 403–406v; TP01534, ff. 1491–1492; TP01935, ff. 781–786, 845v).

Although there are many examples of women who used their property right to their dowry and *arras* (and half of any financial gain during the period she was married), the bankruptcy arrests of Juan Ángel Cernúsculo, one of the wealthiest Milanese merchants in Castile at the time, his wife, Doña Catalina Cernúsculo, and their business partner Doña María de Victoria produced a complicated series of actions by Doña Catalina, the twists and turns of which are fascinating but too complicated for discussion here. Her agency in the crisis of their general partnership started with the use of some of her property to secure a bond from other merchants (discussed earlier). However, the big payoff for having a large dowry and other property came when she asked the royal Council of Castile for protection of her rights. Specifically, she petitioned to stop the auction of her husband's property because some of the items included by the alcalde mayor, Dr Gago de Castro, belonged to her, and the royal council accepted her petition on 30 July 1567 and blocked the sale (Sello, July 1567, f. 806). When the lawsuit of another group of creditors had reached the point where Dr Gago de Castro would auction the property of Juan Ángelo, Doña Catalina, and another partner, Lorencio Cernúsculo, the three again blocked the sale, this time with an order of 5 December 1567 from to the royal council to take testimony in Toledo for proceedings before the superior royal appeals tribunal (*Chancillería*) of Valladolid (Sello, Dec. #2 1567, f. 590).

A mother's property rights to her dowry and *arras* could even protect her children from being despoiled by the creditors of her husband after her death. In Toledo, on 20 September 1565, Hernando de Hurtado, son of Hernando Hurtado and his deceased wife, María Ortiz, appeared before municipal judge (*alcalde ordinario*) Juan de Arce, using authority delegated by the corregidor. The son appeared on his own behalf and that of two brothers and three sisters. Creditors had sued the father to get payment of his debts, but the first satisfaction remained that the father pay to the six children of María Ortiz, the amount of her dowry, *arras*, and paraphernalia and inherited property. The son's petition, prepared by an attorney, requested that the judge question witnesses about the matter (TP01530, ff. 980–984v). I do not know the result, or if the petition served to preserve property which could be used to keep the father and some of the children in business, which was a likely family goal.

Widows' agency in business management

On 7 August 1565, Teresa de San Pedro, vecina of Toledo, arranged an accounting of what was owed to various parties as a result of the death of her husband Francisco Sánchez de Cisneros. He had a general partnership with Hernando Álvarez de Cisneros, also deceased, and the company was continued by Guiomar de la Fuente, Hernando's wife, and by the jurados Alonso de Cisneros and Juan de Cisneros, their sons. Apparently, the two women decided to dissolve the partnership and separate their respective interests. As an example of how confusing the names make efforts to spot relatives: Teresa provided support for the marriage of her daughter Beatriz de Cisneros to Juan de la Torre Ortiz and for that of her daughter María de Herrera to Juan Sánchez Ortiz. Also, Teresa took some property from the company when Diego de Cisneros became engaged to Elvira de Herrera, daughter of jurado Pedro López de Cisneros (TP01530, ff. 477–481).

As widows, women were often revealed as significant business leaders, something that got hidden behind the actions of their late husbands. For example, in Madrid, 10 July 1565, the Treasury Council ordered Francisco de Águilar, vecino of Toledo and farmer of royal taxes on livestock, to appear or have his solicitor appear before royal chief accountants (*contadores mayores*) and the justices (*oidores*) of the council to respond to an appeal of a judgement by a commissioned investigating judge looking into payment of these taxes. That judge had sentenced Mari González, widow of

Pascual Villareal and vecina of Albacete, to the loss of 700 sheep she grazed in the jurisdiction of the city of Chinchilla (Sello, July 1565, f. 829). The economically dominant people, men and women, in this part of the Marquisate of Villena and Kingdom of Murcia were the large-scale livestock owners (Lemeunier 1992; 2002). González was clearly one of them because if these 700 sheep were all the animals she possessed, she would not have had the resources to carry an appeal to the Treasury Council in Madrid.

Transfer of property to others

Final testaments provide the best examples of a woman's ability to transfer property. On 30 May 1566, María de San Pedro, widow of jurado Alonso Álvarez, willed that her slaves be freed, either immediately after her death or after a period of service to some relative she named. Many of these slaves were among the four sons and two daughters of her slave Juana de la Fuente, and María de San Pedro dedicated six clauses to the futures of these slaves (TP00015, ff. 344–345v).

Perhaps less noteworthy by our standards, but still interesting as an example of a woman transferring property because her husband was alive, is the will of Catalina Suárez, wife of the merchant Juan López. She left money to her father and several other people, including a girl who had been helping her, but the major transfer occurred when she took advantage of the inheritance law to increase the share of her estate for two of her daughters. She asked her husband to place the daughters in a convent until they were old enough to *tomar estado* (marry or become nuns). With this major transfer to her daughters, she names as her other heirs her three sons (TP00015, ff. 242–243v).

Finally, an undated testament of 1566 returns us to the example of the marriage of Doña Petronila de la Fuente and Don Pedro Bazán of the Military Order of Santiago. Ldo. Hernán Pérez de la Fuente was one of Doña Petronila's brothers who contributed to her dowry. His wife was Doña Francisca de Ponte, who fell ill and made her will, giving us a clear example of a woman transferring a substantial amount of property (TP01789, ff. 254–257v). She left a large sum – 12,400 ducados – to a niece to help her enter a convent or to marry, and to her brother, Hernán Ruiz, she left a principal house, which had belonged to her grandparents and parents. Hernán's daughter with Doña Mariana Téllez, Doña Francisca de Ponte, would receive 1000 ducados for her dowry or to enter a convent. Hernán and his wife were to receive all of Doña Francisca's jewels and she provided substantial support to her mother, to be assisted by her brother. Doña Francisca (the testator) had two sisters who were nuns in different convents, Doña Juana and Doña Isabel, to whom she left bequests of 50 ducados each, and she made bequests to other nuns, who do not seem to have been relatives. Nice bequests were made to her five female and three male servants and to a male servant who had served her uncle. One of her male servants was to receive 100 ducados. However, the big expenditure was the establishment of a perpetual chaplaincy in her parish church, for which her first husband, Bartolomé Conejo, had also left some money, and she arranged to complete other bequests by Conejo. For whatever was left after all the clauses in the will had been fulfilled, her husband Ldo. Hernán Pérez was her heir.

Agency in economic and judicial initiatives

Of course, women's actions discussed above could easily have been placed here. Membrado (2019) provides a comprehensive examination of the agency of women in Ávila at the end of the 15th century, along '[m]últiples frentes de batalla'. However, several women from Murcia in the mid-1560s showed great courage in pursuing lawsuits against the Inquisition tribunal of the Bishopric of Cartagena (with its see in Murcia), so steeped in racism that, until checked by the Supreme Council in Madrid, it had been ordering people killed and devastating the lives of others on the basis of clearly unreliable testimony and the extensive use of torture. For these years, the Sello section, which serves as a documentary basis for much of this chapter, contains many documents related to these initiatives by women, who often won. Their victories required determination. One example, involving Murcia's merchant community, will serve for all.

In Madrid, on 27 November 1567, the Supreme Council of the Inquisition issued its sentence favorable to Francisca Hernández, the wife of Pedro Hernández, the chief notary of Murcia's Civic Council, in her attempt to recover property seized by Murcia's tribunal upon the arrest of her father, Francisco Algazí, burned at the stake in 1562. This favorable judgment also encompassed Luis and Lorenzo Algazí and Catalina Hernández, children of Francisco Algazí, and of Beatriz López, his first wife, and Francisco, Sebastián, and Jerónima Algazí, his minor children with Luisa Garri, his second wife (Sello, Nov. 1567, f. 909). Francisco Algazí and his son Diego Algazí were prominent New Christian merchants condemned in 1562 by Murcia's Inquisition tribunal to death and to life in prison respectively for practicing Judaism (García Servet 1978; Blázquez Miguel 1987). The successful plaintiffs had claimed a portion of the seized property because it formed part of the dowries, *arras*, and halves of the gains of their mothers, wives of Francisco Algazí. Their triumph built on an earlier judgment of 17 October 1566, which was favorable to them (Sello, Oct. 1566, f. 812). Furthermore, on 5 November 1566, Ana de Medina received a favorable judgment in her attempt to recover her property, which had been confiscated with those of her husband, Diego Algazí, and the executed Francisco Algazí. At issue in this lawsuit were some of the latter's houses in the parish of Santa Catalina, and in addition to the Inquisition, she demanded the return from Ginés Sancho, public notary, who had purchased them, as well as other houses that had belonged to Diego Algazí, because they formed part of her dowry and her half of the economic gains of the couple (Sello, Nov. 1566, f. 743). Through dogged determination, these women recovered substantial property, with which those thus rewarded could shape their economic futures.

Violence against women and the royal Council of Castile

Sadly, violence against women remains a deplorable reality, and it could be used in the 16th century to harm the ability of women to conduct their business affairs or shape their family life (De la Pascua Sánchez 2002; Feci and Schettini 2017). Although the first of such cases discussed in this section involves members of the territorial aristocracy, it reveals an attitude on the part of some men that they could abuse their wives violently to obtain property that belonged by law to the women.

While searching for examples of violence used to discipline the actors in clandestine economic networks, a shocking case popped up. On 11 November 1566, the Council of Castile (Sello, Nov. 1566, f. 191), from Madrid, ordered Don Diego de Zúñiga, Toledo's corregidor, to intervene in a case of an abused wife. The Mariscal of Castile, Don Juan de Ribadeneiva, vecino of Toledo, was badly abusing his wife, Doña Francisca de Silva, even to the point of confining her in the fortress of Caudilla, where her husband gave her nothing to eat and forced her to sleep on the floor without any sort of bed. She was confined so strictly that she presumed that he wanted to kill her, as he had said. The Council ordered Zúñiga to go to the fortress himself with the staff of royal justice, without giving the job to anyone else, and remove Doña Francisca. The corregidor was ordered to take her to Toledo and arrange to house her in either the Convent of Madre de Dios or the Convent of Santa Isabel. The Council ordered the mother superior and the nuns of the selected convent to allow her to stay until other arrangements were made.

It appears that the Mariscal became abusive as his precarious financial situation deteriorated. In Toledo, 20 June 1565, he registered a series of powers of attorney, first to his father-in-law, Don Hernando de Silva, and his wife, both residents of Toledo, to request of the Crown that he be permitted to sell some of the property of his entailed estate. Immediately following, he empowered his father-in-law and wife to administer his property and issued an additional document ratifying these powers of attorney. Then, he registered an additional power of attorney that included two solicitors to handle the judicial work at Court, as well as before the Council and the superior appeals tribunals (*Chancillerías*) (TP01530, ff. 3–8).

Perhaps if the Crown did not give him the permission he sought, he could have resorted to pressuring his wife to surrender part of her dowry for sale. Earlier, something similar happened to Doña Teresa de Zúñiga, Duchess of Béjar, when she initially refused her consent for the sale of property she had inherited from her mother. Without enough resources to continue his defence against lawsuits of Córdoba and Toledo, the Duke of Béjar would have lost almost all the property he brought to the marriage. The Duke locked the Duchess in isolation to force her to relent and she claimed later that she feared he would have killed her if she protested the treatment and sale of the property (Owens 2005a: 140 and n. 61). Because she did not protest, she received from the Council of Castile, in Valladolid on 7 February 1545, the requested permission to sell parts of her entailed estate (Sello, Feb. 1545, f. 328).

Doña Francisca de Silva subsequently sued the Mariscal for divorce but she saw the proceedings before the vicar of Toledo, as the ecclesiastical judge, bog down. Worse, the vicar had excommunicated parties to the lawsuit. She petitioned the Council of Castile to order the trial sent elsewhere and the councillors obliged by telling the vicar, and any other justices who had intervened, to send all documents to the Chancillería of Valladolid within 15 days of receiving the order. Within 80 days the vicar had to lift all excommunications (Sello, Dec. 1567, f. 157).

Although I was searching for evidence about any use of force to compel obedience within the clandestine smuggling networks, this spectacular case prompted an examination of documents related to violence against women within the Marquisate of Villena. The Council of Castile appeared willing to receive petitions about the abuse of women within this huge royal lordship, as though the protection of women formed part of the responsibilities of the monarch as the seigneurial lord of the Marquisate. However, the councillors also responded to crimes that took place in the region outside of the Marquisate.

One example among many will show the royal council's concern about the use of threats to interfere with a woman's freedom to create and carry out her economic and social strategies. From Madrid, on 9 November 1566, the royal council sent an order to the governor of the Marquisate of Villena (whose powers were like those of a corregidor but over a much larger territory), whose residence was the town of San Clemente. Catalina García, the widow of Miguel de Herreros, vecina of San Clemente, filed a criminal complaint against Dr Herreros, Miguel Sainz Herreros the Elder, regidor Sancho López de los Herreros, Francisco de los Herreros, Bach. Alonso Ruiz de Villamediana, and others included in the complaint. Her solicitor described her as a principal person, honorable, rich, of good life and fame, honest, and sheltered. This group became great enemies of Catalina because she would not give her legitimate, unmarried daughter, Inés de Alarcón, who had more than 12,000 ducados for her dowry, in marriage to Ldo. Ramírez, nephew of Dr Herreros. Because of her refusal, the group subjected Catalina to all sorts of abuse, attempting to destroy Catalina and defame her daughter, including the posting of malignant notices in the town's public places. She characterized her tormentors as men who were accustomed to intimidating others. The royal council listed all the claimed harassment in the order, telling the governor to investigate and try anyone found guilty. He had to submit a report within 15 days of receiving the command (Sello, Nov. #1 1566, f. 638). The day before, the royal council sent another order from Madrid to the governor in response to a complaint from Hernán Vázquez de Haro, vecino of San Clemente, about the same group. Vázquez de Haro had recently served as a municipal judge (*alcalde ordinario*) and during his term of office, he had tried the accused and some of their relatives. In response, the Herreros and others defamed him and his family, including in libelous notices posted publicly at night. The councillors ordered the governor, without delegating responsibility to anyone else, to investigate the charges, arrest and jail those who appeared guilty, and punish them, sending his report within 15 days of receiving the royal letter (Sello, Nov. #2, f. 694). Clearly, the Council of Castile was in no mood to tolerate the attempt by a gang of prominent people to intimidate their fellow citizens, including women, with impunity.

Such intimidation could end in violence. From Madrid, on 10 June 1565, the royal council acted on a complaint by Gil de Manés, who was a vecino of both the town of

Jorquera, just west of Alcalá del Río, and the city of Chinchilla. Manés told how the previous April, Damián de Luna Rubia and Miguel Jiménez, vecinos of both Jorquera and the town of Albacete, and others, up to 15 total and armed, attacked him in his house in the village of Latoz, jurisdiction of Jorquera, while he was ill. Against his wishes and those of a woman in the house, Juana de Onrrubia, the men seized her, rolled her up in some clothing and other things, put her over a horse, and took her where they wanted. The clear implication is that she was raped. Moreover, they stole a good horse from Manés. The Council of Castile, in the king's name and under his seal, ordered the alcalde mayor of Jorquera to capture the delinquents, including in Albacete or any other jurisdictions where they might be found (Sello, June 1565, f. 152). In this case, the superior authority of the Crown of Castile made it clear that the monarch would not tolerate violence against women. However, much of the violence and intimidation of women likely involved spouses, and because of marriage's sacramental character, such case went to an ecclesiastical court, leaving royal officials in the dark about such attacks.

Seeing women requires different models?

In 1989, a clandestine Jewish community in the town of Belmonte, Portugal, officially announced their presence, which had been continuous since King Manuel, in 1497, ordered all Jews either to leave the domains of the Crown of Portugal or convert to Christianity. One notable aspect of the Belmonte community was that women exercised authority (Huerga Criado 1994; García 1999; Canelo 2001). Gitlitz (2002) has demonstrated that the clandestine Jewish communities he has studied often adopted practices which deviated from those elsewhere. King Manuel intentionally permitted Jews to depart only through Lisbon, with limitations on what property they could take. Even though there were ample ports in the more densely populated north of Portugal, including Porto, Jews there had little choice but to convert if they wanted to escape destitution (Soyer 2007; 2008; Poutrin 2015).

Nalle has done a great deal of research using the personal narratives required by Cuenca's inquisitors of anyone they detained and examined (for example, 2017). She brought to my attention the file of a Portuguese New Christian, Joseph Enrriquez de Acosta (as the Inquisition's notary recorded the spelling) who was arrested in Villanueva de la Jara in 1680, in the Marquisate of Villena, where Dr Valencia had conducted some of his investigations in 1565. Nalle was struck by Joseph's extraordinary memory and the details he provided about his family members and their activities. A possible pattern emerged from the points of information in this dossier.

Joseph was a tobacconist within the Crown's monopoly, living in San Clemente. The Inquisition charged him with judaizing, but his case was suspended without explanation. He was born in Guimarães, Portugal, in 1652, to Anna Henriquez and Henrique Mendes de Acosta, Anna's second husband. She was born in 1620 and in 1633, married Manuel Lopes Pardo, of the town of Covilha (modern Covilhã), considerably south of Guimarães, in the Bishopric of Guarda. Manuel maintained a store and took commissions from others and in other places to buy requested merchandise to send to his clients. He died in 1640. Perhaps because Anna married so young, her first two children, both girls, were born dead. It was not until the birth of Beatriz at the end of 1636 (baptised on 1 January 1637) that she started to bare living children, and a lot of them. The second, Ysabel, was born in 1638 and married eventually another man from Covilha, Belchior Rodrigues Rios, who died in 1708, leaving a testament with useful family information. Understandably, clandestine Jewish groups, if small, might have trouble finding marriage partners locally and, therefore, interacted with similar groups in other towns. I was attracted to their activities and felt that there might be a form of economic organization headed by the mother as the central family authority, Anna Henriquez, until her death.

While Anna, and possibly some of her daughters, appeared to anchor the family in Guimarães, the male children all took positions elsewhere, some of them moving frequently to take other posts. Keep in mind that, from 1640, Portugal was waging a war of independence against the Hispanic Monarchy, which ended successfully for the Crown of Portugal with the Treaty of Lisbon in 1688. The eldest male for which I have a record was João Lopes Pardo; born in 1639, he was described as an 'administrador de los puertos', perhaps some of Portugal's 'dry ports' with Castile and Galicia. The second son, Manuel de Quiros, born in 1640, assisted his brother, returned to Guimarães to handle the government monopoly on tobacco and aguardiente, before establishing himself in the port of Corunna to handle English and French goods for four years. After that, he went to Madrid for three years. The third son, Gaspar Henriquez, born in 1648, worked with his brother Manuel in Corunna before administering a customs port, which Manuel had started, in Miranda do Duero, on the Portuguese border near Zamora. Following that experience, he went to Madrid and then to San Clemente. The fourth brother, Duarte Rodrigues Nuñes, born in 1650, assisted the customs administration in Ponte da Barca, at the border with Galicia, but after three or four years, he returned to Guimarães and did not leave again, except to visit his brother in Corunna and a trip to Madrid and San Clemente to buy saffron. Thomas Enriquez ended life badly. Born in 1654, he had to leave Guimarães while still young because he was implicated in a murder. He stayed with his brother in Ponte da Barca, conveniently near the border with Galicia should he have to flee. He continued his brief journey to Miranda do Douro and Monçao, on the border with the Galician town of Salvaterra de Miño only 12 km away. His year of adventures ended when he died in Castel Branco, south of Guarda and only 50 km from the town of Covilhã.

Joseph Enrriquez left his mother's home when he was about 15 or 16, when he was called to Lisbon by his brother Miguel, for whom I found no records in Guimarães, and after two or three months, he joined his brother Manuel, who had 'farmed' the customs posts for Alentejo and Algarve in the south of Portugal. Joseph returned to Lisbon for some work, until he was called home by his mother when Thomas was accused of murder. He remained in Guimarães, except for trips to Braga and Porto.

He wanted to journey to Corunna to see his brothers there but he was never able to go. About 1678, after his mother's death, he left Guimarães for Madrid to see Manuel, who was seeking the post of 'farmer' of the sales tax. From there, he went to San Clemente to see his brother Gaspar. At some point, he also went to Ponte da Barca to see his brother Duarte.

I do not have enough information about this family to judge what its members were doing. In addition to the Inquisition file provided by Nalle, my other information comes from the Arquivo Municipal Alfredo Pimenta (AMAP) of Guimarães from the birth, marriage, and death records of the Parish of São Sebastião. There I met Rui Faria, a doctoral student in history at the Universidade do Minho, who served as a research assistant for a project, directed by Norberta Amorim, Professora Catedrática of that university. Faria kindly introduced me to a digital database project in which they are digitising all surviving parish registers. The project is known as NEPS (Núcleo de Estudos de População e Sociedade), which is now part of the program of CITCEM (Centro de Investigação Transdisciplinar 'Cultura, Espaço e Memória' [http://www.ghp.ics.uminho.pt]). With so much information about individuals and families, one could apply different models of people's activities in a digital exploration to see if the Belmonte model of female authority would guide us to other clandestine Jewish groups, which did not survive into the 20th century, and particularly ones in which women formed the base of commercial operations, which could have extended to overseas domains of the Crown of Portugal and to northern Europe.

Of course, the frequent proximity of the males to places along the border suggests a possible tie to smuggling (Escobedo 2003). However, I would like to suggest that if we have a different model of a women's involvement in a *self-organizing trading network*, we might see opportunities for interesting research when this variant model points toward a different type of activity, including in a trading diaspora.

Acknowledgements and/or funding sources

The author expresses his gratitude to multiple fundings sources, which directed their support to this study of 16th century smuggling or to related issues. The major direct support came from consecutive fellowships from the U.S. National Endowment for the Humanities (NEH; 2004–2005) and the John Simon Guggenheim Memorial Foundation (2005–2006). As an outcome of the latter, Owens created and co-coordinated the multi-national, multi-disciplinary project 'Dynamic Complexity of Cooperation-Based Self-Organizing Commercial Networks in the First Global Age' [DynCoopNet] as part of the European Science Foundation's EUROCORES (European Collaborative Research) Scheme programme 'The Evolution of Cooperation and Trading' (TECT). Owens's leadership and research were supported by the U.S. National Science Foundation [NSF] (Grant No. SES-0740345 [$394,000; 2007–2010]). In order to improve the DynCoopNet technical supports, specifically database management systems [DBMS], geographical information systems [GIS], Semantic Web technologies, and social network analysis

[SNA], Owens created, with experts in these technology fields, an NSF-funded multidisciplinary project 'Understanding Social Networks within Complex, Nonlinear Systems: Geographically-Integrated History and Dynamics GIS [SOCNET]' (Grants No. 0941371 [$1,290.704; lead project Principal Investigator Dr J.B. Owens, Idaho State University] and No. 0941501 [$471,193; Principal Investigator Dr May Yuan, University of Oklahoma (now University of Texas, Dallas)], for a total award of $1,761,897 [2009–2013; extended to 2014].

References and bibliography

Maps

The two maps for this chapter were created by Anderson Sidles, MA in Historical Resources Management, MS in Geographic Information Systems, Owens's former research assistant at Idaho State University, now of Seattle, Washington, USA. Because we wished to have map data that corresponds to the 16th century, especially for territorial boundaries and the locations of municipalities and rivers, we selected as our primary source a map from 1802 (in its second edition from 1810), prepared by Tomás López de Vargas Machuca (1730–1802). This map is online with the list number 11510.011, and the short title, *Composite map: A-D. Mapa General de España*, as part of the David Rumsey Historical Map Collection, https://www.davidrumsey.com/home [Accessed 30 September 2020]. The base map was georeferenced to modern coordinates so that contemporary data could be used to position municipalities. However, the two maps are not survey-grade quality and are provided only to help readers orient themselves to places mentioned in this chapter.

Abbreviations

Because the coronavirus pandemic shuttered library services, this chapter was created on the basis of a large collection of archival documents. To avoid distracting the reader by complicated citations, the following system is used to cite the few documents found to be essential for discussing the practices of the men and women who participated in clandestine commercial activities.

In Spain's *Archivo General de Simancas* (AGS), near Valladolid, the collection used is known as the *Registro General del Sello*, which is the repository for copies of documents issued under the seal of the monarch, as though he himself had sent it, by entities such as the Council of Castile, the Treasury Council, or the Supreme Council of the Inquisition. There is not yet an index of the years covered by this chapter. The documents are ordered by year and month. The bundle for some months has been divided in two because the original bundle was so large. Regardless of its length, each document is given a folio number. Therefore, the citations in this chapter follow this form:

Sello, month (+ number if two bundles) year, folio number

Other citations from Simancas collections give the complete name.

The other type of document heavily used in this chapter is the notarial registry, known as a *protocolo*. The parts of the collection used are cared for by two archives: the *Archivo Histórico Provincial de Cuenca* and the *Archivo Histórico Provincial de Toledo.* The citations follow the same pattern, differing only in a letter to indicate to which archive the register belongs.

For Cuenca: CP [for Cuenca Protocolo] a four-digit number for the register [for example: 0176], followed by a folio number or a range of folios. Because folios were numbered only on one side, the letter 'v' [*verso*] is employed to indicate the reverse side [for example, ff. 253–253v].

For Toledo: TP [for Toledo Protocolo] a four-digit number for the register, followed by a folio number or a range of folios.

Other abbreviations

Bach.	*Bachiller*, the first university degree
Dr	*Doctor*, in this chapter, usually a doctorate in Law
Ldo.	*Licenciado*, the second university degree
NR	*Nueva Recopilación*, a legal collection (see below for the version used)

Alexander, J.C. (1988). *Action and Its Environments: Toward a new synthesis.* New York: Columbia University Press.

Amrán, R. (2020). Cristianos nuevos y viejos tras las rebeliones toledanas de 1449: Juan II de Castilla y el 'perdón real'. *eHumanista/Conversos* 8, 245–253.

Aranda Pérez, F.J. (1992a). *Poder municipal y cabildo de jurados en la edad moderna (Siglos XV-XVIII).* Toledo: Ayuntamiento.

Aranda Pérez, F.J. (1992b). Los mercaderes de Toledo en el seiscientos: bases económicas y status sociopolítico. *Investigaciones históricas: Época moderna y contemporánea* 12, 71–96.

Aranda Pérez, F.J. (1997). Judeo-conversos y poder municipal en Toledo en la Edad Moderna: una discriminación poco efectiva. In: Mestre, A., Fernández Albaladejo, P. and Giménez López, E. (eds) *Disidencias y exilios en la España moderna: Actas de la IV Reunión Científica de la Asociación Española de Historia Moderna. Alicante. 27-30 de mayo de 1996*, Vol. 2. Alicante: Universidad de Alicante, 155–168.

Asenjo González, M. (1988). Participación de las mujeres en las compañías comerciales castellanas a fines de la Edad Media: los mercaderes segovianos. In: Segura Graíño, C. and Muñoz Fernández, Á. (eds) *El trabajo de las mujeres en la Edad Media hispana. V jornadas de investigación interdisciplinaria sobre la mujer*. Madrid: Asociación cultural Al-Mudayna, 223–234.

Aslanian, S.D. (2011). *From the Indian Ocean to the Mediterranean: The Global Trade Networks of Armenian Merchants from New Julfa.* Berkeley CA: University of California Press.

Ballard, R. (2005). Coalitions of reciprocity and the maintenance of financial integrity within informal value transmission systems: The operational dynamics of contemporary hawala networks. *Journal of Banking Regulation* 6(4), 319–352.

Barkey, K. and Parikh, S. (1991). Comparative perspectives on the state. *Annual Review of Sociology* 17, 523–529.

Battigalli, P. and Maggi, G. (2002). Rigidity, discretion, and the costs of writing contracts. *American Economic Review* 92(4), 798–817.

Bejarano Rubio, A. and Molina, A.L. (1989). *Las ordenanzas municipales de Chinchilla en el siglo XV*. Murcia: Academia Alfonso X el Sabio, Universidad de Murcia.
Benito Ruano, E. (1976). *Los orígenes del problema converso*. Barcelona: Ediciones El Albir.
Birriel Salcedo, M.M. (2008). El cónyuge supérstite en el Derecho hispano. *Chronica Nova* 34, 13–44.
Blázquez Miguel, J. (1987). Catálogo de los procesos inquisitoriales del Tribunal del Santo Oficio de Murcia. *Murgetana* 74, 5–109.
Bouzada Gil, M.T. (1997). El privilegio de las viudas en el Derecho castellano. *Cuadernos de Historia del Derecho* 4, 203–224.
Burgin, M. and Cárdenas-García, J.F. (2020). A dialogue concerning the essence and role of information in the world system. *Information* 11(9), 406 [https://doi:10.3390/info11090406] accessed 28 September 2020.
Calafat, G. (2011/2). Familles, réseaux et confiance dans l'économie de l'époque moderne: diasporas marchandes et commerce interculturel. *Annales. Histoire, Sciences Sociales* 66, 513–531.
Canelo, A.D. (2001). *Os últimos criptojudeus em Portugal* (2nd edition). Belmonte: Câmara Municipal de Belmonte.
Cárdenas-García, J.F. and Ireland, T. (2020). Bateson information revisited: a new paradigm. *Proceedings* 47(1): 5 [https://doi.org/10.3390/proceedings2020047005] accessed 28 September 2020.
Caro Baroja, J. (1978). *Las formas complejas de la vida religiosa: religión, sociedad y carácter en la España de los siglos XVI y XVII*. Madrid: Akal.
Carrilero Martínez, R. (1997). *Ordenanzas de Albacete del siglo XVI: Edición crítica y estudio documental*. Albacete: Instituto de Estudios Albacetenses.
Casado Alonso, H. (2003). *El triunfo de Mercurio: La presencia castellana en Europa (siglos XV y XVI)*. Burgos: Cajacírculo.
Casado Alonso, H. (2013). El papel de las colonias mercantiles castellanas en el Imperio hispánico (siglos XV y XVI). In: Ruiz Ibáñez, J.J. (ed.) *Las vecinidades de las Monarquías Ibéricas*. Madrid: Fondo de Cultura Económica, 355–374.
Chacón Jiménez, F. (ed.) (2000). *Censo de población de 1533: Reino de Murcia*. Murcia: Universidad de Murcia.
Chang, P. (1991). The first Chinese diaspora in Southeast Asia. In: Ptak, R. and Rothermund, D. (eds) *Emporia, Commodities and Entrepreneurs in Asian Maritime Trade, c. 1400–1750*. Stuttgart: Steiner, 14–19.
Chaudhuri, S. (2005). Trading networks in a traditional diaspora: Armenians in India, *c.* 1600–1800. In: McCabe, I.B., Harlaftis, G. and Minoghou, I.P. (eds) *Diaspora Entrepreneurial Networks: Four centuries of history*. Oxford: Berg, 51–72.
Clavero, B. (1989) [1974]. *Mayorazgo: propiedad feudal en Castilla, 1369–1836* (2nd edition). Madrid: Siglo XXI de España.
Clemente, A. (2018). Il racconto del mercato globale e la crisi della storicità. Sul ritorno della storia económica. *Storica* 72, 7–52.
Corral García, E. (1988). *Ordenanzas de los concejos castellanos: Formación, contenido y manifestaciones (s. XIII–XVIII)*. Burgos: Gráficos Diario de Burgos.
Court, R. (2004). *Januensis ergo mercator*: Trust and enforcement in the business correspondence of the Brignole family. *Sixteenth Century Journal* 35(4), 987–1003.
Court, R. (2014). *De fatigationibus*: what a merchant's errant son can teach us about the dynamics of trust. In: Biorci, G. and Court, R. (eds) *Il registro di lettere di Giovanni Francesco di Negro (1563–1565): Regole e prospettive di un mondo non clamoroso*. Novi Ligure: Città del silenzio, 49–130.
Court, R. (2018). *Honore et utile*: the approaches and the practice of sixteenth-century Genoese merchant custom. In: Pihlajamäki, H., Cordes, A., Dauchy, S. and De Ruysscher, D. (eds) *Understanding*

the Sources of Early Modern and Modern Commercial Law: Courts, statutes, contracts, and legal scholarship. Leiden: Brill Nijhoff, 55–86.

Cox, A. (2005). What are communities of practice? A comparative review of four seminal works. *Journal of Information Science* 31(6), 527–540.

Crivelli, B. (2017). *Commercio e finanza in un impero globale. Mercanti milanesi nella Penisola Iberica (1570–1610).* Rome: Edizioni di Storia e Letteratura.

Curtin, P.D. (1984). *Cross-Cultural Trade in World History.* Cambridge: Cambridge University Press.

Dale, S.F. (2002). *Indian Merchants and Eurasian Trade, 1600–1750.* Cambridge: Cambridge University Press.

De la Pascua Sánchez, M.J. (2002). Violencia y familia en la España del Antiguo Régimen. *Estudis* 28, 77–100.

Doria, G. (1986). Conoscenza del mercato e sistema informativo: il 'know-how' dei mercanti-finanzieri genovesi nei secoli XVI e XVII. In: De Maddalena, A. and Kellenbenz, H. eds *La repubblica internazionale del denaro tra XV e XVII secolo.* Bologna: Il Mulino, 57–121.

Escobedo, R. (2003). Sospechosos habituales: contrabando de tabaco y comerciantes extranjeros en los puertos españoles. In: Villar García, M.B. and Pezzi Cristóbal, P. (eds) *Los Extranjeros en la España Moderna. Actas del I Coloquio Internacional, Celebrado en Málaga del 28 al 30 de Noviembre de 2002*, Vol. 1. Málaga: Portadilla, 313–323.

Establés Susán, S. (2018). *Diccionario de mujeres impresoras y libreras de España e Iberoamérica entre los siglos XV y XVIII.* Zaragoza: Universidad de Zaragoza.

Feci, S. and Schettini, L. (2017). Storia e uso pubblico della violenza contro le donne. In: Feci, S. and Schettini, L. (eds) *La violenza contro le donne nella storia. Contesti, linguaggi, politiche del diritto (secoli XV–XXI).* Rome: Viella, 7–41.

Fortea Pérez, J.I. (1990). *Monarquía y Cortes en la Corona de Castilla: Las ciudades ante la política fiscal de Felipe II.* Salamanca: Cortes de Castilla y León.

Fregulia, J.M. (2015). Stories worth telling: women as business owners and investors in early modern Milan. *Early Modern Women* 10(1), 122–130.

García, M.A. (1999). *Judaísmo no Feminino: Tradição popular e ortodoxis em Belmonte.* Lisbon: Universidad Nova de Lisboa.

García Martínez, S. (1977). *Bandolerismo, piratería y control de moriscos en Valencia durante el Reinado de Felipe II.* Valencia: Universidad de Valencia.

García-Prieto, E. (2016). La gestión femenina del patrimonio nobiliar. Doña Teresa de Saavedra y Zúñiga, condesa de Villalonso: una aristócrata en los reinados de Felipe II y Felipe III. *Cuadernos de Historia Moderna* 41(1), 109–128.

García Servet, J. (1978). *El humanista Cascales y la Inquisición murciana.* Madrid: José Porrúa Turanzas.

Garés Timor, V.M. (2015). Antella, Tous y Sumacàrcer: una encrucijada del comercio y el contrabando entre los reinos de Valencia y Castilla. In: Iglesias Rodríguez, J.J., Pérez García, R.M. and Fernández Chaves, M.F. (eds) *Comercio y Cultura en la Edad Moderna.* Seville: Universidad de Sevilla, 1069–1082.

Gherardi, S. (2012). Why do practices change and why do they persist? Models of explanation. In: Hager, P., Lee, A. and Reich, A. (eds) *Practice, Learning and Change: Practice-Theory Perspectives on Professional Learning.* Dordrecht: Springer, 217–231.

Girón Pascual, R.M. (2018). *Comercio y poder: mercaderes genoveses en el sureste de Castilla durante los siglos XVI y XVII (1550–1700).* Valladolid: Universidad de Valladolid.

Gitlitz, D.M. (2002). *Secrecy and Deceit: The religion of the Crypto-Jews.* Albuquerque NM: University of New Mexico Press.

Gneezy, U. and Rustichini, A. (2000). A fine is a price. *Journal of Legal Studies* 29, 1–17.

González Arce, J.D. (ed.) (2000). *Ordenanzas de la Ciudad de Murcia (1536).* Murcia: Universidad de Murcia.

Habib, I. (1971). The system of bills of exchange ('Hundis') in the Mughal Empire. *Proceedings of the Indian History Congress* 33, 290–303.

Haj-Mohamadi, P., Fles, E.H. and Shteynberg, G. (2018). When can sharing attention increase affiliation? On the bonding effects of co-experienced belief affirmation. *Journal of Experimental Social Psychology* 75, 103–106.

Haken, H. (1983). *Advanced Synergetics: Instability Hierarchies of Self-Organizing Systems and Devices.* Berlin: Springer.

Herrero Sánchez, M. (2017). The business relations, identities and political resources of Italian merchants in the early-modern Spanish monarchy. In: Brilli, C. and Herrero Sánchez, M. (eds) *Italian Merchants in the Early-Modern Spanish Monarchy. Business Relations, Identities and Political Resources.* London & New York: Routledge, 1–12.

Hildreth, P. and Kimble, C. (2004). *Knowledge Networks: Innovation through communities of practice.* Hershey PA: Idea Group.

Huerga Criado, P. (1994). *En la raya de Portugal: Solidaridad y tensiones en la comunidad judeoconversa.* Salamanca: Universidad de Salamanca.

Israel, J.I. (2002). *Diasporas within a Diaspora: Jews, Crypto-Jews, and the world of maritime empires (1540–1740).* Leiden: Brill.

Jiménez Zamora, I. (2016). La actuación política de la Emperatriz Isabel (1528–1538). *Espacio, Tiempo y Forma* 29, 163–185.

Kamen, H. (1997). *Philip of Spain.* New Haven & London: Yale University Press.

Kueh, J.E.S. (2014). The Manila Chinese: Community, Trade and Empire, *c.* 1570–*c.* 1770. Unpublished Ph.D thesis, Georgetown University.

Ladányi, É. and Kobolka, I. (2014). The Hawala system. *Interdisciplinary Management Research* 10, 413–420. [http://www.efos.unios.hr/repec/osi/journl/PDF/InterdisciplinaryManagementResearchX/IMR10a30.pd0]. Accessed 25/09/2020.

Ladero Quesada, M.Á. (1998). Las ordenanzas locales: siglos XIII a XVIII. *En la España Medieval* 21, 293–337.

Lamikiz, X. (2017). Social capital, networks and trust in early modern long-distance trade: a critical appraisal. In: Herrero Sánchez, M. and Kaps, K. (eds) *Merchants and Trade Networks in the Atlantic and the Mediterranean, 1550–1800: Connectors of commercial maritime systems.* London: Routledge, 39–61.

Landes, D.S. (1998). *The Wealth and Poverty of Nations: Why some are so rich and some so poor.* New York: W.W. Norton.

Lapeyre, H. (1981). *El comercio exterior de Castilla a través de las aduanas de Felipe II.* Valladolid: Universidad de Valladolid.

Lascaux, A. (2015). Crowding out trust in the informal monetary relationships: the curious case of the Hawala system. *Forum for Social Economics* 44(1), 87–107.

Lemeunier, G. (1976). La Part de Dieu: Recherches sur la levée des dimes au Diocése de Carthagène-Murcie d'après les visitas des Tercias (XVIII–XIX). *Melanges de la Casa de* Velázquez 12, 357–386.

Lemeunier, G. (1977). Les 'Extremeños', ceux qui viennent de loin: contribution à l' étude de la trashumance ovine dans l' Etat Castillan (XVI–XIX siècles). *Melanges de la Casa de Velázquez* 13, 321–360.

Lemeunier, G. (1982). Las ordenanzas municipales de Calasparra (1583–1622). *Áreas: Revista internacional de ciencias sociales* 2, 179–206.

Lemeunier, G. (1992). Concejos, Hermandades et Mesta: l'organisation de la dépaissance en Murcie au début de l'Époque Moderne. *Melanges de la Casa de Velázquez* 28(2), 175–186.

Lemeunier, G. (2002). La organización del espacio ganadero en la España mediterránea, siglos XVI–XVIII. In: Muñoz Buendía, A. and Díaz López, J.P. (eds) *Herbajes, trashumantes y estantes: la ganadería en la Península Ibérica (épocas medieval y moderna).* Almería: Instituto de Estudios Almerienses, 83–90.

Lemeunier, G. and Rodríguez Llopis, M. (eds) (1983) 1713. *Ordenanzas de Lorca* [1713]. Murcia: Academia Alfonso X El Sabio.
Levi, S. (2007). Multanis and Shikarpuris: Indian diasporas in historical perspective. In: Oonk, G. (ed.) *Global Indian Diasporas: Exploring trajectories of migration and theory*. Amsterdam: University of Amsterdam, 31–65.
Macaulay, S. (1963). Non-contractual relations in business: a preliminary study. *American Sociological Review* 28(1), 55–67.
Marchant Rivera, A. and Barco Cebrián, L. (2017). Participation of women in the notarial public deed of the 16th century: from the constriction of the marital licence to the fullness of widowhood. *European Scientific Journal* 13(11), 1–17. [http://dx.doi.org/10.19044/esj.2017.v13n11p1]. Accessed 25/09/2020.
Marcos Martín, A. (2017). Las ferias de Medina del Campo después de la crisis financiera de 1575–1577. In: Casado Alonso, H. (ed.) *Simón Ruiz y el mundo de los negocios en Europa en los siglos XVI y XVII*. Valladolid: Universidad de Valladolid, 167–193.
Martin, M. (2009). Hundi/Hawala: the problem of definition. *Modern Asian Studies* 43(4), 909–937.
Martín Gamero, A. (ed.) (1858). *Ordenanzas para el buen régimen y gobierno de la muy noble, muy leal é imperial ciudad de Toledo*. Toledo: José de Cea.
Martín Romera, M.A. (2009). Mujeres de mercaderes, *mujeres mercaderes*: testimonios de iniciativas femeninas en el ámbito comercial a finales del siglo XV. *La España Medieval* 32, 273–296.
Martz, L. (2003). *A Network of Converso Families in Early Modern Toledo: Assimilating a minority*. Ann Arbor MI: University of Michigan Press.
McCabe, I.B. (2005). Global trading ambitions in diaspora: The Armenians and their Eurasian silk trade, 1530–1750. In: McCabe, I.B., Harlaftis, G. and Minoghou, I.P. (eds) *Diaspora Entrepreneurial Networks: Four centuries of history*. Oxford: Berg, 27–50.
McCarthy, C.J. (1970). Slaughter of Sangleys in 1639. *Philippine Studies* 18(3), 659–667.
McCloskey, D.N. (2016). Max U versus Humanomics: a critique of Neo-Institutionalism. *Journal of Institutional Economics* 12, 1–27.
McCloskey, D.N. (2017). Neo-institutionalism is not yet a scientific success: A reply to Barry Weingast, *Scandinavian Economic History Review* 65, 116–123.
McLean, P. and Padgett, J.F. (2004) Obligation, risk, and opportunity in the Renaissance economy: Beyond social embeddedness to network co-constitution. In: Dobbin, F. (ed.) *The Sociology of the Economy*. New York: Russell Sage, 193–227.
Membrado, S. (2019). Múltiples frentes de batalla: estrategias femeninas, patrimonio y justicia. Una aproximación a la agencia de las mujeres de Ávila en los escenarios judiciales de fines del Siglo XV. *Clio & Crimen* 16, 415–444.
Méndez Apenela, E. (2009). Notas sobre la circulación del señorío de Albudeite. *Murgetana* 120, 9–68.
Mitchell, M. (2009). *Complexity: A guided tour*. Oxford: Oxford University Press.
Montemayor, J. (1996). *Tolède entre fortune et déclin (1530-1640)*. Limoges: Pulim, Presses Universitaires de Limoges.
Montenach, A. (2020). Género, economía ilícita y estrategias de supervivencia: las mujeres y el contrabando en el sureste de Francia en el siglo XVIII. *Historia Social* 96, 79–96.
Moreno García, J.C. (2018). Microhistory. In Grajetzki, W. and Wendrich, W. (eds) *UCLA Encyclopedia of Egyptology*. Los Angeles CA: University of Calfornia-Los Angeles, 1–20. [http://digital2.library.ucla.edu/viewItem.do?ark=21198/zz002kczsg]
Muñoz Navarro, D. (2015). Las dinámicas de cooperación y competencia entre los agentes comerciales de origen italiano en el puerto de Alicante a comienzos del siglo XVII. *Jerónimo Zurita* 90, 113–132.
Nalle, S.T. (1992). *God in La Mancha: Religious Reform and the People of Cuenca, 1500-1650*. Baltimore: Johns Hopkins University Press.

Nalle, S.T. (2015). A forgotten campaign against the conversos of Sigüenza: Pedro Cortés and the Inquisition of Cuenca. In: Ingram, K. and Pulido Serrano, J.I. eds *The Conversos and Moriscos in Late Medieval Spain and Beyond*, Vol. 3, *Displaced Persons*. Leiden: Brill, pp. 6–28.

Nalle, S.T. (2017). Cross and cross again: first-hand accounts of 1492 exiles' return to Castile. In: Kaplan, Y. ed. *Early Modern Ethnic and Religious Communities in Exile*. Newcastle upon Tyne: Cambridge Scholars Publishing, pp. 144–174.

Nirenberg, D, (2009). Was there race before modernity? The example of 'Jewish' blood in late medieval Spain. In: Eliav-Feldon, M., Isaac, B. and Ziegler, J. (eds) *The Origins of Racism in the West*. Leiden: Brill, 232–264.

North, D.C. (1991). Institutions. *Journal of Economic Perspectives* 5(1), 97–112.

North, D.C. (1995). The paradox of the west. In: David, R.W. (ed.) *The Origins of Modern Freedom in the West*. Stanford CA: Stanford University Press, 7–34.

North, D.C. and Thomas, R.P. (1973). *The Rise of the Western World: A new economic history*. Cambridge: Cambridge University Press.

Nueva Recopilación (1982). *Recopilación de las leyes destos reynos hecha por mandado de la Magestad Católica Rey don Felipe Segundo ...* [1640], 3 vols. Valladolid: Editorial Lex Nova [facsimile reprint].

Owens, J.B. (2005a). *'By My Absolute Royal Authority': Justice and the Castilian Commonwealth at the Beginning of the First Global Age*. Rochester NY: University of Rochester Press.

Owens, J.B. (2005b). Smuggling through Spain: A neglected sixteenth-century commercial connection between the Mediterranean and the Atlantic. In: Asociación Española de Historia Económica (Santiago, A Coruña, Vigo, Spain), 15 September 2005, *Proceedings*, B24 [www.usc.es/estaticos/congresos/histec05/b24_owens.pdf.] Accessed 30/09/2020.

Owens, J.B. (2011a). What kind of system is it? The DynCoopNet Project as a tribute to Andre Gunder Frank (1929–2005). In: Mukherjee, R. (ed.) *Networks in the First Global Age 1400–1800*. New Delhi: Primus Books, 3–9.

Owens, J.B. (2011b). Social networks of Milanese merchants in sixteenth-century Castile. In: Mukherjee, R. (ed.) *Networks in the First Global Age 1400–1800*. New Delhi: Primus Books, 199–227.

Owens, J.B. (2012a). Dynamic complexity of cooperation-based self-organizing commercial networks in the First Global Age (DynCoopNet): What's in a name? In: Crespo Solana, A. and Alonso García, D. (eds) *Self-organizing Networks and GIS Tools: Cases of use for the study of trading cooperation (1400–1800)*. Bucharest: Scientific Papers, 25–51.

Owens, J.B. (2012b). Narrating stories about the world system of the First Global Age, 1400–1800. In: Babones, S. and Chase-Dunn, C. (eds) *Routledge International Handbook of World-Systems Analysis: Theory and research*. Abingdon: Routledge, 147–154.

Owens, J.B. and Kantabutra, V. (2020) A research scheme for a world history of the world. *Entremons: UPF Journal of World History* (Universitat Pompeu Fabra, Barcelona) 11, 69–98.

Pardo Molero, J.F. (2010). Le gouvernement du Royaume de Majorque et la régulation de la défense de la Méditerranée occidentale (1500–1550). In: Brogini, A. and Ghazali, M. (eds) *Des marges aux frontières: les puissances et les îles en Méditerranée à l'époque moderne*. Paris: Éditions Classiques Garnier, 121–157.

Pérez Picazo, M.T. (1990). *El Mayorazgo en la historia económica de la región murciana: Expansión, crisis y abolición (s. XVII–XIX)*. Madrid: Ministerio de Agricultura, Pesca y Alimentación.

Phillips, C.R. and Phillips, W.D. Jr. (1997). *Spain's Golden Fleece: Wool production and the wool trade from the Middle Ages to the nineteenth century*. Baltimore MD: Johns Hopkins University Press.

Poutrin, I. (2015). Éradication ou conversion force? Les expulsions ibériques en débat au XVIe siècle. In: Poutrin, I. and Tallon, A. (eds) *Les expulsions de minorités religieuses dans l'Europe des XIIIe–XVIIe siècles*. Pompignac, Fr: Bière, 45–67.

Puu, T. (2003). *Attractors, Bifurcations and Chaos: Non-linear Phenomena in Economics* (2nd edition). Berlin and Heidelberg: Springer.

Reid, A. (2005). Diaspora networks in the Asian maritime world. In: McCabe, I.B., Harlaftis, G. and Mainoglou, I.P. (eds) *Diaspora Entrepreneurial Networks: Four centuries of history*. Oxford: Berg, 353–358.
Revel, J. (1996). Micro-analyse et construction du social. In: Revel, J. (ed.) *Jeux d'échelles: La micro-analyse à l'expérience*. Paris: Gallimard-Seuil, 15–36.
Ringrose, D.R. (1997). La ciudad y su entorno en la Época Moderna. *Manuscrits* 15, 221–245.
Ringrose, D.R. (2018). *Europeans Abroad, 1450–1750*. Lanham MD: Rowman & Littlefield.
Rodríguez de Gracia, H. (2003). Mercaderes y financieros: los genoveses de Toledo entre 1561 y 1621. In: Villar García, M.B. and Pezzi Cristóbal, P. (eds) *Los extranjeros en la España moderna*, tomo I. Málaga: Universidad de Málaga, 597–610.
Rodríguez-Salgado, M.J. (1988). *The Changing Face of Empire: Charles V, Philip II, and Habsburg Authority, 1551–1559*. Cambridge: Cambridge University Press.
Roitman, J.V. (2011). *The Same but Different? Inter-cultural Trade and the Sephardim, 1595–1640*. Leiden-Boston: Brill.
Salazar Acha, J. De (2013). El requisito de la limpieza de sangre en las Ordenes Militares. *Revista de las Ordenes Militares* 7, 41–56.
Salvador Esteban, E. (1972). *La economía valenciana en el siglo XVI (Comercio de importación)*. Valencia: Universidad de Valencia.
Sanz Ayán, C. (2019). Negocio, dinero y mujer: empresarias en la primera época moderna (S. XVI–XVII). *Boletín de la Real Academia de la Historia* 216(2), 149–169.
Sella, D. and Capra, C. (1984). *Il Ducato di Milano dal 1535 al 1796*. Turin: Unione Tipografico-Editrice Torinese.
Shteynberg, G. (2015a). Shared attention at the origin: on the psychological power of descriptive norms. *Journal of Cross-Cultural Psychology*, 1–7. [doi: 10.1177/0022022115600260 jccp.sagepub.com].
Shteynberg, G. (2015b). Shared attention. *Perspectives on Psychological Science* 5, 579–590.
Shteynberg, G. (2018). A collective perspective: shared attention and the mind. *Current Opinion in Psychology* 23, 93–97.
Shteynberg, G. and Galinsky, A.D. (2011). Implicit coordination: sharing goals with similar others intensifies goal pursuit. *Journal of Experimental Social Psychology* 47, 1291–1294.
Shteynberg, G., Hirsh, J.B., Apfelbaum, E.P., Larsen, J.T., Galinsky, A.D. and Roese, N.J. (2014a). Feeling more together: Group attention intensifies emotion. *Emotion* 14, 1102–1114.
Shteynberg, G., Hirsh, J.B., Galinsky, A.D. and Knight, A.P. (2014b). Shared attention increases mood infusion. *Journal of Experimental Psychology: General* 143, 123–130.
Shteynberg, G., Hirsh, J.B., Bentley, R.A. and Garthoff, J. (2020). Shared worlds and shared minds: A theory of collective learning and a psychology of common knowledge. *Psychological Review* 127(5), 918–931.
Sicroff, A. (1960). *Les controversies des statutes de 'pureté de sang' en Espagne du XVe au XVIIe siècle*. Paris: Marcel Didier.
Soyer, F. (2007). *The Persecution of the Jews and Muslims of Portugal: King Manuel I and the end of religious tolerance (1496–7)*. Leiden: Brill.
Soyer, F. (2008). King Manuel I and the expulsion of the Castilian Conversos and Muslims from Portugal in 1497: New perspectives. *Cadernos de Estudos Sefarditas* 8, 33–62.
Sperling, J. (2004). Marriage at the time of the Council of Trent (1560–70): clandestine marriages, kinship prohibitions, and dowry exchange in European comparison. *Journal of Early Modern History* 8(1–2), 67–108.
Sperling, J. (2007). Dowry or inheritance? Kinship, property, and women's agency in Lisbon, Venice, and Florence (1572). *Journal of Early Modern History* 11(3), 197–238.

Straub, V.J., Tsvetkova, M. and Yasseri, T. (2020). The cost of coordination can exceed the benefit of collaboration in performing complex tasks. [https://*arXiv*: 2009.11038v1].

Studnicki-Gizbert, D. (2009). *La Nación* among the nations: Portuguese and other maritime trading diasporas in the Atlantic, sixteenth to eighteenth centuries. In: Kagan, R.L. and Morgan, P.D. (eds) *Atlantic Diasporas: Jews, Conversos, and Crypto-Jews in the age of mercantilism, 1500–1800*. Baltimore MD: Johns Hopkins University Press, 75–98.

Tirole, J. (1999). Incomplete contracts: Where do we stand? *Econometrica* 67(4), 741–781.

Torres Fauaz, A. (2013). L'enquête judiciaire au Moyen Âge: Techniques d'information et forms de communication. Bourgogne XIIe – XIIIe siècles. Communication réalisée dans le cadre de l'atelier doctoral de recherche « Formen mittelältlicher Kommunikation », Institut Historique Allemand, Paris, 10 juillet.

Torres Fontes, J. (1953). La conquista del Marquesado de Villena en el reinado de los Reyes Católicos. *Hispania* 50, 38–151.

Trivellato, F. (2009). *The Familiarity of Strangers: The Sephardic Diaspora, Livorno, and cross-cultural trade in the early modern period*. New Haven CO: Yale University Press.

Ulloa, M. (1977) [1963]. *La Hacienda Real de Castilla en el Reinado de Felipe II* (2nd edition). Madrid: Fundación Universitaria Española.

Vela Santamaría, F.J. (2013–2014). La penetración extranjera en la economía castellana bajo Felipe II: el observatorio sevillano. *Yakka. Revista de Estudios Yeclanos* 20, 433–447.

Venkatesh, S.A. (2008). *Gang Leader for a Day: A rogue sociologist takes to the streets*. London: Penguin Press.

Wenger, E. (1998). *Communities of Practice: Learning, meaning, and identity*. Cambridge: Cambridge University Press.

Wenger, E., McDermott, R. and Snyder, W. (2002). *Communities of Practice: A guide to managing knowledge*. Cambridge MA: Harvard Business School Press.

Wills, J.E. (ed.) (2011). *China and Maritime Europe, 1500–1800: Trade, settlement, diplomacy, and missions*. Cambridge and New York: Cambridge University Press.

Chapter 8

Market performance in the grain market of late medieval Western Europe (*c.* 1300–1650)

Bas van Leeuwen and Robin C.M. Philips

Introduction

Well-functioning markets, defined as having low price volatility, are often considered to be a crucial pre-condition for economic growth as they enhance both specialization and innovation (McMillan 2003; Studer 2008; Baumol 2014). This has led to an extensive literature on the impact of markets on economic development (*e.g.* Jacks *et al.* 2011) with periods of fast economic growth arguably being accompanied by rising market performance.

Yet, various authors have placed question marks at the role of grain markets in calculating market performance. First, there are those studies that, following Polanyi (1944; 1957), argued that ancient markets do not function according to standard economic principles. Yet, whereas some have tried to find a middle way by arguing for the existence of market-types between ancient and modern markets (*e.g.* Bang 2008), other studies have been more favorable towards applying economic concepts like market performance to history (van der Spek *et al.* 2014). Besides scholars doubting the existence of market rules, a second group points out that, even in competitive markets, well performing markets might negatively affect growth. For example, Jacks *et al.* (2011) shows that increased market performance leads to increased economic specialization. This leads in certain regions to the specialization in highly volatile commodity production and, consequently, lower market performance. Likewise, it is argued that, even in well-functioning markets, grain may flow to richer regions thus increasing volatility in the poorer areas (Dijkman and van Leeuwen 2019: 4). Third, yet other authors do not argue for a negative relation but rather claim it is unconnected to growth. For example, Clark (2015) claimed that the effect of market performance on the beginning of sustained economic growth were limited while Bateman (2011) found no evidence of long-run rises in market integration.

Historiography

As discussed above, in the various studies markets are seen as, to a certain extent, 'integrated', 'efficient', or 'performing'. Yet, whereas the first concept looks at trade, and the second one at information, market performance covers the combined effect of storage, market integration through trade, and better institutions on price volatility (Földvári and van Leeuwen 2014: 19–20). This also implies that, in order to obtain proper estimates of market performance, first unrelated, region-specific, factors such as price rises and cropping structure need removing (Földvári and van Leeuwen 2011). Yet, even with these removed, it still includes income and specialization as time-varying factors driving market performance.

Not only do we find various definitions of well-working markets, empirical studies have also presented widely divergent results. Bateman (2011) and Federico (2011) find little evidence for rising market performance in Europe before 1800. Clark (2015) finds high, though stable, market performance up to 1500 in England. Yet, he concludes that, even though in England market performance might be high, institutional and other factors make this not necessarily true for Europe as a whole. For the in-between period, Földvári and van Leeuwen (2011) find that the way in which volatility is estimated often makes it difficult to compare price volatility across regions or over time for two reasons. First, if prices are non-stationary, the variance is inflated. Second, the variance of commodity prices contains information on a number of region- and time-specific factors that are not related to market efficiency. Hence, the popular coefficient of variation and related indicators are not adequate measures of the efficiency of markets and are incomparable across regions. As a solution, we suggest using a conditional heteroscedasticity model to estimate the residual (conditional on region-specific factors) and find slow but gradual integration since 1500.

A third factor causing debates in the literature concerns differences in the causes of increasing market performance they identify. So, is the increase in market integration explained by increasing trade (Jacks 2000), institutions (Clark 2015), or geography (Chilosi *et al.* 2013), whereas the study of Földvári and van Leeuwen (2011) find evidence for a range of these time-varying factors while they remove the region-specific effects from their analysis.

Taking a more long-term and balanced perspective, van Leeuwen *et al.* (2014) trace the increasing market integration back to 300 BC. In this perspective, in particular increased yields improved market performance after the 10th century AD (Persson 1991), whereas a reduction of *c.* 20% in transaction and trade costs removed many barriers to trade (Földvári *et al.* 2011). Yet, during the late medieval period, trade contacts remained relatively limited which, aggravated by urban concentration – increasing trade distance – limited market performance. When, after 1500, transaction and transport costs started to decline, the negative effect of urban concentration diminished (see for a similar evolution in Ancient Greece also Pirngruber in this volume).

A case study: Pre-industrial Europe during 1300–1650

We compile a dataset of grain prices in approximately 60 cities in Austria, France, Germany, Italy, the Low Countries, Spain, and the United Kingdom for the period 1300–1650. For this, we draw on the data of the *Allen-Unger Global Commodity Prices Database* (Allen and Unger 2018). In order to obtain estimates of market performance, we ran a regression, for 50 year periods, on the first difference of the log of the price. In this way, we filtered out both region-specific effects and inflation. We took 1 minus the standard error of the regression as our measure of market performance. That is, the higher the value, the higher market performance.

We report all our observations in Appendix 8.1. Whilst we can only draw from a limited number of observations in the 1300–1400 period, we have a good sample size for the period of 1400–1650. In Table 8.1, we report a sample of our dataset, presenting a set of cities for which we have observations consistently throughout most of the 1300–1650 period. A first observation we can make is that the coefficient of variation declined over time, indicating a strong trend of increasing convergence in the European grain market prices. Here, a small nuance has to be indicated, given the drastic decline in the coefficient of variation during 1400–1450 period, which most probably can be attributed to the different sample size in the benchmark years before. As such, our results affirm the findings of Clark (2015), who found a similar evolution in the grain market of pre-industrial England. In addition, as for regional development, we find that the city of Firenze in Italy ranked consistently lowest in market performance compared to the other cities in Europe. During the 14th and 15th century, the cities in England ranked the highest in market performance, whereas this title was taken over by the city of Amsterdam during the 16th and 17th centuries.

Figures 8.1–8.7 provide a broader view on the regional evolutions of market performance in 50 year periods from 1300 to 1650. During the 14th century

Table 8.1. Values market performance for a selection of cities and coefficient of variation

	Dates	*1300–1350*	*1350–1400*	*1400–1450*	*1450–1500*	*1500–1550*	*1550–1600*	*1600–1650*
Country	*City/region*							
France	Douai	0.60	0.75	0.67	0.57	0.64	0.62	0.73
England	Exeter	0.72	0.71	0.73	0.77	0.61	0.58	0.80
	Southern England	0.67	0.74	0.70	0.79	0.68	0.61	0.79
Low Countries	Lier			0.70	0.72	0.73	0.70	0.71
	Amsterdam				0.65	0.76	0.76	0.88
Italy	Firenze	0.44	0.57	0.71	0.73	0.56	0.70	0.71
	Tuscany	0.67	0.62	0.66	0.69	0.61	0.67	0.78
Coefficient of variation		0.16	0.10	0.03	0.10	0.08	0.07	0.05

Sources: estimates of market performance based on Allen and Unger (2018). For details on methodology, see text.

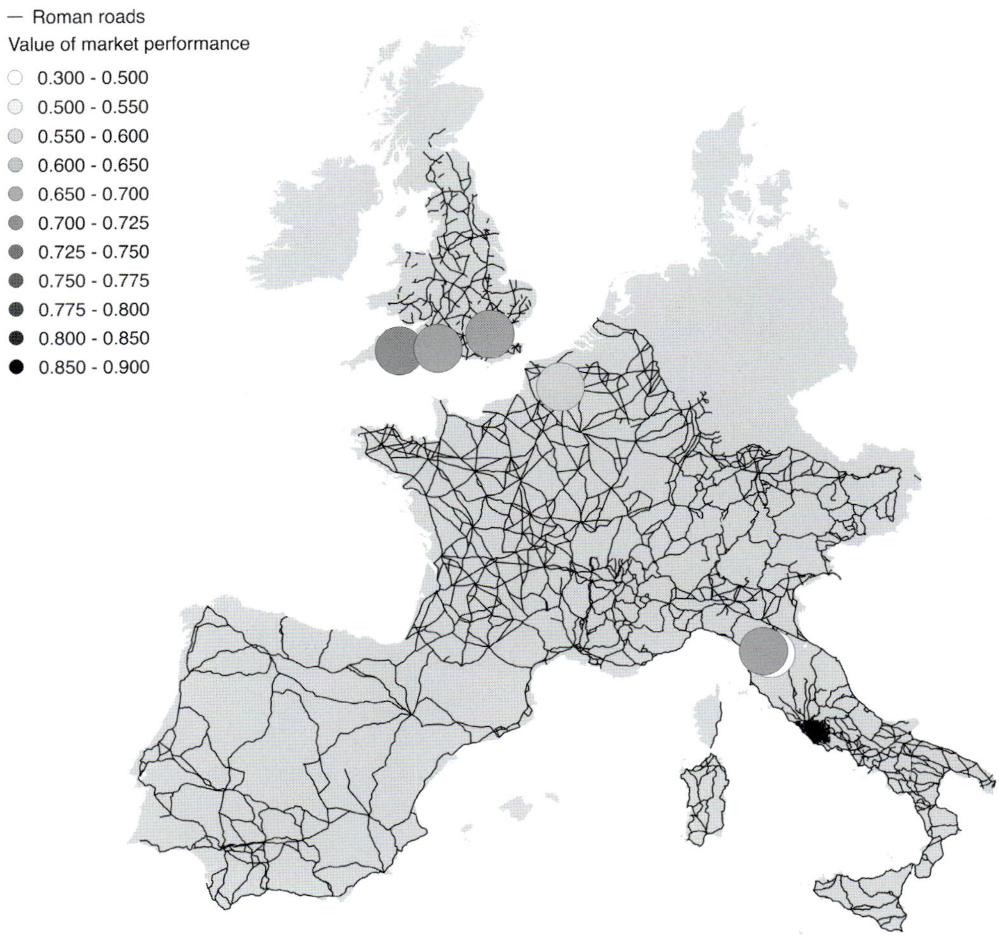

Figure 8.1. Map of market performance in major European cities, 1300–1350. Estimates of market performance based on Allen and Unger (2018). Roman road network derived from McCormick et al. (2013). For details on methodology, see text.

(Figs 8.1 and 8.2) we notice not only a lower market performance in the northern Italian cities compared to the cities in England and the Low Countries, but also an increase of the gap between those regions. During the 15th century (Figs 8.3 and 8.4), this trend of divergence is halted and reversed with a convergence in market performance across the European cities. During this period we not only notice a high market performance in Exeter, London, and southern England, but also the Spanish city of Valencia. During the 16th century (Figs 8.5 and 8.6) and the first half of the 17th (Fig. 8.7), we find a continuation of this process: where the highest market performance can be found in the cities of Valencia and Barcelona in

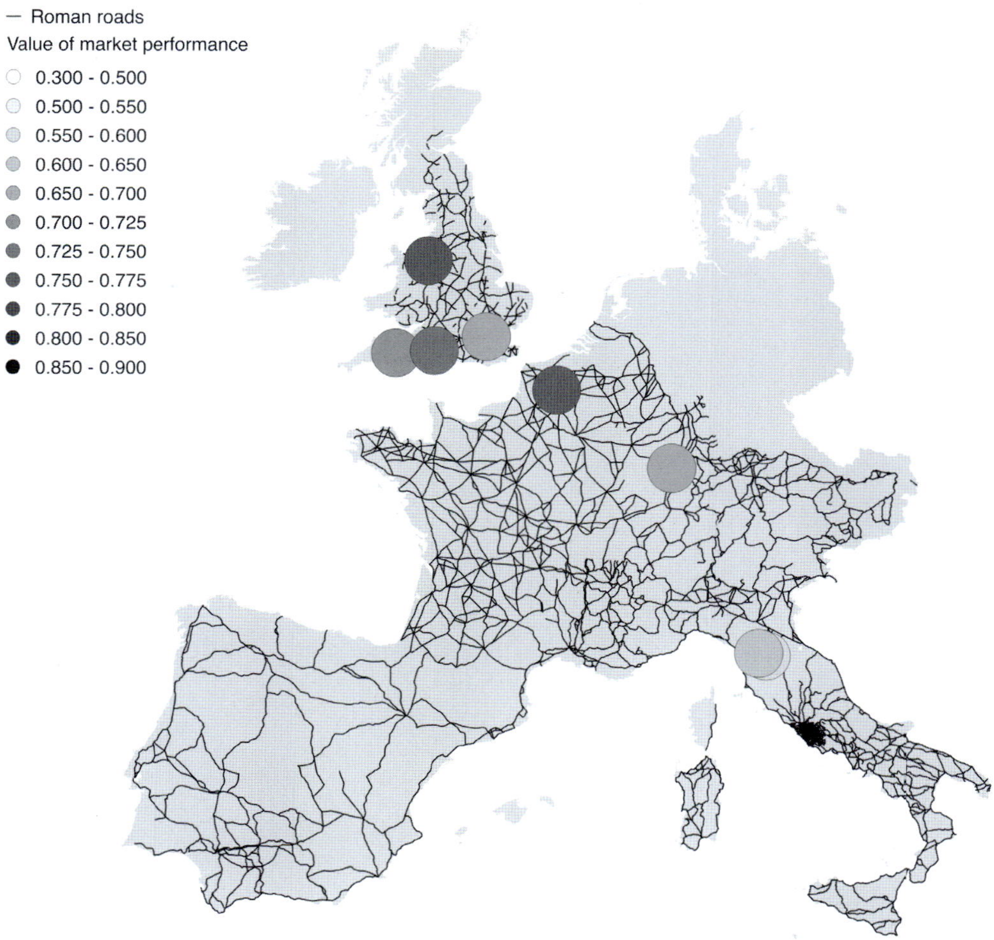

Figure 8.2. Map of market performance in major European cities, 1350–1400. Sources: see Fig. 8.1.

Spain, both with access to the Mediterranean Sea, they competed with the cities of Northwestern Europe, in particular the Netherlands: Leiden and Amsterdam. Conversely, most of the cities in France, Italy, and Germany had a relatively low market performance. So, our estimates are in line with most recent Gross Domestic Product (GDP) reconstructions, which indicate that economic growth accelerated in Northwestern Europe compared to the rest of Europe, causing an economic divergence between these regions from the late medieval period onwards (*e.g.* de Pleijt and van Zanden 2016).

As an investigation into the factors that can explain market performance, we perform on our panel dataset – including the estimates of market performance for all years and regions as a dependent variable – a fixed effect estimation, to control

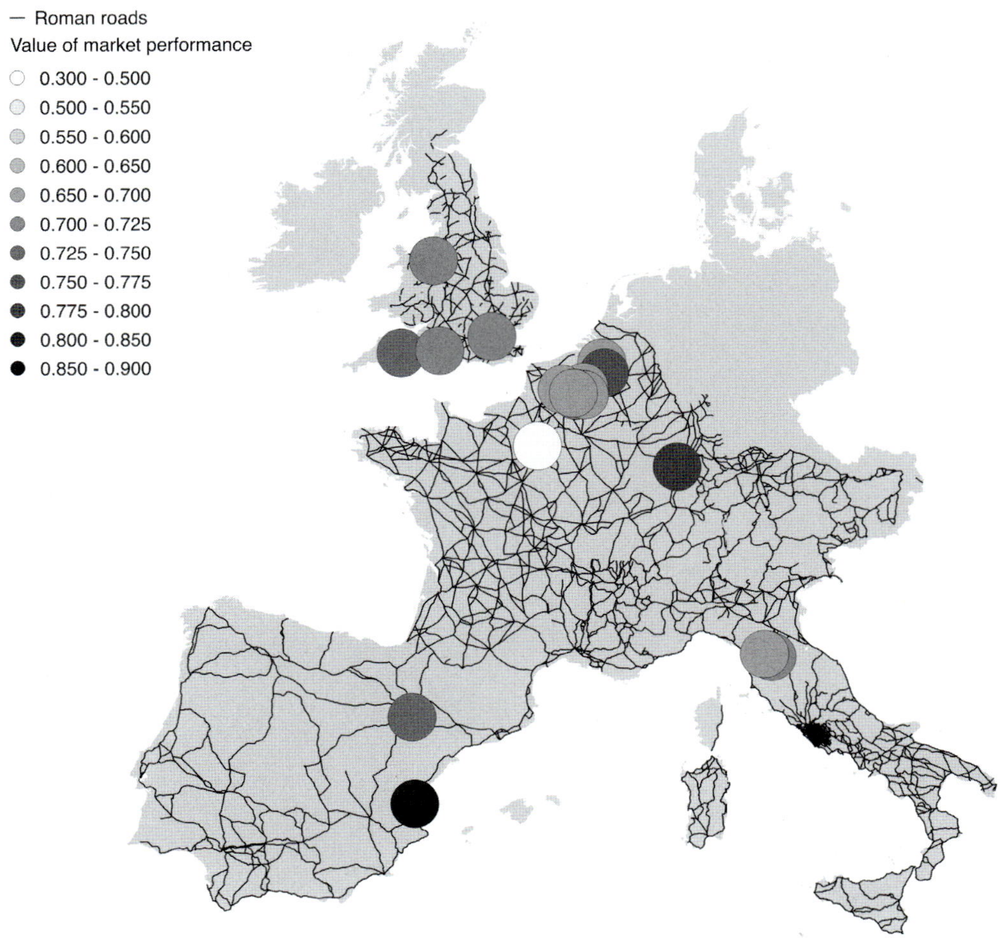

Figure 8.3. Map of market performance in major European cities, 1400–1450. Sources: see Fig. 8.1.

for year-specific effects. We include three explanatory factors. First, we add a spatial lag of the market performance of the cities, by constructing a binary spatial matrix with the distance band set at the smallest maximum distance between spatial units, in line with the construction of spatial regression estimates of Pisati (2001). In other words: we test whether being located in the vicinity of other cities with a high market performance can increase the market performance of the city itself. Second, we introduce a proxy for urbanization by using the estimates of Bosker *et al.* (2013) for all cities in our dataset and using a 3000 population threshold for those cities which could not be found in this database (cities with a population of 5000 or less were excluded from the dataset of Bosker *et al.* 2013). Third, to capture

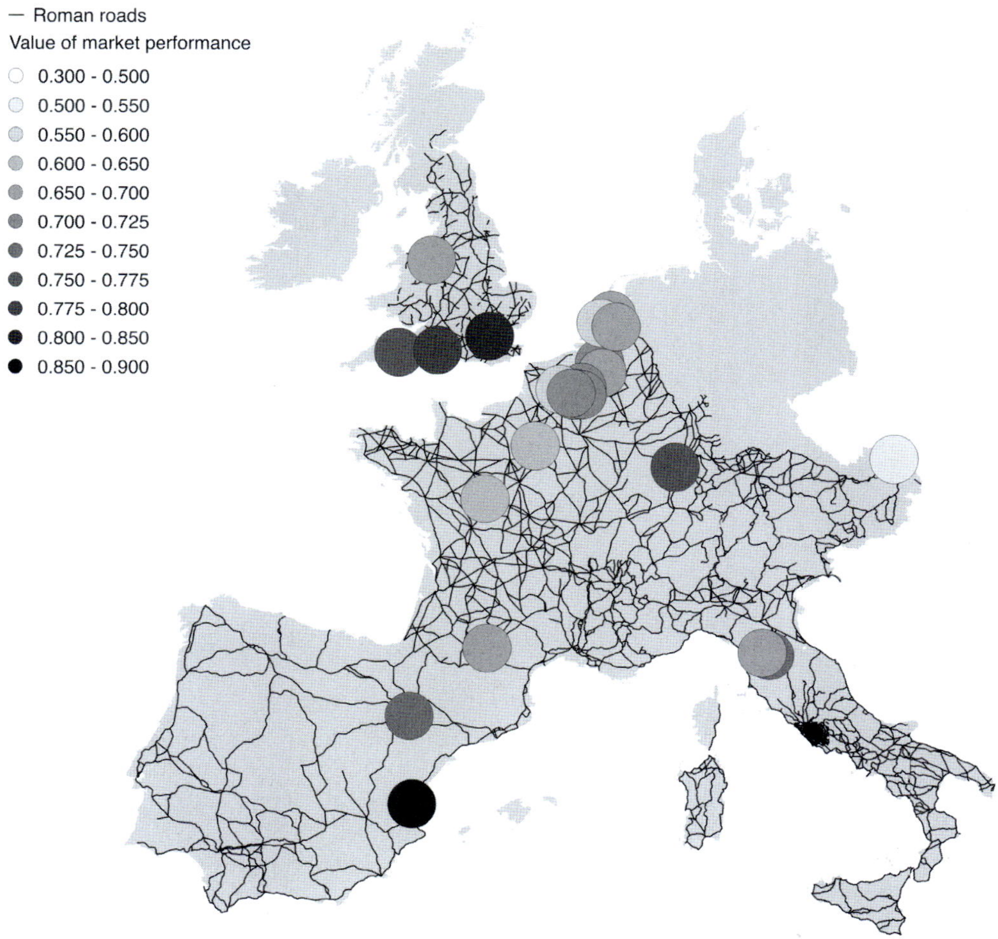

Figure 8.4. Map of market performance in major European cities, 1450–1500. Sources: see Fig. 8.1.

the effect of previous trade networks, we use the Roman road network digitized by McCormick *et al.* (2013), where we use as a proxy the length of the road network in the radius of 100 km from the city.

The results are reported in Table 8.2. We include all observations in column 1. In addition, to explore changes in the effect of the explanatory variables over time, we perform an Ordinary Least Squares (OLS) including only the benchmark years of 1350–1550 in column 2, and only the benchmark years of 1550–1650 in column 3. For 1350–1550, we find that urbanization has a significant negative effect, indicating that particularly small cities had a high market performance and that larger cities – with high levels of specialization and relatively more production in highly volatile

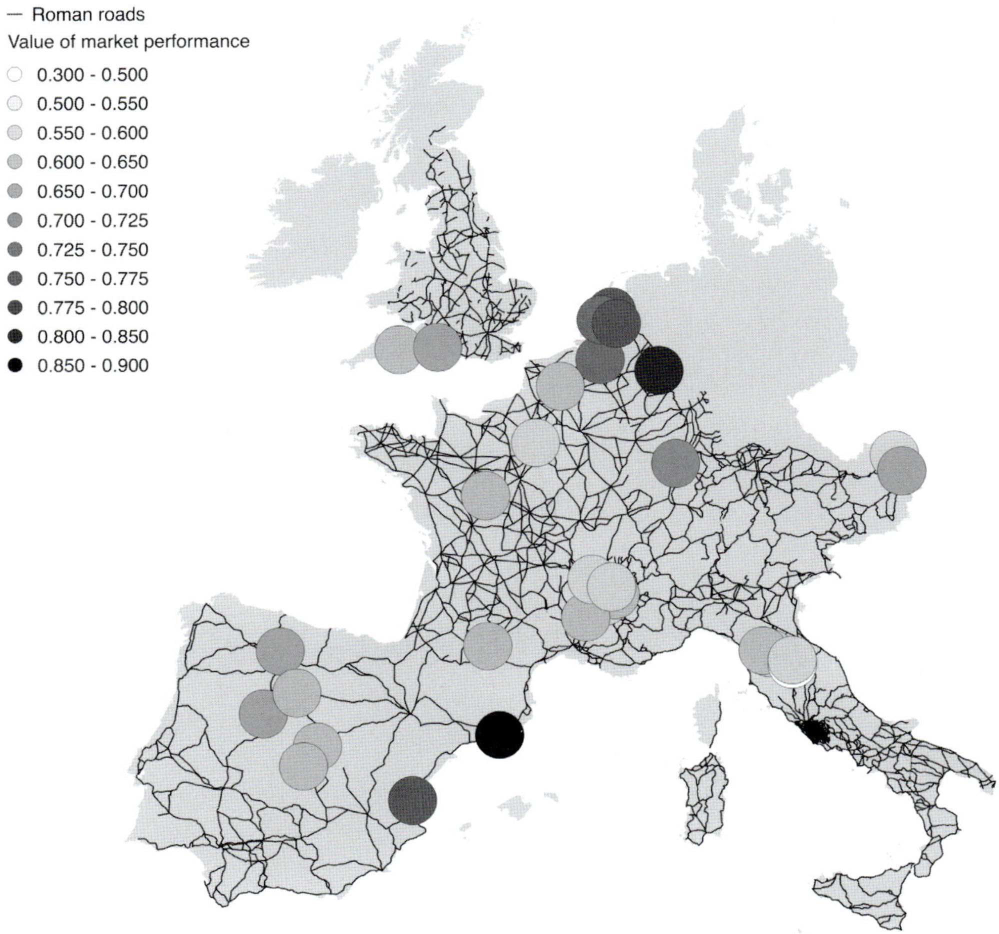

Figure 8.5. Map of market performance in major European cities, 1500–1550. Sources: see Fig. 8.1.

goods – faced high volatility in grain prices, hindering their market performance. Furthermore, we find a significant, positive effect of the spatial lag, whereas the density of the roman roads has a low, but significant, negative effect. For 1550–1650, we find that neither urbanization levels nor roman road density has a significant effect, indicating that the aforementioned difference between small and large cities diminished over time. Yet, also, we find a strong significant effect of the spatial lag. Overall, for the 1350–1650 period, we find that only the spatial lag of market performance can significantly explain the level of market performance in the pre-industrial European cities, indicating the role that economic geography can play in explaining these patterns.

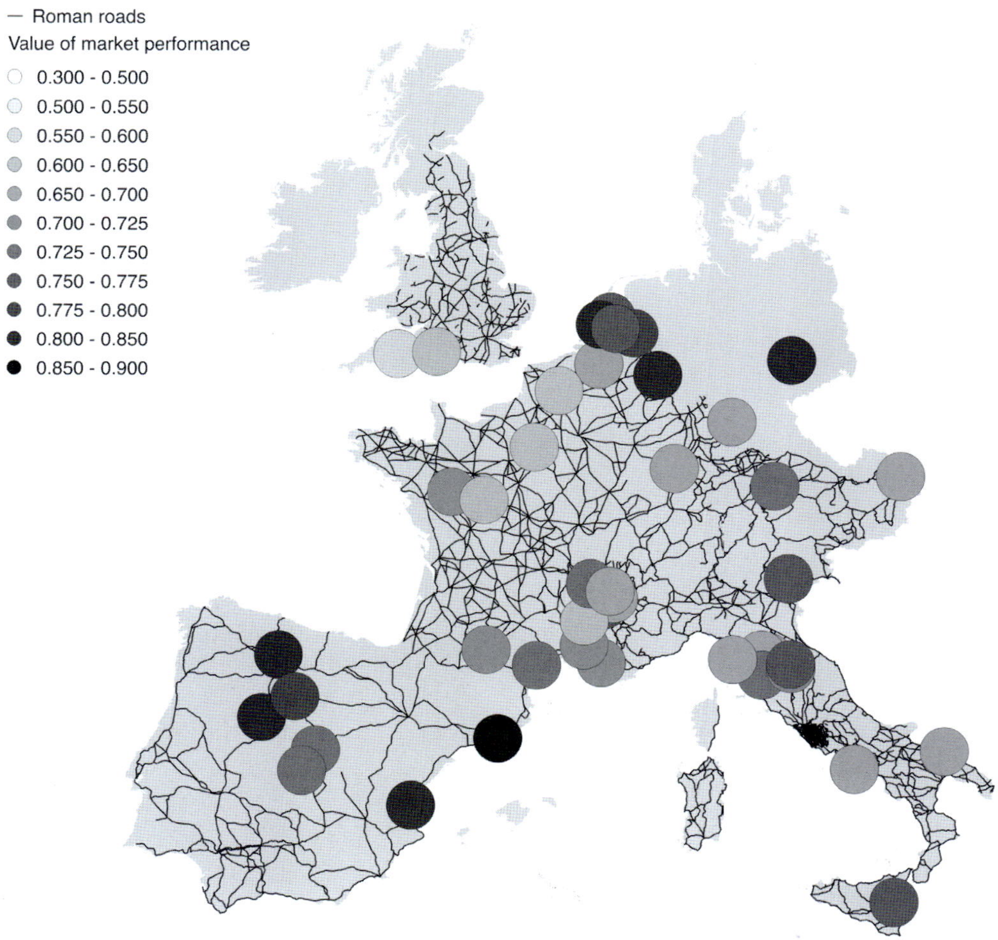

Figure 8.6. Map of market performance in major European cities, 1550–1600. Sources: see Fig. 8.1.

Conclusion

The notion that rising market performance enhances economic growth has been widely accepted. Yet, recent debates have arisen regarding the strength of market integration over time and its main determinants. In this paper, we aimed to provide an overview of the latest empirical studies on the pre-industrial period. Overall, these studies affirm the view that the economic performance of pre-industrial societies has been enhanced by market integration, although authors have debated the scale of market performance and the channels through which market integration was enforced.

Using data from the dataset of Allen and Unger (2018), we offer a contribution to this branch of literature, by measuring the strength of market performance

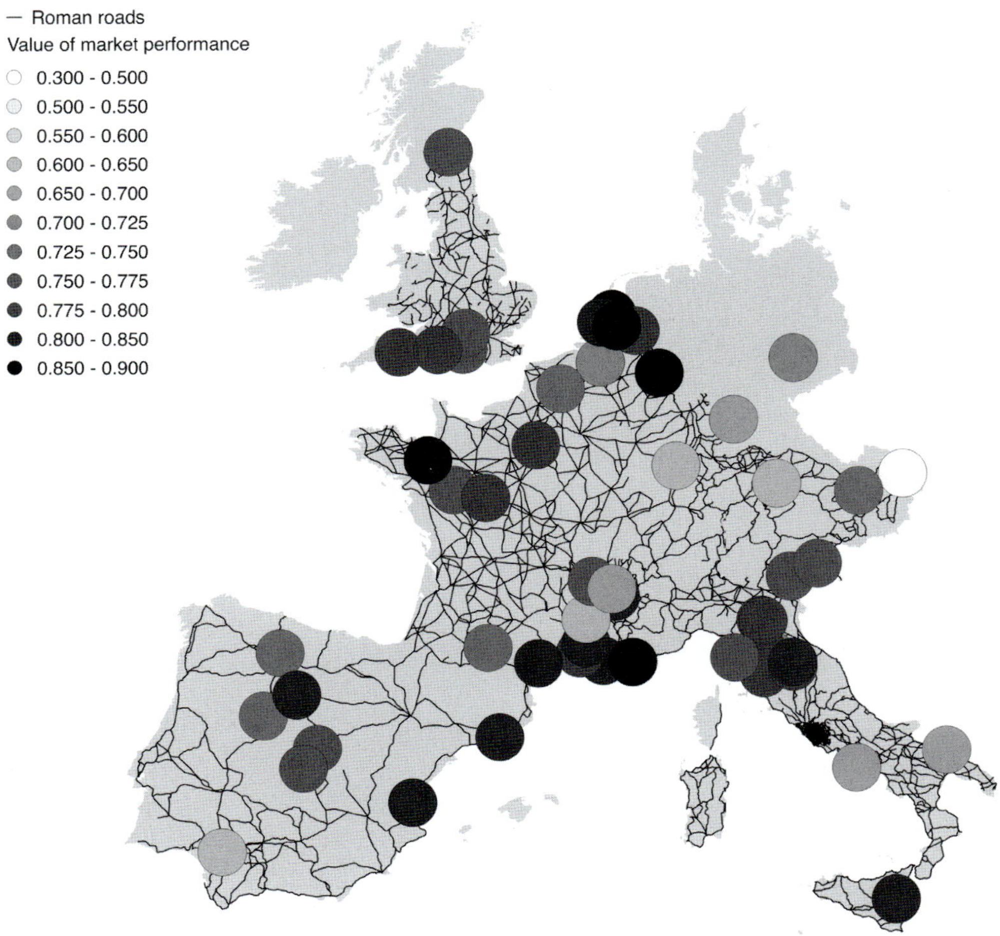

Fig. 8.7: Map of market performance in major European cities, 1600–1650. Sources: see Fig. 8.1.

in various regions of Northern, Southern and Western Europe during 1350–1650. Our findings reveal a gradual but slow increase of market performance during the studied period, whereas the variation in market performance declined. Breaking down our results on a more regional level, market performance improved less in the Italian city-states, whereas highest values were noted in Northwestern Europe – the Low Countries and England – and the Spanish cities along the Mediterranean Sea. To explore the determinants of market performance in these regions, we tested for three effects: a spatial lag of market performance, the density of the Roman road network to control for inland trade, and the urbanization level to control for market potential. In particular, our results revealed a particular role for the first effect, affirming that cities, surrounded by other urban regions with high market

Table 8.2. Fixed-effects estimation to explain market performance (Ordinary Least Squares, OLS)

	(1) OLS all years	(2) OLS 1350–1550	(3) OLS 1550–1650
	dependent variable: market performance		
W Market performance	0.411***	0.443***	0.368***
	(0.0825)	(0.124)	(0.109)
ln Urbanization level	-0.000341**	-0.000591***	-0.000148
	(0.000141)	(0.000192)	(0.000209)
ln Roman road density	-0.249	-0.254**	-0.216
	(0.261)	(0.122)	(0.277)
Constant	0.425***	0.396***	0.475***
	(0.0597)	(0.0868)	(0.0824)
Year-specific effects	yes	yes	yes
Observations	188	89	99
R-squared	0.158	0.259	0.119

Notes: All variables are in logarithm, using ln(x+1), except for values of market performance. The spatial weight matrix (W) of market performance was calculated with the STATA commands for spatial regressions of Pisati (2001), constructing a binary spatial matrix with the distance band set at the smallest maximum distance between spatial units. The asterisks denote significance levels, respectively for *** p<0.01, ** p<0.05, and * p<0.1. Sources: see text.

performance, also featured on average higher levels of market. This hints at the value the economic geography literature could play in this line of historiography.

Bibliography

Allen, R. and, Unger, R. (2018). *The Allen Unger Commodities Dataset.* [https://hdl.handle.net/10622/3SV0BO, IISH Data Collection, V1].

Bang, P.F. (2008). *The Roman Bazaar.* Cambridge: Cambridge University Press.

Bateman, V.N. (2011). The evolution of markets in early modern Europe, 1350–1800: A study of wheat prices. *Economic History Review* 64(2), 447–471.

Baumol, W.J. (2014). *Free-Market Innovation Machine.* Princeton NJ: Princeton University Press.

Bosker, M., Buringh, E. and van Zanden, J.L. (2013). From Baghdad to London: Unraveling urban development in Europe, the Middle East, and North Africa, 800–1800. *Review of Economics and Statistics* 95(4), 1418–1437.

Chilosi, D., Murphy, T.E., Studer, R. and Coşkun Tunçer, A. (2013). Europe's many integrations: Geography and grain markets, 1620–1913. *Explorations in Economic History* 50(1), 46–68. [https://doi.org/10.1016/j.eeh.2012.09.002].

Clark, G. (2015). Markets before economic growth: The grain market of medieval England. *Cliometrica* 9(3), 265–87. [https://doi.org/10.1007/s11698-014-0117-7]

de Pleijt, A. and van Zanden, J.L. (2016). Accounting for the 'Little Divergence': What drove economic growth in pre-industrial Europe, 1300–1800? *European Review of Economic History* 20(4), 387–409.
Dijkman, J. and van Leeuwen, B. (2019). Resilience to famine ca. 600 BC to present. An introduction. In: Dijkman, J. and van Leeuwen, B. (eds) *An Economic History of Famine Resilience.* Abingdon and New York: Routledge, 1–13.
Federico, G. (2011). When did European markets integrate? *European Review of Economic History* 15(1), 93–126. [https://doi.org/10.1017/S1361491610000146]
Földvári, P. and van Leeuwen, B. 2011. What can price volatility tell us about market efficiency? Conditional heteroscedasticity in historical commodity price series. *Cliometrica* 5(2), 165–186. [https://doi.org/10.1007/s11698-010-0055-y.]
Földvári, P. and van Leeuwen, B. (2014). Market performance in early economies: Concepts and empirics, with an application to Babylon. In: van der Speck R.J., van Leeuwen, B. and van Zanden, J.L. (eds) *A History of Market Performance: From Ancient Babylonia to the modern world.* Abingdon and New York: Routledge, 19–44.
Földvári, P., van Leeuwen, B. and van Zanden, J.L. (2011). Long-run patterns in market efficiency and the genesis of the market economy: Markets around the Mediterranean from Nebuchadnezzar to Napoleon (580 BC and 1800 AD). London: CEPR Discussion Paper 8521.
Jacks, D. (2000). Market integration in the North and Baltic Seas, 1500–1800. Economic History Working Paper, London School of Economics and Political Science. [https://econpapers.repec.org/paper/ehlwpaper/22383.htm].
Jacks, D.S., O'Rourke, K.H. and Williamson, J.G. (2011). Commodity price volatility and world market integration since 1700. *Review of Economics and Statistics* 93(3), 800–813. [https://doi.org/10.1162/REST_a_00091].
McCloskey, D.N. and Nash, J. (1984). Corn at interest: The Extent and cost of grain storage in medieval England. *American Economic Review* 74(1), 174–187.
McCormick, M., Huang, G., Zambotti, G. and Lavash, J. (2013). *Roman Road Network* (version 2008). Cambrdige MA: DARMC Scholarly Data Series, Data Contribution Series #2013-5.
McMillan, J. (2003). *Reinventing the Bazaar.* New York: W.W. Norton.
Persson, K.G. (1991). Agrarian productivity in medieval agriculture: Tuscany and the 'Low Countries.' In: Campbell, B.M.S. and Overton, M. (eds) *Land Labour and Livestock: Historical studies in European agricultural productivity.* Manchester: Manchester University Press, 124–143.
Pisati, M. (2001). SG162: Tools for spatial data analysis. *Stata Technical Bulletin* 60, 21–37.
Polanyi, K. (1944). *The Great Transformation.* Boston MA: Beacon Press.
Polanyi, K. (1957). Marketless trading in Hammurabi's time. In: Polanyi, K., Arensberg, C.M. and Pearson, H.W. (eds) *Trade and Market in the Early Empires. Economies in History and Theory.* Glencoe IL: The Free Press & The Falcon's Wing Press, 12–26.
Studer, R. (2008). India and the great divergence: Assessing the efficiency of grain markets in eighteenth- and nineteenth-century India. *Journal of Economic History* 68(2), 393–437. [https://doi.org/10.1017/S0022050708000351].
van der Spek, R.J., van Leeuwen, B. and van Zanden, J.L. (2014). An introduction. Markets from Ancient Babylonia to the Modern World. In: van der Spek, R.J., van Leeuwen, B. and van Zanden, J.L. (eds) *A History of Market Performance: From Ancient Babylonia to the modern world.* Abingdon and New York: Routledge, 1–16.
van Leeuwen, B., Földvári, R. and van Zanden, J.L. (2014). Long-run market performance in the Near East, the Mediterranean and Europe from Antiquity to *c.* AD 1800. In: van der Spek, R.J., van Leeuwen, B. and van Zanden, J.L. (eds) *A History of Market Performance: From Ancient Babylonia to the modern world.* Abingdon and New York: Routledge, 506–526.

Appendix 8.1. Estimates of market performance in pre-modern European cities

	Dates	*1300–1350*	*1350–1400*	*1400–1450*	*1450–1500*	*1500–1550*	*1550–1600*	*1600–1650*
Country	*City/region*							
Austria	Stiftkloster Neuberg				0.51	0.56		
	Vienna					0.67	0.69	0.33
France	Aix-en-Provence						0.72	0.83
	Angers						0.71	0.77
	Arles							0.8
	Avignon						0.72	0.83
	Beziers						0.74	0.82
	Bavay			0.69	0.71			
	Die					0.57	0.76	
	Douai	0.6	0.75	0.67	0.57	0.64	0.62	0.73
	Draguignan							0.85
	Grenoble					0.62	0.7	0.82
	Le Quesnoy			0.71	0.72			
	Maubeuge			0.67	0.71			
	Montelimar					0.61	0.62	0.65
	Paris			0.38	0.64	0.6	0.61	0.78
	Rennes							0.85
	Strasbourg		0.7	0.8	0.76	0.72	0.69	0.65
	Toulouse				0.68	0.65	0.72	0.73
	Tours				0.65	0.63	0.65	0.8
	Valence					0.63	0.71	0.86
	Valenciennes			0.66	0.7			
	Vienne					0.6	0.73	0.77
	Voiron					0.6	0.69	0.69
Germany	Cologne					0.81	0.82	0.85
	Leipzig						0.83	0.71
	Munich						0.75	0.64
	Weyer							0.75
	Würzburg						0.68	0.66

(Continued)

Appendix 8.1. Estimates of market performance in pre-modern European cities (Continued)

Country	City/region	1300–1350	1350–1400	1400–1450	1450–1500	1500–1550	1550–1600	1600–1650
Italy	Arezzo					0.5	0.72	0.8
	Bari						0.7	0.66
	Bassano						0.77	0.77
	Bologna							0.8
	Cantania						0.77	0.8
	Firenze	0.44	0.57	0.7	0.73	0.56	0.7	0.71
	Lucca	0.67	0.62	0.66	0.69	0.61	0.67	0.78
	Modena				0.6	0.54	0.77	0.8
	Naples						0.68	0.7
	Pisa						0.69	0.76
	Sansepolcro					0.59	0.76	0.81
	Siena						0.74	0.79
	Udine							0.77
Low Countries	Amsterdam				0.65	0.76	0.76	0.88
	Arnhem						0.79	0.8
	Leiden				0.59	0.74	0.82	0.81
	Lier			0.70	0.72	0.73	0.7	0.71
	Louvain			0.76	0.67			
	Mons			0.68	0.71			
	Utrecht				0.65	0.76	0.76	0.88
Spain	Barcelona					0.88	0.86	0.83
	Leon					0.7	0.82	0.73
	Madrid					0.61	0.75	0.76
	New Castille					0.61	0.75	0.76
	Old Castile					0.7	0.81	0.73
	Seville							0.6
	Valencia			0.84	0.85	0.76	0.83	0.83
	Valladolid					0.64	0.78	0.83
	Zaragoza			0.73	0.74			

(Continued)

Appendix 8.1. (Continued)

	Dates	*1300–1350*	*1350–1400*	*1400–1450*	*1450–1500*	*1500–1550*	*1550–1600*	*1600–1650*
Country	*City/region*							
United Kingdom	Chester		0.76	0.72	0.66			
	Edinburgh							0.76
	Eton							0.77
	Exeter	0.72	0.71	0.73	0.77	0.61	0.58	0.8
	London	0.68	0.68	0.71	0.81			
	Southern England	0.67	0.74	0.7	0.79	0.68	0.61	0.79
	Winchester							0.76

Chapter 9

Two tales of pre-modern contraction: Wage differentials in late medieval and early modern Japan

Osamu Saito

Introduction

In the modern world, whenever job markets for the less-skilled become tight, customary wage differentials between skilled and less-skilled occupations tend to shrink in liaison with rising *per capita* incomes. As population growth slows down or comes to a standstill a labor reserve will eventually be dried out. As a result, a noticeable increase in the level of wages for the less-skilled relative to the skilled will take place if the labor demand for the latter group of workers remains more or less unchanged. This actually happened in the process of modern economic growth among today's advanced nations.[1] While this is a stylized fact for the age of industrialization, it is sometimes implied that such a contraction of wage differentials never happened in pre-modern times, a view held by many historians and social scientists. In reality, however, there are pre-modern episodes in which both the increase in *per capita* income and the decline in wage differentials occurred well before the onset of fully-fledged industrialization. Probably the most spectacular of all those is the period after the Black Death in Europe. With a significant decline in population totals, real wages rose over the period from the late 14th to the mid-15th century and, across the European region from Amsterdam and London to Florence and Istanbul, the rise was distinctly higher for the unskilled than those for the skilled.[2] However, it was caused by an external shock, *i.e.* the arrival of a pathogen in 1346. Given Phelps Brown's famous assertion that the skilled-to-unskilled ratio for southern England in the period between 1412 and 1914 was 'never far from 3 to 2', the rule of customary forces seems to have overridden that of market forces over the 500-year period since the disastrous pestilence (Phelps-Brown 1977).

Prevailing as this view might be, one could argue that there were episodes of internally generated erosion of customary wage differentials even before the industrial revolution. If this were really the case, such episodes of pre-modern contraction would enable us to have a better understanding of the workings of labor markets, and hence market systems in general, in a pre-modern setting.

This chapter provides a couple of much less-spectacular cases of contracting wage differentials in pre-modern Japan, one medieval, and the other Early Modern. The medieval findings are based on wage data for building trades while the early modern ones are the results from village-level sources for agricultural laborers and carpenters. Both occurred in the capital region of Japan before 1868, with the medieval case covering a period before 1600 when Japan was a peripheral partner of intra-Asian trade, and the early modern contraction being a phenomenon that took place under a self-imposed seclusion policy. Moreover, forces at work were diagonally different. The medieval contraction was associated with changes in monetary factors, whereas the early modern episode was conditioned by long-running agrarian progress. How to place these contrasting cases in a longer-term context of market growth is the issue I would like to explore in this paper.

Contrasting market systems

In 1600 there was a battle at Sekigahara between two camps of *daimyo* (samurai lords exercising territorial control), which led Tokugawa Ieyasu to the formation of a new shogunate in 1603. Since the mid-15th century the country had been plagued by nearly constant military conflict between daimyo states; a move towards the consolidation of powers began and its whole process was completed with the 1600 battle. The establishment of the Tokugawa shogunate has long been regarded as the beginning of a new 'early modern' era and was often contrasted with the medieval situation with respect to the differing levels of market growth. Early modernists tended to portray the Tokugawa economy as a system with markets making inroads into the peasant sector, in contrast with pre-Tokugawa command economy-type relations with a mass of subsistence farmers. For the past decades, however, medievalists have unveiled a good deal of contrary evidence: from the 14th century onwards the volume of market transactions grew steadily in provincial as well as metropolitan economies (Saito 2020; see also Sakurai 2008; Segal 2011). In both time periods, therefore, peasants were involved in market exchanges, generating the demand for money at lower levels of society.

Monetary systems

That said, however, there remains a contrast between the late medieval and early modern patterns in relation to institutional frameworks of market systems.[3] The use of coins in the medieval period began with an influx of copper coins from China (*zeni*, or *qian* in Chinese). By the 14th century, payments of annual tributes in many estates were commuted into cash. Among the coins used, most numerous were those issued in Song China. Soon, however, forged coins were found in the imports and between the 14th and the 16th centuries domestically manufactured ones were also brought to markets. Although Chinese coins kept coming in, currencies in circulation increasing consisted of coins which were not genuinely Chinese – forged Chinese coins, home-made coins, and other 'inferior' metal objects. This created problems. In 1485 the governor of one province issued Japan's first anti-shroffing (anti-counterfeiting) edict, followed by the Muromachi shogunate's in 1500, which indicates that the circulation of inferior coins was on the increase. Some of those were accepted, some rejected, and others received by mixing them with genuine ones. Whenever accepted as a medium of official payment those inferior coins were valued on a par with the genuine ones. However, the currency was in short supply overall. The period between the mid-15th century and the third quarter of the 16th was a time of unmistakable deflation but there took place a sudden turn in the late 1560s. The import of Chinese coins came to a complete cessation resulting in an acute shortage of genuine ones. The money market reacted to this emergency by raising the value of low-quality coins (collectively called *bita* by contemporaries, which means 'bad'). This triggered inflation. By the 1590s, as the pace of inflation soared, however, the *bita* gradually gained the status of a conventional standard. Since there existed no centrally designed institutions of currency supply, the course of change in the 16th century money market differed considerably from region to region. The above account of the unexpected revaluation of the *bita* is based largely on what happened in the Kinai, the region centred on Kyoto and the ancient city of Nara, but it is worth noting that when the Tokugawa state formally issued the first copper coin in 1636, it inherited the standard value that the *bita* had acquired during the turbulent quarter century of the 16th.

Apparently, the medieval state had no motivation to issue currency on its own, suggesting that we may characterise the late medieval money economy as badly coordinated (Sakurai 2008: 58).[4] Deflation, inflation, revaluation of the *bita*, and the lack of systemic stability are the products of this uncoordinated monetary system.

In contrast, the early modern monetary system was largely a product of conscious efforts made by the Tokugawa shogunate in the early 17th century.[5] The shogunate issued gold and silver currencies in 1601, immediately after the victory at Sekigahara. The choice of these two new metals reflected the growing trend in domestic mine production since the 16th century. Particularly, the output of silver grew strongly following the introduction of a Korean technique in 1533, enabling Japan to become an active partner of Asia-wide trade in which silver was a *de facto* standard. A third currency, copper, was integrated into the shogunate's monetary system a little later. It was in 1636 when a new *zeni* was issued on a par with the *bita*, keeping the *zeni* suitable for petty-cash, daily transactions. All the three became legal tenders with the mines placed under shogunal monopoly.

This difference in the timing of issuance of the three currencies suggests that the shogunate paid more attention to daimyo's fiscal needs than to domestic market demands for small change in the initial stage. Because of the geography of mineral deposits, with more gold mines in the east and more silver deposits in the west, the country's eastern half became gold-using and the western half silver-using. The period from the end of the 16th into the early 17th century saw many castle towns constructed by daimyo lords, making their demand for cash urgent. On the other hand, the government's concern for small denomination coins surfaced only in 1635 when the shogunate forced every daimyo to make an alternate residence between his castle town and Edo, the capital: the daimyo family's travel suddenly increased demands for petty cash to be used during their long journey. This emphasis on public finance over the private sector's was inherited by Ieyasu's successors and it took a century for the shogunate to shift its monetary policy to meet the common people's demand for the medium of market transaction.

By the time of the eighth shogun, the great mining boom had been over, under which Japan had opted for the withdrawal from the Asian market by placing overseas trade under tight governmental control. The shogunate of 1716–1745 inherited a fiscal trouble caused by strong money and price deflation. In order to redress this imbalance, the shogun took the decision in 1736 to reflate the economy by increasing money supply. What the shogunate did was, first, to debase gold and silver currencies without attempting to gain recoinage proceeds, second, to supply the market with iron-made 'copper' coins, and, finally, to allow daimyo's territorial governments to issue paper notes for their domain economies. This policy orientation for the nominalisation of metallic currencies was passed on to subsequent administrations. In the 1770s and also in the 1818–1832 period, new coins of smaller denomination were created. They were all 'gold' currencies but some of them were made of silver, with the smallest being 1/16th *ryō*.[6] From the 1730s, therefore, both the shogunate and territorial governments became more concerned with satisfying the private sector's demand for money. As a result of all this, the share of small denomination currencies in the shogunate money stock increased. According to Iwahashi's estimates, the share stood at 7.5% in 1695, which declined to 5% in 1714 but went up back to 10% in 1736. Since then, the share increased to 30% in 1818 and to 46% in 1866. Although the paucity of statistical data concerning daimyo's domain notes does not allow us to include the stock of paper money in this calculation, it seems certain that the number of daimyo administrations who successfully kept domain note supply on the rise from the 18th–19th century (Iwahashi 2019).[7] Given a finding that many of those daimyo notes were linked to the *zeni* with the same face value as on its metallic currency, the tempo of increase in the actual share of small denomination currencies over the period from the 1730s onwards must have been even higher (*ibid.*).[8]

If we focus on the period after 1730, therefore, it is safe to conclude that the early modern market economy was in operation within a reasonably well functioning institutional framework. The system itself was still a little too complicated and the degree of regional integration remained relatively low, but with the state's willingness to meet the common people's demand for money, the market was no longer constrained by money-supply volatility as in the late medieval period.

Macro-economic contexts

Economic historians have recently expanded their quantification effort to Japan's ancient and medieval past, focusing primarily on the estimation of gross domestic product (GDP), its sectoral distribution, and GDP *per capita*. Table 9.1 summarizes the estimates of average annual growth rates of GDP *per capita*, population and sectoral output, with the sectoral share of agriculture (for the medieval period) and primary-sector output (for the early modern).

Growth in medieval times was sluggish by modern standards, but its level of the annual rate of growth was not entirely negligible. The growth-rate level stood at 0.02% for the period before 1450, which went up to 0.13% for the post-1450 period. Population was stagnant throughout the period from the mid-10th to the mid-12th century, and the most recent of all estimates for 1150 suggests that there had been a substantial setback from the 8th century.[9] Since then, recovery took place, especially in the period after 1280, with growth-rate levels being a little higher than 0.3% per annum. In the 1280–1450 period agricultural production barely managed to keep up with the population increase while the non-agricultural sector's performance was a little better, so that the rate of growth in GDP *per capita* did not fall into negative territory. After 1450, the tempo of growth increased. Both sectors grew, but the rate of growth was higher in the industrial and service sector, reflecting a proliferation of non-agricultural occupations and commodities which was in progress over the late medieval period.[10]

What remains uncertain is the performance of agriculture. Figure 9.1 displays how the frequency of famines changed from the mid-14th century. The measure I have employed is based on the count of famines, but each famine is weighted by

Table 9.1. Macro-economic performances in the medieval and the early modern period

Period	*Annual rate of growth (%)*				*Share in GDP (%)*
Medieval	*GDP per capita*	*Population*	*Agricultural output*	*Non-agricultural output*	*Agricultural output*
1280–1450	0.02	0.31	0.31	0.37	70
1450–1600	0.13	0.35	0.41	0.62	66
Early modern	*GDP per capita*	*Population*	*Primary sector output*	*Non-primary sector output*	*Primary sector output*
1600–1721	0.01	0.51	0.38	0.80	68
1721–1846	0.23	0.02	0.25	0.26	63

Notes: 1) For the medieval period, forestry and fisheries are included in the non-agricultural sector, whereas for the early modern period, they constitute a subsector of the primary sector. In 1600, for which both estimates are available, the share of this subsector in GDP was 12 %; 2) The sectoral share in GDP for each period is the average of estimates for the start and end years

Sources: For the medieval period, Nakabayashi *et al.* (2020: tables 1–3); and for the early modern period, Bassino *et al.* (2019: tables 6 and 8).

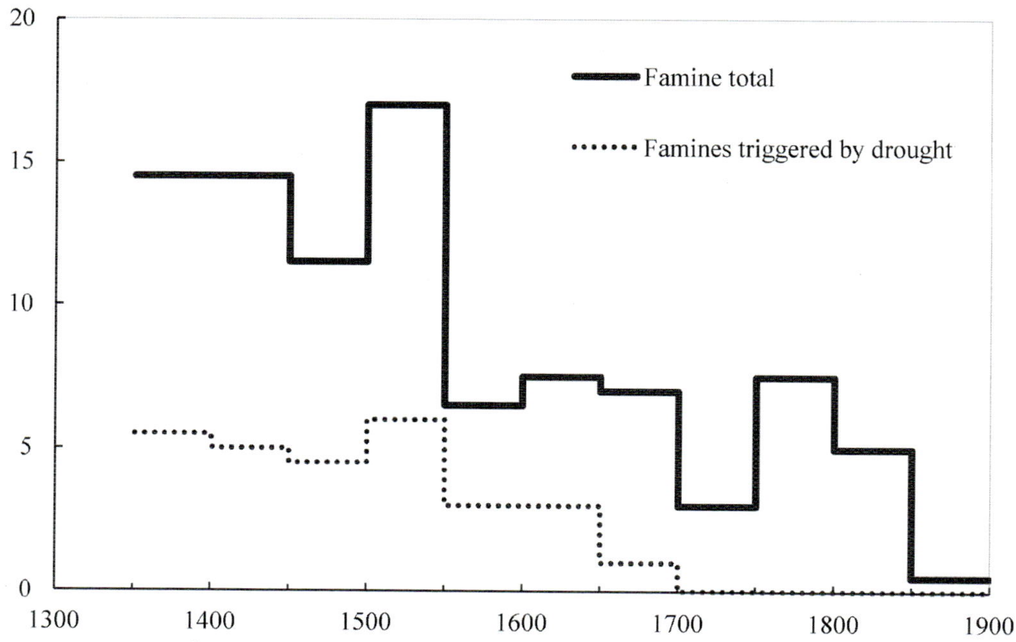

Figure 9.1. Famine frequency and drought as a trigger, 1350–1900. Notes: 1) In counting famines, 1 point is given to a cross-regional occurrence for which records exist across more than several provinces, 0.5 points to famines apparently confined to a few provinces, and 0 to genuinely local famines. The results are weighted by the number of years affected. The famine frequency series shows points by half-century; 2) In the period before 1550, the proportion of famines triggered by drought or cold summer is about 50%.. The other half were cases of unknown cause or those triggered by causes other than drought and cold summer. On average, it turns out to be 51% before 1550 as against 19% for the post-1550 period, although in the late 17th century the percentage is exceptionally high (57%). Thus, the drought-triggered famine counts for the 1350–1550 and 1650–1700 periods are likely to have been somewhat understated (after Saito 2015, table 11.2 and its source data. The estimate for the late 16th century is corrected from 7 to 6.5 points).

both geographical areas and the number of years affected (its graph shows changes in the number of famine points by half century). As such, it is expected to reflect the frequency of excess death better than that of crop failure, although, together with the information about the number of famines triggered by drought, it is also hoped that the graph will show how agriculture was transformed in the long-run (Saito 2015). From Figure 9.1, it is clear that there was a sharp drop in the famine frequency during the 16th century. Before 1550, on average, the frequency was once every three to four years, but in the middle of the warring states period it declined to once every seven years.

This finding has two implications. One is that there was no hint of gradual decline in the frequency of famine until the mid-16th century; the other is that the break with the famine-stricken past came before the establishment of a regime labelled early modern. This mid-16th century breakthrough cannot be explained by climate change. Summer temperature fell from the second quarter of the century onwards (Nakatsuka *et al.* 2020), implying that despite this unfavorable trend in climate the number of famines declined. The mid-16th century witnessed the localization of famine under warring daimyo's domain rule, which suggests that actions taken by the daimyo administration was instrumental in preventing any poor harvest from developing into a cross-regional famine, since the warlords paved the way to the consolidation of power over their territory by paying greater attention to land clearance and investment in infrastructures, such as dykes, waterways, and roads, than their predecessors. The sharp decline in the frequency of famines was an unintended consequence of state formation efforts by those warring daimyo (Saito 2015). Towards a better understanding of both macro-economic and systemic features of the medieval market economy, therefore, much of this half-century period should be separated out from the centuries-long past.

Turning to the first half of the early modern era, on the face of it, the trends were just a continuation from the previous 150 year period. Population grew at even a higher rate: between 1600 and 1721 the country's population nearly doubled. While the primary sector grew at a marginally lower pace than agriculture of the previous period, the growth of industrial and commercial activities was comparatively brisk in the 17th century. As a result, *per capita* GDP growth remained stagnant until the early 18th century. Behind the strong growth of the secondary and tertiary sectors, however, was an equally strong drive for urbanization. By 1721, the total population living in towns with at least 10,000 residents more than tripled. This growth of urban population was driven by daimyo's construction of castle towns across the country, which in turn acted as a stimulus for both the proliferation of non-primary sector occupations and the urban demand for manufactured goods and services. Despite the near-zero growth of *per capita* GDP, therefore, the 17th century was a time of change in sectoral composition and increased monetization.

Contraction of wage differentials

Having surveyed differences in monetary systems and macro-economic contexts between the two time periods, we can now turn to the issue of contraction in wage differentials. In both late medieval and early modern times there emerged a period in which wage differentials narrowed between skilled and unskilled workers when the level of real wages for the unskilled was on the rise. This section examines the patterns of change in real wage levels and skill differentials in each time period. Then in the next section, the two episodes of contraction in wage differentials will be explored in relation to the previous section's comparative findings on market forces which were at work under two contrasting sets of circumstances.

All source data for both wages and prices come from one single region, the Kinai, which literally means 'within the capital region': ancient cities of Nara, Osaka (formerly

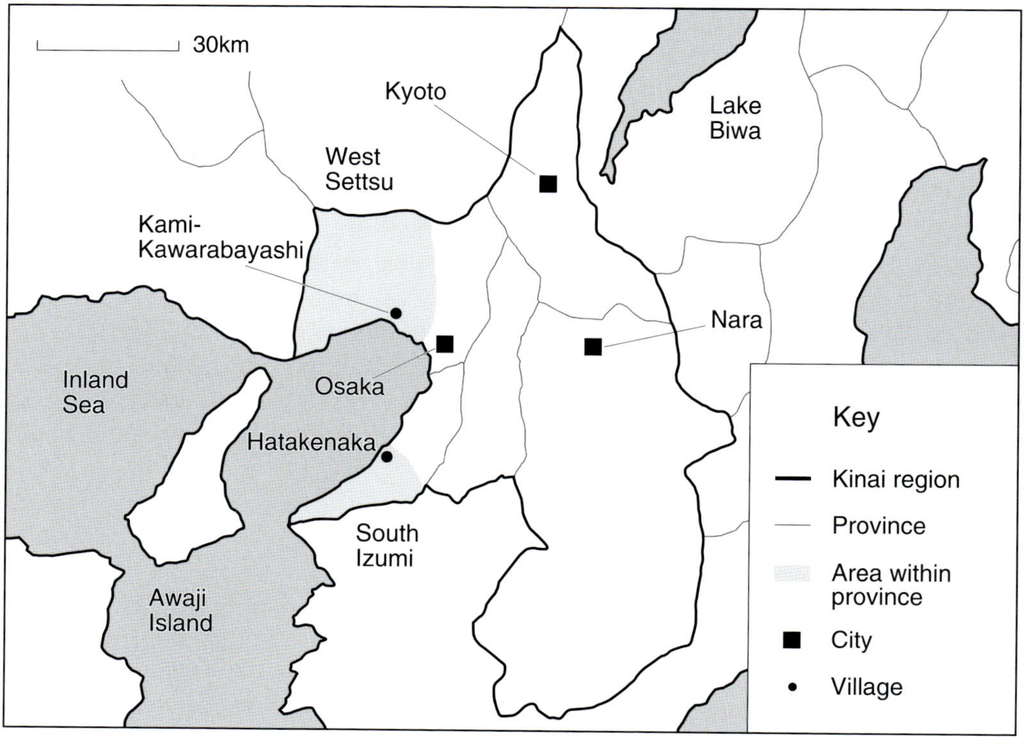

Figure 9.2. Map of the Kinai region.

Naniwa), and Kyoto are all located in this region. The Kinai consists of five provinces including Settsu and Izumi. Our medieval wage data are taken from a comprehensive dataset for pre-1600 prices and wages (known as the Rekihaku database), from which data for Kyoto and Nara and surrounding locations are selected. Early modern wage data come from two villages, one from Kami-Kawarabayashi in west Settsu, 12 km west of Osaka, and the other from Hatakenaka in south Izumi, 30 km south of Osaka (see Fig. 9.2). The price index series are constructed on the basis of data from Kyoto and Nara (for the medieval) and from Kyoto and Osaka (for the early modern).[11]

Figures 9.3 and 9.4 set out change in real wages and wage differentials for the two time periods. There are some differences between the two in the nature of data and ways in which real wages were computed. For the medieval real wage series calculation is made with reference to the price of rice only and for the early modern series with a bundle of commodity prices. The medieval unskilled are represented by builders' laborers and the early modern unskilled by agricultural laborers, be they day laborers or one-year farm servants, while carpenters are chosen for the skilled in both periods. There are also some differences with respect to the meaning of the wage rate. In both cases, wage payments often included sums added to the amount agreed by the two parties: in most cases board and lodging were added. But in the

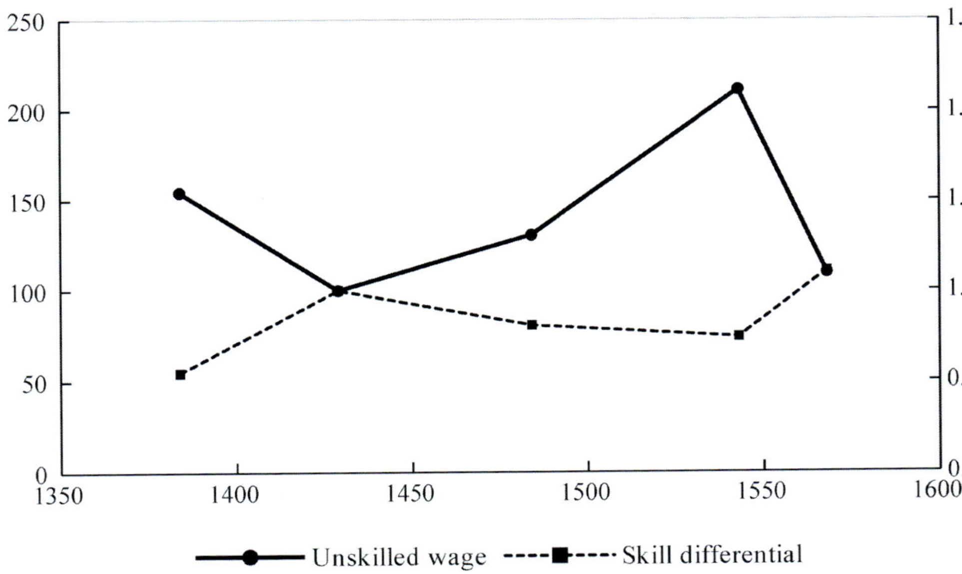

Figure 9.3. Rice wages for laborers and the skilled:unskilled differentials: Kanai 1384–1568. Notes: 1) 'Unskilled wage' refers to an index of building laborers rice wages (1427–31=100). Rice wages are wages expressed in a capacity measure of rice; 2) 'skill differential' is defined as the ratio of building craftsmen's nominal wage to that of building laborers' rice wage (1427–31=1); 3) all figures are five year averages centered on the year concerned (after Saito and Takashima 2020, appendix table. Some of the estimates are revised).

medieval building trade, contractors frequently received a non-negligible amount of extra wages, a practice which was rarely observed in early modern times. According to scattered late medieval cases, the proportion of extra wages to the agreed pay rate varied from 17% to 80%, depending, probably, on the technicalities of the work contracted as well as the skill level of individual workers (Saito and Takashima 2020).[12] Finally, while the early modern ratio of carpenters' to agricultural day workers' wages stood at 5:2, the medieval ratio of carpenters' to common laborers' wages was as high as 10:1. Did the laborers also earn extra wages when the task was hard or the employer was generous? Unfortunately, very little is known about actual practices surrounding contract and pay in the medieval labor market.

Considering these differences, indexation is applied to both graphs so that we can focus on the direction of change when examining the real wage and its skill differential series in both periods. For the medieval series, an index is measured in relation to 1427–1431 and for the early modern it is to 1802–1804. In both Figures 9.3 and 9.4, a five year average is shown as a value for the year on which the calculation is centered.

From the two graphs, it is evident that in each time frame there was a lengthy period in which a contraction of the differential index took place together with rising real wages for the unskilled. In the medieval age it was a 114 year long period

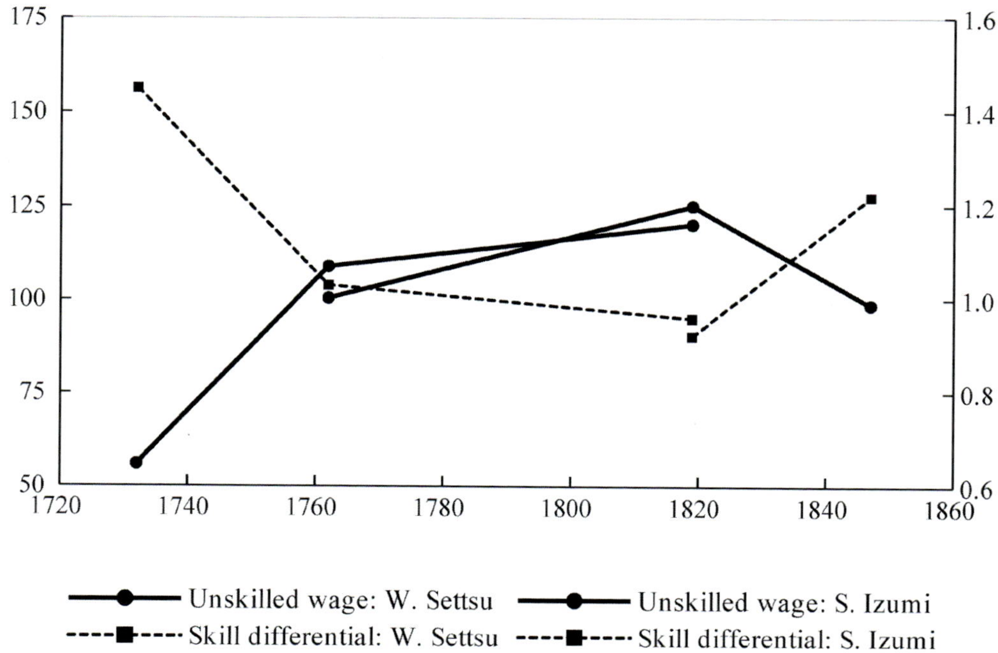

Figure 9.4. Real wages for agricultural workers and the skilled:unskilled differentials: west Settsu and south Izumi 1732–1847. Notes: 1) 'Unskilled wage' refers to an index of agricultural laborers' real wages (1802–04=100). Real wages are calculated in reference to the Kyoto-Osaka general price indies; 2) 'Skill differential' is defined as the ratio of carpenters' nominal wage to agricultural laborers' (1804–04=100). In the case of west Settsu, data for both skilled and unskilled wages correspond to carpenters and agricultural day laborers employed by the same farm household in the area. For south Izumi, while unskilled wages refer to one year farm servants employed by a farm household in that area, skilled wages are taken from urban data, i.e. carpenters' daily wage rates in Kyoto; 3) all figures are 5 year averages centered on the year concerned except for west Settsu carpenters in 1730–1734, and for south Izumi farm servants in 1817–1821 and 1845–1849 (wages are taken from Saito (2009: table 1) and Mandai (2009: appendix tables 7–8). Price data are from Miyamoto's Kyoto-Osaka general price indices, reproduced in Fukao et al. 2017: appendix table 4.A).

of 1429–1543, while in the early modern era it was from 1732 to 1819, a little shorter than the medieval counterpart. In the medieval period the average annual rate of wage growth stood at 0.7%, accompanied by a decrease of only 0.05 points in the differential index. In the early modern, the average growth rate of Kami-Kawarabayashi wages was 0.9% per annum over the entire period, but the first half of the 87 year period saw an even higher rate of growth, 2.2%, while in the second half the rate of growth slowed down to 0.2%. Changes in the magnitude of decline in the differential index for the Kami-Kawarabayashi series – a 0.5 point decline in the first half and a 0.07 point decline in the second – mirror the pattern of change in the corresponding real wage series. The Hatakenaka series of real wages is short and the accompanying differential series even shorter, which makes the comparison of the two difficult for the period before 1819. However, what happened to the two series in the subsequent period of real wage decline suggests that changes in the Hatakenaka differential index in the pre-1819 period may well have been similar to the Kami-Kawarabayashi pattern.

To summarise the observations from Figures 9.3 and 9.4, in both periods of 1429–1543 and 1732–1819 real wage growth for the unskilled was accompanied by a contraction of the wage differential with the skilled; however, the magnitude of contraction was much less pronounced in the medieval than in the early modern period of wage growth. The question is what accounts for this difference between the two time periods.

Contrasting contexts

Background factors and market forces at work

For the unskilled wage level to narrow the gap with the skilled, the most likely scenario in historical contexts is for population to cease to grow. As hinted in the introductory section, this must have been what Lewis had in mind when he thought about the transition from 'unlimited' to 'limited' labor in relation to modern economic growth. However, it should not be assumed that such a turning point arrived only once in human history. The post-Black Death labor market in Western Europe is a classic case. Although it was a product of an exceptionally disastrous pandemic, a similar situation may well have emerged in any pre-modern labor market, be it in the western or the eastern part of Eurasia. From the Japanese history, the second half of the Tokugawa era is a case in point. As Table 9.1 has made it clear, the population hardly grew during this 125 year period. Although a couple of serious famines, which hit the archipelago in the 1780s and the 1830s, held back population totals from increasing, it was not a period of macro-economic disaster. It was a long phase which saw output growing at a slow but steady pace while the total labor force hardly grew.

Thus, output growth can be another important background factor. In peasant society where a vast majority was agricultural population, output growth in agriculture had a considerable impact on the supply of labor. In my 1978 article, which explored the same labor-market question based on the Kami-Kawarabayashi evidence, I proposed to see this macro-economic effect in a micro-economic framework of farm household behavior. According to this micro-economic framework it is implied that any rise in agricultural productivity on the peasant's farm will *ceteris paribus* lead to an increase in that farm household's asking price of labor in the outside job market (Saito 1978: 94–98).[13] Do we have evidence of productivity growth in agriculture for the period after the 1720s?

Table 9.2 summarizes two kinds of productivity-related evidence: one for land productivity growth in rice growing and the other for labor productivity growth in

Table 9.2. *Productivity growth in the primary sector: land and labor, 1600–1850*

Period	*Average annual rate of growth (%)*	
	Land productivity of rice cultivation	*Labor productivity in the primary sector*
1600–1720	0.11	0.01
1720–1800	0.16	0.25
1800–1850	0.09	0.18

Note: Periodization is slightly different between the two estimates. The sectoral labor productivity estimates are for 1600–1721, 1721–1804, and 1804–1846.
Sources: Land productivity estimates are from Mandai and Nakabayashi (2017: table 3.1); and labor productivity estimates from Settsu and Takashima (2020: table 6).

the entire primary sector, both covering the period from 1600 to 1850 with three sub-periods. The growth of output per unit of rice field was steady throughout the 250 year period, while that of labor productivity was more articulated – when population increase was considerable in the first sub-period its growth rate was almost zero, which turned positive in the second and third phases. Given the labur-intensive nature of paddy rice cultivation, 0.25% per annum recorded in the 18th century was non-negligible. Also worth emphasizing is that from 1720 onwards the growth of labor productivity consistently outperformed that of land productivity. All this refers to national aggregates with no breakdowns by region. For the Kinai and adjoining provinces, there are a good deal of land productivity records for rice fields at the individual farm level but none of them allows us to compute the corresponding estimates of labor productivity. Nevertheless, it is interesting to note that collectively the level of rice output per unit of land in the Kinai was substantially higher than the national average. In the case of the Okamoto farm of Kami-Kawarabayashi land productivity in rice cultivation kept increasing until 1830 with the average annual rate of growth reaching 0.5%; on the other hand, while records from the Kaname family of Hatakenaka showed much slower productivity growth, it is Kaname's tenant farmers who achieved higher land productivity. What these pieces of evidence suggest is that behind the productivity performance in Kinai agriculture there was technological progress and also that most of the superior cultivation methods were shared by small to medium sized farmers as well as large landowners' home farms.[14] Considering the tendency that most of agricultural laborers were supplied from families of tenants farmers of the record-keeping landowner family, therefore, it is this agrarian progress that was the underlying economic factor for the observed rise of agricultural workers' real wages in the 18th century Kinai.

Such agrarian development was less apparent in medieval times. According to Table 9.1 above, agricultural output increased at the average annual growth rate of 0.4% over the 1450–1600 period while population simultaneously grew at a lower rate of 0.35%. On the face of it, there seems to have been a non-negligible increase in agricultural labour productivity. However, we have to be cautious in accepting it as a stylised fact. First, most recent estimates of agricultural output proposed by Nakabayashi *et al.* (2020) are based largely on Midorikawa's (2019) new figures for land productivity and total arable land; but while Bandai and Nakabayashi's estimates (2017) of rice output per unit of land for early modern benchmarks give 0.96 *koku* for 1600, Midorikawa's for 1585 stands at 2.1 *koku* with the average growth rate being 0.3% for 1414–1585. Even allowing for the coverage difference that the early modern estimates are for rice (excluding non-rice grains such as barley, wheat and millet), the level of the medieval estimates are apparently too high.[15] Second, it is difficult to find landmark innovations in medieval agriculture, except for the introduction of Champa rice, a variety of non-*japonica* type resistant to both flood and drought, thus enabling to turn floodplains of the river deltas into rice fields, and the pioneering adoption of better irrigation facilities in the Kinai and a few other provinces (Farris 2006: 132–136; Saito 2015).[16] Finally, as we have seen in Figure 9.1, there was no breakthrough in the frequency of famines until the mid-16th century, and as suggested earlier, while the number of serious famines declined, it was not a product of agri-technological progress but an unintended consequence of daimyo administrations' effort to consolidate power and authority over the territory they acquired.

Thus, there is little room for the aforementioned productivity-wage link to work in the medieval agricultural sector. What we have to consider next is the effect of monetary instability on the labor market for, especially, skilled workers, to which I shall now turn.

Monetary instability and its impact on market behaviour

The history of late medieval money features the emergence of low quality copper coins and its sudden acceptance as a standard means of transaction in the period after the late 1560s. Anti-shroffing edicts were issued by both Kyoto and local governments. Many of those edicts were an attempt to enforce the circulation of low quality but acceptable copper coins (*i.e. bita*) on a par with the proper Chinese ones, which actually meant that merchants in marketplaces were desperate to separate an unacceptable, lowest-low one from the genuine or the acceptable *bita*. Such a risk was high for anyone who was not familiar with the most up-to-date market information but was to receive wage payments in cash from the employer. They probably knew that a long-term trend was for the genuine to become scarcer, as a result of which the general level of prices would fall and, hence, their real wages would rise; but, in the short-run, the risk of getting fooled by accepting an unusable coin must have been non-negligible.

When good quality coins became extremely scarce after the 1560s, one obvious consequence of the expanding circulation of the *bita* was inflation. Another reaction to this exigency was the revival of commodity money. Rice and cloth had long been used as currency before the 13th century when metallic coins had been in extremely short supply. The comeback of rice in the late 16th century was also a reaction to the scarcity of coins; this time, however, the economy was more marketized. An analysis of Nara and Kyoto records confirms that the use of rice in buying of goods suddenly increased from the late 1560s and lasted until the end of the 1590s (Uranagase 2001). In warring daimyo states, there was also the return to a system under which land was expressed in terms of the amount of rice with tax collection in rice (Honda 2017: 113–114).

It is particularly worth noting in this context that a list of those goods and services traded in rice included wage payments. Judging from the rice-to-coin ratios calculated from a Nara temple's payment records,[17] the share of payments in rice increased from the level of 21% in the 1560s to 79% in the 1570–1596 period. This shows not only that the change was sudden, but also that those who received wage payments in rice had not been nil even before the final years of the 1560s: such workers must have always existed throughout the ancient and medieval periods.

It is well known that pre-modern labor markets tended to exhibit a nominal rigidity of wages. This is concerned usually with wages paid in money and thus meant the corresponding real wages changed according to the prices of consumables. The ancient and medieval Japanese custom of paying wages in rice showed much the same tendency of rigidity, but note that in this case the workers' real wages were expressed in terms of the amount of rice. The Rekihaku database contains a small number of rice wages for both building craftsmen and laborers. A close look at those cases reveals, first, that all the rice-denominated cases for laborers appeared in a province outside the Kinai during a relatively short period before 1450, suggesting that this was not an option for the unskilled in the late 16th century monetary crisis. Second, skilled wages paid in rice seem to have increased from a centuries old level of 6 *shō* to 10 *shō* between *c.* 1250 and 1350, but since then remained at that level until the end of the 16th century. Third, this pattern of change was considerably different from that for the skilled wages paid in money. During the phase of wage growth, 1429–1543, while the real wages of the former group of building craftsmen remained at the customary level of 10 *shō*, the latter group enjoyed a more-than-doubled rise in real wages, or at 0.8% per annum. To use Sakurai's metaphor, the baseline money wage rate for the skilled 'got off its lazy butt' and shifted up from 100 *mon* to 110 *mon* during the 15th century, behind which there must have been pressures from vociferous craft guild organizations (Sakurai 2017: 219).[18] This pattern of wage growth was similar to that for the unskilled; in fact, the growth was a little faster than the growth of the unskilled wages. In other words, if focused only on workers who received wages in coins, the wage differentials between the skilled and unskilled widened slightly. Simply, the existence of a small group of fellow craftsmen who preferred to fix their wage earnings in rice allowed the overall differential index to turn in the opposite direction. Given the length of that period of wage growth, they may have been too risk-averse, but when price levels turned upwards in the late 1560s and inflation ticked up, it was they who were able to avoid a drastic fall in real earnings.

The root cause of such violent fluctuations in the late medieval labor market was the lack of stability in money supply. Japan's early modern regime was able to greatly reduce the level of this instability by introducing both gold and silver as the major means of exchange and by defining the relationships with the age-old copper currency. However, this does not necessarily mean that the Tokugawa shogunate monopolized money supply and fully monetized the taxation and financial systems. While keeping rice based taxation intact, the central government allowed local daimyo administrations to issue paper money; and in the daimyo territory local merchants were licenced to issue notes to supplement monies supplied by the public sector. Such flexibility eventually enabled the governments to meet the local demand for means of small-scale transactions. From the late 18th century onwards, moreover, the central government started to mint gold denominated smallish coins by silver, again, in order to satisfy the private sector's growing demand for market transactions. Thus, the early modern labor markets were free from any monetary instability problems – until the final decade of the regime, when the nation was forced to open up the economy by the Western powers, causing acute exchange-rate problems and hyperinflation.[19]

Concluding remarks

The exploration in the previous section has revealed that the medieval and the early modern episodes of contraction in wage differentials should not be seen in the same light. The medieval case was an unexpected consequence of the co-existence of two differently behaving groups of craftsmen – one very risk-averse and the other much less so – in a situation where the level of prices was falling the supply of acceptable currency was not reliable and hence the level of prices falling. The former group of risk-averting skilled workers opted for wages paid in rice. As their real wages remained stationary, their choice meant that the overall wage differential index turned negative against the unskilled in the period of wage growth. In contrast, the early modern contraction took place in a period population was static while in agriculture productivity of both land and labor grew at a moderate rate. In the context of Japan's 18th century when there was neither urbanization drive nor building boom, this combination of factors meant a rise in the peasant family's supply price of labor, which pushed up the bottom level of wage layers in the local labor market. Market forces in this particular situation thus resulted in a gradual reduction in the wage gap between the skilled and unskilled.

From these two tales of pre-modern contraction of wage differentials, it is possible to draw several implications for historical studies on markets, money, and economic development.

First, a stable and adequate supply of means of transaction is crucial for market growth. The supplier was in most cases the state but local authorities and even non-state institutions, if willing, might also be able to meet the private sector's demand for money, thus keeping the market at work without trouble. Japan's transition from the medieval monetary regime, in which no one was responsible for meeting this condition, to the early modern one is a case in point. Second, participants of the market should not be restricted to the privileged. The more involved peasants were in transactions the better did any pre-modern markets work. Third, in pre-modern societies custom often played a greater role in social and economic life than in modern times. However, there could be changes of a kind that would break up the rule of custom. In the early modern Kinai, Japan, market forces had already begun to work for the good of peasants who supplied labour to the local market for less-skilled jobs.

Finally, this pre-modern 'transition' should not be fitted into a unilinear framework of historical narratives. During the industrial revolution, for example, the wage differential index tended to widen, rather than shrink, because industrialization, technological innovation, and population growth, all changed the balance between competing forces. In the pre-modern context too, it will be no surprise if more tales of contraction are found in different countries in different time periods.

Notes

1. This view has been associated with a thesis of the unlimited supply of labor developed by Lewis in his 'Economic Development' paper (1954). While debates are focused on economic mechanisms of the transition and the identification of a turning point in a specific country's development process, it is worth noting that when Lewis set out a diagram showing when leading countries crossed the turning point, he apparently based his judgement on the chronology of modern population growth in each country (Lewis 1958: 28–29). This effect of population growth on the pay structure is also touched upon by Phelps Brown in his discussion on the course of change in pay differentials in Britain and several other countries since the late 19th century (Phelps Brown 1977: 68–81).
2. The account is based on a more recent dataset of historical wages (Pamuk 2007: 297–299). Although the author does not make any specific comment, the graphic comparison makes this apparent.
3. The following draws largely on Sakurai (1017, chap. 5); Honda (2017); Takagi (2018); and Kuroda (2020: 104–107).
4. It is worth noting that despite the situation in the money market, the use of credit was early: bills of exchange and promissory notes emerged from the late 13th century and developed further. However, Sakurai points out that the state showed no interest in the use of any form of credit for their own finance.
5. The following account draws on Miyamoto and Shikano (2003) and Takagi (2018).
6. With this measure, silver was relegated to the status of a subsidiary currency. It is widely agreed that this policy was deliberately taken, reflecting the shogunate's another orientation, *i.e.* one for a gold standard. See Miyamoto and Shikano (2003: 179).
7. See chapters 2 and 6, especially table 2.2 for the changing shares of small denomination currencies, and table 6.1 for a list of daimyo administrations who issued notes by time period.
8. In chapter 10, it is pointed out that even among silver denominated notes, there were a sizeable number of cases in which the unit printed on the note was that of the *zeni*, not the unit of silver.
9. It stood as low as 3.9 million, a 36% decline from the ancient peak of 6.1 million in 730, according to Nakabayashi *et al.* (2020: table 1); *cf.* Farris (2006: 262; 2009: 19, 26), for earlier estimates of population totals for 730 and 1150.
10. See Saito (2020) where it is argued that signs of Smithian growth can be identified in the 16th century.
11. For the construction of the early modern 'general price index' series, see Miyamoto (2004: 121–122).
12. Saito and Takashima (2020: 130).

13. The model enables us to see how the allocation of household's labor force is made when a job opportunity is offered from outside, and how an increase in agricultural productivity on the home farm influences on the household's labor supply to the outside job market. For wider contexts in which rural labour markets worked, see Saito (2009).
14. For the evidence concerning the Okamoto family in Kami-Kawabayashi, west Settsu, see Imai and Yagi (1955:105), and the Kaname family in Hatakenaka, south Izumi, see Mandai (2019: 171–176). Land productivity estimates for wealthy farmers' farms in the Kinai are summarised in Mandai and Nakabayashi (2017: table 3.2). According to Mandai and Nakabayashi's estimate for Japan in 1800, rice output per unit of land, *tan*, was 1.2 *koku*. For Okamoto's family farm, it stood at 2.2 *koku* in 1800–1806. In the case of Hatakenaka, while the value for Kaname's home farm was 1.9 *koku* for the same period, his tenants achieved generally high land productivity. There were nine annual records for which the two productivity figures can be compared; of the nine, seven years saw the average of tenants' land productivity higher than Kaname's family farm's, with the average margin of 16%. Note that all output values are in *koku*, a capacity measure (like the metric system, this traditional Japanese units use base 10; thus, one *koku* is equal to 100 *shō*). One *koku* equals 180 litres, which in the case of brown rice weighs approximately 150 kg. As for *tan*, an area measure, one *tan* equals 0.099 hectares.
15. This comparison is based on Nakabayashi *et al.* 2020: appendix table I.2), and Midorikawa (2019: table 4). As the former article does not provide land productivity figures, they are calculated from estimates of output total given by Nakabayashi *et al.* and for total land areas by Midorikawa. For the measures, *koku* and *tan*, see note 18 above.
16. In the advanced Kinai, the coming of the new technologies was earlier. In many other regions, however, progress was late and uneven.
17. The shares are calculated from Uranagase (2001: table 1.3), who presents year-by-year ratios of payments in rice to those in coins. Unfortunately, the number of cases is not reported except for 1588 and 1589. In both years, the number of cases reported is very small, one in 1588 and seven in 1589, none of which was in rice. In my calculation of the average for the second period, the former is excluded but the latter is not. If the latter should also be excluded, the average will increase to 83%.
18. And for some evidence concerning the activities of craftsmen's guilds (*za* according to the medieval terminology), see Sakurai (1996: pt 1, chaps 1–2).
19. For this period of hyperinflation, see Miyamoto (2004: 136–138).

Bibliography

Bassino, J.-P., Broadberry, S., Fukao, K., Gupta, B. and Takashima, M. (2019). Japan and the Great Divergence, 730–1874. *Explorations in Economic History* 72, 1–22.

Farris, W.W. (2006). *Japan's Medieval Population: Famine, Fertility, and Warfare in a Transformative Age*. Honolulu: University of Hawai'i Press.

Farris, W.W. (2009). *Daily Life and Demographics in Ancient Japan*. Ann Arbor MI: Center for Japanese Studies, University of Michigan.

Fukao, K., Saito, O., Takashima, M. and Imamura, N. (2017). Seisan, bukka, shotoku no suitei. In: Fukao, K., Nakamura, N. and Nakabayashi, M. (eds) *Iwanami kōza nihon keizai no rekishi*, vol. 2. Tokyo: Iwanami Shoten, 283–300.

Honda, H. (2017). Chūsei kahei: toraisen no jidai. In: Fukao, K., Nakamura, N. and Nakabayashi, M. (eds) *Iwanami kōza nihon keizai no rekishi*, vol. 1. Tokyo: Iwanami Shoten, 92–116.

Imai, R. and Yagi, A. (1955). *Hōken shakai no nōson kōzō*. Tokyo: Yūhikaku.

Iwahashi, M. (2019). *Kinsei kahei to keizai hatten*. Nagoya: Nagoya Daigaku Shuppankai.

Kuroda, A. (2020). *A Global History of Money*. London: Routledge.

Lewis, W.A. (1954). Economic development with unlimited supplies of labour. *Manchester School* 22, 139–191.
Lewis, W.A. (1958). Unlimited labour: Further notes. *Manchester School* 26, 1–32.
Mandai, Y. (2019). *Kinsei Kinai no gōnō keiei to hansei*. Tokyo: Hanawa Shobō.
Mandai, Y. and Nakabayashi, M. (2017). Kinsei no tochi hōsei to jinushi keiei. In: Fukao, K., Nakamura, N. and Nakabayashi, M. (eds) *Iwanami Kōza Nihon Keizai no Rekishi*, vol. 2. Tokyo: Iwanami Shoten, 150–176.
Midorikawa, K. (2019). Nihon kodai-chūsei no suiden seisanryoku. *Shakai-keizaishigaku* 85, 113–134.
Miyamoto, M. (2004). Prices and macroeconomic dynamics. In: Hayami, A., Saito, O. and Toby, R.P. (eds) *Emergence of Economic Society in Japan 1600–1859*. Oxford: Oxford University Press, 119–158.
Miyamoto, M. and Shikano, Y. (2003). The emergence of the Tokugawa monetary system in East Asian international perspective. In: Flynn, D.O., Giráldez, A. and von Glahn, R. (eds) *Global Connections and Monetary History, 1470–1800*. Farnham: Ashgate, 169–186.
Nakabayashi, M., Fukao, K., Takashima, M. and Nakamura, N. (2020). Property systems and economic growth in Japan, 730–1874. *Social Science Japan Journal* 23(2), 147–184. [https://doi.org/10.1093/ssjj/jyaa023].
Nakatsuka, T. and members of the Historical Climate Adaptation project (2017). Impact of climate change on social transformations in Japan and beyond. Unpublished paper presented at the *RHIN International Symposium on Asia's Transformations to Sustainability*, held at the Research Institute for Humanity and Nature, Kyoto, 10–11 March, 2017.
Pamuk, S. (2007). The Black Death and the origins of the 'Great Divergence' across Europe, 1300–1600. *European Review of Economic History* 11, 289–317.
Phelps Brown, H. (1977). *The Inequality of Pay*. Oxford: Oxford University Press.
Saito, O. (1978). The labor market in Tokugawa Japan: Wage differentials and the real wage level, 1727–1830. *Explorations in Economic History* 15, 84–100.
Saito, O. (2009). Land, labour and market forces in Tokugawa Japan. *Continuity and Change* 24, 169–196.
Saito, O. (2015). Climate, famine, and population in Japanese history: A long-term perspective. In: Batten, B.L. and Brown, P.C. (eds) *Environment and Society in the Japanese Islands: From prehistory to the present*. Corvallis OR: Oregon State University Press, 213–229.
Saito, O. (2020). The medieval origins of Smithian growth: The proliferation of occupations and commodities in Japan, 1261–1638. *Social Science Japan Journal* 23 (2), 205–224. [https://doi.org/10.1093/ssjj/jyaa003].
Saito, O. and Takashima, M. (2016). Estimating the shares of secondary- and tertiary-sector output in the age of early modern growth: The case of Japan, 1600–1874. *European Review of Economic History* 20, 368–86.
Saito, O. and Takashima, M. (2020). Chūsei kōki Nihon no jisshitsu chingin: hendō to kakusa. *Keizai kenkyū* 71, 129–143.
Sakurai, E. (1996). *Nihon chūsei no keizai kōzō*. Tokyo: Iwanami Shoten.
Sakurai, E. (2008). Currency and credit in medieval Japan. *International Journal of Asian Studies* 5: 53–70.
Sakurai, E. (2017). *Kōkan, kenryoku, bunka: hitotsu no Nihon chūsei shakai-ron*. Tokyo: Misuzu Shobō.
Segal, E. (2011). *Coins, Trade, and the State: Economic growth in early medieval Japan*. Cambridge MA: Harvard University Asia Center.
Settsu, T. and Takashima, M. (2020). Labour productivity growth in the long run: Japan, 1600–1909. *Australian Economic History Review* 60, 5–26.
Takagi, H. (2018). The monetary system of Japan in the Tokugawa Period. In: Battilossi, S., Cassis, Y. and Yago, K. (eds) *Handbook of the History of Money and Currency*. Singapore: Springer. [https://doi.org/10.1007/978-981-10-0622-7_53-2]
Uranagase, T. (2001). *Chū-kinsei Nihon kahei ryūtsūshi: torihiki shudan no henka to yōin*. Tokyo: Keisō Shobō.

Chapter 10

Markets, transactions, and ancient Egypt: New venues for research in a comparative perspective

Juan Carlos Moreno García

Recent research in archaeology, economic history, anthropology, and ancient history has led to a thorough re-evaluation of the role played by markets and market transactions in the circulation of goods, in the commercial operations led by traders, and in the overall economic structure of the societies where they are documented. Markets and traders appear more and more as indispensable mediators in ancient societies. In the case of traders, former assumptions about their practically complete subordination to institutions are gradually giving way to more nuanced approaches. It becomes more evident that, in many cases, they carried out their own commercial business alongside the missions that economic institutions trusted to them. More precisely, their activities left a durable mark in the economies of the ancient Near East. This was particularly evident in areas such as the commercialization of part of the temple and palace production (textiles, agricultural produce), the use of precious metals in transactions and in the diffusion of weight systems spread over vast areas. At the same time, the revalorization of markets and market transactions exposes the epistemological limits implicit in currently dominant economic models. According to these, modern mentalities, values and attitudes are thought as universally valid, as deeply rooted in the human mind and, consequently, as the most developed, efficient or, at least, rational way to carry out business, irrespectively of the society studied. More particularly, neo-institutional models have popularized concepts like 'rational behavior', 'transaction costs', etc., and interpreted pre-modern markets and economies in their light, as if the gradual expansion of trade, markets, private transactions, and investments should ineluctably lead to an economic mentality and a social consideration of efficiency and profit similar to those prevailing in our world (see Chapter 1 of this book).

On the contrary, the papers gathered in this book show that markets and market transactions could and did follow other distinctive paths, neither less rational nor efficient because they were based on different values and priorities. Commercial operations carried out over very long distances, for instance, benefited from some security provided not only by political powers but also by autonomous networks of traders based on ethnic and religious affiliations or, simply, on trust and reputation. In this light, research on pre-modern markets in different areas of the world also reveals that they cannot be interpreted as mere steps in a gradual, general move toward increasingly market-oriented economies, capable of breaking down former political, social, and economic structures as an ineluctable trend aiming to replace them by more 'market-friendly' oriented ones. It is easy to see behind these interpretations the shadow of the Western myths of 'progress' and Western 'exceptionalism/uniqueness', marking the path to follow to other areas of the world in their elevation toward Modernity. Pre-modern markets were often fragile and, where market transactions took a greater impetus and extension leading to limited 'capitalist' moves in some areas and periods of the world, usually under the form of commercial capitalism, they failed to initiate a sustained and irreversible ascension towards capitalism as it happened in some European regions in the late Middle Ages.

Such moves should not be underestimated either, because they open fascinating perspectives about the limits imposed by social and political structures but also about the very organization of mercantile activities and the role played by investment, monetization, trade ventures, organization of entrepreneurial activities, prices, and price formation, or about the ability of traders to create autonomous institutions capable of influencing decisively in political decision-taking. What is more, whereas such moves were relatively limited in geographical and chronological terms, they can be identified in periods more and more remote, to the point that early 'globalization' and periods of intense exchanges are detectable across Eurasia and East Africa since the Bronze Age. Such phenomena usually resulted in a process of gradual integration of more and more areas, of regional productive specializations, and in complex articulations of peoples and productions, able to incorporate mobile and sedentary populations, highly urbanized areas, loosely populated steppes, etc.

Obviously, it would be impossible to treat so many topics in only a few pages. Many recent discussions on ancient and pre-modern economies are contributing to renew our comprehension of the role played by markets, market transactions, and traders both in the economic and political spheres. One cannot but regret that pre-Hellenistic Egypt is too often absent from these discussions. That is why I would like to focus the following thoughts on four relevant topics inspired by the evidence presented and discussed in the previous chapters. These topics may show how much Egyptian sources could and should contribute to a better comprehension of these topics. At the same time, Egyptologists could enlarge their perspectives of research and integrate models, conceptual tools, and the experience accumulated by neighbor disciplines to analyze their own sources under a new light and, in so doing, to review their potential for more sophisticated interpretations of the pharaonic economy. Comparative research should not but gain from such fruitful collaboration between diverse disciplines and distinctive corpus of evidence.

Gathering places, 'silent' markets, and meeting points

The Egyptian term *meryt* 'quay' usually meant 'market' too and, in fact, some of the rare representations of markets and trading areas found in the rich pharaonic iconography took place, precisely, at quays (Eyre 1998). It is probably not by chance that another term linked to navigation, *demi* 'harbor, the harbor area of a town', appeared more or less at the same time, at the very late 3rd millennium BC, a period when exchanges expanded along the Nile and beyond. It was also a time that witnessed the expansion of the use of private seals and mentions to sealed documents in commercial agreements involving the sales of land, slaves, or the purchase of specialized services, like funerary rituals (an example: Landgráfová 2011: 36–38 no. 12). Given the particular geographical characteristics of Egypt, a long narrow floodplain crossed by the Nile and surrounded by a harsh desert environment, the river constituted the main pathway for the circulation of peoples and goods. Harbors and fluvial facilities distributed at regular distances were thus ideal places for exchanges, so quays became synonyms of 'market' and it was there that agriculture products, wood, textiles, wool, etc., were gathered and collected or bought and sold. Egypt was not unique in this respect, and the Akkadian term *kārum* conveyed both meanings too, 'quay, harbor' as well as 'trading area'. The inscription of the leader of Elephantine Sarenput I (*c.* 1950 BC), for instance, refers to his duties as overseer of ships and cargoes mooring at the quays/markets of the province. That is why inscriptions from different periods record ships as one of the most prized possessions in private hands, used to transport grain, cattle, and other goods. Administrative papyri from the 2nd millennium BC record the itineraries followed by small fleets at the service of institutions and traders, as well as the quays and other fluvial facilities where they moored to collect and exchange goods (Moreno García 2019a; 2019b). Lastly, archaeological discoveries at Tell el-Dab'a, Kerma (Nubia) and Wadi el-Jarf (Red Sea) confirm this picture as they have revealed sizeable harbour facilities as well as huge storage areas within them.

Temples were also meeting points in which exchanges took place. Several inscriptions from the early 1st millennium BC refer to traders that met representatives of the temples at the gates of the sanctuaries (Moreno García 2019b: 92–93). It was also common that a 'superior of the traders' intervened as a mediator between temples and traders. Earlier monuments mention them too, as in the case of Huy, a trader and 'superior of trader(s) of the temple of Aten', who lived in times of king Akhenaten (1352–1336 BC; Ockinga and Binder 2013; *cf.* also Valloggia 2018). The reason for the close association between traders and temples is that the latter became massive economic institutions from the second half of the 2nd millennium BC onwards. Apart from their cultic activities, they managed and accumulated substantial economic assets (fields, herds, mines, workshops, etc.), partly devoted to meet their own needs (provision of offerings, building projects, remuneration of priests and personnel, etc.) and partly commercialized through the mediation of traders who supplied temples with other goods too. In the end, markets and demand were substantial enough so as to absorb part of this production and to provide institutions with specialized, labor-intensive goods that complemented their own production, like textiles, wine, dates, and others.

Egyptian temples included facilities like warehouses and workshops and were surrounded by residential areas that hosted a diverse population made of priests, farmers, and craftspersons (Janssen 1992). Egyptologists have frequently interpreted enclosures combining cultic and productive areas as fortresses or temple-towns, especially when they were founded outside the Egyptian borders. An alternative view consists in considering them as multifunction centres used, among other purposes, to facilitate contacts between different peoples arrived there to trade, and that some kind of divine sanction at a sacred environment was considered indispensable to formalize the transactions that occurred there. In the case of mining and harbor sites, for instance, Egyptians and foreigners alike, given the particular favor enjoyed by Hathor among non-Egyptian peoples, attended sanctuaries erected in honour of goddess Hathor. Her temples provided a common cultic ground frequented and shared by different populations, a sacred area in which not only could they pray and perform rituals, but also negotiate, make agreements and collaborate, as evidence from the Hathor sanctuaries at Byblos, Serabit el-Khadim, or Timna shows (Fig. 10.1). In other cases, it seems that distinctive female portable figurines played a similar role, a sort

Figure 10.1. Temple of Hathor at Serabit el-Khadim (Wikipedia commons: https://commons.wikimedia.org/wiki/File:Serabit_el-Chadim_020.JPG).

of amulets recognizable by different peoples. They have been found along the trade routes of the Near East and the Aegean and discovered in mining sites too, like Gebel Zeit in Egypt (Moreno García 2017a).

So, massive enclosures that included a sanctuary and that were founded abroad probably aimed to concentrate flows of wealth and to facilitate contacts and exchanges between Egyptians and their foreign partners. One can think, for instance, of the isolated and short-lived 'fortress' of Zawiyet Umm el-Rakham, built in times of Ramesses II at a rather untenable military location on the Mediterranean coast, some 300 km west of the Delta and 25 km west of Marsa Matruh. There, the Egyptians erected a limestone temple inside a massive brick wall (140 × 140 m), together with storerooms, a governor residence, and a major provisioning area for production of bread and beer. A senior military officer ruled the complex but there is evidence that the local Libyan population provided at least part of the foodstuff consumed at the site, thus playing an important role in the viability of the Egyptian community settled there. Pottery finds revealed a substantial presence of Cypriot and Mycenaean vessels as well as Levantine goods, so international commerce seems, in fact, one of if not *the* main reason for building this enclosure at such a remote location. The site may be better understood as a jumping-off/arrival point in the maritime route that connected Crete with Egypt. At the same time, the presence of Libyans there and the textual mentions in the Egyptian sources of the Late Bronze Age of desert routes in the hands of Libyans, through which gold, ivory, and other precious items circulated, suggest that the 'fortress' was probably a factory or trading outpost founded at a meeting point frequented by Libyans, sailors, and Egyptians (Snape 2013; Moreno García 2014c; Nielsen 2017; Hulin 2018; *cf.* a parallel from Roman North Africa in Shaw 1995: 40–44). Archaeological evidence reveals similar enclosures built in the Western Delta, another border area between 'Libyans' and Egyptians. Finally, judging from the published reports and the plans of Zawiyet Umm el-Rakham, it appears that much of the enclosure lacks any substantial architectural remains. Perhaps the open spaces available served to lodge caravans, sailors, and passing travellers and to provide them a suitable place to stay and trade under the supervision of Egyptian authorities, a sort of caravanserai. If this was the case, then Zawiyet Umm el-Rakham shows functional similarities with the Nubian fortresses built in the early 2nd millennium BC as well as with the 'temple-towns' built by the Egyptians in the same region five centuries later.

The Nubian 'temple-towns' of the Late Bronze Age consisted of substantial enclosures where the temple only occupied a relatively reduced area of the total walled space. As for their geographical distribution pattern, they were built principally at strategic crossroads, close to gold production zones. It seems then that their main role was not simply cultic and that they intended perhaps to concentrate exchanges and flows of wealth at particular spots. No wonder that such a combination of cultic, economic, administrative, storage, and military functions have led researchers to doubt the definition of these sites: temple towns, fortified towns, or temple-based settlements? (Vieth 2018). Perhaps the term 'factory' is closer to reality too, a sort of trading meeting point in which divine sanction was considered essential to guarantee and solemnize exchanges between partners arriving from very different territories and cultural backgrounds (a general comparative overview in Delgado Hervás 2014: 284–287). Only the massive aspect of these enclosures and their walls may give the equivocal impression of a predominantly military function to modern eyes. However, walls of this kind usually conveyed different values for ancient audiences (Kemp *et al.* 2004).

Under this perspective, the Nubian 'temple-towns' played a role very similar to that of the 'fortresses' of the early 2nd millennium BC, when trade, navigation facilities and mining operations justified the foundation of impressive fortified sites at strategic spots in Nubia (Fig. 10.2) (Knoblauch 2019). Any real defensive role was perhaps secondary, more dissuasive than purely military in nature. 'Temple-towns' appear thus as links in a circuit that connected Egypt with Nubia and that facilitated the circulation of coveted goods. The rock decree of pharaoh Sety I (1294–1279 BC) at Nauri, in Nubia, just north of the third Nile cataract, mentions ships that belonged to the temple of Osiris at Abydos and that traded in Nubia (Kitchen 1993: 38–50). Foreign merchants (*šwtyw n ḫ3st* 'merchants of foreign countries') were at the service of this temple too. Another passage from the same decree forbids the commanders of a fortress built by Sety I near Nauri from stopping or taking goods from the ships of the temple of Osiris when they returned from Nubia. Finally, another section of this text forbids the superintendent of the *khetem* (=a fort and checkpoint that monitored the circulation of people and goods) at Bigeh, just south of Elephantine, to take anything from the 'tribute of Nubia' carried from Nubia to Abydos by the ships of the temple, mainly gold, pelts, hides, exotic skins, ochre, and plants (perhaps ivory and ebony

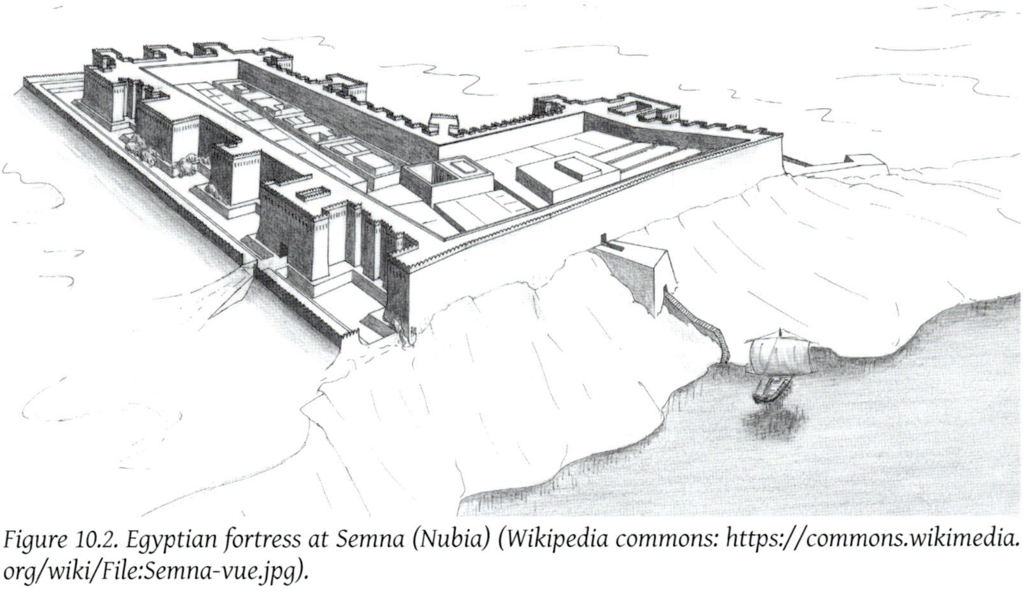

Figure 10.2. Egyptian fortress at Semna (Nubia) (Wikipedia commons: https://commons.wikimedia.org/wiki/File:Semna-vue.jpg).

too, but the passage is fragmentary; Moreno García in press a). So, *khetem* were a sort of fort-like buildings, a kind of checkpoints where Egyptian authorities levied taxes, monitored flows of wealth, controlled peoples, and, perhaps, held markets and fairs.

'Temple-towns' and 'fortresses' founded as remote trading outposts correspond to a very particular modality of exchanges, one that served the interests of the monarchy, which built, supplied, and operated such huge facilities. Nevertheless, it is possible to guess another modality, more informal and less institutionally oriented, based on meeting places and seasonal markets, which facilitated contacts between mobile and sedentary populations, or between itinerant merchants and local populations. One example is Khor Dawd, an archaeological site used between 3500–3200 BC and situated in Lower Nubia, about 100 km south of Aswan, and only 9 km north of the entrance of Wadi Allaqi, rich in gold deposits. There were uncovered 578 storage pits but no surface structures or hearths. Seventy-four pits contained Egyptian pots – many of them empty and turned upside down, whereas many pits contained abundant pieces of ostrich eggshell. Other organic finds consisted of some date stones and a small quantity of barley and wheat. Hafsaas-Tsakos interpreted the site of Khor Dawd as an early transit market, a place where Egyptians and people of the Nubian A-Group met to exchange their products on a 'neutral' ground. The Egyptian-imported pots consisting of jars and open bowls were most probably used as containers for imported cereals, beer, wine, and olive oil (Hafsaas Tsakos 2009: 25–26). Whereas the pits may, alternatively, correspond to the storage facilities of a nearby community, the huge quantity of Egyptian imports discovered there, precisely at the entrance of a gold-producing area, may suggest interregional trade and the existence of meeting points where Egyptians and Nubians exchanged goods. These meeting points were a sort of remote precedent of the Nubian fortresses discussed previously (Gatto 2019: 276–277).

Perhaps not by chance this was the very area in which the pharaohs of the early 2nd millennium BC built the fortress/emporia of Qubban, while another one was located slightly to the north, at Buhen. Buhen was founded as a fortified settlement about 2550 BC and was in use for 100 years, before being re-occupied again in the early 2nd millennium BC. Its main goal seems to have controlled access to gold mining areas and quarries of gneiss (Raue 2019: 295–296). When considering that Qubban and Buhen were not abandoned after the end of the Middle Kingdom monarchy (*c*. 1750 BC), and that an Egyptian community remained there (Knoblauch 2019: 382), we can conclude that their main goal was not defensive but commercial and that their very existence did not depend on the needs and the logistic support of the Egyptian monarchy. In fact, Ka, an official who lived then at the fortress of Buhen, claimed to be loyal to the ruler of Kush (Kubisch 2008: 36–87). No wonder then that these centres controlled the movements of small caravans and Nubian ships that arrived at the fortresses to trade (Kraemer and Liszka 2016). As for the magnitude of these commercial activities, one has to consider the existence of a sizeable non-fortified 'open town' adjacent to the fortress/factory of Mirgissa, occupied from the Middle Kingdom through the Second

Intermediate Period, where hundreds, even thousands of people lived. It comprised a cluster of houses with sinusoidal precinct walls and a dry-stone enclosure wall, quite distinct from the main town/fort, as well as a large swathe of garden plots (Spencer 2019: 444). As for the string of *khetem* that controlled the desert route between the Eastern Delta, the northern Sinai and the Levant, there is evidence of huts and small seasonal settlements built by mobile populations close to the forts. The purpose of these settlements was, perhaps, to trade or collaborate with the garrison as scouts, guides and suppliers of foodstuff and other goods (Hoffmeier *et al.* 2016).

These examples reveal the use of meeting points as seasonal or occasional markets by peoples that arrived there from different horizons. One can also think, for instance, about the inscription of Pharaoh Mentuhotep II at Jebel Uweynat, a remote area in the Eastern Sahara, where Egyptians obtained aromatic plants and other products (Diego Espinel 2013). As a matter of fact, an official who lived probably in the early 2nd millennium claimed that he had followed the route of the desert 'to meet the people of the oasis', but the purpose of the encounter is not made explicit. Nubian pottery and cemeteries of the Pan-Grave culture are well attested in the oases of the Western Desert and the Egyptian Nile Valley, respectively, about 1800–1550 BC. While they are usually interpreted as evidence of Nubian mercenaries and desert peoples patrolling at the service of the Egyptians, the fact that their necropolies were used by reduced domestic groups points to other alternatives. For instance, wandering herders and traders that sold aromatic plants and products of the desert in Egypt and that offered magical 'services' (Gatto *et al.* 2012; Manassa 2012; for a magic text mentioning 'the Nubian woman who has come from the desert', *cf.* Koenig 1987). In the case of Nag el-Qarmila (Gatto *et al.* 2012), the discovery of ostrich shells, beads, and other ornaments provides further evidence about the kind of goods exchanged. This site confirms that small communities of Nubians frequented particular spots in Egypt for generations and were buried in distinctive cemeteries there.

In the end, small caravans of mobile peoples circulated freely in Egypt, even across the routes of the oases in the early centuries of the 2nd millennium BC, with the aim of trading with desert goods that included minerals too. Literary, iconographic, and archaeological sources, such as the caravan led by the protagonist of the tale of *The Eloquent Peasant* (Parkinson 1997: 54–88), the Asiatic and Libyan caravans depicted in the tombs of Beni Hassan, the participation of Nubians and nomadic peoples in the extraction of minerals (Avner 2014; Liszka 2017; Moeller and Marouard 2018a: 175; 2018b: 39–40; Tassie 2018) or the circulation of scrap metal throughout Egypt's history (Rehren and Pusch 2012), support this view. Almost 1000 years earlier, several Bedouins lived in the villages around Gebelein, whereas desert peoples settled there in a town again at the very late 2nd millennium BC (Moreno García 2018a: 159). Finally, discoveries at Bates Island, an isolated anchorage near Marsa Matruh that served as an encounter place for mariners, Libyans and Egyptians, have revealed semi-permanent buildings as well as storage areas with Cypriot, Aegean, Canaanite, and Egyptian pottery. Many small fragments of ostrich shells confirm the presence of Libyans involved in small trade activities with foreign sailors, even in small-scale metallurgy and craft production (Hulin 2011; 2018).

Inversely, Egyptians also led small caravans abroad in an apparently non-institutional context. For instance, Egyptian herders lived in southern Palestine among Levantine agriculturalists in the late 4th millennium BC (Nicolle 2009: 38–40) whereas people from the Western Desert crossed the Delta and even reached Ashkelon. Tell el-Farkha, a locality in the Eastern Delta, imported wine, olive oil, copper, and bitumen from the southern Levant and exported grain and pork meat there. Many localities in this region show abundant traces of Egyptian presence and culture (Czarnowicz 2011). Formerly interpreted as 'colonies', they probably represent in fact nodal points in trade routes through which copper and valuable local produce (wine, olive oil, resins) were imported into Egypt. The disappearance of such centres, as well as the decline of Tell el-Farkha, coincides with the consolidation of the united monarchy in the Nile Valley and, quite probably, with the capture and centralization of formerly autonomous exchange networks (Moreno Garcia 2014d: 240). Shortly afterwards, animals and other goods were still exchanged between Egypt and the southern Levant around 2850–2550 BC. Area E of Tell eṣ-Ṣâfi/Gath (Israel) was a domestic residential neighborhood occupied by merchant families involved in regional and interregional exchange systems. The analysis of donkey and goat remains reveals a substantial network of exchange based on donkey caravans that criss-crossed the southern Levant and linked this region with Egypt. The animals were born and raised in Egypt, brought to Canaan, and slaughtered soon after their arrival at the site. Such 'hidden exports' cast thus some light on commerce based on relatively archaeologically-invisible products (Greenfield *et al.* 2020). Finally, many localities that flourished in the eastern Nile Delta in the late 4th and the 3rd millennia could have been meeting places for trade partners of different origins, such as Southern Levantines and Egyptians. The logistics of exchange, including transport, may have been carried out jointly by several settlements/parties (Dębowska-Ludwin *et al.* 2012; Mączyńska 2014; Tassie 2018).

May it be possible that ritual gathering places, frequented by nomads, played a similar role? Locality HK64, near Hierakonpolis, is a good candidate in view. Nubian mobile populations and Egyptians seem to have interacted there and participated together in celebrations in honour of goddess Hathor about the middle of the 2nd millennium, at the time of the Nile inundation (Friedman 1992; 2000). According to Friedman, Hathor's return, during the hottest part of the year, would have coincided with the northern seasonal migration of desert pastoralists. Another piece of evidence comes from a scene found at Wadi el-Hol, dating perhaps from the early 2nd millennium. It depicts a cow and two men bearing feathers on their heads, apparently two celebrants honoring Hathor. One of them has a beard and bobbed hair, thus suggesting a Libyan, while the other is depicted as an Egyptian official, bearing a necklace, a stick, and a long skirt (Darnell 2002: 126–127). Wadis used as desert routes were ideal connecting pathways, as in the case of the 'Way of cattle' (*t3 mj.t n jḥ.w*), mentioned in inscriptions of Taharqa from Bab Kalabsha, about 50 km south of Aswan, a departure point to the oasis of Kurkur. So the arrival points of the routes used by Nubians and Libyans in their (seasonal?) movements across the desert and into the Nile Valley, following perhaps seasonal transhumance itineraries, were ideal settings for exchanges between sedentary and mobile peoples too.

Finally, colonies of foreign traders operated in Egypt, in localities founded at strategic crossroads between Egyptians, desert populations, and merchants from other regions of the Near East, like Elephantine or Middle Bronze Age Tell el-Dab'a. Kom el-Hisn, in the Western Delta, probably played a similar role. It was there that another Ramesside enclosure similar to that discovered at Zawiyet Umm el-Rakham was built in the late 2nd millennium. However, this locality had previously known a long history of contacts between Egyptians and foreigners. Ruled by a series of 12 overseers during the second half of the 3rd millennium, their activities included control of movements across the desert and the Nile Valley and regulation of access to grazing areas in the Delta. Kom el-Hisn was thus a sort of checkpoint for desert peoples arriving into Egypt from Marmarica and the desert areas west of the Delta. When the monarchy collapsed about 2150 BC, Kom el-Hisn flourished instead, together with other localities of westernmost Lower Egypt. The traces of prosperity and the elite monumental buildings they displayed seem related to the intensification of maritime trade between Egypt and the Aegean (Moreno García 2015). The unique discovery at Kom el-Hisn of many 'warrior-tomb' burials, of Levantine style, suggests the presence of a substantial colony of traders who arrived there from Canaan in the late 3rd millennium BC (Wenke *et al.* 2016: 348–350). Slightly later, during the early second millennium BC, women from Kom el-Hisn and the Western Delta were involved in commercial (?) missions at Wadi Korosko, about 190 km south of Aswan (Žába 1974: 38, 56–57). In other cases, peoples from the Levant settled in Middle and Lower Egypt and were employed as warriors, to the point that some officers buried at Heracleopolis in the late 3rd millennium led military contingents of *Aamu* or 'Asiatic' soldiers.

Trade diaspores

In a seminal article published in 2001, Holladay analyzed the potential traces of merchant diaspores operating in the ancient Near East, that is to say, networks of merchants issued from a particular locality, state, ethnic group, or religious community who operated over long distances. In some cases, they developed institutions intended to protect their activities and interests in foreign territories. Whereas some of the examples he adduced are rather well known, such as the colony of Assyrian merchants settled at Kanesh/Kültepe (Anatolia), he also proposed that Egyptian traders were organized and operated with similar principles in the Levant and elsewhere during the Late Bronze Age. So, the houses discovered in Canaan but built according to an Egyptian plan might be interpreted as evidence of Egyptian traders active in this region who kept, nevertheless, their Egyptian lifestyle. Hence, these buildings were not necessarily used by Levantine egyptianized elites (Holladay

2001: 143, 166–174). Another consequence is that there is no proof that *any* Egyptian involved in commercial missions abroad was forcibly a specialized official trusted with a very particular *administrative* task – getting precious commodities. An alternative interpretation is that they were quite often merchants who worked on their own and carried out their own business in foreign lands. Their experience and contacts justified that kings used their services on special occasions, for example, when they needed a large shipment of specific items. Unfortunately, the nearly complete absence of archives produced and kept by traders, coupled with the surprising scarcity of references to merchants in pharaonic Egypt and their apparent reluctance to present themselves as traders in their own monuments (some rare exceptions: Ockinga and Binder 2013; Valloggia 2018), makes it extremely difficult to study their transactions: were they purely private, limited to the crown's demands, or a mix of both? Were they individual or organized as joint ventures, even in the framework of 'companies'? The same is true about the scope of their interests and the impact of their activities in the Egyptian economy. Still, some evidence suggests that Egyptian trade diaspores in the Levant are far from inconceivable and that Egyptian exchanges abroad did not necessarily depend on the state demand and the expeditions organized by the Pharaohs.

To begin with, a corpus of cuneiform tablets from Ebla (Syria) refers to the commercial contacts maintained by the royal palace with a foreign territory called Dugurasu (identified with Egypt) about 2500–2250 BC, through the mediation of Dulu (quite probably Byblos). The transactions included the export of lapis lazuli, tin, and textiles to Dugurasu/Egypt and the import of gold, ivory, and linen. According to these documents, the exchanges were in the hands of private merchants, as a commercial activity of their own among others. Furthermore, these merchants belonged to a very reduced number of families, including at least an Egyptian one formed by a certain Awa/Urwa and his son Gara (or Aib) (Biga and Steinkeller in press; cf. the case of two traders, sons of Hori, and two other traders, sons of Seniri, mentioned in a papyrus of the late 2nd millennium: Peet 1930: 90). Later, Egyptian ships and, possibly, traders (the term used is simply *kemetiu* 'people from Kemet [=Egypt]) involved in timber exports operated in Lebanon in the early 2nd millennium (Allen 2008), whereas the annals of Pharaoh Amenemhat II (1911–1877 BC) record considerable shipping cargoes that arrived in Egypt from the Levant (Marcus 2007; Altenmüller 2015). This was also a time in which contacts between Egypt and Ebla continued, led by their royal courts and in some cases by private people (Enea and Fiorentino 2018). The discovery of raw materials and luxury objects from Egypt, including an elaborate textile and fine hippopotamus ivory at Acemhöyük (Lassen 2014: 259–260) in southeastern central Anatolia, is considered as proof of an Eblaite trade network that dominated the southwestern corner of Central Anatolia in this period. This network would ensure the circulation of Egyptian commodities into Anatolia, a region then divided into three different regional spheres of commerce, dominated respectively by Assyria, Ebla, and the Mesopotamian city of Sippar (Barjamovic 2019).

Given the emphasis in the official record on commercial missions organized by the monarchy abroad, one cannot but regret that our knowledge about the social background of some of the most important expeditionary leaders is so poor. One can think, for instance, of Iny, a dignitary who led several maritime missions to Byblos and other localities in the Levant. On those missions he obtained silver, lead/tin, some kind of oil, and lapis lazuli, as well as Asiatic *(Aamu)* men and women, during the reigns of pharaohs Pepi I, Merenre, and Pepi II (around 2300 BC: Marcolin and Diego Espinel 2011). Unfortunately, the inscription in which he describes his travels appeared in the antiquities market, fragmented in several blocks, and the location of his tomb remains unknown. The biographies of both Iny and Herkhuf, a caravan leader of Elephantine (Strudwick 2005: 328–333), refer to a predecessor, an official called Werdjededba who lived a century earlier and whose commercial missions stood up as a model. Only in some cases is it possible to guess that the leaders of some localities specialized in foreign trade apparently controlled their own networks of contacts abroad. Therefore, when kings decided to dispatch a commercial mission to another territory, they called on their experienced services, according to a model well attested in Mesopotamia too (*cf.* for instance Garfinkle 2020).

One of such localities was Elephantine, the traditional Egyptian gateway to Nubia. The inscriptions of their leaders between 2300 and 2000 BC provide a unique insight into the missions they commanded abroad. While most expeditions were directed to Nubia, others took place by sea, to the land of Punt (southern Red Sea) and Byblos, far away from their usual theater of operations. The fact that they continued their activities when no king ruled over Egypt suggests that their commercial activities did not depend on royal commands. Hence, Setka of Elephantine (about 2100 BC) provided precious African and Levantine goods to the regional Heracleopolitan kingdom, which ruled then over some areas of Lower and Middle Egypt. Having imported myrrh from Byblos, gold and copper from Punt, incense from Nubia (Yam) as well as precious items like ebony, ivory, and exotic animals from other countries, he shipped them off to Heracleopolis in the north, across areas nominally controlled by a rival kingdom centered at Thebes (Edel 2008: 1743–1744). Another clue is that some people from Elephantine were apparently involved in trading activities with the Levant on a purely private basis from the 23rd century BC onwards (Forstner-Müller and Raue 2008). Therefore, the scope of action of the leaders of Elephantine was in no way limited to Nubia. As skilled specialists in foreign trade, it seems that they had their own interests, networks, and contacts both in Egypt and abroad making them unavoidable agents in commercial expeditions to other regions of Africa and the Near East. Apart from Elephantine, it seems that the leaders of Beni Hassan and Bersheh, in Middle Egypt, played a similar role in the first centuries of the 2nd millennium, as they were involved in exchanges, contacts, and expeditions to Punt (Fig. 10.3) and the Levant too (Moreno García 2017b). Unfortunately, evidence about the organization of the networks used by all these leaders in their contacts with foreign territories, including the possible presence of their own agents there, is missing.

Figure 10.3. Incense trees at Punt (Wikipedia commons: https://commons.wikimedia.org/wiki/File:Incense_trees_transport._Punt_relief._Mortuary_Temple_of_Hatshepsut,_Deir_el-Bahari.jpg).

Only in the Late Bronze Age does evidence about Egyptian merchants operating in foreign territories increase. One can think, for instance, of the 20 Egyptian traders in Cyprus mentioned in the Amarna letter no. 34 (Moran 1992: 105–106, and n. 9), the 13 Egyptian merchants murdered in southern Canaan for whom a local ruler paid 1400 shekels of silver in compensation (*ibid.*: 346–347), or the fleets of apparently wealthy private merchants evoked in the *Story of Wenamun*. They owned dozens of ships that traded between Egypt and the Levant, such as Werekter and the 50 ships in the harbor of Sidon that did business with his 'house' (Ritner 2009: 87–99). Special areas in the harbors of important cities (Memphis, Tell el-Dab'a) were settled with foreign merchants and 'messengers' involved in diplomatic and trading activities with Egyptian officials. Thus, a papyrus referring to a ship that carried out commercial exchanges and was dispatched from Thebes to the *meryt* (market/quay) of Memphis, mentions the 'account of trading' made 'in the language of Kharu [= Syria, Levant]'.

Temples built to honor the gods Baal and Astarte are well attested at the harbor of Memphis, Peru-Nefer, while papyrus St Petersburg 1116 mentions food delivered to Baal of Peru-Nefer as well as to messengers of several Asian cities settled there. The harbor/quay at Memphis was thus a meeting point for traders arriving from Egypt and from abroad. The same is true for Pi-Ramesses, in the Eastern Delta, as its markets were frequented by foreign merchants: 'Pleasant is the place of distribution/market-place with its money/silver there, mainly the vine tendrils (?) and business/commerce (*t-m-k-r-i-t*). The chiefs of every foreign country come in order to descend with their products' (Moreno García 2019b: 94).

Egyptian traders may have operated along similar conditions in foreign territories. In any case, Levantine temples with a strong presence of Egyptian material, as it happened at the Ba'alat Gebal temple and the Obelisk Temple at Byblos, probably point to a local community of Egyptian merchants settled there or that frequented this harbor. It might be possible that they enjoyed some kind of protection from Pharaohs, who presented votive offerings there. The fact that Egyptian deities (Hathor, Herishef-Re) were worshipped in both sanctuaries is particularly relevant (Diego Espinel 2002; Bietak 2019), especially since they were associated with traders abroad and, in the case of Herishef-Re, with Heracleopolis, an Egyptian locality involved in the commerce of aromatic plants about 2100 BC. Having in mind that both temples consisted of many contiguous shrines, each with distinctive objects deposited there, Wengrow has concluded that such assemblages represent the coming together of a specific group of individuals for a particular purpose that involved marking their unity through a collective act of object sacrifice. Furthermore, he considers it conceivable that a routine association existed at Byblos between the construction and use of stone monuments, the performance of collective ritual dedications, and the mounting of individual sea voyages. Finally, the assemblage of Egyptian stone vessels from the temple comprised many provincial forms, something coherent with the presence of a provincial deity like Herishef-Re (Wengrow 2009: 151–157; Moreno García 2019a). A final point to consider is that, as discussed in previous pages, temples and their gateways were meeting points where commercial exchanges took place, including foreign peoples and merchants (Moreno García 2019b: 92–93).

Finally, specialized Late Bronze Age estates in the Levant, erroneously interpreted as Egyptian 'governors' residences' due to their Egyptian-like architectural features may correspond, in fact, to centers that produced particular items highly appreciated by Egyptian elites and exported to Egypt, such as wine (Gadot 2010) or, alternatively, centers that monitored large pasturages (Blakely 2018). Their smooth decline during the Late Bronze Age, in most cases with no sign of a violent end (Millek 2018), may suggest that their fate was closely linked to a declining Egyptian market. As for the Egyptian objects and imitations found there, they suggest the presence of Egyptian or Egyptianized managers. Other architectural structures found in the Levant and related to the Egyptian presence there in the Late Bronze Age raise similar interpretability challenges too. It is the case, for instance, of the Amman Airport structure, a sort of fortified way station, fort tower and redispersal center, probably manned by Egyptians or Egyptianized locals accompanied by local-regional auxiliaries, which formed part of an important trade network (Mumford 2015). These examples can be compared with later buildings in the Negev, interpreted cautiously as caravanserais, which included small niches or wayside shrines where travelers left votive offerings (Hadley 1993).

Markets, small landholders, and peasant strategies

The dominant model about the nature and organization of the pharaonic economy highlights its alleged redistributive and centralized structure under the tight control of the royal administration. According to this interpretation, the state collected taxes in kind (grain, cloth, other agricultural produce) and labor (as corvée work), subsequently spent on socially useful measures (distribution of foodstuff in case of famine, hydraulic works, clearing and tilling of uncultivated land), and in civilian and culturally significant equipment (fortresses, monumental architecture). Under these conditions, markets occupied a marginal position at best in the circulation and distribution of wealth, submerged by an overwhelming bureaucratic control of economic activities and distribution of 'rations'. However, the empiric basis of such a view is surprisingly meagre, mostly based on rhetorical claims about providing food to the poor or workers employed in very specific projects of the crown, such as expeditions to quarries and building programs. That is why its limits have been rightly outlined by alternative models in which markets and private transactions play a more active role (Moreno García 2014a; 2014d; 2016a; Warburton 2016; Muhs 2018).

To begin with, in an economy based on agriculture it was not uncommon that land itself was sold and bought and that private initiatives sought either to acquire land or to maximize the profitability of one's agricultural assets. In the first case, many inscriptions from the very end of the 3rd millennium mention private acquisitions of fields by officials and wealthy individuals. Inversely, private letters and moralizing texts evoke the loss of family land assets because of debts. So rhetorical and biographical claims may co-exist in private inscriptions. The former emphasize help provided to needy neighbors and poor people in hard times, to avoid them the loss of their fields and freedom, while the latter boast about the acquisition of fields and serfs (Moreno García 2000). Land appears thus as a tempting investment, particularly for the people that had accumulated precious metals. When a soldier from Edfu called Ha-ankhef (*c.* 1550 BC) returned from Nubia after having obtained 26 pieces of gold and a servant girl as payment for his military services for six years, he invested his wealth in the purchase of three plots of land, one for himself, another for his wife, and the last one for his children (Redford 1997: 12). Penone, a sandal maker who lived in the Ramesside period, acquired 17 *nbyw* (?) of land in exchange for gold (Hassan and Ouda 2018: 100). As for the famous robberies of the late New Kingdom, when huge amounts of silver and gold were stolen from temples and royal tombs, the robbers used the booty to acquire, among other goods, fields, slaves, grain, and cattle, usually through the mediation of merchants (Peet 1930: 118, 144, 149, 152, 157). Thus the overseer of the field of the temple of Amun, Akhenmenu, received 1 *deben* of silver (=91 g) and 5 *kite* of gold (=45.5 g) 'in exchange for land.' However, the scribe Amenhotep 'called Seret', of the temple of Amun, received 2 *deben* (=182 g of silver) in exchange for land, for 40 *deben* of copper and for ten sacks of barley (Peet 1930, 144; the ratio silver:copper at this time was 1:60). The fact that enormous quantities of precious metals could be absorbed and laundered through commercial transactions and, what is more, easily exchanged for common goods, means that their circulation, as well as the activities of traders, were far from uncommon in the local sphere, even among the people of modest condition (Castle 1992: 256–263; Moreno García 2014a; 2014b; 2016a). This was the case, for instance, of a group of traders, apparently at the service of a temple, who exchanged gold for foodstuff (papyrus Boulaq XI: Peet 1934; Megally 1974; 1975; Ali 1997), or a group of independent tenants who paid directly their taxes to the treasury of the pharaoh in gold (Wente 1990: 130–131).

In other cases, access to royal and temple fields was another way to accumulate a substantial land portfolio, either as agricultural 'entrepreneurs' who cultivated the fields owned by institutions or as a reward for performing specialized services to the temples or the king. In both cases, the rights over the possession or cultivation of institutional fields were bought and sold, a process in which the rather intricate accumulation of multiple rights over a single piece of land might bring about occasional conflicts between holders. In the end, holding scribal, military, or priestly functions gave access to institutional fields. As a coveted source of wealth, local elites, wealthy peasants, or people of some importance sought avidly for the income, power, and prestige derived from the possession of temple and crown land. So, the patrimony of the elite consisted of a mix of private/patrimonial land and institutional fields, and their strategies sought to preserve and increase both sources of wealth (Moreno Garcia 2014b; 2016b). To put an example, a land record like the Wilbour Papyrus (*c.* 1146 BC) enumerates more than 2400 holders of such fields in a section of about 140 km of the Nile Valley, roughly south of Fayyum. The landowning institutions included the domains of gods Amun, Re, Ptah, smaller temples, a few secular landowners (*e.g.*, the Treasury of Pharaoh), and royal land (called *khato*). However, modern social categories such as 'priests' or 'officials' conceal far more complex conditions. Holders of ritual functions like the *choachytes* (they took care of the ceremonies and cult for the dead in exchange for a fee), pursued other lucrative activities, like leasing temple land individually or collectively as members of a group of shareholders. In other cases, they invested in slaves, houses, building plots, loans, fields, or cattle, as the archives of Djekhy, a lady called Tsenhor and Petebaste reveal (Donker van Heel 2012; 2014; Moreno García 2016b).

Private landowners sought for maximizing the profitability of their agricultural assets, as the examples of Heqanakhte and Thutmose reveal (early and late 2nd millennium, respectively). Heqanakhte, for instance, addressed several letters to his subordinates with very precise instructions about the management of his land and the allocation of resources to the members of his household. What emerges from these documents is that his agricultural choices were guided by purely private interests, as he sought to obtain the best possible returns. A plot previously planted with flax was to be grown with barley unless a big inundation came because, in that case, emmer would best suit the soil; another plot, left in pasture, had to be hoed; and more land was to be leased in order to be cultivated despite his being a holder of a substantial landed portfolio (some 15–30 ha). Other accounts from his archive reveal that one of the main concerns of his agricultural activities was flax production. He owned considerable pasturage land too (about 3.8 ha) that should be hoed, quite probably with the intention to be planted (Allen 2002). As for Thutmose, he owned two categories of land, one which explicitly belonged to him and his son ('our own land'), the administrative status thereof being difficult to identify (privately held fields on temple land or simply private property?), and the other which quite probably consisted of estates pertaining to temples or secular institutions. As it happened with Heqanakhte, the administrative or juridical nature of Thutmose's fields were a secondary concern: his main goal was managing the land so as to obtain the best agricultural yield. Both Heqanakhte and Thutmose behaved like managerial landlords, closely watching over all the details of agricultural operations, and they were certainly not absentee landlords who delegated the management of their fields to subordinates preoccupied only with the revenue generated. Their interests extended over a district too. In the case of Thutmose, his letters refer to grain stored in magazines in several villages, thus suggesting that other cultivators living nearby worked the estate alongside household members. In fact, the men laboring in the fields were perceived as having the same level of importance as his son and his family as if they were part of his household. Links with temples also emerge in one of his letters, in which Thutmose mentions chariot-pulling donkeys that, apparently, belonged to a temple (Antoine 2015; Moreno García 2019b: 99). As for Heqanakhte, he held land in several zones and many people owed grain to him, from local administrators and scribes to landowners. Other documents reveal similar strategies, in which profitability and careful land management and accumulation guided the actions of certain individuals (Fig. 10.4). The papyrus Brooklyn 16.205 (around 770 BC) deals with the acquisition of several plots of land made by a certain Ikeni in a year of hard times. The plots are quite small (in three cases hardly more than half an *aroura* or 1400 square meters) and, in several cases, they are described as located next to 'the well of Ikeni' (Parker 1962: 49–52, pls 17–19). It seems as if Ikeni followed a calculated strategy of purchase, seeking to acquire plots around a well that bore his own name or that of a member of his kin, even of an ancestor. Given the location and small surface of the tenures, it is possible that they were both devoted to horticultural production instead of the cultivation of cereals and represented then a profitable investment.

Finally, Heqanakhte also stands out for another reason. His wealthy agricultural enterprise enabled him to lend grain to numerous neighbors. Having in mind how little we know about peasant credit in ancient Egypt (Bleiberg 2002), some documents

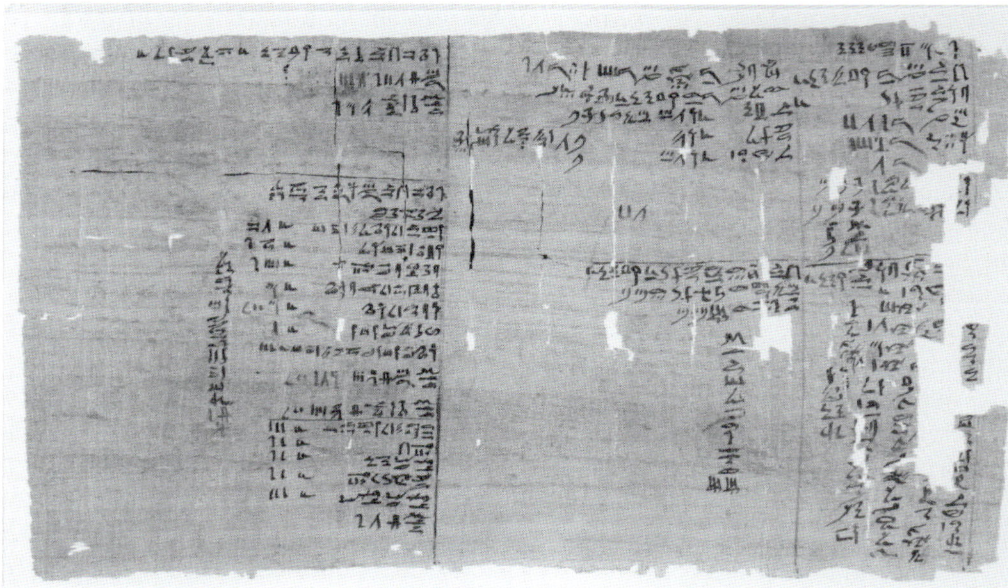

Figure 10.4. Heqanakhte letter (Wikipedia commons: https://commons.wikimedia.org/wiki/File:Heqanakht_Letter_V_MET_EG37_22.3.517-crop.jpg).

from his archive prove invaluable in this respect. Thus, accounts V and VI record the names of 22 debtors and the amounts of grain related to them, which may represent loans of cereals (Allen 2002: 19–20, 163–185). Debts provided wealth and social power to wealthy landowners. A letter from the late 3rd millennium states that the debts contracted by an individual and not reimbursed led to the seizure of some fields held by his family (Wente 1990: 211–212). A satirical composition of the late 2nd millennium refers to peasants in need forced to resort to traders in order to get a loan, whereas another passage from the same text refers that 'the merchants travel downstream and upstream. They are as busy as can be, carrying goods from one town to another. They supply him who has wants' (Lichtheim 1976: 170).

This reference suggests that traders not only transported, bought, and sold goods and helped convert agricultural produce into precious metals and *vice versa*. They also provided loans to peasants and their commercial operations along the Nile involved institutions as well as commoners too. In fact, the commercialization of crops may explain the massive deliveries of silver made annually by the servants of the royal mortuary temple of Ramesses III (1184–1153 BC) and subsequently granted to other temples during his reign. Along with remittances in nature (grain, linen, cattle, agricultural goods, metals, etc.), the text also mentions enormous quantities of silver, a metal not produced in Egypt and that, consequently, only arrived in the Nile Valley by trade and tribute. Only the Theban temples, for example, received three assignments of silver for an amount of, respectively, 997.8 kg, 328 kg, and 382 kg (Grandet 1994: 238, 325). How those servants obtained such huge quantities of silver is unfortunately never mentioned but it seems reasonable to think that the commercialisation of part of the harvests of the temples procured substantial amounts of silver to these people, so they could pay their taxes in silver on a regular, annual basis. In fact, the texts of the late 2nd millennium reveal that Egypt exported grain, partly at least in the context of agreements between states. A letter sent from Egypt to Ḫatti during the reign of Ramesses II mentions a Hittite delegation sent to Egypt with the mission to procure a vital shipment of grain to the Anatolian kingdom (Edel 1994 II: 276–277). These exports of grain may explain the depreciation of the value of silver in Egypt around the reign of Merenptah (from a ratio silver:copper of 1:100 to only 1:60 *deben*), perhaps because huge quantities of silver were arriving then into Egypt as payments for the cereals delivered (Liverani 1990: 235–236). In other cases, it was individuals who commercialized their crops and obtained precious metals in exchange. According to a letter of the late 2nd millennium, some affluent farmers delivered their taxes in gold directly to the royal treasury (Wente 1990: 130–131). In another instance, however, a scribe wrote to a colleague to forbid him to behave in such a reprehensible way again as he had done in the past, when he set aside part of the rations/wages under his care in order to convert them into silver (*ibid.*: 114). Fishermen also exchanged their captures for silver, as they paid their taxes with this metal and officials ordered to buy fish carried with them large amounts of this metal as well (*ibid.*: 118–119, 120–122). Markets and traders appear indispensable in all these transactions.

How did markets guide the agricultural choices and strategies of small peasants? Given the nearly complete absence of archives produced by small landholders, only some administrative records derived from institutions (temples, etc.) reveal that farmers produced crops not only for their own subsistence but also for markets and institutions. This was the case particularly with labor-intensive crops because their costs of production (specialized workforce, long term returns, continuous irrigation, etc.) were too high for institutions. Dates represent a good example. The papyrus Louvre E 3226 (*c.* 1420 BC) records the operations carried out along the Nile by several ships belonging to the Granary, that is to say, the institution in charge of collecting and stocking grain. Several sections of this papyrus show that the Granary employed two teams of agents called *bnryw* or 'those in charge of dates' (Megally 1977). The Granary supplied barley to both teams and they exchanged grain for dates at several points along their itinerary. Unfortunately, papyrus Louvre E 3226 never reveals how the *bnryw* obtained the dates but comparable papyri reveal that small fleets dispatched by temples and royal institutions traveled around the Nile and collected dates and other goods from particulars (women seem particularly active in these exchanges), like cereals, flowers, wine, cattle, and cloth (Janssen 1961; 2004; Condon 1984; Wente 1990: 92–93, 119–122, 128, 180; Castle 1992; Hagen 2008; Hassan 2016). A document from around 1500 BC records, for instance, that in one case such ships delivered some pieces of silver to a woman at a *mryt* 'quay, marketplace' (Condon 1984: 63–65). In fact, institutional agricultural records only rarely refer to plantations of date palms, the exception being recreational basins in temples and palaces in which date palms grew together with many other types of trees. That is why only a single palm plantation is enumerated among the massive donations of fields, gardens, and other goods recorded in the papyrus Harris I (Grandet 1994: 261), whereas, in sharp contrast, huge quantities of dates were donated to the temples (*ibid.*: 251, 273, 275), even ropes made of palm fiber (*ibid.*: 244).

Other administrative documents referring to the cultivation of vegetables and the payment of rents in these goods, such as the Wilbour Papyrus, confirm that horticulture and small irrigation became a common feature in the 2nd millennium BC, but they were mostly restricted to private landholdings. This was a period that witnessed the introduction of irrigation devices like the *shaduf* that made possible perennial irrigation of small gardens. Not by chance, many references in administrative and literary texts of the second half of the 2nd millennium evoke a peri-urban landscape made of gardens and villas, provided with every kind of wealth, from fields to herds of cattle, even able to import goods from the Levant in their own ships (Caminos 1954: 137–138, 164–165, 412–413). Quite significantly, the literary genre known as 'Praise of the City', with its vivid descriptions of the rich peri-urban horticultural landscapes around some of the most important Egyptian metropolies, also appeared at this time (Ragazzoli 2008). Other agricultural innovations consisted in the introduction of new fruit crops such as pomegranate, almond tree, apple tree, etc., around 1600 BC. As it happened in Mesopotamia, date palm plantations were usually in private hands and they represented a lucrative investment for urban landowners and rural potentates. That is why some land sales enumerate date palms together with basins and wells and the quality of the fields sold. In other cases, letters and administrative documents record instructions given to plant plots with fruit (Wente 1990: 175–176) or evoke fields planted with vegetables and that delivered rents in vegetables too, sometimes alternating with grain (Kitchen 1970: 804,15; 805,5; 806,5; Wente 1990: 46, 209). However, things were different with vineyards and olive plantations. They were part not only of private gardens (as archaeological, iconographic, and written evidence from this period shows: Fig. 10.5), but also constituted huge institutional plantations, from which considerable amounts of oil and wine were collected (Moreno García in press b).

In all these cases, a new kind of private wealth seems to be based on private small-scale irrigated agriculture and lucrative crops oriented toward urban markets – at least partly. One may only infer that traders played again an essential role in such operations and the commercialization of crops, both private and institutional. According to the Papyrus Lansing, a scribal composition of the late 2nd millennium:

> the merchants travel downstream and upstream. They are as busy as can be, carrying goods from one town to another. They supply him who has wants. But the tax collectors carry off

Figure 10.5: Garden Tomb of Minnakht (Wikipedia commons: https://commons.wikimedia.org/wiki/File:Funeral_Ritual_in_a_Garden,_Tomb_of_Minnakht_MET_DT10880.jpg).

> the gold, that most precious of metals. The ships' crews from every house (of commerce), they receive their loads. They depart from Egypt for Syria, and each man's god is with him. (Caminos 1954: 390; Lichtheim 1976: 170).

Furthermore, the Great Abydos Inscription of Ramesses II (lines 34–35) mentions merchants at the service of the funerary temple of Seti I at Abydos in the commercial operations it conducted abroad:

> and I gave to you a mnš-ship bearing deliveries on the Great Green [=the Eastern Mediterranean], bringing in for you great [marvels of] God's Land [=the southern Red Sea], while traders trade with their consignments, and their revenue thereof being gold, silver and copper. (Kitchen 1970: 332–333; Castle 1992: 250–251)

Inversely, foreign merchants were involved in agricultural exchanges along the Nile. A passage from a papyrus referring to a ship involved in riverine trade and dispatched from Thebes to the *mryt* (market/harbor) of Memphis mentions the 'account of trading' made 'in the language of Kharu [=Syria, Levant]' (Janssen 1961: 72–73).

The report of Wenamun (end of the 2nd millennium) describes a commercial mission abroad that involved the exchange of crops. This text records the demands made by the king of Byblos to the Egyptian rulers in exchange for the delivery of timber. Together with precious items such as five gold and silver vessels and several garments of fine linen, Wenamun mentions more prosaic goods sent to the Lebanese city too, including 500 linen mats, 500 ox-hides, 500 ropes, 20 sacks of lentils, and 30 baskets of fish (Ritner 2009: 96). Another aspect mentioned by Wenamun is that Egyptian '(commercial) houses' of traders (like those mentioned in the Papyrus Lansing or in papyrus BM 10068 recto: Peet 1930: 90) operated then in the Levant. Hence, 20 ships in Byblos traded with pharaoh Smendes, while another 50 ships in Sidon did business with a certain Werket-el (probably a Levantine partner or agent of Smendes) and had sailed to his 'house' (Liverani 1990, 247–254; Ritner 2009: 94). Finally, traders from foreign lands arrived in Egypt to exchange their goods for grain too, as in the case of the sailors from the land of Punt who brought incense, ebony, monkeys, etc., to an Egyptian harbor, according to a scene from around 1400 BC (Bradbury 1996). In some cases, royal commercial expeditions intended to bypass intermediaries. Queen Hatshepsut, for instance, organized a direct naval expedition to Punt just to avoid the sort of difficulties encountered by her forebears when they brought precious goods from this exotic land but 'in exchange of numerous payments' (Sethe 1961: 344).

Grain, markets, and private economy

Papyrus Turin 1887 (*c.* 1150 BC) describes, among other crimes, the charges raised against a merchant and ship's captain named Khnumnakht. He connived with the scribes, inspectors, and cultivators of the temple of god Khnum at Elephantine and embezzled nearly 6724 sacks of grain (=516,403 litres) that were destined for the temple over a ten-year period (1151–1142 BC), including 1000 sacks delivered by two individuals, Remet and Pawekhed, during the same period (50 sacks per year each of them). Furthermore, he also stole 0.63 kg of gold from the sanctuary (Porten 1996: 53–55). Shortly afterwards, another papyrus from Elephantine describes the protest of a mayor of this locality against a tax claim made by an agent of the royal administration, concerning 100 sacks of grain from a crown field located to the north, in the Island-of-Ombos. He swore that it was not cultivated by him but by some private tenants who made their payments in gold directly and regularly to the Royal Treasury (Porten 1996: 57–59). Both documents raise several important questions. On the one hand, it was apparently quite easy to make disappear or launder more than 256 tons of grain (or 25.6 tons/year), thus implying the existence of markets capable of absorbing substantial quantities of cereals. Not by chance, Khnumnakht was a merchant and ship's captain. On the other hand, part of the land owned by the state or by temples was cultivated through intermediaries that paid their taxes either in grain or in gold, thus implying again that crops were commercialized.

Two new elements seem to characterize the agricultural economy of the Late Bronze Age in Egypt. Since 1550 BC temples became massive economic institutions, owners of extensive landed assets. Yet the actual management and cultivation of these fields were partially assured by 'agricultural entrepreneurs', usually wealthy peasants, with interests extending over several villages or a district. As for the second element, it was the first mention of traders in administrative texts and documents. The two elements seem connected, on the one hand, the indirect exploitation of land that opened the possibility to make business with institutions; and, on the other hand, the existence of traders who commercialized the crops produced by institutions and transformed them into precious metals. In contrast, a network of royal agricultural, production and storage centres scattered all over the country in previous centuries had made it possible to produce and deliver goods to royal agents directly when needed. However, this system was partly replaced by a new one about 1550 BC, when temples, not royal centers, raised to a prominent economic position in what appears as indirect management of crucial economic assets. It was at temple gateways that agents of the sanctuaries and traders met and made transactions.

Under these conditions, the cereals produced by great institutions stimulated private economic activities and exchanges that profited wealthy peasants, managers, and other producers. As evoked previously, fleets of temples and institutions like the Granary collected goods from individuals (fruits, cloth, cereals, dates, vegetables, cattle) who delivered grain too, either as managers, suppliers, or, simply, tenants subject to taxes and rents. The fact that the interaction between the institutional and the private economic spheres intensified since 1550 BC meant that labor-intensive activities (horticulture, weaving, etc.) were partially left into private hands, so institutions could get specialized productions too costly for them when needed. A new category of population flourished then, the *nemehu* or 'free/independent men', people whose private wealth did not derive from any service to the state. The decree of King Horemheb, for instance, aimed to protect their property against any abuse by any agent of the crown, particularly the illegal seizure of their boats, serfs/slaves, hides, fodder, grain, linen, and vegetables from their houses and their boats (Kruchten 1981: 198). These measures reveal a category of person, owners of a subordinate workforce, who possessed boats (for previous periods, *cf.* Moreno García 2019a: 193–194) and carried goods in them, and that included cattle and horticulture among their property. They were thus not mere peasants but people relatively affluent. Women took part in this move too and 'ladies' (the imprecise translation of the Egyptian term *ʿnḫt nt nwt* 'living one of the city'), that is to say, women involved in independent economic activities, are frequently referred to as protagonists of exchanges and holders of temple land.

It was probably to this social sector that the owners of private villas called *bekhen* and of the rich agricultural economy centered around them belonged. To take an example, the late Ramesside Wilbour Papyrus provides a unique glimpse into the settlement structure in a rural area of Middle Egypt, where it records 51 mounds, 37 houses, 29 villages, and 17 'villas' (*bekhen*). As Kemp observes, these centers were not evenly spread out within the area covered by this document: 'villas' cluster in zones marked by larger towns, whereas houses tend to be more numerous in zones where there were fewer larger towns (Kemp 1991: 312). Having in mind that the Wilbour Papyrus records the fields and agricultural domains held by temples and the crown in this area, this document seems to confirm the symbiosis between affluent landowners and institutions and the mutual benefits gained from their collaboration in the cultivation of institutional land. Not by chance, more than 2500 plots of institutional land listed in this document were in the hands of what could be defined as local sub-elites, a social sector made of officers, priests, affluent farmers, 'ladies', etc., who paid taxes in grain in exchange for these fields (cf. temple warehouses: Fig. 10.6).

Another link between the private and the institutional sphere was the implementation of the '*ihuti*-system' in the cultivation of temple and crown fields (Moreno García 2016b). The *ihuti* were farmers forced to till fields and deliver quotas of grain, usually standard plots of 20 arouras (=5.5 ha) and standard quotas of 200 sacks of grain (=15,360 liters). The institution for which they worked also provided for a yoke of oxen. Their serfdom-like status explains why temples and the crown affected prisoners of war, deportees, criminals, etc., as *ihuti* to their fields, a system that grew considerably in the Late Bronze Age thanks to the imperial expansion of Egypt and the regular flow of foreign forced workers to the Nile Valley. It seems that substantial areas of Egypt were now put under cultivation and that extensive cereal farming was the option preferred for areas insufficiently irrigated by the annual flood of the

Figure 10.6. Ramesseum and its warehouses (Wikipedia commons: https://commons.wikimedia.org/wiki/File:SFEC_AEH_-ThebesNecropolis-2010-RamsesII-021.jpg).

Nile. It is not probably by chance that some of the most detailed inventories of fields from this period (the Wilbour Papyrus, the Baldwin and Amiens papyri, etc.) concern Middle Egypt, a region with abundant potential agricultural land. However, the term *ihuti* also designed wealthy farmers who assumed the cultivation of substantial fields of crown and temple land. In the case of the Wilbour Papyrus, for example, they tilled agricultural domains of considerable size, about 60 ha or more. This means that they had enough workforce, tools, and assets at their disposal to till fields that exceeded the capacities of modest peasant families. Unfortunately, the sources are rather elusive about the profit obtained by this particular category of *ihuti*- 'rural entrepreneurs' from their activities. The Wilbour Papyrus and other institutional documents reveal, nevertheless, that they were granted temple fields of the type usually held by the local sub-elites as a reward or remuneration for their services. Access to influential institutions helped them thus to strengthen their prestige and importance in the local society. In fact, they appear as men of influence over districts that encompassed several villages, like the *ihuti* Amenmose (Gardiner 1941: 57) or the *ihuti* Patjauemdiamun, concerned by several oracular decisions taken at several villages that involved numerous witnesses as well as his companions and members of his personnel (Kitchen 1989: 416–418). As temples received then not only enormous amounts of grain but also of silver, it seems rather probable that the *ihuti*-system and its expansion during the Late Bronze Age was a fundamental source of revenues for the temple and the crown and that it boasted the production of grain subsequently commercialized.

In this perspective, institutional grain fuelled quite probably a private economy as well as urban markets in the Late Bronze Age, a period of expanding urbanism in Egypt. Traders appear thus as the third pillar of this economic system together with landed institutions and private landholders. They helped commercialize agricultural production and, at the same time, institutions provided merchants with silver and gold in order to acquire precise items. This not only means that metals were used in transactions, but also that temples and other institutions needed a regular income in precious metals to exchange them for other goods and services, even to pay taxes in silver and gold (Janssen 1991; Traunecker 2005). The papyrus Boulaq XI, for instance, contains accounts of the sale of small quantities of goods, principally beef and wine. The majority of the transactions appear to be debits entered against the names of various traders who, in some cases, paid for their purchases in gold. These transactions seem to involve retailers making purchases from a wholesaler, apparently a temple. Another document mentioning the same traders (Papyrus Cairo CGC 58081) shows that they co-operated among themselves and that when a number of goods and/or precious metals was due to one of them, another colleague could receive it in his name (Megally 1974; 1975; Ali 1997). In another case, a temple provided several quantities of gold, silver, and copper 'for the rations of the Necropolis' (Kitchen 1983: 612). In other cases, the sources refer to grain for sale, as when a female servant was given two *deben* copper to buy barley (Hölzl *et al.* 2018: 19; compare with a coppersmith that received one *deben* of copper to buy tin or lead: *ibid.*: 13). Another document mentions a considerable amount of silver delivered to several ship captains in order to get fish and wool (Wente 1990: 120–122), and it was not rare that fishermen leased their boats to people who transported other cargoes (*ibid.*: 174)

Traders also made loans to modest peasants, according to the Papyrus Lansing cited previously. They were not unique in this role, as private individuals made loans to people in need too, particularly in grain. Papyrus Turin 1881, for instance, mentions a loan of grain made at the very high interest of some 100% yearly. In ostracon Gardiner 137 two policemen take an oath that they will repay a grain debt or pay a penalty – double the amount owed (Kitchen 1983: 251), whereas papyrus Cairo 58056 mentions the reimbursement of a service or favor that could be made either in 80 *deben* of copper (1 *deben*=91 g) or in 80 sacks of emmer (Wente 1990: 117). If debtors failed to reimburse their debts, they lost their fields or their property and, in some cases, they or some members of their families (usually young girls) were reduced to serfdom, according to texts from different periods (Moreno García 2000).

The inconclusive evidence about early commercial capitalism in Egypt

Recent research shows that some early forms of commercial capitalism emerged in several parts of the world and that they preceded its blossoming in Europe in the late Middle Ages (Van Bavel 2016; Banaji 2020). However, these precocious developments did not crystallize in the consolidation of capitalist relations of production as dominant in their respective economic systems. The ancient Near East was not alien to these trends and the study of markets and their impact on the ancient Near Eastern economies have made significant contributions to these discussions (see Chapter 1). Unfortunately, Egyptian evidence, both archaeological and textual, about the role and activities of merchants, their investments, their modalities of capital accumulation, and the potential boost they gave to other economic sectors is so meagre that one can only speculate, at best, about the path followed (if any) by this early commercial capitalism in the land of the pharaohs.

The fate of several towns with substantial commercial activities might cast some light on this question. Elephantine, for instance, was founded in southernmost Egypt as the departure point for caravans dispatched into Nubia. Many seals from around 2600 BC reveal that men and women from Elephantine were involved in trading activities and that gold was of paramount importance in the exchanges that took place there. Some centuries later, the leaders of this locality described in their tombs the expeditions they led into Nubia, the goods transported, the difficulties they encountered, and the rewards obtained from the king. They certainly built huge tombs, a sort of prestige investment that visualized their wealth and status, and their activities never stopped when the monarchy collapsed about 2160 BC. In fact, they continued to flourish in the next centuries. However, Elephantine, apparently, never became a major Nilotic market. Its leaders did not accumulate substantial capital, subsequently reinvested in manufactures, in expansive commercial networks, etc., but this impression may be misleading. A particular type of small globular jar known as 'Elephantine pink ware' was probably produced there in the first centuries of the 2nd millennium. Its technological uniformity and homogeneity suggest that it is likely to have originated from a single workshop or one group of workshops. These jars must have been considered a precious, as well as a luxurious, commodity because they are found far from the borders of Egypt, from the Levantine coast to Nubia, as far away as the Fourth Cataract of the Nile. In fact, the quantity of the Elephantine Pink Ware ceramics found in Nubian cemeteries alone is considerably higher than that in the Middle Kingdom Egyptian settlements and necropolies combined. Hence, it appears likely that the majority of these jars were manufactured specifically for export. Another group of pottery, the Elephantine Black Ware, has been identified alongside the Pink Ware, although it is less numerous and less homogenous than the Pink Ware and it seems inspired by Nubian ceramics. As for the products contained in the jars, they remained unknown (Rzeuska 2012). As trade specialists, the role of the leaders of Elephantine was likely indispensable for the monarchy (they led missions to Punt and Lebanon too) but their activities remained somewhat modest. The very reduced size of Elephantine and many other cities from the 3rd and early 2nd millennia, judging from their archaeological vestiges, suggests that the commercial elites they produced were small and that, consequently, they may have found it quite hard to assert their interests before the state and its tax system or even before other local elites. According to a Ramesside papyrus, the local elite that controlled the temple of god Khnum despised a candidate to the local priesthood because he was the son of a merchant (Porten 1996: 47–48).

Avaris, on the contrary, provides a different scale. It was one of the most important commercial harbors in the Eastern Mediterranean in the late Middle Bronze Age, around 1600 BC. Pharaoh Kamose, who led a raid into this city, boasted about his campaign in these terms:

> I haven't left a plank to the hundreds of ships of fresh cedar which were filled with gold, lapis, silver, turquoise, bronze axes without number, over and above the moringa-oil, incense, fat, honey, willow, box-wood, sticks and all their fine goods – all the fine products of Retenu – I have confiscated all of them! (Redford 1997: 14)

Ships and caravans arrived there loaded with products from the Aegean and the Levant, and the seals and a fragmentary cuneiform tablet found there, reveal that traders from Mesopotamia frequented this locality and may have established some kind of diplomatic or commercial agreement with its Hyksos rulers. At the same time, the Nubian presence attested at Avaris might correspond, at least partially, to commercial reasons at a time when contacts between Avaris and the Nubian kingdom of Kush are well documented. Finally, the discovery of Hyksos seals at Edfu points to the export of commodities from Avaris to Upper Egypt (Moeller and Marouard 2011). According to a Late Bronze Age ostracon, the nearby locality of Pi-Ramesses was 'the outpost of all foreign countries, the hinterland of Egypt', and the text continues saying: 'pleasant is the place of distribution/market-place with its money/silver there, mainly the vine tendrils (?) and business/commerce (t-m-k-r-i-t). The chiefs of every foreign country come in order to descend with their products' (Fischer-Elfert 2016). Such foreign chiefs and merchants occupied positions of influence in Ramesside Egypt, to the point that a son of Ramesses II married the daughter of a Syrian ship owner. As for Memphis and its burgeoning harbor, it received traders and diplomats from the Levant too, whereas the palace accounts of Pharaoh Sety I (1294–1279 BC) reveal that traders and Egyptians of high status shared the same residential areas of the city. Hence, both cities, Avaris/Pi-Ramesses and Memphis operated on a different scale than Elephantine, but the nearly complete invisibility of rich merchants in the monumental archaeological record (mainly tombs) suggests that their social esteem was not very high, and that their capacity to influence the state policy was probably reduced too.

A passage from the Papyrus Lansing (late 2nd millennium) may provide another approach to the study of commercial capitalism in Egypt:

> the merchants travel downstream and upstream. They are as busy as can be, carrying goods from one town to another. They supply him who has wants. But the tax collectors carry off the gold, that most precious of metals. The ships' crews from every house (of commerce), they receive their loads. They depart from Egypt for Syria, and each man's god is with him. (Caminos 1954: 390; Lichtheim 1976: 170)

Is it possible that these activities included some sort of precocious putting-out system, for instance in the production of textiles, when traders at the service of temples or other institutions collected and delivered raw material to private producers or granted loans to them and obtained in exchange pieces of cloth? Papyrus Gebelein IV verso, from about 2500 BC, lists the household heads of two villages in this area of Upper Egypt together with accounts of textiles (Posener-Krieger 1977; Posener-Krieger and Demichelis 2004). Several centuries later, a hieratic record fro m Elephantine, from the early 2nd millennium, records the wages/rations delivered by the overseer of a production center of the crown to a group of female weavers, the women's wages being twice as high as those of girls. Other activities of the center concerned the production of cattle and agricultural goods. In both examples people produced textiles directly for an institution of the crown or a high dignitary (Von Pilgrim 1996: 285–300).

However, other modalities of textile production are well attested as well in the second half of the 2nd millennium. According to the Papyrus Brooklyn 35.1453A (*c.* 1300 BC), a ship docked at different places and collected goods from women, usually pieces of cloth and honey, but also small quantities of silver and copper, while a woman received a piece of silver at a *mryt* 'quay/market' (Condon 1984). Other papyri from the late 2nd millennium record the activities of ships at the service, apparently, of temples. They delivered cloth and other goods in exchange for sesame oil obtained from women and other people (Janssen 1961). These documents reveal a system of exchanges in which women delivered textiles to ships and paid and were paid during the transactions, while other ships exchanged the pieces of cloth they transported for goods delivered by other individuals. The verso of papyri Amiens and Baldwin (*c.* 1150 BC) registers, among other transactions, ships that received small amounts of grain from individuals and households, and an account of garments from various villages (Janssen 2004: 50). Finally, the rich documentation from Deir el-Medina records a scribe called Qenhirkhopshef who arrived at the 'quay/market' in order to deliver some textiles to a certain Amenemwia in the presence of several 'ladies' and to receive some cloths that he brought back to Deir el-Medina in return (Kitchen 1982: 159). In general, the inhabitants of this locality not only frequented the 'quay/market' but, in some cases, they also possessed a *'t* 'house' there, perhaps a sort of small shop and/or workshop (Burkard 2003: 14).

What this evidence reveals is that women produced textiles and cloth for institutions and traders as independent producers, apparently on a private basis, and that they were paid for their work (Fig. 10.7). Other sources confirm this impression. Several fragmentary Ramesside papyri from Ilahun (erroneously referred to as coming from Gurob), near Fayyum, contain lists of high-quality garments elaborated for royals and members of the elite (an activity, by the way, also attested there around 1800 BC, when slave-women weaved high quality clothes and received rations/wages: Wente 1990: 82–83). Then, the garments were withdrawn from the storeroom of, presumably,

Figure 10.7. Textile workshop tomb Meketre (Wikipedia commons: https://commons.wikimedia.org/wiki/File:Meketre,_maquette.jpg).

the Royal Harem at nearby Gurob and part of them were sent to the royal residence in the Delta (fragments G, T, U: Gardiner 1948: 20–24). Fragment Y lists many houses involved in what appears as deliveries of pieces of cloth (*ibid.*: 24–26), while fragment K mentions deliveries of fish to 'ladies' (*ʿnḫ(t) nt nwt*) made by the overseer of the Royal Harem (*ibid.*: 28–29), with the particularity that one entry (col. 2, line 2: *ibid.*: 29) mentions a female slave (*ḥmt*) owned by a 'lady.' In my opinion, these fragments may refer to households that delivered quotas of textiles, while 'ladies', who received wages (including fish) for their work, made the actual weaving labour. In some cases they owned slaves to perform this task in their place. This interpretation may find some support in Papyrus Cairo JdE 65739, found at Thebes (Gardiner 1935; Muhs 2016: 139–140), in which a 'lady' who elaborated cloths bought a Syrian slave-girl from a merchant. She paid in return with several pieces of cloth and many objects in bronze brought by other ladies, priests, and officials (a loan or a share anticipated from the production expected from the slave?), for a total amount of 4 *deben* and 1 *kite* in silver (=0.37 kg; for another example of a slave woman sold by a merchant, *cf.* Wente 1990: 129–130). This model of production, based on the work of women and household production, reminds Papyrus Gebelein IV *verso*, an administrative book-keeping account which records a list of the inhabitants of two villages committed to deliver a certain amount of textile production (around 2500 BC). Each column of the text mentions, first, the function and name of the person supposed to deliver the garments (quite probably the head of a household) and, second, the person who actually performed the duty – usually, a woman defined as 'daughter' or 'wife' or simply having her name followed by the feminine hieroglyphic sign (Posener-Kriéger and Demichelis 2004: pl. 35; about quota-system for textiles: Kemp and Vogelsang-Eastwood 2001: 427–436).

Such domestic activities may explain the interest shown by private individuals to acquire not only slaves, as in the examples mentioned, but also to rent out their 'workdays' (lit. 'day of slave/serf') for considerably high prices (Navailles and Neveu 1989). An excellent example comes, again, from Ilahun (around 1360 BC), where a chief herdsman called Mesuy purchased but also rented out 'work days' of three slave-women over several years. Quite significantly, he paid in grain, livestock, and silver for his first acquisition of 'work days', but subsequently in cattle *and cloth* (Murnane 1995: 43–47). Given the substantial quantities of garments he handed over for his purchases, it may be quite possible that the slaves were committed to produce cloth that was later sold or used as a means of payment. In some cases slaves were owned collectively, either by a city (Porten 1996: 35–37) or by two or more people (Černy 1934). Hiring and sharing slaves, even part-time, might have been a profitable investment in textile production. An unfortunately fragmented ostracon from Deir el-Medina records a woman who had taken a certain amount of wool (?) from a neighbor lady and requested the services of a 'free woman'. In exchange for the wool and the services, she was ready to pay 5 *deben* of copper (Wente 1990: 156).

What seems clear is that the elaboration of textiles in Egypt cannot be reduced either to a purely domestic activity, aiming only for self-consumption, or to an institutional sphere. It encompassed other modalities of production and exchange too. Many texts and scenes from different periods evoke weavers working in an institutional context, who elaborated high quality cloths for dignitaries, members of the royal court and temples, and who received wages and rewards for their work (an example: Küllmer 2017). In some cases, small textile workshop models were buried in the tombs of wealthy Egyptians, among other offerings. Yet textiles were also produced in the domestic sphere and then sold and exchanged. This activity was particularly important in an economy that used textiles as means of exchange and reward and that exported cloth and linen to other regions of the Mediterranean and the Near East according to the tablets from Ebla or the record of Wenamun. Another point to consider is that it was 'ladies' (*'nḫt nt nwt*) who were involved in the manufacture and sale of textiles, so temples, institutions, and merchants turned to domestic production to obtain this commodity. This activity, among others, may explain the apparent independent economic status of 'ladies', a sort of businesswomen. As for traders, they may have supplied them with linen and wool. A Ramesside letter records ships loaded with wool and transactions involving considerable amounts of silver to acquire wool and fish (Wente 1990: 120–121). Administrative evidence, such as signs of quality, shows that linen was graded and assessed by specific criteria, which would have included at least the density of the weave and the fineness of the yarn (Jones 2010).

However, domestic production was in no way limited to cloth and linen. The excavation of the city of Tell el-Amarna, the ephemeral capital city of Pharaoh Akhenaton, has revealed abundant evidence about the production of finished and unfinished glass, faïence, and metal artifacts as well as sculpture. Raw glass, for example, was elaborated in specialized workshops under central control while actual glass working took place in the small houses. Similarly, faïence was made in specialized workshops and household contexts. In general, Tell el-Amarna reveals a three-level system of production and exchange that included specialized workshops close to state buildings, multi-purpose workshops in larger elite compounds (the larger estates seem to have been places of control and distribution), and a household-based 'cottage industry' located throughout the city with a decreasing degree of specialization and state control. Specialized workshops operated thus alongside a cottage industry. By contrast, highly organized large-scale glass, faïence, and metal factories have been discovered at Pi-Ramesse, the Egyptian capital in the Eastern Nile Delta around 1292–1070 BC (Quirke and Tajeddin 2010; Vanthyune 2012–2013; Hodgkinson 2018: 263–284). The site of Elephantine has provided evidence of domestic production in several houses around 1800 BC. The activities documented concerned the elaboration of beads and jewelry, partly with semi-precious stones (carnelian and amethyst, the latter mined in Wadi el-Hudi, 35 km to the south), partly with organic materials such as ostrich eggshell, bone, and mother of pearl (Sigl and Kopp 2020: 21–22). Evidence from a possibly local bronze casting workshop from the middle of the 1st millennium BC has been recovered from a tomb at Qubbet el-Hawa, adjacent to Elephantine (Fitzenreiter *et al.* 2016).

Another economic sector that may have known some kind of entrepreneurial organization is fisheries. Several references from the Late Bronze Age and the Early Iron Age reveal that fishermen paid taxes and contributions in silver, thus implying the commercialization and 'monetization' of their captures. This is the case of Ramesside ostracon Gardiner 86, in which workers involved in herding and gathering in the Delta delivered animals, salt, natron, and plants while fishermen paid instead a fixed amount of silver each – 3 *deben* or 0.27 kg each (Wente 1990: 118–119). A papyrus from the reign of Ramesses II described a considerable amount of silver (46 bars) delivered to a group of ship captains in order to acquire wool and fish, the latter evaluated at 760 *deben* or 69.16 kg (*ibid.*: 120–121). Fish evaluated in silver *kite* (=9.1 g) is referred to in administrative records of the same period (Warburton 1997: 175). Later, when Kushite Pharaoh Taharqa endowed a sanctuary in the Memphite region, part of the revenue consisted of silver delivered by fishermen as taxes (Ritner 2009: 515). Moreover, when Herodotus evoked, centuries later, the Egyptian tribute paid to the Persian treasury, it consisted of 700 talents of silver as well as silver delivered by the fishermen of Lake Moeris. Archaeological evidence shows that Nile perch was exported all over the Levant and Anatolia between the Middle Bronze Age and the Iron Age, that is, in periods of both intense and declining international trade. As a modest commodity, its demand apparently did not fit the culinary preferences of the elite of these sites (Van Neer *et al.* 2004; Linseele *et al.* 2013; Routledge 2015). Recent archaeological research at the Egyptian garrison of Beth Shean, in Palestine, reveals the presence of fish from the Nile as well as of small quantities of silver buried in domestic areas of this locality. Economic circuits involving fish and silver might thus be traced back between Egypt and the Levant (Thompson 2009). Wenamun, who transported fish to Byblos at the very late 2nd millennium (Ritner 2009: 96), confirms this circumstance. Finally, fishermen trusted with the supply of the workers' community at Deir el-Medina delivered considerable amounts of fish, more than 400 and 500 *deben* in two cases (Warburton 1997: 156), 380 in another case and 50 *deben* daily provided by three fishermen each over a year (*ibid.*: 239). However, it seems certain that these quantities refer to weight, not value (Janssen 1997: 37–54; Warburton 1997: 307 n. 1157; Antoine 2006). Finally, fishermen worked as part-time transporters, carrying goods in their ships for institutions, usually grain, wool, and papyrus (Wente 1990: 121, 174, 180).

To conclude this section, there is evidence that some modalities of 'cottage industry', even of a putting-out system, were operative in pharaonic times alongside the much better documented institutional production that took place in temple and state workshops. Traders collected textiles and other goods from domestic producers and, as a counterpart, they may have provided the raw materials needed (flax, wool, semi-precious stones, raw glass, copper, and bronze, etc.) as well as loans, but little is known about this aspect of their business, not to speak about the financial tools used in their transactions, if any. Yet occasional references to promissory notes, for instance, are not completely unknown in Ramesside times (Allam 1967; 1983, with references; Wente 1990: 118; *cf.* also Pappa 2017). Traders carried goods between cities, agricultural domains, and temples, granted loans, operated within the framework of commercial 'houses' and trade diaspores, but their real impact on the Egyptian economy still remains to be explored.

Conclusion

The evidence discussed in the previous pages provides many possibilities for comparative research about the role played by markets and exchanges and the dynamics they promoted in the economic life of the Nile Valley. The old redistributive paradigm, in reality, a strange mixture of literal interpretations of rhetoric Egyptian statements and a reductionist application to ancient Egypt of the Polanyian model, may explain, at best, the circulation of some goods and services under very specific conditions. Such conditions were, nevertheless, fundamental for the tax system implemented by the monarchy, therefore its over-representation in the documentary record, mostly produced by institutions. Yet they only correspond to some sectors of the ancient Egyptian economy. Other sectors, insufficiently documented, emerge nevertheless from the archaeological record as being of paramount importance in the overall economic structure of ancient Egypt. A world of itinerant traders, mobile populations, women involved in diverse business, independent craftsmen, rural 'entrepreneurs', even of 'cottage industry', may explain some paradoxes of the ancient pharaonic history. One of them is that it followed closely the historical cycles that crossed all the ancient Near East, thus implying a certain integration of their economies, so changes or problems touching some sectors or geographical areas extended their influence over other, far away regions. Another one is that when central authority entered one of its recurrent periods of crisis, the economic activity not only failed to collapse too but, on the contrary, it flourished and inaugurated a time of expansive urbanism, trade, and integration in international circuits. It also seems that control over the flows of wealth that crossed Egypt and neighboring areas was a major stimulus in the balance of power and the policies followed, first, by some Egyptian regions and, later, by the pharaohs themselves. The political impact of economic activities and economic actors in shaping the geography of power of ancient Egypt opens fascinating possibilities still to be approached (Moreno García 2017b; 2018b; 2019b; Barjamovic and Yoffee 2020). Finally, ancient Egypt offers many parallels with other regions of the ancient Near East that should stimulate both comparative research and an analysis of Egyptian evidence under more comprehensive and sophisticated perspectives (Warburton 2016). Far from the alleged exceptionalism and utter bureaucratic centralism of the land of the pharaohs, many other actors and productive sectors still await an in-deep study (or, simply, to be discovered) in order to get a more balanced general understanding of the Egyptian economy.

Of course, the reduced scope of this volume makes it completely utopian to deal with many other topics crucial nevertheless for a better comprehension of markets and ancient Egypt, from pre-monetary forms of use of precious metals to international trade. If the results presented here and the stimulus provided by the authors who have contributed to this volume help open new perspectives of comparative research, then the integration and contribution of ancient Egypt to economic history may prove to be as fruitful as this volume already shows.

Bibliography

Ali, M. S. (1997). Der Papyrus Kairo 58078 – ein Teil von Papyrus Boulaq 11? *Lingua Ægyptia* 5, 1–12.

Allam, S. (1967). Silber=Leistung (in Form von beweglichen Vermögensgegenständen). *Orientalia* 36, 416–420.

Allam, S. (1983). Papyrus Boulaq XIV und die Silber-Schrift. *Die Welt des Orients* 14, 22–29.

Allen, J.P. (2002). *The Heqanakht Papyri*. New York: Metropolitan Museum of Art.

Allen, J.P. 2008. The historical inscription of Khnumhotep at Dahshur: Preliminary report. *Bulletin of the American Schools of Oriental Research* 352, 29–39.

Altenmüller, H. (2015). *Zwei Annalenfragmente aus dem frühen Mittleren Reich*. Hamburg: Helmut Buske.

Antoine, J.-C. (2006). Fluctuations of fish deliveries at Deir el-Medina in the Twentieth Dynasty. A statistical analysis. *Studien zur altägyptischen Kultur* 35, 25–41.

Antoine, J.-C. (2015). Landholding and agriculture in late Ramesside Theban documents. *Zeitschrift für Ägyptische Sprache und Altertumskunde*, 142, 104–119.

Avner, U. (2014). Egyptian Timna – reconsidered. In: Tebes, J.M. (ed.) *Unearthing the Wilderness. Studies on the History and Archaeology of the Negev and Edom in the Iron Age*. Louvain, Paris and Walpole MA: Peeters, 103–162.

Banaji, J. (2020). *A Brief History of Commercial Capitalism*. Chicago IL: Haymarket Books.

Barjamovic, G. (2019). Silver, markets and long-distance trade in the Konya Region, 2400–1700 BCE. In Maner, Č. (ed.) *Crossroads. Konya Plain from Prehistory to the Byzantine Period*. Istanbul: Ege Yayınları, 71–81.

Barjamovic, G. and Yoffee, N. (2020). Working at home, traveling abroad: Old Assyrian trade and archaeological theory. In: Mas, J. and Notizia, P. (eds) *Working at Home in the Ancient Near East*. Oxford: Archaeopress, 107–116.

Bietak, M. (2019). The Obelisk Temple in Byblos and its predecessors. In: Pieńkowska, A., Szeląg, D. and Zych, I. (eds) *Stories Told Around the Fountain. Papers Offered to Piotr Bieliński on the Occasion of his 70th Birthday*. Warsaw: University of Warsaw Press; PCMA UW, 165–185.

Biga, M.-G. and Steinkeller, P. (in press). In search of Dugurasu. *Journal of Cuneiform Studies* 73.

Blakely, J.A. (2018). Tell el-Hesi: A type site for re-evaluating so-called 'Egyptian governors' residencies' of the South. *Palestine Exploration Quarterly* 150, 217–295.

Bleiberg, E. (2002). Loans, credit, and interest in ancient Egypt. In: Hudson, M. and Van de Mieroop, M. (eds) *Debt and Economic Renewal in the Ancient Near East*. Bethesda MD: CDL Press, 257–276.

Bradbury, L. (1996). *Kpn*-boats, Punt trade, and a lost emporium. *Journal of the American Research Center in Egypt* 33, 37–60.

Burkard, G. (2003). 'Oh, diese Mauern Pharaohs!' Zur Bewegungsfreiheit der Einwohner von Deir el Medine. *Mitteilungen des Deutschen Archäologischen Instituts, Abteilung Kairo* 59, 11–39.

Caminos, R.A. (1954). *Late-Egyptian Miscellanies*. Oxford: Oxford University Press.

Castle, E.W. (1992). Shipping and trade in Ramesside Egypt. *Journal of the Economic and Social History of the Orient* 35, 239–277.

Černy, J. (1934). Parchemin du Louvre n° AF 1577. In: *Mélanges Maspero. Vol. I: Orient Ancien*. Cairo: Institut Français d'Archéologie Orientale, 231–239.

Condon, V. (1984). Two account papyri of the late Eighteenth Dynasty (Brooklyn 35.1453 A and B). *Revue d'Égyptologie* 35, 57–82.

Czarnowicz, M. (2011). Between core and periphery – early contacts between Egypt and the southern Levant in light of excavations at Tell el-Farkha, eastern Nile Delta. In: Mynářová, J. ed. *Egypt and the Near East - The Crossroads*. Prague: Czech Institute of Archaeology, 117–138.

Darnell, J.C. (2002). *Theban Desert Road Survey in the Egyptian Western Desert, Volume 1: Gebel Tjauti rock inscriptions 1-45 and Wadi el-Hôl rock inscriptions 1-45*. Chicago IL: Oriental Institute Press.

Dębowska-Ludwin, J., Rosińska-Balik, K., Czarnowicz, M. and Ochał-Czarnowicz, A. (2012). Trade or conquest? The nature of Egyptian-South Levantine relations in Early Bronze I from the perspective of Tell el-Farkha, Egypt and Tel Erani, Israel. *Recherches Archéologiques, nouvelle série* 4, 113–122.

Delgado Hervás, A. (2014). Cultura material, etnicidad y contacto cultural en la arqueología tartésica. In: García Alonso, E. (ed.) *Movilidad, contacto y cambio. II Congreso de Prehistoria de Andalucía*. Sevilla: Consejería de Educación, Cultura y Deporte de la Junta de Andalucía, 279–291.

Diego Espinel, A. (2002). The role of the temple of Ba'alat Gebal as intermediary between Egypt and Byblos during the Old Kingdom. *Studien zur altägyptischen Kultur* 30, 103–119.

Diego Espinel, A. (2013). The tribute from Tekhebeten (a brief note on the graffiti of Mentuhetep II at Jebel Uweinat). *Göttinger Miszellen* 237, 15–19.

Donker van Heel, K. (2012). *Djekhy & Son: Doing business in Ancient Egypt*. Cairo and New York: American University in Cairo Press.

Donker van Heel, K. (2014). *Mrs. Tsenhor: A female entrepreneur in Ancient Egypt*. Cairo and New York: American University in Cairo Press.

Edel, E. (1994). *Die agyptisch-hethitische Korrespondenz aus Boghazkoi in babylonischer und hethitischer Sprache, Band I-II*. Opladen: Westdeutscher.

Edel, E. (2008). *Die Felsgräbernekropole der Qubbet el-Hawa bei Assuan. I. Abteilung, Band 2*. Paderborn: Ferdinand Schöningh.

Enea, A. and Fiorentino, R. (2018). Nota su un unguentario in alabastro dalla Residenza Occidentale di Ebla. In Vacca, A., Pizzimenti, S. and Micale, M.G. (eds) *Contributi e materiali di archeologia orientale XVIII: A oriente del Delta. Scritti sull'Egitto ed il Vicino Oriente antico in onore di Gabriella Scandone Matthiae*. Rome: Scienze e Lettere, 247–258.

Eyre, C. (1998). The market women of Pharaonic Egypt. In Grimal, N. And Menu, B. (eds) *Le commerce en Égypte ancienne*. Cairo: Institut Français d'Archéologie Orientale, 173–191.

Fischer-Elfert, H.-W. (2016). In praise of Pi-Ramesse – A perfect trading center (including two new Semitic words in syllabic orthography; Ostr. Ashmlean Museum HO 1187). In: Collombert, P., Lefèvre, D., Polis, S. and Winand, J. (eds) *Aere Perennius. Mélanges égyptologiques en l'honneur de Pascal Vernus*. Leuven, Paris and Walpole MA: Peeters, 195–218.

Fitzenreiter, M., Willer, F. and Auenmuller, J. (2016). *Materialien einer Gusswerkstatt von der Qubbet el-Hawa*. Berlin: EB-Verlag.

Forstner-Müller, I. and Raue, D. (2008). Elephantine and the Levant. In: Engel, E.-M., Müller, V. and Hartung, U. (eds) *Zeichen aus dem Sand. Streiflichter aus Ägyptens Geschichte zu Ehren von Günter Dreyer*. Wiesbaden: Harrassowitz, 127–148.

Friedman, R.F. (1992). Pebbles, pots and petroglyphs: Excavations at HK64. In: Friedman, R.F. and Adams, B. (eds) *The Followers of Horus. Studies Dedicated to Michael Allen Hoffman*. Oxford: Oxbow Books, 99–106.

Friedman, R.F. (2000). Pots, pebbles and petroglyphs, part II: 1996 excavations at Hierakonpolis Locality HK64. In: Leahy, A. and Tait, J. (eds) *Studies in Ancient Egypt in Honour of H.S. Smith*. London: Egypt Exploration Society, 101–108.

Gadot, Y. (2010). The Late Bronze Egyptian estate at Aphek. *Tel Aviv* 37, 48–66.

Gardiner, A.H. (1935). A lawsuit arising from the purchase of two slaves. *Journal of Egyptian Archaeology* 21, 140–146.

Gardiner, A.H. (1941). Ramesside texts relating to the taxation and transport of corn. *Journal of Egyptian Archaeology* 27, 19–73.

Gardiner, A.H. (1948). *Ramesside Administrative Documents.* Oxford: Oxford University Press.
Garfinkle, S.J. (2020). The house of Ur-saga: Ur III merchants in their non-institutional context. In: Mas, J. and Notizia, P. (eds) *Working at Home in the Ancient Near East.* Oxford: Archaeopress, 71–82.
Gatto, M.C. (2019). The later prehistory of Nubia in its interregional setting. In: Raue, D. (ed.) *Handbook of Ancient Nubia.* Berlin and Boston MA: De Gruyter, 259–291.
Gatto, M.C., Gallorini, C. and Roma, S. (2012). Pan-Grave pottery from Nag el-Qarmila and Sheikh Mohamed cemeteries in Gharb Aswan. In: Forstner-Müller, I. and Rose, P. (eds) *Nubian Pottery from Egyptian Cultural Contexts of the Middle and Early New Kingdom.* Vienna: Österreichisches Archäologisches Institut, 83–102.
Grandet, P. (1994). *Le Papyrus Harris I (BM 9999). Vol. I.* Cairo: Institut Français d'Archéologie Orientale.
Greenfield, H.J., Greenfield, T.L., Arnold, E., Shai, E., Albaz, S. and Maeir, A.M. (2020). Evidence for movement of goods and animals from Egypt to Canaan during the Early Bronze of the Southern Levant: A view from Tell eṣ-Ṣâfi/Gath. *Ägypten und Levante* 30, 377–397.
Hadley, J. (1993). Kuntillet 'Ajrud: Religious centre or desert way station? *Palestine Exploration Quarterly* 125, 115–124.
Hafsaas-Tsakos, H. (2009). Hierarchy and heterarchy: The earliest cross-cultural trade along the Nile. In: Hafsaas-Tsakos, H. and Tsakos, A. (eds) *Connecting South and North: Sudan studies from Bergen in honour of Mahmoud Salih.* Bergen: University of Bergen, 19–40.
Hagen, F. (2008). A Ramesside administrative document (P. Cambridge University Library MS. Add. 4167). *Zeitschrift für ägyptische Sprache und Altertumskunde* 135, 30–39.
Hassan, K. (2016). An 18th dynasty wooden board in the Egyptian Museum of Cairo JE 95750-CG 25366. *Egyptian Journal of Archaeological and Restoration Studies* 6(2), 125–132.
Hassan, K. and Ouda, A.M.M. (2018). Ramesside hieratic stela of the sandal maker Penōne in the Egyptian Museum Cairo (TR. 27.6.24.3). *Journal of the American Research Center in Egypt* 54, 93–106.
Hodgkinson, A.K. (2018). *Technology and Urbanism in Late Bronze Age Egypt.* Oxford-New York: Oxford Studies in Egyptian Archaeology.
Hoffmeier, J.K., Davis, T.W. and Hummel, R. (2016). New archaeological evidence for ancient Bedouin (Shasu) on Egypt's eastern frontier at Tell el-Borg. *Ägypten und Levante* 26, 285–311.
Holladay, J.S. (2001) Toward a new paradigmatic understanding of long-distance trade in the ancient Near East: From the Middle Bronze II to Early Iron II – a sketch. In: Daviau, P.M.M. and Weigl, M. (eds) *The World of the Arameans. Studies in Language and Literature in Honour of Paul-Eugène Dion*, Vol. II. Sheffield: Sheffield Academic Press, 136–195.
Hölzl, R., Neumann, M. and Demarée, R.J. (2018). *The Notebook of Dhutmose. P. Vienna ÄS 10321.* Leiden and Boston MA: Brill.
Hulin, L. (2011). Pragmatic technology: Issues in the interpretation of Libyan material culture. In: Duistermaat, K. and Regulski, I. (eds) *Intercultural Contacts in the Ancient Mediterranean.* Leuven, Paris and Walpole MA: Peeters, 101–114.
Hulin, L. (2018). Marsa Matruh revisited: Modelling interaction at a Late Bronze Age harbour on the Egyptian coast. In: Manzo, A., Zazzaro, C. and De Falco, D.J. (eds) *Stories of Globalisation: The Red Sea and the Persian Gulf from late prehistory to early modernity.* Leiden and Boston MA: Brill, 53–64.
Janssen, J.J. (1961). *Two Ancient Egyptian ship's logs: Papyrus Leiden I 350 verso and Papyrus Turin 2008+2016.* Leiden: Brill.
Janssen, J.J. (1991). Requisitions from Upper Egyptian temples (P. BM 10401). *Journal of Egyptian Archaeology* 77, 79–94.
Janssen, J.J. (1992). A New Kingdom settlement: The *verso* of Pap. BM. 10068. *Altorientalische Forschungen* 19, 8–23.
Janssen, J.J. (1997). *Village Varia. Ten Studies on the History and Administration of Deir el-Medina.* Leiden: Nederlands Instituut voor het Nabije Oosten.
Janssen, J.J. (2004). *Grain Transport in the Ramesside Period. Papyrus Baldwin (BM EA 10061) and Papyrus Amiens.* London: British Museum Press.

Jones, J. (2010). Some observations on the dimensions of textiles in the Old Kingdom linen lists. In: Woods, A., McFarlane, A. and Binder, S. (eds) *Egyptian Culture and Society. Studies in honor of Naguib Kanawati*, Vol. II. Cairo: Conseil Suprême des Antiquités de l'Égypte, 247–262.

Kemp, B.J. (1991). *Ancient Egypt: Anatomy of a civilization*. London and New York: Routledge.

Kemp, B.J. and Vogelsang-Eastwood, G. (2001). *The Ancient Textile Industry at Amarna*. London: Egypt Exploration Society.

Kemp, B.J., Gascoigne, A.L., Moeller, N. and Spence, K.E. (2004). Egypt's invisible walls (the late Roman and early Islamic urban enceinte). *Cambridge Archaeological Journal* 14(2): 259–288.

Kitchen, K. (1970). *Ramesside Inscriptions: Historical and biographical II: Ramesses II, royal inscriptions.* Oxford: Blackwell.

Kitchen, K. (1982). *Ramesside Inscriptions: Historical and biographical IV: Merenptah and the late Nineteenth Dynasty.* Oxford: Blackwell.

Kitchen, K. (1983). *Ramesside Inscriptions: Historical and biographical VI: Ramesses IV to XI and contemporaries.* Oxford: Blackwell.

Kitchen, K. (1989). *Ramesside Inscriptions: Historical and biographical VII: Addenda.* Oxford: Blackwell.

Kitchen, K. (1993). *Ramesside Inscriptions Translated and Annotated: Translations. Vol. I: Ramesses I, Sethos I and contemporaries.* Oxford: Blackwell.

Knoblauch, C. (2019). Middle Kingdom fortresses. In: Raue, D. (ed.) *Handbook of Ancient Nubia*. Berlin and Boston MA: De Gruyter, 367–391.

Koenig, Y. (1987). La Nubie dans les textes magiques. 'L'inquiétante étrangeté'. *Revue d'Égyptologie* 38, 105–110.

Kraemer, B. and Liszka, K. (2016). Evidence for administration of the Nubian fortresses in the Late Middle Kingdom: The Semna Dispatches. *Journal of Egyptian History* 9, 1–65.

Kruchten, J.-M. (1981). *Le Décret d'Horemheb. Traduction, commentaire épigraphique, philologique et institutionnel.* Bruxelles: Éditions de l'Université de Bruxelles.

Kubisch, S. (2008). *Lebensbilder der 2. Zwischenzeit. Biographische Inschriften der 13.-17. Dynastie.* Berlin and Boston MA: De Gruyter.

Küllmer, H. 2017. 'Das Verteilen von Gold' – Einige Überlegungen zu den Webereien des Alten Reiches. In: Bárta, M., Coppens, F. and Krejčí, J. (eds) *Abusir and Saqqara in the Year 2015*. Prague: Czech Institute of Egyptology, 185–199.

Landgráfová, R. (2011). *It is My Good Name that You Should Remember. Egyptian Biographical Texts on Middle Kingdom Stelae.* Prague: Charles University.

Lassen, A.W. (2014). Wool in Anatolia in the Old Assyrian period. In: Breniquet, C. and Michel, C. (eds) *Wool Economy in the Ancient Near East and the Aegean*. Oxford: Oxbow Books, 255–263.

Lichtheim, M. (1976). *Ancient Egyptian Literature, A Book of Readings. Volume II: The New Kingdom.* Berkeley CA, Los Angeles CA and London: University of California Press.

Linseele, V., van Neer, W. and Bretschneider, J. (2013). The mysteries of Egyptian Nile perch (*Lates niloticus*). The case of Tell Tweini (Syria, Middle Bronze Age – Iron Age). In: De Cupere, B., Linseele, V. and Hamilton-Dyer, S. (eds) *Archaeozoology of the Near East X. Proceedings of the tenth international symposium on the archaeozoology of South-Western Asia and adjacent areas.* Peeters: Leuven, Paris and Walpole MA, 209–226.

Liszka, K. (2017). Egyptian or Nubian? Dry-stone architecture at Wadi el-Hudi, Wadi es-Sebuia, and the Eastern Desert. *Journal of Egyptian Archaeology* 103, 35–51.

Liverani, M. (1990). *Prestige and Interest. International Relations in the Near East ca. 1600–1100 BC.* Padoue: Sargon Press.

Mączyńska, A. (2014). Some remarks on the visitors in the Nile Delta in the 4th millennium BC. In: Mączyńska, A. ed. *The Nile Delta as a centre of cultural interactions between Upper Egypt and the Southern Levant in the 4th millennium BC.* Poznan: Poznan Archaeological Museum, 181–216.

Manassa, C. (2012). Middle Nubian ceramics from Umm Mawagir, Kharga Oasis. In: Forstner-Müller, I. and Rose, P. (eds) *Nubian Pottery from Egyptian Cultural Contexts of the Middle and Early New Kingdom.* Vienna: Österreichisches Archäologisches Institut, 129–148.

Marcolin, M. and Diego Espinel, A. (2011). The Sixth Dynasty biographic inscriptions of Iny: More pieces to the puzzle. In: Bárta, M., Coppens, F. and Krejčí, J. (eds) *Abusir and Saqqara in the Year 2010*. Prague: Czech Institute of Egyptology, 570–615.

Marcus, E. (2007). Amenemhat II and the sea: maritime aspects of the Mit Rahina (Memphis) inscription. *Ägypten und Levante* 17, 137–190.

Megally, M. (1974). À propos du papyrus CGC 58070 (Papyrus Boulaq XI). *Bulletin de l'Institut Français d'Archéologie Orientale* 74, 161–169.

Megally, M. (1975). Le papyrus CGC 58081. Suite du papyrus CGC 58070 (Papyrus Boulaq XI). *Bulletin de l'Institut Français d'Archéologie Orientale* 75, 165–181.

Megally, M. (1977). *Recherches sur l'économie, l'administration et la comptabilité égyptiennes à la XVIIIe dynastie d'après le papyrus E 3226 du Louvre*. Cairo: Institut Français d'Archéologie Orientale.

Millek, J.M. (2018). Destruction and the fall of Egyptian hegemony over the Southern Levant. *Journal of Ancient Egyptian Interconnections* 19, 1–21.

Moeller, N. and Marouard, G. (2011). Discussion of Late Middle Kingdom and early Second Intermediate Period history and chronology in relation to the Khayan sealings from Tell Edfu. *Ägypten und Levante* 21, 87–121.

Moeller, N. and Marouard, G. (2018a). Tell Edfu 2017. *Oriental Institute Anual Report 2017–2018*: 156–180.

Moeller, N. and Marouard, G. (2018b). The development of two early urban centres in Upper Egypt during the 3rd millennium BC. The examples of Edfu and Dendara. In: Budka, J. and Auenmüller, J. (eds) *From Microcosm to Macrocosm. Individual Households and Cities in Ancient Egypt and Nubia*. Leiden: Sidestone Press, 29–58.

Moran, W.L. (1992). *The Amarna Letters*. Baltimore MD and London: Johns Hopkins University Press.

Moreno García, J.C. (2000). Acquisition de serfs durant la Première Période Intermédiaire: Une étude d'histoire sociale dans l'Égypte du IIIe millénaire. *Revue d'Égyptologie* 51, 123–139.

Moreno García, J.C. (2014a). Penser l'économie pharaonique. *Annales. Histoire, Sciences Sociales* 69, 7–38.

Moreno García, J.C. (2014b). L'organisation sociale de l'agriculture pharaonique: quelques cas d'étude. *Annales. Histoire, Sciences Sociales* 69, 39–74.

Moreno García, J.C. (2014c). Invaders or just herders? Libyans in Egypt in the 3rd and 2nd millennia BCE. *World Archaeology* 46(4), 610–623.

Moreno García, J.C. (2014d). Recent developments in the social and economic history of ancient Egypt. *Journal of Ancient Near Eastern History* 1, 231–261.

Moreno García, J.C. (2015). *Ḥwt jḥ(w)t*, the administration of the Western Delta and the 'Libyan question' in the 3rd millennium. *Journal of Egyptian Archaeology* 101, 69–105.

Moreno García, J.C. (2016a). Economies in transition: trade, 'money', labour and nomads at the turn of the 1st millennium BC. In: Moreno García, J.C. (ed.) *Dynamics of Production in the Ancient Near East, 1300–500 BC*. Oxford: Oxbow Books, 1–39.

Moreno García, J.C. (2016b). Temples and agricultural labour in Egypt, from the Late New Kingdom to the Saite Period. In: Moreno García, J.C. (ed.) *Dynamics of Production in the Ancient Near East, 1300–500 BC*. Oxford: Oxbow Books, 223–256.

Moreno García, J.C. (2017a). Métaux, textiles et réseaux d'échanges à longue distance entre la fin du IIIe et le début du IIe millénaire: les *'Paddle dolls'*, un indice négligé? In: Favry, N., Ragazzoli, Ch., Somaglino, Cl. and Tallet, P. (eds) *Du Sinaï au Soudan: Itinéraires d'une égyptologue (Mélanges offerts au Professeur Dominique Valbelle)*. Paris: De Boccard, 173–194.

Moreno García, J.C. (2017b). Trade and power in ancient Egypt: Middle Egypt in the late third/early second millennium BC. *Journal of Archaeological Research* 25(2), 87–132.

Moreno García, J.C. (2018a). Elusive 'Libyans': Identities, lifestyles and mobile populations in NE Africa (late 4th–early 2nd millennium BCE). *Journal of Egyptian History* 11, 147–184.

Moreno García, J.C. (2018b). Divergent trajectories on the Nile: Polities, wealth and power between 4000–1600 BCE. In: Meller, H., Risch, R. and Gronenborn, D. (eds) *Surplus Without State - Political forms in Prehistory*. Halle: Landesmuseum für Vorgeschichte Halle (Saale), 337–372.
Moreno García, J.C. (2019a). Marketplaces, customs and hubs of trade in Bronze Age Egypt. In: Rahmstorf, L. and Stratford, E. (eds) *Weights and Marketplaces from the Bronze Age to the Early Modern Period*. Kiel and Hamburg: Wachholz Verlag & Murmann Publishers, 185–202.
Moreno García, J.C. (2019b). *The State in Ancient Egypt: Power, challenges and dynamics*. London and New York: Bloomsbury.
Moreno García, J.C. (in press a). Taxes, contrôle des routes et trafic fluvial en Égypte pharaonique (3100–700 avant J.-C.). In: Cifani, G. and Zurbach, J. (eds) *Tolls and Ancient Economies*. Paris: Hermann.
Moreno García, J.C. (in press b). Wells, small-scale private irrigation and agricultural strategies in the 3rd and 2nd millennium BC. In: Rost, S. (ed.) *Irrigation in Early States: New Directions*. Chicago: Oriental Institute of the University of Chicago.
Muhs, B. (2016). *The Ancient Egyptian Economy 3000–30 BCE*. Cambridge: Cambridge University Press.
Mumford, G. (2015). The Amman Airport Structure: A re-assessment of its date-range, function and overall role in the Levant. In: Harrison, T.P., Banning, E.B. and Klassen, S. (eds) *Walls of the Prince: Egyptian interactions with Southwest Asia in Antiquity. essays in honour of John S. Holladay, Jr.* Leiden and Boston MA: Brill, 89–198.
Murnane, W.J. (1995). *Texts from the Amarna Period in Egypt*. Atlanta GA: Scholar Press.
Navailles, R. and Neveu, F. (1989). Qu'entendait-on par 'journée d'esclave' au Nouvel Empire? (*hrw m ḥm(t), hrw n bꜣk*). *Revue d'Égyptologie* 40, 113–123.
Nicolle, C. (2009). Aux marges du Levant sud. Quelques considérations sur l'expansion 'égyptienne' dans la seconde moitié du IVe millénaire. In: Durand, J.-M. and Jacquet, A. (eds) *Centre et périphérie: Approches nouvelles des orientalistes*. Paris: Librairie d'Amérique et d'Orient Jean Maisonneuve, 29–46.
Nielsen, N. (2017). Cereal cultivation and nomad-sedentary interactions at the Late Bronze Age settlement of Zawiyet Umm el-Rakham. *Antiquity* 360, 1561–1573.
Ockinga, B. and Binder, S. (2013). Fragments of an Amarna-age stele in the Teti Pyramid Cemetery North. *Études et Travaux* 26, 501–516.
Pappa, E. (2017). 'You give me letters instead of money?' Commercial transactions in the Near East and the Western Mediterranean ca. 1100–600 BCE: social innovation and institutional inhibition of Phoenician commerce. *Revista do Museu de Arqueologia e Etnologia* 28, 1–30.
Parker, R.A. (1962). *A Saite Oracle Papyrus from Thebes in the Brooklyn Museum (Papyrus Brooklyn 47.218.3)*. Providence NJ: Brown University Press.
Parkinson, R.B. (1997). *The Tale of Sinuhe and Other Ancient Egyptian Poems, 1940–1640 BC*. Oxford: Oxford University Press.
Peet, T.E. (1930). *The Great Tomb-Robberies of the Twentieth Egyptian Dynasty. Vol. I: Text*. Oxford: Clarendon Press.
Porten, B. (1996). *The Elephantine Papyri in English. Three Millennia of Cross-Cultural Continuity and Change*. Leiden, New York and Köln: Brill.
Posener-Kriéger, P. (1977). Les mesures des étoffes à l'Ancien Empire. *Revue d'Égyptologie* 29, 86–96.
Posener-Kriéger, P. and Demichelis, S. (2004). *I papiri di Gebelein: Scavi G. Farina 1935*. Turin: Ministero per i Beni e le Attività Culturali - Soprintendenza al Museo delle Antichità Egizie.
Quirke, S. and Tajeddin, Z. (2010). Mechanical reproduction in the age of the artwork? Faience and 5000 moulds from 14th-century BC Egypt. *Visual Communication* 9, 341–362.
Ragazzoli, C. (2008). *Éloges de la ville en Égypte ancienne. Histoire et littérature*. Paris: Presses de l'Université Paris-Sorbonne.

Raue, D. (2019). Cultural diversity in Nubia in the late 3rd–Mid 2nd millennium BC. In: Raue, D. (ed.) *Handbook of Ancient Nubia*. Berlin and Boston MA: De Gruyter, 293–333.

Redford, D.B. (1997). Textual sources for the Hyksos period. In: Oren, E.D. (ed.) *The Hyksos: New historical and archaeological perspectives*. Philadelphia: Museum of Archaeology and Anthropology, 1–44.

Rehren, T. and Pusch, E.B. (2012). Alloying and resource management in New Kingdom Egypt: The bronze industry at Qantir–Pi-Ramesse and its relationship to Egyptian copper sources. In: Kassianidou, V. and Papasavvas, G. (eds) *Eastern Mediterranean Metallurgy and Metalwork in the Second Millennium BC – A Conference in Honour of James D. Muhly, Nicosia, 10th–11th October 2009*. Oxford: Oxbow Books, 215–221.

Ritner, R.K. (2009). *The Libyan Anarchy. Inscriptions from Egypt's Third Intermediate Period*. Atlanta GA: Society of Biblical Literature.

Routledge, B. (2015). A fishy business: The inland trade in Nile perch (*Lates niloticus*) in the Early Iron Age Levant. In: Harrison, T., Banning, E.B. and Klassen, S. (eds) *Walls of the Prince: Egyptian interactions with Southwest Asia in Antiquity. Essays in honour of John S. Holladay Jr.* Leiden and Boston MA: Brill, 212–233.

Rzeuska, T. (2012). Elephantine – a place of an end and a beginning. In: Schiestl, R. and Seiler, A. (eds) *Handbook of the Pottery of the Egyptian Middle Kingdom. Volume II: The regional volume*. Vienna: Verlag der Österreichischen Akademie der Wissenschaften, 312–359.

Sethe, K. (1961). *Urkunden des ägyptischen Altertums: Urkunden der 18 Dynastie. Historisch-biographische Urkunden*. Berlin: Akademie.

Shaw, B.D. (1995). Fear and loathing: The nomad menace and Roman Africa. In: Shaw, B.D. *Rulers, Nomads, and Christians in Roman North Africa*. Aldershot: Variorum, Chapter VII.

Sigl, J. and Kopp, P. (2020). Working from home – Middle Kingdom daily life on Elephantine Island, Egypt. In: Hodgkinson, A.K. and Tvetmarken, C.L. (eds) *Approaches to the Analysis of Production Activity at Archaeological Sites*. Oxford: Archaeopress, 8–24.

Snape, S. (2013). A stroll along the corniche? Coastal routes between the Nile Delta and Cyrenaica in the Late Bronze Age. In: Förster, F. and Riemer, H. (eds) *Desert Road Archaeology in Ancient Egypt and Beyond*. Cologne: Heinrich-Barth-Institut, 439–454.

Spencer, N. (2019). Settlements of the Second Intermediate Period and New Kingdom. In: Raue, D. (ed.) *Handbook of Ancient Nubia*. Berlin and Boston MA: De Gruyter, 433–464.

Strudwick, N.C. (2005). *Texts from the Pyramid Age*. Atlanta GA: Society of Biblical Literature.

Tassie, G.J. (2018). The Sinai connection from 10,000 to 2,000 BC. In: De Trafford, A., Tassie, G.J., el Daly, O. and Van Wetering, J. (eds) *A River Runs Through It: Studies in honour of Professor Fekri A. Hassan on the occasion of His 75th birthday*. Vol. 1. London: Golden House, 133–178.

Thompson, C.M. (2009). Three 20th Dynasty silver hoards from the Egyptian garrison. In: Panitz-Cohen, N. and Mazar, A. (eds) *Excavations at Tel Beth-Shean 1989-1996*. Vol. III. Jerusalem: Israel Exploration Society and Institute of Archaeology, Hebrew University of Jerusalem, 597–607.

Traunecker, Cl. (2005). Amenhotep IV, Precepteur royal du Disque. In: *Akhénaton et l'époque amarnienne*. Paris: Khéops, 145–182.

Valloggia, M. (2018). La stèle du marchand Nefermenou parmi les dessins de Henri Wild. In: Blöbaum, A.I., Eaton-Krauss, M. and Wüthrich, A. (eds) *Pérégrinations avec Erhart Graefe. Festschrift zu seinem 75. Geburtstag*. Münster: Ugarit, 537–543.

van Bavel, B. (2016). *The Invisible Hand? How Market Economies Have Emerged and Declined since AD 500*. Oxford: Oxford University Press.

van Neer, W., Lernau, O., Friedman, R., Mumford, G., Poblome, J. and Waelkens, M. (2004). Fish remains from archaeological sites as indicators of former trade connections in the Eastern Mediterranean. *Paléorient* 30(1): 141–147.

Vanthyune, B. (2012–2013). Amarna factories, workshops, faience moulds and their produce. *Egypt and the Levant* 22–23: 395–423.

Vieth, J. (2018). Urbanism in Nubia and the New Kingdom temple towns. In: Budka, J. and Auenmüller, J. (eds) *From Microcosm to Macrocosm: Individual households and cities in Ancient Egypt and Nubia*. Leiden: Sidestone Press, 227–238.
von Pilgrim, C. (1996). *Elephantine XVIII: Untersuchungen in der Stadt des Mittleren Reiches und der Zweiten Zwischenzeit*. Mainz: Zabern.
Warburton, D.A. (1997). *State and Economy in Ancient Egypt: Fiscal vocabulary of the New Kingdom*. Fribourg-Göttingen: University Press Fribourg Switzerland & Vandenhoeck und Ruprecht.
Warburton, D.A. (2016). *The Fundamentals of Economics. Lessons from the Bronze Age Near East*. Grand-Saconnex: Recherches et Publications.
Wengrow, D. (2009). The voyages of Europa: Ritual and trade in the eastern Mediterranean circa 2300–1850 BC. In: Parkinson, W.A. and Galaty, M.L. (eds) *Archaic State Interaction: The Eastern Mediterranean in the Bronze Age*. Santa Fe NM: SAR Press, 141–160.
Wenke, R.J., Redding, R.W. and Cagle, A.J. (ed.) (2016). *Kom el-Hisn (ca. 2500-1900 BC): An Ancient Egyptian Settlement in the Nile Delta*. Atlanta: Lockwood Press.
Wente, E.F. (1990). *Letters from Ancient Egypt*. Atlanta GA: Scholars Press.
Žába, Z. (1974). *The Rock Inscriptions of Lower Nubia. Czechoslovak Concession*. Prague: Czechoslovak Institute of Egyptology.